The Evidence-Based Internship

The Evidence-Based Internship

A Field Manual

Edited by

BARBARA THOMLISON
and KEVIN CORCORAN

OXFORD
UNIVERSITY PRESS
2008

OXFORD

UNIVERSITY PRESS

Oxford University Press, Inc., publishes works that further
Oxford University's objective of excellence
in research, scholarship, and education.

Oxford   New York
Auckland   Cape Town   Dar es Salaam   Hong Kong   Karachi
Kuala Lumpur   Madrid   Melbourne   Mexico City   Nairobi
New Delhi   Shanghai   Taipei   Toronto

With offices in
Argentina   Austria   Brazil   Chile   Czech Republic   France   Greece
Guatemala   Hungary   Italy   Japan   Poland   Portugal   Singapore
South Korea   Switzerland   Thailand   Turkey   Ukraine   Vietnam

Published by Oxford University Press, Inc.
198 Madison Avenue, New York, New York 10016

www.oup.com

Oxford is a registered trademark of Oxford University Press

Library of Congress Cataloging-in-Publication Data
The evidence-based internship : a field manual / edited by Barbara Thomlison and Kevin Corcoran.
     p. cm.
Includes bibliographical references and index.
ISBN 978-0-19-532350-4
1. Social work education.   2. Social service—Study and teaching (Internship)
3. Evidence-based social work.   4. Criminal justice, Administration of—Study
and teaching (Internship)   5. Practicums.
I. Thomlison, Barbara.   II. Corcoran, Kevin
HV11.E965 2007
361.3071'55—dc22   2006028568

9 8 7 6 5 4 3 2 1
Printed in the United States of America
on acid-free paper

Once again, for Sug Olivetti, and our cats: Olivia, Elizabeth, and Harley.
And to _____ [your name goes here] _____, as I promised you.

— KC

To Ray, Lynn, and Breanne for support and patience, and to the
students and supervisors who contributed to this volume.

— BT

PREFACE

The goal of this book is to provide students entering their internships with the tools necessary to have a successful, rewarding, and enjoyable field experience. However, this book is not the ordinary field book consisting of an overview of roles and expected behaviors and advice on how to work in a field setting. This book is unique in that it both offers students the practical information needed to be successful in their internships and provides the theoretical foundation for practice with clients, which uses an evidence-based methodology. This book will familiarize students, field instructors, supervisors, and even seasoned practitioners and faculty members with the processes and approaches to using the best research for practice.

Why should you engage in evidence-based practice? There are several compelling reasons. First, the use of an evidence-based practice approach is currently considered the industry standard in many helping disciplines, from medicine to managed care to human services. Professionals involved in complex and challenging issues need access to approaches that support sound decisions based on the best available information. Second, in the years after graduating, keeping knowledge and skills up-to-date is important and necessary—but, frankly, not the highest priority. A professional needs to stay on top of new developments, new interventions, and practice frameworks as they occur, while at the same time getting acclimated to a new job, new colleagues, and possibly even a new town or city. Thus keeping abreast is very challenging.

It is not social workers' job to know everything, even in their area of expertise, but it is their job to be able to find the information when they and their clients need it. This book teaches students how to identify and locate the latest protocols and methods of evidence-based practice.

Third, evidence-based practice is driven by performance and accountability concerns, as well as by ethical considerations. Evidence-based practice provides the social worker with the tools to find new and important research easily and to determine its usefulness for a problem and target population. In this book, the structure and policies of agencies and the information and guidelines required for evidence-based practice in a variety of human service, social work, juvenile and criminal justice settings are made available for students and supervisors. Evidence-based information in this text gives students knowledge and shows them how to use these resources to enhance skills through practice and supervision for continuous learning.

EVIDENCE-BASED PRACTICE AND THE INTERNSHIP

Our research and experience indicates that internships now require increased rigor and conceptual depth from students and that agencies and field instructors expect students to be able to provide clients with the best evidence-based practice methods currently available. In order to do this, students cannot "sit back" and rely on random knowledge to make timely and critical decisions. It is recognized now that during their internships students are required to incorporate specific knowledge, skills, values, and attitudes of the highest standards for their particular professional service activity. Evidence-based practice is the logical extension of learning about evidence-based knowledge in the classroom, and this practice begins during the internship by implementing information on evidence-based programs, assessment measures, treatment protocols, and interventions in human service and other interdisciplinary settings.

Many students become anxious about starting their internships because they do not think they have enough knowledge or skills. We assume that students are at varying levels of knowledge and experience, and for that reason students will find that this book delivers content suitable for practice situations that require a range of resources, from beginning to advanced. Our book addresses a wide range of populations and settings that emphasize science-informed theory and practice. We present in this book the most commonly accepted best practices for these real-life settings and situations in which client safety and care is critical. We expect that students will heighten their skills under supervised practice and build competence. The content in the book provides both foundation and advanced knowledge, so all students can quickly begin to use the resources. We present a solid grounding in evidence-based practice, best practice guidelines, exemplary models, and cases for study. We demonstrate how to locate information about state-of-the-art practices through research, both online and in the library, on commonly presented challenges that will be presented by clients and by the demands of the internship environment.

Faculty and supervisors, as field educators, agree that one of the defining characteristics of professional practice today is the integration of science with practice in the provision of services. Such integration is not so easy to accomplish as a student. This book provides students with supervision resources to assist them in developing evidence-based practice competencies, attitudes, and skills that support these various knowledge bases and their applications to individual cases in a professional and ethically sound approach. Through the process of supervision, students learn skills of observation and critical appraisal and are able to test understanding in real-life situations during the internship. The evidence-based framework of science-to-service will assist students to weigh information for preferred practice decisions. The authors identify best practices for positive client outcomes and for a successful internship experience by selecting essential knowledge and skills for learning. Moreover, all students will develop their practice models based on the best practices and evidence from the field experience. This is an asset for students transitioning from the educational setting to employment, as resumes are often not sufficient in a competitive job market in which the candidate must stand out.

HOW TO USE THIS BOOK

Before beginning, we want to make several important points about the organization and use of this book that will strengthen the student's learning during the internship. Noteworthy features of the book are as follows:

1. The book is a *resource manual*. The book is set up as a resource manual of commonly encountered topics and practice challenges that students are likely to face during the internship in human service settings. The theme of each chapter is evidence-based best practices; however; each topic or chapter can stand alone. Because each chapter is independent, it is not necessary to read the chapters in sequence. Readings may be selected based on needs, issues, or challenges that you are facing or most interested in learning about during the internship.
2. The book is *concise, practical,* and *theoretical.* The 16 chapters are organized into three parts:
   - Part I: Defining Evidence-Based Practices for Internships. Chapters 1 through 4 provide an overview of the essential terms and definitions of evidence-based practice and why it is important for practitioners to implement best practices.
   - Part II: Evidence-Based Practice Skills and Interventions for Internships. Chapters 5 through 12 present selected evidence-based interventions

for commonly experienced problems and conditions of children, youth, and adults.

- Part III: Using Evidence in Practice. Chapters 13 though 16 discuss the transition from intern to professional.

  Students will find each chapter to be a concise summary of practice issues, with helpful references including Internet resources and websites. Chapters are relevant to interdisciplinary needs and to the current approach to practice in many settings.

3. The book contains *applied learning activities* and *case studies*. The end of each chapter presents exercises or applied learning activities to reinforce chapter learning. Each chapter has an originally prepared case study written by a well-known practitioner, field educator, or academic scholar. We are delighted that these colleagues have agreed to collaborate with us and share their expertise about clients, students, and practice to make the student's learning more relevant.

4. The book, as a whole, provides an overview of *selected evidence-based practice interventions*. It presents up-to-date resources, skills, protocols, and theory to help students identify and apply best practices throughout the internship experience in all phases and contexts, including supervision. Not all challenging behavior and problems are presented, but we teach skills to handle those that are not included in this book.

5. The book is *skill based*. Knowledge, skills, and strategies focus on getting started, on supervision, on the settings, and on the essential laws, values, and attitudes for professional practice. Skills for interviewing under different contexts—including assessment, readiness to change (i.e., motivational interviewing), and working with clients who have mental health and problems in juvenile and criminal justice areas—are included. The student will learn skills for documentation and writing in different contexts. An increasingly important component for students includes developing a portfolio of resources suitable for another internship or to support the transition to employment.

6. The book can *supplement other courses* beyond the internship. This resource manual can support internship seminars, practice methods courses, or any course that introduces students to the evidence-based skills for identifying evidence-based practices.

UNIQUE PEDAGOGY

The book's teaching framework uses adult education approaches to maximize the various learning styles of students, their field instructors, and supervisors. Each learning activity involves reflection, knowledge retrieval, and skill or application strategies for teaching and learning. The range of learning activities will help students to recognize and describe communication and interpersonal skills and will teach them to select skills for engaging, assessing, and analyzing interviews and principles of standardized assessment and of evaluating client change. The content is didactic yet highly practical, focusing on developing interpersonal skills for self-improvement, motivational enhancement, and personalized feedback, all within a best-practice framework.

FINAL THOUGHTS

We are keenly aware that combining social work and criminal justice may seem like shaking oil and water: sometimes they just don't mix that well. We recognize the degree of professional distinction, stereotyping, and perhaps even contempt and envy that may prevail among professionals in the two fields. The criminal justice professional may be seen as the "law and order" black-and-white thinker who has watched too many episodes of *CSI*, and the social worker may be dismissed as the pushy-gamushy, liberal softy and do-gooder. To us, professionals can no longer practice with such outdated belief systems. What is far more important is to recognize that these two disciplines often work in the same settings, have the same clients and the same employers, and may think and act similarly in many ways, especially with skills acquired in the professional internship. For these reasons, we think it is better to address both criminal justice and social work together, and we have done so throughout this book.

Throughout the book we also emphasize the interaction between skills and knowledge acquired within supervision and within the setting. We have gathered the best available evidence about these processes and realize the limitations of research in various internship settings in this area. We appreciate that learning is continuous, and what is presented here serves as the foundation for the student's experiences. We hope that students enjoy the learning this book brings to them as much as we enjoyed developing the content. Our students have inspired us in many ways, and we thank them for presenting us with challenges.

Finally, take some extra time to savor the wealth of knowledge found in the case studies from our collaborators, who added so much to the content. We would like to thank each and every author for his or her insight, knowledge, and commitment. Without them, as well as Mandy Davis, who served the valuable role of "case editor," this book would not have been possible. We hope readers are as grateful for their efforts as we are. And last we would like to thank our readers for using this book, and we welcome feedback as we continue to look for ways to improve the field experience.

CONTENTS

THE EDITORS AND AUTHORS

Barbara Thomlison is a professor in the School of Social Work and director of the Institute for Children and Families at Risk at Florida International University in Miami.

Kevin Corcoran is a professor in the Graduate School of Social Work at Portland State University.

Jennifer Abeloff, MSW, MS
School of Social Work
Florida International University
Miami, FL

Elizabeth Mayfield Arnold, PhD
Assistant Professor
Department of Psychiatry and
    Behavioral Medicine
Wake Forest University School
    of Medicine
Winston-Salem, NC

José B. Ashford, MSW, PhD, LCSW
Professor and Associate Director
School of Social Work
Affiliate Professor
School of Justice and Social Inquiry
Arizona State University
Tempe, AZ

Jennifer Becker, MSW
School of Social Work
Florida International University
Miami, FL

Dan Coleman, PhD
Assistant Professor
Graduate School of Social Work
Portland State University
Portland, OR

Mandy Davis, MSW
Child Welfare Partnership
Graduate School of Social Work
Portland State University
Portland, OR

Catherine N. Dulmus, PhD
Associate Professor and Director
Buffalo Center for Social
    Research
School of Social Work
State University of New York
Buffalo, NY

Marian Dumaine, PhD
Coordinator of Field Practicum
School of Social Work
Florida International University
Miami, FL

Joel Fischer, DSW
Professor
School of Social Work
University of Hawai'i
Honolulu, HI

Cynthia G. S. Franklin, PhD
Professor of Social Work;
Stiernberg/Spencer Professor in
   Mental Health
School of Social Work
University of Texas
Austin, TX

Patricia B. Higgins, MSW, LCSW
Clinical Social Work Supervisor
Western State Hospital
Staunton, VA

Robin J. Jacobs, PhD
School of Social Work
Florida International
   University
Miami, FL

Catheleen Jordan, PhD
Professor and Chair
Direct Practice Sequence
School of Social Work
University of Texas
Arlington, TX

Melissa Kupferberg, MSW
Mitigation Specialist
Integrated Mitigation and
   Investigations
Phoenix, AZ

Gerard LaSalle, MA, PhD
Assistant Professor
Department of Criminal Justice
East Stroudsburgh University
East Stroudsburgh, PA

Jill S. Levenson, PhD, LCSW
Assistant Professor of Human Services
Lynn University
Boca Raton, FL

Tammy Linseisen
Clinical Assistant Professor
University of Texas
Austin, TX

Doris Layton MacKenzie, PhD
Professor and Director, Evaluation
   Research Group
Department of Criminology and
   Criminal Justice
College of Behavioral and Social Sciences
University of Maryland
College Park, MD

Nikki D. Mowbray, MSW
Addictions Counselor
Alcohol and Drug Center
Cecil County Health Department
Elkton, MD

Jennifer Powers, MSW
Graduate School of Social Work
Portland State University
Portland, OR

Brian C. Renauer
Assistant Professor
Criminology and Criminal Justice
College of Urban and Public Affairs
Portland State University
Portland, OR

Christopher P. Rice, PhD
Associate Professor
School of Social Work
Florida International University
Miami, FL

Phyllis Solomon, PhD
Professor
School of Social Policy and Practice
University of Pennsylvania
Philadelphia, PA

Karen M. Sowers, PhD
Dean and Professor
The University of Tennessee
College of Social Work
Knoxville, TN

David W. Springer, PhD
Professor and Associate Dean of
    Academic Affairs
University Distinguished
    Teaching Professor
School of Social Work
University of Texas
Austin, TX

Victoria Stanhope, MSW, LSW
School of Social Policy and Practice
University of Pennsylvania
Philadelphia, PA

Kim Strom-Gottfried, PhD
Professor
School of Social Work
University of North Carolina
Chapel Hill, NC

Barbara Thomas, LCSW
Linkage Coordinator
Ohio State University
Columbus, OH

Stephen J. Tripodi
School of Social Work
University of Texas
Austin, TX

Bruce A. Thyer, PhD
Professor
College of Social Work
Florida State University
Tallahassee, FL

M. Elizabeth Vonk, PhD
Associate Professor
School of Social Work
University of Georgia
Athens, GA

Thomas Alexander Washington, PhD,
MSSW, LGSW
Assistant Professor
Morgan State University
Baltimore, MD

Shannon C. Wright, MSW
Intensive Services Team
    Program Manager
Region Ten Community
    Services Board
Charlottesville, VA

Part I Defining Evidence-Based Practice for Internships

1 WHAT ARE EVIDENCE-BASED PRACTICES AND EVIDENCE-BASED INTERNSHIPS?

KEVIN CORCORAN *and* BARBARA THOMLISON

In this chapter you will learn (1) what is meant by evidence *in the behavioral and social sciences; (2) how evidence has emerged in the history of science; (3) that the quality of evidence is chiefly a matter of how persuasive it is; (4) what is meant by* evidence *according to the American Psychological Association; (5) three types of evidence-based practices—systematic reviews, practice guidelines, and expert consensus; and (6) guidelines for implementing evidence-based practices.*

It is now the time to actually apply what you have been learning in the classroom. You are about to start your internship or field practicum. That is, you are about to start developing the skills of a professional social worker or criminal justice worker. This learning opportunity should be one of the most exciting experiences in your educational process. It is critical to your initial professional development. It should be your crowning hour! At least, we hope it is, and we hope this book helps make that happen.

The purpose of this book is to provide you an overview of the knowledge and skills needed to make for a successful internship, regardless of whether you are studying criminal justice or social work. We are emphasizing these two disciplines because the social services delivered by criminal justice and by social work are similar and often overlap, regardless of your field of study or final college degree. In fact, depending on how well you integrate the scope of your education and interests in the future, you may be learning aspects of criminal justice and social work simultaneously. We hope you find this book to be a resource guide with practical learning activities, cases, and information that make education in your field an academically sound, professionally developmental, and, most of all, fun and rewarding experience. We also hope to help you acquire the knowledge and skills of a competent and confident practitioner. In our opinion, this means structuring your practicum or internship to acquire the best practices in the field, those that are evidence-based, and to develop the skills of applying these interventions systematically and successfully in order to help your clients change and improve their quality of life and well-being.

WHAT DO WE MEAN BY *EVIDENCE* IN EVIDENCE-BASED PRACTICE?

We hope to facilitate making your field education one based on the best evidence. But, what do we mean by evidence? Evidence-based practices are those interventions that are derived from sound research methodologies in which the outcome findings consistently show that the interventions actually help clients change and improve (Drake et al., 2003). In the words of the former Surgeon General of the United States, David Satcher, "Evidence-based treatment is treatment based upon the best available science" (as cited in Thyer, 2002).

Because the best available practice interventions are derived from convincing evidence, we need to know what we mean by *evidence*. To answer this, let's take a brief look at the history of the source of evidence, namely, science. The *evidence* in evidence-based practice (EBP) reflects part of historical development in the scientific revolution, as noted by Corcoran and Vandiver (2004). For convenience, most historians of science date the beginning of the scientific revolution from the publication of Copernicus's *On the Revolution of Celestial Bodies* and Andreas Vesalius's *On the Structure of the Human Body,* which, coincidentally, both occurred in 1543.

The scientific revolution is characterized by improved methods in which the accuracy of the answer was more important than the way in which one thought things out, which had been the defining method of the prescientific thinkers and philosophers. Prior to this dramatic change in how we viewed the way knowledge is ascertained, methods of answering questions were more important than the accuracy of the answer (Dear, 2001). Here is an illustration. One of us (KC) had a roommate in college, Ernie Lidquest, who complained that he ran out of marijuana before his monthly allowance arrived from home so he could purchase more. Thanks to Zeno, the Greek philosopher, I informed Ernie that the problem was not that he was smoking too much marijuana (which he was) but that he was defining the problem incorrectly. Instead of smoking all his marijuana, all Ernie needed to do in order not to run out was to simply smoke half of it first. Once that was gone, all he had to do was smoke half of what was left; and then half of that, and so on. Because all space is infinitely divisible, an axiom we had just learned in our math appreciation course, if Ernie followed this advice, he would always have some marijuana left and, therefore, would never run out! Ernie, being under the influence of marijuana at the time, thought this was an excellent idea and was grateful for the prescientific methodology—until, that is, he ran out of marijuana a couple of days later.

In contrast to the concern over how the question was asked, the scientific approach changed the method of answering the question. This, in turn, improved

the soundness of the methods and increased the likelihood of more accurate observations. The improved methods tended to provide more persuasive evidence, as
the observations were more objective and not as greatly influenced by the method
of asking the question. Ernie would have been better served by the objective observation that he should smoke less. This type of inquiry and reasoning changed
greatly with the scientific revolution, although admittedly the change was very
slow. This pace is clear when we consider that resistance still exists to evidence-
based practice, to single-case empirical clinical evaluations, and sometimes even
to research in general.

The improvement in methodology does not, however, mean that science actually had much immediate impact on practice. The effort to integrate research in
practice and to transfer science into routine practice has had—in fact—a rather
long history in the behavioral, social, and medical sciences. Much like the pace of
acceptance of scientific methods, the adaptation of scientific procedures was also
quite slow. This history, also, has been neither easy nor terribly successful. Often,
new scientific developments are slow to reach the front-line practitioner who
labors with clients every day. In medicine, for example, more than 2,000 years
passed between the time of Hippocrates (born around 460 B.C.E.) and the introduction of science into medicine.

Even though the earlier pioneers in health care based their practices on observation of nature, they did not do so with much accuracy. Chief among the
observational procedures was watching blood dry, which resulted in the notion
that there are four types of bodily fluids, or humors—namely, blood, phlegm, bile,
and black bile. As Barry (2004) points out, this idea was consistent with the Greek
quadratic world view of four seasons, four components of the environment (i.e.,
hot, cold, wet, dry), and four elements in the universe (i.e., earth, wind, fire, and
water).

It would be 600 years before any advance was made by way of Galenic medicine, which was named after the Greek physician Galen, who lived from around
130–200 C.E. It would appear that Galen simply tinkered with the Hippocratic
notions; but he did so with a critically different method, active observations. Two
examples of Galen's active observations are his first dissections of animals and his
studies of human anatomy by treating the deep wounds of gladiators, somewhat
similar to human vivisections. Galen was quite influential. His works were available in Latin and Arabic, and both Near Eastern and Western medicine would wait
another 1,500 years before any noticeable advancement would occur.

Even though the Greek and Galenic approaches were based on observations,
the resulting theory of balance and imbalance in the body system (i.e., the four
body humors being out of balance) produced such interventions as bloodletting,
sweating, urinating, defecating, vomiting, and other methods of purging to restore

the balance between blood, phlegm, bile, and black bile, the body humors. Not until around 1550 would much advancement occur, and this happened when a Flemish anatomist named Vesalius (1514–1564) did one of the first human dissections. At about the same time, Fracastorius, an astronomer and mathematician, as well as a botanist and a poet, concluded that Galen's observations on infrahuman animals did not apply to humans. It was Fracastorius who theorized that illnesses were not the result of imbalance but of contagion from one person to another.

As radical and critical as these advances were, they had very little, if any, impact on the practice of medicine for more than 200 years. Even William Harvey's delineation of the circulation of blood in 1628, which some consider to be medicine's "greatest achievement until the late 1800s" (Barry, 2004, p. 21), did not have much effect on the interventions of the times, chiefly bloodletting. Many practitioners, it seems, preferred this method of establishing a balance in the humors over defecation, urination, and vomiting, for fairly understandable reasons.

When we ask why there was so little progress for more than 2,000 years, at least three answers emerge. First, the Galenic theory that existed at the time was logical and internally consistent. Second, the interventions or procedures based on the theory often produced the desired results. That is, the evidence was that they appeared to be effective. "Yet a patient's improvement, of course, does not prove that a therapy works" (Barry, 2004, p. 23). Third, like social work and criminal justice, medicine includes the human emotions of both provider and patient; most providers prefer to at least try to help a client.

If all of this is not sufficient to illustrate that even the revered discipline of medicine has not done well in integrating research into practice, let's consider another example, the thermometer. Physicians at the "Paris clinical school," a revolutionary approach to medicine established by the French government after the Revolution, did not start taking patients' temperatures until the 1820s, and they were the first to think it might be worthwhile to monitor patients' body temperatures. The thermometer, however, had been invented between 1615 and 1625, one of the first having been invented by Galileo (Gribbin, 2002). Imagine that: 200 years between the invention of what would become a basic and essential medical technology and the first time it was put into a patient's mouth (or so we assume its first application was in this direction).

Clearly, the efforts to integrate research in practice, including medical practice, have not been impressive. Even "evidence-based medicine," in which much of the current evidence-based practice movement had its start, has not pervasively integrated research in practice. Hellman and Hellman (1991), in the laudable *New England Journal of Medicine*, has even argued against science by asserting that research may be unethical because it often excludes clinical judgment. They aver that because clinical judgment plays a critical role in so much of the practice of medicine, to study an intervention without it is misguided and lacks external validity. That is, it simply is not the reality of practice, and to study the efficacy of an intervention without the role of clinical judgment asserts conclusions that are not realistic in everyday practice.

EVIDENCE OF ALL SORTS

The current effort at "evidence-based practice" is based on medicine, in spite of its constipated history of movement. We believe that the very term *evidence-based* is a rather misrepresentative name. After all, the medical history previously noted was based on observations, "evidence" if you will. Even primitive interventions, such as trephining, exorcism, and some psychotherapies, were backed by some, though not necessarily good, evidence.

By *good evidence* we mean persuasive evidence for which the probative value outweighs the limitations and uncertainties. When we use the term *evidence,* we mean the results of observations that have probative, or substantiating, value. For various interventions in criminal justice and social work, the evidence that has probative value is that which may convince one that the procedures are likely to be effective in helping a client change (Corcoran & Vandiver, 2004). They are likely based on rigorous observations using scientific methods—or at least the best evidence available.

One thing you will learn from this book is that evidence comes in all sizes and shapes. Like law, evidence may be beyond reasonable doubt; it may be clear and convincing; or the preponderance of the weight of the evidence may suggest a degree of persuasion. Some of the evidence used in criminal justice and social work internships will be beyond doubt, and at other times it will be less convincing. There will even be times in your field setting when there appears to be no evidence whatsoever.

Evidence-based practice is based on this same scientific revolution, a revolution that advanced the methods we used to answer questions. The evidence we use is derived from randomized controlled trials—that is, experiments—and research designs that have some degree of rigor. Evidence-based practice is rarely the result of a single study. As we discuss later in this chapter, typically, evidence-based interventions are derived from a number of studies, and the studies are integrated or synthesized into a corpus of evidence on the effectiveness of an intervention. The goal of evidence-based practice is to select the most accurate information derived from the best available research methods and to apply the information with fidelity. By *accurate* we simply mean valid information. This may, as is often the case for theory development, be an in-depth description of a single case or a few cases. There are many familiar examples of case studies for theory development, including Jean Piaget's studies of children; J. B. Watson's study of conditioning; Skinner's small coop of pigeons and his only daughter, who was raised as an infant in the conditioned environment of the "Skinner box"; and even Freud's case studies. Although the accuracy of these examples varies considerably, what is common to them all is the use by social scientists of more rigorous methods to test, support, refute, and revise these and other areas of case assessment in the behavioral and social sciences.

As new and more rigorous studies emerge, the choices of what evidence is the "best" evidence for the most accurate interventions increase exponentially. Evidence-based practice is a way for clinicians to select from the corpus of the available evidence the most useful information to apply to a particular client who has sought services. Because there are so many publications and a variety of different research methodologies in the social sciences, evidence-based practice has tried to corral the information by categorizing research by the degree of rigor and, therefore, the probative value of the results. The most widely accepted view is delineated by the American Psychological Association's (APA) Division 12, the Society of Clinical Psychology (APA, 1995). The standards for an intervention to be considered effective, as discussed by Division 12, include no less than two studies with positive results derived from between-group comparisons in a randomized controlled trial. The results must illustrate that one intervention consistently produces better outcomes than another or better than a placebo condition; as an alternative, the two studies would be considered clear and convincing if an experimental condition was equivalent to an already established intervention. Moreover, the two research studies are to be conducted by independent research teams and in different research settings. However, sometimes the evidence is acceptable without the independent check and balance, such as Linehan's (1993) dialectic behavior treatment for borderline personality disorders and Henggeler's (Henggeler, Schoenwald, Borduin, Rowland, & Cunningham, 1998) multisystemic therapy for antisocial conditions such as juvenile delinquency and its concomitant family dysfunction.

Of course, randomized controlled trials are not always available. This is especially so with innovative interventions for difficult conditions to treat, such as schizoaffective disorders in psychiatry, gang membership in criminal justice, and poverty in social work. In the absence of a randomized controlled trial, the APA considers 10 or more single case studies using rigorous experimental designs, such as those discussed in chapter 11 of this book, to be an acceptable alternative.

The APA also sets the standard that the persuasive evidence of effectiveness should include manuals to implement the interventions. Manuals are important, as they help ensure fidelity when the interventions are used by others. Further, the research participants in the studies, randomized control trials, or single case studies should be from specific client populations and from a reliable nomenclature so that the sample in the study can be assessed. The research participants must be specific and well defined, not just clients who happen to walk into the agency. This specificity allows you to determine whether the intervention is likely to fit the nuisances, preferences and context of your client.

Additional criteria include using well-established and meaningful outcome measures, appropriate and properly done statistical procedures, and a blind assessment in which the person doing the evaluation is not biased by knowing the client's treatment condition. The last criterion further protects against bias by keeping the assessor blind to the hypothesis of the study. Taken together, these criteria are, frankly, rather restrictive and might even chill the development of new and more effective interventions. Some of the problems with these criteria include the fact that all randomized controlled trials and single case studies are not equal. In order for randomized control trial findings to be sufficient, there must be randomized assignment, and the dropout rate, called attrition, must not exceed 20%. This condition is particularly problematic for work in substance abuse, in which the attrition rate averages more 25% after just 6 months (Ribisl et al., 1996). As you can imagine, it is difficult to establish much effectiveness in the treatment of drugs and alcohol with such a short-term follow-up and low continuous-participation rate.

The criteria also have a limitation in terms of external validity, that is, the application of the results to routine practice in social work and criminal justice. The uniformity of a research study may not consider such things as the cost of the interventions and its relative cost, such as Viagra at $10 a pill, compared with various behavioral interventions or medical procedures, such as a penal implant. Similarly, the criteria do not consider such critical aspects of real-life service delivery as the availability of practitioners trained in the intervention and client preference. An effective intervention, such as electroconvulsive therapy (ECT) with major depression that is resistant to psychotropic medication, is of zero value if no one will agree to the treatment. As noted by Hellman and Hellman (1999), most research excludes the seminal aspect of clinical and professional judgment, as well as experience. And, finally, regardless of the verisimilitude of the study, in all likelihood your client will be different in some—if not many—respects from the participants in a research study (Thyer, 2002). As Rosenthal (2004) notes, there is an important distinction between the actual research and the question of whether or not the intervention will work with your particular client.

This is what you will struggle with as you begin to master evidence-based interventions in criminal justice and social work settings. It is rather easy to resolve these conflicts by drawing on Satcher's original definition (as cited in Thyer, 2002) of evidence-based practice; namely, interventions derived from the best *available* evidence. These standards are the ideal that we strive for, though frequently fail to obtain. Therefore, your job in selecting interventions for the clients you see in your internship is to select those with the best evidence, even if that evidence does not rise to the standard delineated by the APA.

THREE TYPES OF EVIDENCE-BASED PRACTICE

The use of an evidence-based-practice approach is currently considered the industry standard in many helping disciplines, from medicine to managed mental health care. It is as if we had just gotten comfortable with the notion of "best practices" and now use a different and yet more contemporary term. As a consequence, the very definition of evidence-based practice has become more elusive, if not ambiguous (e.g., Reid & Colvin, 2005). Some restrict the term to systematic reviews using meta-analytic procedures, which is a quantitative procedure in which different results are compared by converting outcomes to standardized scores. A standardized score is also called a z score. It is typically the average for the experimental group minus the comparison and divided by the standard deviation of the comparison group. As such, a z score ranges from -3 to $+3$ with a mean of zero. The z score or standardized score, estimates the size of the effects of an intervention relative to some control or comparison group. Positive effect sizes mean that the intervention works better than the control condition, and negative scores mean that it is less effective. A z score is easily transformed into a percentile using Table 1.1. By using a z score and the percentile rank, you can determine the degree of improvement that is likely to result from the intervention. It is a powerful way to estimate the benefits of interventions (e.g., Smith, Glass, & Miller, 1978).

Others use a wider scope in determining what evidence-based practices are, including less rigorous studies and more influential case studies (Vandiver, 2002), such as the standard of 10 well-conducted single case studies. The credibility of the evidence-based on systematic reviews is clearly derived from the most rigorous methods evaluated with sound quantitative procedures; namely, the randomized control trial, which has an experimental condition and a comparison group.

In addition to systematic reviews and case studies, evidence is delineated by a group of experts in an area or intervention, who in turn produce guidelines

Table 1.1 Z Score and Percentile Equivalents

Z Score	Proportion of Score		Z Score	Proportion of Score	
	Lower than	Higher than		Lower than	Higher than
−3.0	.13	99.87	.1	53.98	46.02
−2.9	.19	99.81	.2	57.93	42.07
−2.8	.26	99.74	.3	61.79	38.21
−2.7	.35	99.65	.4	65.54	34.46
−2.6	.47	99.53	.5	69.15	30.85
−2.5	.62	99.38	.6	72.58	27.42
−2.4	.82	99.18	.7	75.80	24.20
−2.3	1.07	99.93	.8	78.81	21.19
−2.2	1.39	98.61	.9	81.59	18.41
−2.1	1.79	98.21	1.0	84.13	15.87
−1.9	2.87	97.73	1.1	86.43	13.57
−1.8	3.59	96.41	1.3	90.32	9.68
−1.7	4.46	95.54	1.4	91.92	8.08
−1.6	5.48	94.52	1.5	93.32	6.68
−1.5	6.68	93.32	1.6	94.52	5.48
−1.4	8.08	91.92	1.7	95.54	4.46
−1.3	9.68	90.32	1.8	96.41	3.59
−1.2	11.51	88.49	1.9	97.13	2.87
−1.1	13.57	86.43	2.0	97.73	2.27
−1.0	15.87	84.13	2.1	98.21	1.79
−.9	18.41	81.59	2.2	98.61	1.39
−.8	21.19	78.81	2.3	98.93	1.07
−.7	24.20	75.80	2.4	99.18	.82
−.6	27.42	72.58	2.5	99.38	.62
−.5	30.85	69.15	2.6	99.53	.47
−.4	34.46	65.54	2.7	99.65	.35
−.3	38.21	61.79	2.8	99.74	.26
−.2	42.07	57.93	2.9	99.81	.19
−.1	46.02	453.98	3.0	99.87	.13

known as expert consensus guidelines. This source of evidence-based practice may be designed with less restrictive inclusion criteria in order to make it a broader source of information. Expert consensus guidelines may include quasi-experimental designs, such as a matched comparison groups, or descriptive single case studies.

The broader scope of studies that are included in expert consensus guidelines should not lead you to think that they are less valuable than systematic reviews of randomized controlled studies. One would assume, for example, that the experts who compiled the guidelines were thorough enough to have incorporated the same sources considered in the systematic reviews. Based on this assumption, we believe that the guidelines probably have the same studies used for quantitative synthesis and additional ones that systematic reviews exclude. They are, unquestionably, broader in scope.

In summary, for the intern who is beginning to see clients and who frequently faces unfamiliar and challenging cases, it is useful to consider three sources of information on how to deliver the best intervention available that is also the most useful in helping your client change. The three general sources are (1) *systematic reviews,* (2) *practice guidelines,* and (3) *expert consensus guidelines.*

Systematic Reviews

For the typical practitioner the critical concern is not simply the best intervention available but the one that is most useful for the client's circumstances. This concern is reflected in Gibbs and Gambrill's (2002) review of evidence-based practice, which asserts that "evidence applies to the client(s) at hand" in the context of "the values and expectations of the clients" (p. 453). The intervention, then, even with sound evidence, must be adapted to the client's unique or particular circumstances. It would be folly to think that your client would conform to those in a research study. There may be similarities, but the differences need to be acknowledged by fitting the procedures to the peculiarities of your client—or fitting the form of the intervention to the client's fuss or context.

The chief source of systematic reviews in the broad areas of health is the Cochrane Library (http://www.cochrane.org), which contains over 1,500 systematic reviews of medical, nursing, and health procedures. In the behavioral and social sciences, the Campbell Collaboration (http://www.campbell.gse.upenn.edu) provides systematic reviews in the areas of crime and delinquency, education, and social welfare. It is noteworthy that education is often the intersection between social welfare needs and delinquency issues, with truancy so important that it was the subject of one of the Campbell Collaboration's first reviews. Many more have followed, and you will find that the best way to manage the massive information is to regularly visit these and other web pages discussed in chapter 3. We suggest no less than once every 2 weeks, and more often as you start your field internship.

Reviews are also frequently available through professional journals. This is nicely illustrated by Wilson, Lipsey, and Soydan (2003), who published a systematic review of juvenile justice with minority youth. Additionally, many journals, such as *Evidence-Based Mental Health, Research on Social Work Practice, The Journal of Consulting and Clinical Psychology,* and *The Journal of Clinical Psychology* have good track records for publishing systematic reviews. Other critical sources of such evidence are the cutting-edge articles first published in leading peer-reviewed journals. These articles are not only the most up-to-date and available, but they will eventually be incorporated into future systematic reviews. Staying abreast of the best research in the field means that you must be well read. This means a commitment to going to the library and spending a morning or an afternoon in the journal section, a task that is truly formidable and that requires your professional commitment and allocation of time. Easier said than done, we dare to admit.

As may be suggested by the number of sources of systematic reviews that exist, the quality and thoroughness of the reviews may vary. Additionally, the quantitative methods used in data synthesis are not without controversy (e.g., Fischer, 1990). Chief among the problems is the fact that studies with nonsignificant findings are rarely published, and therefore those studies included in a review are biased toward positive results that are at least statistically significant. Systematic reviews are also not terribly new (e.g., Smith et al., 1980).

Inevitably, the same concern exists in applying any evidence on which to build a practice, namely, the *veracity* of the data. Is it persuasive for this particular client, whose problem is similar in some ways and different in many others? What would the reasonable and prudent practitioner in the same situation do with this evidence? The latter question is discussed more thoroughly in chapter 6.

Practice Guidelines

Another source for evidence-based practice is practice guidelines. Practice guidelines are also considered treatment manuals, and they may include expert consensus guidelines. These sources are distinguishable from systematic reviews by their method of integrating the available evidence, and they are reflective of earlier times when practice was guided more by authority than by sound empirical evidence (Gambrill, 1999). Although these and other limitations exist, practice guidelines and expert consensus guidelines are readily available to a wide audience of practitioners in a variety of disciplines, especially in juvenile justice and social work. Additionally, many guidelines and manuals are very practical and direct in facilitating session-to-session activities, exercises, and homework assignments.

Self-help books and workbooks are very thorough resources that are excellent auxiliaries for practice in many criminal justice and social work settings. A large number of workbooks are reviewed by L'Abate (2004), and Norcross, Santrock, Campbell, Smith, Sommer, and Zuckerman (2003) review self-help books. The use of homework in a variety of settings and with various problems is nicely covered by Tompkins (2004). Self-help books, workbooks, and homework are particularly valuable in the face of impediments such as the 50-minute hour, limitations in number of sessions imposed by insurance companies and third-party payment plans, probation time limits, early release and discharge, and cancellations for every conceivable reason. They are excellent supplements for the motivated client who wants to facilitate treatment with a self-change program, and you will find all three personally useful in such programs.

Practice guidelines also refer to statements and recommendations for conducting an intervention. Terms associated with practice guidelines include *treatment protocols, standards, options, parameters, preferred practice,* and *best practice.* There are, of course, important distinctions. Standards are considered a prerequisite to competent practice. Guidelines are more like a set of suggestions for effective interventions. And options are other approaches to consider when no established standard or guideline is available (Havinghurst, 1991). *Preferred practices* and *best practices* seem to be terms used in a variety of ways for various standards, guidelines, and options.

Another valuable source for this form of evidence-based practice are practice texts (e.g., J. Corcoran, 2000; Roberts & Springer, 2007), handbooks (e.g., Roberts & Greene, 2002), and manuals (e.g., LeCroy & Daley, 2005; LeCroy, 2007; Steketee, 1999). Roberts and Greene's *Social Work Desk Reference* (2002) has no less than 33 chapters that are relevant to some definition of evidence-based practice. Most textbooks in production and under contract are likely to describe evidence-based practice, whereas others find the need for an updated edition.

What is striking about these sources is their variety. Some publishers are committed to producing treatment manuals, such as New Harbinger Publications, which has eight diagnosis-specific manuals in production. Texts such as Corcoran's (2000) focus more on intervention, whereas others are more diagnostic related (Roth & Fonagy, 1996), or setting specific (such as juvenile justice; e.g., Fenley, et al, 1993; Sheidow & Henggeler, 2005; Tate & Redding, 2005).

As you can imagine, there are many evidence-based practices to consider in your internship and eventual practice. Some are better than others. They will all likely have some degree of supporting evidence. Thus the challenge now and in the future is to consider the value of that evidence as it pertains to the particular client problem and agency setting. Again, judging the veracity of the evidence is a crucial task.

One thing you will learn from this workbook is that evidence comes in all sizes and shapes. Like law, evidence may be beyond reasonable doubt, or clear and convincing, or perhaps simply the preponderance of the weight of the evidence may suggest a degree of persuasion. Some of the evidence used in criminal justice and social work internships will be beyond doubt, and at other times it will be less convincing.

Expert Consensus Guidelines

Expert consensus guidelines are distinguishable from practice guidelines in that they are typically developed by a broad-based panel of experts. For example, McEvoy, Scheifler, and Francis (1999) *Practice Guidelines for Schizophrenia* surveyed more than 300 experts, including professionals from a variety of disciplines, consumers of services, and family members and advocacy groups.

Despite engaging a wide scope of experts, which potentially strengthens an expert consensus guideline, the guidelines are limited and often fail to consider cultural differences. Frequently, consensus guidelines are marketed by professional organizations, such as the APA. Professional journals, such as *Psychiatry* and the *Journal of Clinical Psychology,* frequently publish expert consensus guidelines. A useful website for a number of psychiatric conditions is http://www .psychguides.com., and additional websites are covered in chapters 3, 4, and 5.

With these three sources of information on evidence-based practice—systematic reviews, practice guidelines, and expert consensus guidelines—we believe that you will find too many rather than too few procedures that will help your clients change. Once you have selected the most appropriate intervention and have adapted it to your client's unique circumstances, you will need to implement it correctly, that is, with fidelity to the integrity of the intervention balanced against fitting the form to your client's circumstances.

IMPLEMENTING EVIDENCE-BASED PRACTICE

Applying evidence-based practice is the end stage of the search for a practice approach to guide a particular intervention with a unique client. It is never as easy as the articles suggest or as the manuals direct (including the suggestions in this chapter). The results of a search for evidence-based procedures will likely provide you several to select and adapt to your client. Thus you must sift through more rather than less information in developing a treatment intervention for the client. Your own client—the one who may be late or overly hostile or affected by the weather or the traffic—is seemingly never as uniform as those in the systematic reviews or the experts' descriptions. Such is the nature of most internships. It is more difficult than we want to admit. Not surprisingly, we believe that one of the first steps in applying evidence-based practice in your internship is for you to carefully consider the credibility of the evidence that will guide the procedures.

As summarized by Vandiver (2002), much more successful work has been done on *developing* evidence-based interventions than on *disseminating* guidelines and protocols, that is, seeing that they are easily available and integrated into routine practice. It seems that it is easier to develop effective interventions than it is to get practitioners to access them and use them.

The burdens of this task, then, fall to you. For an evidence-based practice to be successful, it must first be accessible and then applied. This process is greatly facilitated by those interventions that are manualized (e.g., LeCroy & Daley, 2005; LeCroy, 2007), that are structured in a step-by-step format (e.g., Steketee, 1999, Steketee & Frost, 2007), or that contain treatment protocols, such as those from the Cochrane Library, that provide practical steps, exercises, and procedures for facilitating client change.

All too often, however, evidence-based practice requires that the practitioner structure the intervention into a workable treatment plan, that is, into the session-by-session planning for the particular client. Evidence-based treatment plans reflect an intervention selected from the best available information appropriate to the values and preferences of a particular client.

An evidence-based treatment plan should include seven elements: (1) a bio-psychosocial assessment using standardized procedures and instruments; (2) an accurate and up-to-date diagnosis using all five axes of the *Diagnostic and Statistical Manual of Mental Disorders* (*DSM*; APA, 2000); (3) valid behavioral descriptions of the identified problems or focus of treatment; (4) relevant goals and observable description of the planned target of change; (5) selection of a diagnosis-specific evidence-based guideline derived from systematic reviews, practice guidelines, or expert consensus guidelines and delineating a specific and particular treatment plan; (6) repeated administration of outcome measures of the problem, the goals of treatment, or both; and (7) monitoring client change over the course of treatment and critically evaluating the treatment outcome.

All of this, of course, is done under field supervision and in liaison with your classroom learning. We cover much of this in the following chapters. The most critical component of the treatment plan is that the intervention is guided by evidence and delivered in a systematic manner for targeted and observable outcomes.

In summary, what we consider a predictable continuum in the scientific revolution has, we believe, a Janus face, to borrow from Roman mythology. One side is designed to disseminate the best available knowledge to guide practice, whereas the other side is marked by the lack of centralized and readily available information that can be easily applied by practitioners who see clients day in and day out. This reflects the problem noted earlier, that there has been more success in developing evidence-based practice information than in disseminating the procedures. The challenges of evidence-based practice are made more complex because the information that is available itself has variability in accuracy and utility and thus must be weighed to determine its application. Additionally, all the available information that contributes "evidence" for practice is growing so rapidly that keeping up is a formidable task, even for the most committed practitioner and intern.

Guidelines for Evidence-Based Practice

When thoughtfully applied, evidence-based practice will likely strengthen a treatment plan and, in turn, will increase the likelihood of a client's changing and thereby reaching the goal of the intervention. In other words, an intervention derived from evidence-based practice is likely to enhance treatment effectiveness. Vandiver (2002) suggests four summary guidelines for implementing evidence-based knowledge in practice settings: (1) let the assessment be the guide to selecting the appropriate diagnosis, practice guideline, and intervention; (2) use information from all three sources (i.e., systematic reviews, expert consensus, and practice guidelines) as a guide for determining the most appropriate intervention; (3) if no guideline is available for a particular diagnostic category (e.g., schizoaffective or sociopath), it is necessary to review the professional literature for cutting-edge research or practice articles; and (4) practice guidelines are guides (supplements, if you will) and should never be a substitute for sound clinical judgment, interpersonal skills, and all that makes for a professional in the administration of justice and social work.

WHY ARE CLIENTS NOT GETTING BEST PRACTICES?

Now that we have built up the value of evidence-based practices, we must honestly knock them down a bit. Regrettably, although there is good evidence for a number of best practices, many clients are not getting them. This is as would be expected, in part, from the industry itself: we have had limited success in disseminating evidence-based interventions (Vandiver, 2002). Additionally, the plain fact of the matter is that many agencies are delivering services the way they have been for years without too much change or thought about changing. This is so in social work and criminal justice and, surprisingly, even in medicine. Many providers and agencies simply continue with business as usual, regardless of the advances in the knowledge base. The other simple fact is that it is hard to get agencies and service providers to change. Even many educational aspects of training in corrections and social work remain as they have been for years and will likely continue to be for years to come. In a time of scarce resources and increased competition for these resources, it is understandable, but regrettable, that many agency executives and program directors are more concerned with getting their programs funded and providing services to their clients than they are with determining whether the services are effective and based on the best scientific evidence.

So what do you do when you learn during your internship that an intervention is not effective or that a program is likely to fail? One striking example of this is the Drug Abuse Resistance Education (DARE) program. School administrators, teachers, parents, and police all embrace it. And yet, the research consistently shows not only that the program does not work but also that it might in fact cause harm (Dukes, Stein, & Ullman, 1997; http://www.gao.gov/new.items/ d03172r.pdf). It is imaginable that an internship in a school setting, juvenile justice program, or family services center might include the DARE program in your practicum experience. This type of dilemma is not peculiar to DARE alone but may arise with many boot camps (see effective interventions, cited in chapters 10 and 11) in corrections programs, with one-size-fits-all insight-oriented psychotherapy, and with "scared straight" programs, as examples.

When you are faced with this problem, there are many steps to take to maximize the learning experience. First of all, what you should anticipate is hearing "yes, but our program is different." It might be different. It probably is not that distinguishable. But you won't know until you learn more about the program, which is the very reason for the internship: to learn.

Additionally, the distinction between what you are learning in the classroom and observing in the field makes for marvelous discussions with field faculty, student, and supervisors. Thus we believe the first task is to openly evaluate the components and application of the program or intervention. Maybe it is different. Second, discuss your questions about the intervention or program with your new supervisor, and do not wait until too much time has passed. Bear in mind, as well, that much of the corpus of programs or services is the individuals who deliver them. A new program with an enthusiastic staff that opens its doors for the very first time is different from the same program after a couple of years of working out the procedural details, dealing with staff turnover, and so forth.

Finally, if the agency or services are, in fact, causing harm and are intolerable in your judgment, then you should talk with the faculty liaison about changing placements. We think that this is an extreme circumstance that can easily be prevented by selecting an appropriate practicum in the first place. The exercises at the end of this chapter and parts of chapter 2 are designed to facilitate an appropriate placement and settling in.

EARLY SEARCH FOR EVIDENCE

Joel Fischer

Case Description

This case is one of my early attempts to use the results of research to inform my decisions about the interventions I should use to help a client. The case also involved ongoing monitoring and evaluation using two single-system designs. The case took place in the early 1970s, when the body of evidence on effective interventions was far smaller than it is in the first decade of the twenty-first century. It was also an era when social attitudes about issues were in dramatic flux and, on balance, quite different from attitudes in 2006.

To understand this case, then, students would have to be familiar with three areas: (1) the history of and changes in social attitudes regarding issues such as homosexuality; (2) changes in the amount and quality of evidence supporting effective practice interventions both in the 1970s and today; and (3) the body of knowledge social workers consider important for evaluating practice, such as single-system designs, which were used very rarely by social workers in the 1970s. I chose this case because, although I was not an intern, I was pretty fresh out of my doctoral program; also, many of the issues involved in this case were similar to those an intern might face, including trying to go through the literature to find the best interventions, figuring out how to evaluate this case, and ethical and value issues that were intrinsic to the treatment decisions.

The case involved a 22-year-old man who was referred to me by word of mouth. I was seeing clients in my university office free of charge. It was a time of major changes in the social work knowledge base, and it was important to me to continue seeing clients to support my learning of new techniques as research began supporting their effectiveness.

This client came in with a complaint that he was gay and wanted "to change." He described himself as exhausted from having to deal with the stigma of his gayness; he also said that he was sick of trying to keep his "dirty little secret" from his family and friends. He had read that some therapists were helping to convert gays to being straight and wondered if I would be able to help him do so.

Assessment/Screening and Problem Identification

I was very impressed with the work of Carl Rogers as someone who was both humanistically and empirically oriented, and I was determined to try to communicate high levels of warmth, empathy, and genuineness (WEG) to my clients. That determination might have been the key to the eventual decision the client and I reached about how to define the problem.

As noted, the client came to see me looking rather depressed, beaten down, and discouraged. He was "certain" he wanted out of the gay lifestyle (his words), and our initial discussions centered on why he felt that way and what alternatives there might be for him if he were to choose to try to "change." Because I was focused more closely on his feelings than on solutions, we spent essentially the first two sessions discussing the stress he had been under trying to maintain being gay in secret and the multitude of reasons he had for wanting to "change."

In the third session, however, I noticed a subtle change in what he was saying about his desires to change, plus more openness about discussing his hidden life as a gay man. I had been trying to remain as open as possible to hearing about his conflict between his sexual identity and the family and social pressures he experienced—or anticipated experiencing if he were to be open about it. Gradually, the discussion seemed to change away from the notion of wanting to change his sexual identity and toward the goal of wanting to be more secure and comfortable with his sexual identity, including the desire to tell his family and straight friends.

By the end of the fourth session, we had defined the problem as the need to increase skills and self-esteem and decrease anxiety so that the client could "come out of the closet" and be confident in his dealings with others.

As part of the assessment, although I did not use a formal intake or assessment protocol, I tried to find measures that could be used to assess the current and subsequent state of the client's concerns. This was at a time when the use of such measures was very rare in social work. But I was committed to finding or developing measures because I planned to do ongoing monitoring and evaluation of changes in the target problems before, during, and after the course of intervention.

I tried to tie my measures to the major goals in the case: (1) to decrease his anxiety about discussing his issues with others; (2) to increase his assertiveness, self-confidence, and skills regarding those discussions; and (3) to increase the client's participation in supportive activities to help decrease any sense of isolation in his more open lifestyle.

My search through the measurement literature suggested two scales that would measure at least parts of the first two goals. The first was the Subjective Units of Disturbance Scale (SUDS), a 100-point self-anchored scale that the client and I would use to identify and track his anxiety. This measure was developed by Dr. Joseph Wolpe and was selected in part because this was the primary evaluation tool used with one of the intervention techniques I was considering using. The second measure I found in the literature was for evaluating self-esteem, the Affect Balance Scale (ABS) developed by Bradburn and Noll (available in Fischer & Corcoran, 2007a). This was a 10-point standardized measure that had very good reliability and validity, correlating in predicted ways with life satisfaction (positive) and depression (negative). I asked the client to begin filling out the ABS twice a week starting in the 5th week.

Intervention Selection

My search through the literature for interventions led me to the work of Wolpe. He was the primary developer of systematic desensitization and assertion training (Wolpe, 1969). Not only had I read about this work in my doctoral program, but I also had had some practical experience in using these techniques. I also had read some early reviews of research that suggested that these were effective techniques (Franks, 1969). At the time, these interventions were what I thought to be the best the literature had to offer for the targets we had identified. Many years later, such a search and conclusion would come to be called evidence-based practice.

At the time, I had very little idea about how to directly increase self-esteem, reasoning that increasing skills and decreasing anxiety would have an automatic effect on increasing self-esteem. I recall reading somewhere that having the client say positive things about himself (later called self-affirmations) might help to increase self-esteem, so together the client and I developed positive statements, typed on 3×5 cards and taped to his bathroom mirror. I asked the client to repeat these aloud every time he used the bathroom.

The fourth intervention consisted of a referral to a group I had heard about that met at a community center. The group was designed specifically for gays struggling with their sexual identity. It was a support group with the goal of helping people deal with the crisis of coming out or deciding to stay closeted.

Intervention/Treatment

The client and I met twice a week for $1\frac{1}{2}$ hours per session. The fifth through the seventh sessions were devoted to developing and beginning use of the SUDS measure and training the client in the skills of the intervention techniques. The SUDS requires the client to identify specific situations that he feared, using the theme of "fear of others evaluating him" and putting each on a 3×5 card. The client would then try to evaluate the extent to which each situation created anxiety and then rank those on the 100-point SUDS. I asked the client to do so every day because I wanted a daily measure of anxiety. Thus, over the course of treatment, the rankings on the SUDS varied more than in traditional use, which typically was confined to the treatment sessions alone.

Each session was divided up into sections, starting with approximately 20 minutes of review and discussion to see whether there was any new information and to discuss the support group, 20 minutes of constructing new items for the self-affirmations, and the remaining time divided equally between implementing the desensitization techniques and the assertion training.

Evaluation

To evaluate change, I used two single-system A-B designs (A = Baseline; B = Intervention), one for changes in self-esteem using the ABS as the outcome measure and one for evaluating change in anxiety using the SUDS ratings as the outcome measure. The ABS was used twice a week and the SUDS daily. The designs began with a period of nonintervention, the baseline (A), for a period of about 2 weeks (part of week 5, all of week 6, and part of week 7). The basic assumptions of this evaluation procedure were that changes in self-esteem could occur based on the cumulative impact of all the interventions, whereas changes in anxiety on the SUDS would be mainly due to the technique of systematic desensitization.

The total length of the intervention phase (B) was 10 weeks. At first, the client actually deteriorated on both measures, as his fears appeared to galvanize over the enormity of what he planned to do. But around the 4th week of the intervention phase, a steady drop in anxiety, consistent with progress using the systematic desensitization technique, and an increase in self-esteem on the ABS occurred. During the eighth intervention session, we discussed and practiced how the client might inform his parents, and he did so that very week. He called me excitedly the following day to report that he had started out "a wreck" but was shocked at how easily his family had accepted his coming out. In fact, the client said, his father had responded to the announcement by saying, "Good. I was afraid there was something wrong with you. I'm glad to see there isn't."

In the ninth treatment session, we discussed termination. The client finished the SUDS measure in that session (none of the items, even the most fearful ones, produced undue anxiety) and finished the ABS with superb scores on its two dimensions, positive and negative affect. The last week of treatment was devoted to synthesizing all that we had accomplished, crediting the client for his high motivation and courage, and making plans to meet again in 6 weeks for a follow-up session. I also encouraged the client to continue attending the support group. At the 6-week follow-up, the client reported that he was "happier than he had ever been in his life" and that he had found an incredible amount of support in the community.

Discussion

Several issues were involved in this case. The first was the practitioner's values concerning homosexuality and the professional code of ethics involving client self-determination. I was completely open to the client's desire to change in any way that he wanted, but I have to say that I would not have engaged in "conversion procedures" with the client because I did not believe such endeavors were consistent with the social work code of ethics. Had the client persisted in his desire to convert, I would have been happy to meet with him for several weeks to discuss the pros and cons of conversion, though not to use any conversion techniques myself.

The second issue was the time involved. I had almost unlimited time to meet with the client, and I was willing to take the time necessary to facilitate the client's goals. That may not be customary practice in an actual agency. I also had the time necessary to review the research and literature for techniques that are effective, as well as for measures that could be used in my evaluation.

The third issue was the weakness of the evaluation. I used two A-B designs, one for the SUDS and one for the ABS. Both showed considerable, even amazing, improvement. However, all of the interventions were implemented at the same time. Thus these designs could only more or less objectively monitor and evaluate whether the target problems changed. These designs could not analyze *why* the change occurred, whether it was the cumulative effect of all the interventions or even something that occurred outside of the treatment altogether.

This case took place more than 30 years ago. I have become much more familiar with measurement and numerous effective techniques since then. I know that now I would be much more efficient in planning and implementing the entire process. I would also focus more on cognitive procedures, such as building coping statements into systematic desensitization and use of cognitive restructuring, but I was just beginning to learn these cognitive techniques at the time and did not feel quite ready to use them with a real client.

This case illustrated for me the importance of integrating caring and empathic therapy (WEG) with specific techniques. Had I not displayed the willingness and openness to listen carefully to the underlying message of the client, the outcome of this case could have been disastrous.

▪ ▪ ▪

Activities

A. *Some questions for thought from the case study*

    1. What would your reactions be to a client like this? What are your values and issues concerning sexual identity, especially when the sexual identity of the client is different from yours?

    2. Do you know how to locate and/or develop measures for your clients? Do you routinely develop specific goals, use specific outcome measures, and plan an evaluation design with every case? If not, why not?

    3. Do you know how to engage in evidence-based practice? Do you know how to use the Internet and other forms of literature searches to find the most effective intervention techniques? Do you do so with every client or situation? If not, why not?

B. *Finding an internship*

The seminal first learning experience is to actually find and procure an agency for your internship. Even programs that are fairly strict about who is placed where often offer more than a single choice. To facilitate your task, use the following form:

Step 1. List three agencies you are considering and the contact person:

    A. _____

        contact person: _____

        phone # _____

    B. _____

        contact person: _____

        phone # _____

C. _____

    contact person: _____

    phone # _____

Step 2. What are the primary strengths of each agency?

    A.

    B.

    C.

What are the main limitations of each agency in terms of your learning experience?

    A.

    B.

    C.

The best internship is the one that prepares you for your first job after graduation or, if you're lucky, while you are still in school. The best internship is also the one that best prepares you for the job that defines your career and your goals: making detective, being a superintendent of a correctional facility, administering a public assistance program, being a family therapist, owning a group home—the list is as infinite as the youthful dreams of professionals who are young in experience only. So consider the following:

1. What is your ideal job after you finish your criminal justice or social work degree?

2. What is your ideal long-term job, the one that more or less defines your career?

Step 3. The brief view of things

Which of the three sites you are considering is the best match for your short-term employment goals? Answer by circling the best choice for your A, B, and C internship sites.

A = Best match	2nd best match	3rd best match
B = Best match	2nd best match	3rd best match
C = Best match	2nd best match	3rd best match

Step 4. The long-term view of things

The best internship is also the one that best prepares you for the job that defines your career. So consider the following:

Which of the three sites is the best in terms of your ideal long-term job, the one that more or less defines your career?

A = Best match	2nd best match	3rd best match
B = Best match	2nd best match	3rd best match
C = Best match	2nd best match	3rd best match

Step 5. Rank-order your preferences

Consider all of the foregoing, and once you have thought about it thoroughly, rank-order the three choices.

A. = ___ choice

B. = ___ choice

C. = ___ choice

C. Interviewing potential internship sites

Each internship starts with an interview. This may be with the potential supervisor, but it might include a volunteer coordinator, program directors, administrators, and other personnel. We think it is best to remember that the interview is a reciprocal process. You are just as much interviewing the agency as you are being interviewed. Thus you must be prepared for both. Consider the following.

What are three questions you should expect to be asked at the interview?

1.

2.

3.

As you now anticipate those questions, it is time to answer each. What will you say in response to these questions?

1.

2.

3.

You should also anticipate being asked the following three questions, and we have provided space for you to draft your answers.

1. Why do you want to have a placement with our agency/program?

2. What strengths do you bring to the agency/program?

3. What are your major learning needs that may affect your placement at this agency or program?

You may very likely face the question, "What is your theoretical orientation or perspective toward work with clients?" We think you should have an answer, but one that reflects your current active learning status. That is, your theory is still developing, and hopefully the internship itself will influence that emerging theory. We also want to assure you that, when you hear this question, it typically means the interview or interviewers are out of important questions and the interview is pretty much over. So here goes:

What is your theory?

At some point, you will be able to ask questions about the potential internship. Consider the following.

What are the three most important questions you would like to ask at the interview?

1.

2.

3.

What answers do you hope to hear in response to each question?

1.

2.

3.

The following is a list of questions you might consider asking at the interview.

a. What are the opportunities to work with a variety of staff and other disciplines?

b. What is the practice framework most used in this setting? Or, what is the most important type of learning I will be experiencing at this setting?

c. What educational opportunities are available during the internship, such as attending workshops, seminars, conferences, and in-service trainings?

d. What is your supervisory style? What supervisory formats will I have an opportunity to experience?

e. Will I be assured of _____ hours of supervision? (fill in the blank)

f. Please tell me about the typical client I will be working with in this internship.

Postinterview Activity

Once the interview is over, there is still one step left, and it is really an important one. Be courteous and write the interviewer to thank him or her or them for the interview. There is an added advantage to this letter, as it is also an opportunity for you to correct anything that you may have said that was not correct or expressed as you would have liked. This "thank you" letter is also an opportunity to mention things you may have forgotten, such as that you have had relevant experience or that your dedication can be seen in a volunteer experience that you forgot to discuss. At this point, if it is certain that you are not going to be assigned to the agency for any reason, including your own choice, then it is important to say so in this letter. After all, you may be certain that there will be another student who may be the next choice after you and who is simply waiting and fretting. Consequently, for the sake of another student who is hoping for that particular internship, if you are not going to take that placement, then say so.

SUMMARY

Now that you have read all of the material in this chapter, we hope that you have accomplished two general goals: first, to see the importance of good evidence in determining what you do in your internship; and, second, to have thought and worked through some of the most important aspects of the initial learning phase of the internship. That is, by now we hope that you have been assigned to an internship setting and are about to embark on the applications of social work and criminal justice. We hope that at this point you are about to learn the ropes of your agency.

2 LEARNING THE ROPES OF THE INTERNSHIP SETTING

KEVIN CORCORAN *and* BARBARA THOMLISON
With GERARD LaSALLE

This chapter shows you how to assess the strengths and weaknesses that you bring to the internship and discusses learning the mission and values of your agency and the agency's goals and objectives. You will see how to grasp the policies that govern your agency and its nexus with your academic program. Finally, this chapter shows you how to develop a learning contract that will shape your entire internship experience.

Hopefully, you have a comprehensive understanding of the definition and dynamics of an evidence-based field internship. It is our view that the successful evidence-based internship is the foundation of a successful and professional career in social work and criminal justice. We now consider how to learn the ropes of your field placement agency. You simply must understand how the agency operates in order to perform your expected role. In essence, the initial phase of your placement should focus on the structure and function of the agency and how you may interact in a mutually advantageous role.

Your goal, when first getting assigned to a field internship, is to learn enough to be comfortable as a student and practitioner. Thus the goal of this chapter is to help you learn enough about the field setting to be familiar and comfortable while maintaining the acuity and curiosity that accompanies the feeling of being "uncomfortable." Yes, you will be uncomfortable many times in your field experiences, from the first awkward meeting with your supervisor and the seemingly numerous staff members to trying an intervention numerous times with varying degrees of success to saying good-bye and turning in your staff identification on your last day. You will be uncomfortable chiefly because of your unfamiliarity with practicing social work and criminal justice. We, in fact, want you to be uncomfortable, because that means that you are experiencing and learning new material and professional procedures. Consequently, our goal in this chapter is to help you become comfortable with being uncomfortable.

You might very well ask, though, what evidence is available to help you learn how to be an intern in an agency. Frankly, although considerable writing and some research have been done about field education in criminal justice and social work, little of it concerns how to get used to your internship. Sufficient research has not been done to provide persuasive evidence about what works. We must persevere on with the "best available science," to use the words of David Satcher (as cited in Thyer, 2002), and this is primarily the result of our combined experience and the experiences of our students in the field.

UNDERSTANDING HOW THE INTERNSHIP POLICIES WORK

It is important to understand how the field internship is designed within your academic program. Some criminal justice programs are very large and have sizeable and well-coordinated staffs; others incorporate internship coordinating responsibilities into a faculty member's workload, similar to many undergraduate social work programs. Conversely, most graduate programs have field staffs more comparable in size to those of larger criminal justice programs. There is, in fact, a wide array of institutional structures that guide field internships. Your goal is to understand the relationship between your academic program and the internship placement procedures.

One thing is fairly common in all internships, criminal justice and social work alike, and that is that you will in all likelihood be assigned someone from your educational program who will guide or oversee your field experience. This faculty member is your liaison between the internship agency and the academic program.

Regardless of the structure and composition of the field office in your academic program, someone is responsible in some way for arranging the field assignments, training the field instructors on the particularities of the goals and objectives of field education, and assigning students. Some social work and criminal justice programs allow and encourage students to make the initial arrangements in procuring the internship. Others strictly forbid it. However, both arrangements should have the ultimate objective of ensuring that students become part of the experiential learning process to prepare them for careers in public service or the private sector.

It is critical that you get your field assignment in the appropriate way, even though that may differ from program to program and agency to agency. If you deviate from the academically designed protocol, it may result in adverse personal consequences. Every faculty member in social work and criminal justice knows of students who arranged their own placements, only to be assigned elsewhere. Some of these self-placements seemed educationally appropriate and professionally sound. Most faculty members know of other times when not permitting the placement seems petty, if not punitive.

Though it is imperative that you remain within the guidelines of your academic institution, it is certainly not forbidden to discuss with your academic internship coordinator the benefits of permitting a placement in the agency you have chosen. Self-placements afford several advantages. The agency may be your ultimate career choice, and gaining exposure, or "face time," with them may prove a valuable asset in future interviews and serve as a pathway to future employment. The agency may particularly recognize your initiative in seeking them for placement rather than having the placement emanate from the academic coordinator. Finally, you are more likely to have positive expectations if you have previously researched and selected the agency. Each academic institution may have different protocols for internship assignments, recognizing the differences between social work and criminal justice programs.

We suggest that as you prepare for the internship you consider the following questions, which will help you learn about how your school and the field program function. These questions were designed to help you learn how to establish a successful internship and one that will ensure that you are adhering to the policies and procedures of the academic institution and the agency. It is important to remember that you are the ambassador for your particular academic institution and that future requests by the agency for students may very well depend on your actions and the perception you convey to the sponsoring agency about the school's internship program. Additionally, many of the questions will directly affect the field educational learning contract, which we consider later in this chapter and throughout this manual.

A final word of introduction: This is a field manual—a workbook, if you will. So use it as such. The spaces provided in all the activities are there for you to record your work. We hope that you use this manual in field supervision and class discussion in relevant course work.

■ ■ ■

Does your school or program have a written internship or field manual or course syllabus?   Yes _____   No _____

If yes, obtain a copy.

What is the delineated purpose of the field education experience, as stated in the internship manual, course syllabus, field seminar syllabus?

Is there a policy on how internship placements are assigned?   Yes ___   No ___

If yes, summarize it here:

If no, who makes the decision about the internship assignment?

Faculty name: _____

Office telephone number: _____

E-mail address: _____

Office hours: _____

Questions and topics you wish to discuss with the intern/field coordinator:

1. How are assignments made?

2. My particular interests are:

    a.

    b.

    c.

    d.

3. The four major learning goals I have from the field internship are

    a.

    b.

    c.

    d.

4. Some of the professional skills I wish to acquire include

    a.

    b.

    c.

    d.

5. Based on these interests, what agencies are likely to meet my needs?

    Agency name: _____

Contact person: _____

Telephone/e-mail: _____

Agency name: _____

Contact person: _____

Telephone/e-mail: _____

Agency name: _____

Contact person: _____

Telephone/e-mail: _____

6. Is there any other question I should have asked about?   Yes _____   No _____

Record that question here:

Now record the answers to that question:

What are the next steps in arranging for your field assignment?

Step 1: _____

Step 1 will be completed by what date? _____

Step 2: _____

Step 2 will be completed by what date? _____

Step 3: _____

Step 3 will be completed by what date? _____

Step 4: _____

Step 4 will be completed by what date? _____

Step 5: _____

Step 5 will be completed by what date? _____

ASSESSING YOURSELF AND THE POTENTIAL AGENCY

Although we ended the last set of exercises with an inquiry about what the next steps are, we anticipate and suggest that you complete two steps. One is a personal assessment of what you need to know about yourself and your educational needs; the second is a structured interview form for evaluating the appropriateness of an agency in terms of meeting your educational and professional needs.

By self-assessment, we simply mean understanding your strengths and limitations; that is, the strengths you bring to the agency as a student intern and the limitations that may affect the appropriateness of the agency to meet your particular needs. We suggest that you do this in a very structured way in order to be thorough. If you rely on a free-form self-evaluation, in all likelihood you will either over- or underestimate your strengths and weaknesses and completely overlook some examples of both. A self-assessment should be evidence-based, and we know that structured and semistructured assessments using standardized instruments are more consistent and more accurate (Fischer & Corcoran, 2007a). In the parlance of research and psychometrics, these qualities are referred to as *reliability* (i.e., consistency) and *validity* (i.e., accuracy). As you will see in chapter 10, these qualities are the reason we use standardized instruments for assessing and diagnosing problems.

To help facilitate this personal-educational assessment, we have included the Professional Assessment Inventory (PAI) here. You should use this form as a point of departure in your discussion with a potential field instructor and as the springboard to developing the learning contract or field contract.

Professional Assessment Inventory

This inventory was designed to determine your strengths and weaknesses in a number of areas of your professional development. The purpose is to ascertain those areas that you wish to build on in your internship. It is worthwhile only if you are totally honest with yourself. Once you have answered each item, we suggest that you use the responses in an early field supervision meeting and review the responses with your internship instructor or supervisor. Using the answers on the PAI and the review with your instructor to synthesize your strengths and weaknesses is the point of departure for developing your educational contract.

■ ■ ■

Using the following scale, record your answers in the spaces to the left of the items:

0 = No; I disagree; or I have never done this before
1 = Yes; I agree a little; or I have done this, but very infrequently
2 = Somewhat agree with this; or I have done this on occasion
3 = I agree with this; or I have done this frequently
4 = Strongly agree; or I have done this frequently and am very comfortable with it

Bear in mind that there are no right or wrong answers and that the purpose is to determine what you know, what you are familiar with, and what you need to know. So be totally honest!

___ 1. Have you ever had professional supervision that *critically* evaluates your work with clients or employers?

___ 2. Are you comfortable telling a supervisor of your successes?

___ 3. Are you comfortable telling a supervisor of your failures or errors?

___ 4. Are you comfortable asking for what you want and need in a direct manner?

___ 5. Have you worked with interdisciplinary teams?

___ 6. Are you able to resolve ethical conflicts without second thoughts?*

___ 7. If a personal and professional conflict emerged, would you be able to talk about it openly with a supervisor?

___ 8. Have you worked with individual clients in need of professional services?

___ 9. Are you familiar with the most up-to-date evidence-based interventions with clients in this field internship?

___ 10. I am typically aware of how my feelings, thoughts, and beliefs affect my work with clients in this type of intern setting.

___ 11. When I am angry, sad, or fearful, I am able to keep these emotions out of my work with clients.

___ 12. I have very few biases or prejudices about the typical client in this intern setting.

___ 13. Weak, helpless people or people "caught in the system" usually bring this on themselves.*

___ 14. People in authority are usually too pushy for my liking.*

___ 15. I am comfortable in the presence of people of color.

___ 16. I am comfortable working with European Americans.

___ 17. Gays, lesbians, bisexual, and transsexual persons make me nervous.*

___ 18. I am at ease with people older than I.

___ 19. I am at ease with people younger than I.

___ 20. If I had my preference, I would work only with people of own gender.

___ 21. I am articulate and persuasive in my speech most of the time.

___ 22. I can express my thoughts, beliefs, and opinions in written words.

___ 23. People with physical or mental disabilities make me nervous.*

___ 24. I do not like following the "chain of command."*

___ 25. Once I read a policy or procedure, I retain that information without much trouble.

___ 26. I am good at discerning a client's problem regardless of the amount of tangential information presented in an interview.

___ 27. Once I grasp a client's problem, I know what is the best intervention.*

___ 30. I have worked with a variety of clients with problems similar to those in this agency.

___ 31. When people start talking about how they feel, I get uncomfortable.*

___ 32. I would rarely tell my clients in this agency how I feel.

___ 33. I am able to sense my client's feelings "as if" they were my own without losing that "as if" quality.

___ 34. Most clients in this setting just need a "swift kick in the butt" to get it together.*

___ 35. I have developed contracts for client change that have observable goals/outcomes.

___ 36. I prefer to just "go with the flow" instead of having specific goals of an intervention.*

___ 37. I have no idea what to do with the typical client in this setting.

___ 38. I am familiar with other agencies for referral of the typical client in this agency.

___ 39. I have had experience leading group discussions

___ 40. I can take a large amount of information and summarize it in less than a page.

___ 41. Confronting a client about inappropriate behavior is not my job.*

___ 42. I have worked with families in the past.

___ 43. I am pretty certain about my strengths.

___ 44. I do not like to tell others of my shortcomings or weaknesses.

___ 45. I do not see much use for research with clients in this setting.*

___ 46. I am familiar with the local, state, and federal polices that are germane to the clients at this agency.

___ 47. Most theories about how to work with the clients in this setting are similar.*

___ 48. Hostile or threatening clients scare me.*

___ 49. When the intervention or program is over, there is not much reason to chat about feelings.*

___ 50. It is not necessary to consider a client's strengths, just those areas needing improvement.*

Based on your answers, you will want a field agency that focuses on items you scored as 0, 1, or 2 rather than those scored as 3 or 4. The learning activities that you scored with a 4 probably should not play a large part in your internship. You are there to gain new knowledge and skills; a practicum that focuses on knowledge and skills that you already have will not teach you much. On the other hand, knowing very little and having few of the skills required for an internship may be too challenging. Higher scores on those items marked with an asterisk indicate content or concerns that warrant your attention.

■ ■ ■

How do you decide? First of all, we suggest that you now review the answers on the PAI and recategorize them according to the scores you gave each response.

What item numbers did you score as 0?

_____

What item numbers did you score as 1?

_____

What item numbers did you score as 2?

_____

What item numbers did you score as 3?

_____

What item numbers did you score as 4?

_____

Do the items look fairly balanced, with some in each of the five categories? Based on these assessments and categorizations, you now have important information with which to start your internship and develop your educational contract. Furthermore, as we discuss in chapter 10, evidence-based criminal justice and social work use internal evidence, as well as external evidence that is established by research. Internal evidence is that which you collect to see whether your client's problem is changing or whether the goal of the intervention has been obtained; this evidence is typically observed before and after the intervention. You have the opportunity to do this with your internship. We hope that your responses to the PAI will be quite different at the end of your internship than they are now. Therefore, we suggest that you complete the PAI again after you finish your internship. We think you will be pleased with how much you have learned and developed as a professional social worker or criminal justice worker. In the meantime, the PAI should help identify a good fit between your needs and the potential internship and provide the basis for developing your educational contract.

UNDERSTANDING YOUR FIELD AGENCY'S MISSION AND PROFESSIONAL VALUES

We persevere with the assumption that after having done the preceding exercises, you have been assigned a field internship. Perhaps you have even started your internship. Regardless, you are now thoroughly emerged in learning the ropes of your agency. Your goals are now to determine and delineate the expectations and outcomes of your student-intern role. One of your objectives is to familiarize yourself with the agency's "big picture." An agency's or program's big picture is found in either its mission statement or agency value statement.

To understand your role in an agency, you must understand the agency's actual role or mission and values. Different agencies and programs can have compelling and opposite goals and missions. For example, the intern assigned to a juvenile diversion program emphasizes the value of keeping a youth out of the criminal justice system, whereas the student interning in a victim's rights program or secured facility has the considerably dissimilar mission of keeping a youngster detained. The social worker interning in a battered-women's shelter may have an agency mission of mandatory arrest with a minimum sentence for offenders, whereas another intern in a batterer's intervention program may have the goal of mandatory treatment. Interns in a hospice setting might have an agency mission of easing death; simultaneously, another intern in a state that permits physician-assisted suicide, such as Oregon, may have the mission of aiding death. Agencies and programs, you see, like a poky ball, have many compelling points. Most, but not all, are legitimate competing interests.

Thus it is important for you to understand the mission and goals of your agency or program. Why does it exist, whom does it serve, and with what other agencies does it interact? Imagine the problems that might arise if you have a field placement in political advocacy on teen sexuality and you fail to understand that the goal is to restrict sex education to an abstinence-only model, although you believed it was to promote sex education and safer sex practices. The opposite could also happen. You might be assigned to an agency promoting birth control for teens, whereas you oppose this on religious grounds. In either case, there would be poor fit, and you would be either looking for a new placement or guaranteed a profoundly miserable experience[F1]. For example, a boot camp for youth may focus on punishment and coercive behaviors rather than teaching and education for problem solving and meeting needs of troubled youth. Such a program or setting may pose ethical and professional dilemmas for you and will not be a "good enough fit" for your learning needs.

As you can see, it is important to understand your agency's or program's mission, values, and goals. To help, we suggest that you consider the following questions to facilitate your understanding:

▪ ▪ ▪

1. Does your agency or program have a written mission statement?

   ___ Yes   ___ No

   If no, what documents are available that determine or define the agency's or program's mission, values, and goals? (Record your answers on the following lines).

   _____

   _____

   _____

2. Read thoroughly and carefully the mission statement or the documents you described in question 1. Summarize the mission and values of the agency in the following space.

Mission of agency or program: _____

_____

_____

Values of the agency or program: _____

_____

_____

3. Discuss your answers with your supervisor, classmates, or faculty. Do they see the mission and values in the same manner? If not, revise your answers to reflect your new understanding of the mission and values.

Mission of agency or program: _____

_____

_____

Values of the agency or program: _____

_____

_____

You are now much closer to settling into your agency because you know why it exists and can see whether it is compatible with what you hope to gain from being in a field internship. If you find that the mission and values of the agency or program do not square with your personal beliefs or educational goals, then we suggest you give serious consideration to finding a different placement. This, of course, should be done with open and honest communication with the field supervisor and your faculty liaison.

UNDERSTANDING THE GOALS AND OBJECTIVES
OF YOUR AGENCY OR PROGRAM

Out of the agency's mission will emerge goals and objectives. The words *goal* and *objective* are actually terms with specific meanings. Goals are "specific statements that provide a clear, engaging sense of direction and specify what is going to be accomplished" or "targets for accomplishment" (Lewis, Goodman, & Fandt, 2004, p. 117). Objectives, in contrast, are specific results that are likely to be defined in quantitative and qualitative terms. Objectives will guide "in selecting the appropriate course of action" to reach a goal (Lewis et al., 2004, p. 186); this course of action is a *plan*, such as a treatment plan or your educational plan for what you wish to accomplish in your internship. For example, the goal of a field unit in your agency may be to increase the professional preparation of future practitioners in criminal justice and social work; the objective may be to provide field experiences to two to four students an academic year; and the plan may be to establish a relationship with the social work and criminal justice departments at your university, to recruit four to eight students, to select the two to four best suited for the agency, and to provide various professional and educational experiences, including weekly supervision. As you can see, the objective is dependent on the goal, as it is the operationalization of the goal; and the plan is the means or method of reaching the objectives and goals.

We do not set goals subsequent to an objective; or, at least, we should not if the social service agency or program is to have any sense of integrity. As a consequence, it is important to make sure you use the terms correctly in your internship. Not only will this prevent you from being judged poorly by the agency, but it will also enhance your service to the agency and your actual work with clients. The reason is that your work with clients as an intern will be compatible with the goals and objectives of the agency and will enable you to develop a plan to achieve them. For nearly every client, you will need to have an intervention plan—such as a "treatment plan" in clinical social work, a "release plan" in corrections, or an investigative plan in criminal justice. The intervention plan will delineate goals and objectives. Especially with clients, you will need to be correct and clear about what you wish to obtain (the goal) in observable terms (the objective) and how you intend to obtain it (the plan).

Your learning contract will do the same thing. Like evidence-based practice, your internship should be goal-directed. For example, your goal may be to develop the professional skills and knowledge for practice in social work or criminal justice. The objective may be to learn how to implement a particular intervention, such as group facilitation skills. The plan might be to read a particular book, attend a training seminar, practice the intervention with an actual group of clients, and review your mastery in supervision.

If that were all you did, you would not have a very meaningful internship experience. Thus your learning contract will include a few goals, several objectives, and many plans. With this in mind, consider the following questions for the primary goal, objectives, and plans of your agency or program. Much of this material may be derived from the mission statement and other, similar documents. In some informal agencies, this information may be more difficult to discern, as the case may be that "everyone here knows this" or that past practices have become the norm of the agency or program without being documented. This situation is becoming less and less frequent, however, as most funding agencies require an enumerated mission with specified objectives and plans.

▪ ▪ ▪

1. From all the materials you have gathered so far, what is the primary goal of your agency or program? Write your answer in the space provided.

2. How many objectives specify the goal in objective and observable terms?

   There are _____ objectives.

3. Delineate the four or five predominant objectives of the agency or program that define the primary goal.

   a.

   b.

   c.

   d.

   e.

4. Review the preceding questions and answers with your supervisor and/or faculty advisor. Do they agree with your definitions of the goals, objectives, and plan?

   __ Yes   __ No   __ Somewhat

5. In your own words, what are the plans for reaching the objectives and goals? Record your answer in the space provided.

   a. Revised goal

    b. Revised objectives

    c. Revised plan

  6. a. Now for the hard part. Develop at least two other objectives for the goal, and remember that you want the objectives to be a quantitative and qualitative operationalization of the goal's outcome.

     b. What plan would you develop to obtain the objectives and reach the goal?

From this exercise, we hope you have gained a clear understanding of your agency's or program's goals, objectives, and plan. Remember, though, that just about every agency and program will have more than one goal, several objectives, and many plans. We suggest that you repeat the preceding exercise for all the relevant goals, objectives, and plans. Yes, it will be tedious, but it will certainly help your understanding of your agency or program.

UNDERSTANDING THE AGENCY AND ADMINISTRATIVE STRUCTURE AND POLICIES

Agencies that offer internships are often fairly complex structures that include a number of programs and many policies that govern how the agency and programs work. Few agencies these days have a single program. You may be expected to rotate through a number of programs, as is typical of hospital social work or of juvenile justice settings that have diversion, detention, and a number of programs for incarceration and after release.

Because of the complexity of most agencies, it is critical to understand the structure of the agency, your program within that structure, and the agency's policies. Without this understanding, you will not see the "big picture" of the agency and how your particular program contributes to this picture or how it works or functions pursuant to the policies. Consequently, your learning will be restricted, and you will miss much of the mission of the agency and operational policies.

The first thing you need to know is the organizational structure and the resulting chain of command for administering the agency and your program. The following exercise is designed to help you grasp the organizational structure of the agency. To help with the exercise, ask your supervisor whether there is an organizational chart.

▪ ▪ ▪

1. What is the title of the head of the agency? It might be "chief administrative officer," "chief executive officer," "agency director," or one of many other titles. Record this in the following space.

2. What is this person's name?

3. What is the title and name of the person who is second in command?

4. How many programs are offered by the agency?

5. Where does your internship program fit within this organizational structure?

6. What is the title and name of the person who runs the program?

7. What is the title and name of the person who is second in command in the program?

8. Where does the intern (i.e., you) fit within the program structure?

From this exercise, you should have a grasp of the complexity of the agency, its chain of command, and the place of your internship program within the agency, as well as your particular place within the program or agency. Let's now focus on the relevant policies that outline how the agency and program are supposed to run.

Every agency and program will have many policies. They are all important, but some are more relevant to your internship than others. For example, the policies on documenting your work with a client are probably more important than the policies on how to file an incident report for a paper cut; incident reports for accidents, however, are very relevant and important in settings such as outdoor wilderness programs, boot camps, and hospital settings.

You may very well be asking, "How do I determine which of all the policies are the most important?" The answer is best determined by working directly with your supervisor. We suggest that you gain mastery of the relevant policies by completing the following exercise:

▪ ▪ ▪

Step 1. In conjunction with your field supervisor, identify the three most important or most relevant policies. What is the general title of these policies? If they are unnamed, what is the general focus of the policies?

   1.

   2.

   3.

Step 2. What are the primary purposes of the policies? Why do they exist in the first place?

   1.

   2.

   3.

Step 3. What are the procedures for implementing each of these policies?

   1.

   2.

   3.

Some very important and critical policies are those that govern how you are to interact with other programs within the agency or between your agency and other agencies. These policies may deal with how to make referrals, how to transfer clients from one program to another, or how to coordinate services. There are many forms of and reasons for interprogram and interagency policies.

Does your program have a policy for working with other programs in the agency?

____ Yes   ____ No

If yes, summarize the policy here.

What are the specific procedures for implementing this policy?

Does your program have a policy for working with other programs from other agencies outside the one in which are placed? ___ Yes ___ No

If yes, summarize the policy here.

What are the specific procedures for implementing this policy?

Review the preceding with your supervisor and revise this material based on that discussion. The results of this exercise are twofold. One, you should have a pretty good grasp on how to work with other programs and other agencies. As a result of the discussion with your supervisor, the exercise should give you a brief but workable set of procedures for implementing the policies. Eventually, you will be so familiar with the policies and procedures that they will become rote. That is, initially you might very well need to refer to your answers to the preceding questions as you learn to work within the policies and procedures of your agency and program, but soon, as you interact within the agency, you will be guided by its policies and procedures We hope that the results of the exercises are easier to use as you get started in your internship than trying to use the original policy to determine their purposes and procedures.

But what do you do if there are no such polices for your agency or program? The only solution to this issue is to complete the preceding exercise with your supervisor in terms of his or her guidance or advice. In this case, the answers will capture the standards and practices of the program. If there are no formal policies, then the answers in the exercise are even more important, because you will have to rely on this information and the aid of your supervisor.

Moreover, ask your supervisor whether one of your field assignments might be to write an initial policy for the agency. This is a marvelous way not only to learn about how to write a policy but also to give something back to the agency or program that is giving so much to you.

UNIVERSITY PROGRAM POLICIES THAT MIGHT
AFFECT YOUR INTERNSHIP

One more set of policies is important to your internship: those that relate to the relationship between your field setting and your academic program. Every university or college in the United States and Canada has a number of student policies that will apply to your field setting. That is to say, the rules of the academic program also apply to your role as a student intern. Student codes of conduct, for example, do not stop at the door of your field internship agency. Agency policies, of course, apply to you because you are at the agency in a quasi-professional role and under the authority of the agency in the eyes of the clients. The agency policy may not, however, apply to you at school, even though the university's policy will likely apply to you in the field. For example, federal agencies, many state agencies, and some local programs have prohibitions against endorsing a political candidate. This restriction has a rational basis; after all, if your supervisor has placed campaign material around the workplace, it may pressure you toward the supervisor's advocacy. If nothing else, there could be the perception of undue influence. Such a restriction, incidentally, is not an issue of freedom of speech because what is restricted is considered by the courts to be "conduct," not "speech." If your agency prohibits the conduct of wearing campaign buttons on the job, this does not mean that you cannot wear them to class, even though your professor would likely be prohibited from wearing the same button. After all, he or she is on the job, and you may perceive him or her as having influence over you.

In essence, then, when you review agency policies, pay particular attention to the interagency policies that apply to you as a student as well as a quasi employee. Accordingly, we recommend that you examine the policies of your academic program that apply to you as a student on campus, as well as a student off campus. Many of these policies require paperwork that you will need to complete over the course of your internship.

University and agency policies also intersect in ways that may affect you positively, instead of restricting your behavior. For example, all universities and agencies will have a student policy to protect against sexual harassment. Such a policy typically delineates sexual harassment as a hostile work environment or a quid pro quo sexual exploitation. The definition of a hostile work environment clearly differs between the perspectives of men and women. In spite of this, female students in the field of administration of justice have the right to a safe internship in the field setting, even if it is with hardened criminals in detention. Few agencies these days would claim that this is the way these men are and that women students should "get used to it." Unfortunately, all too many still do attempt to diminish sexual harassment in such a manner, even though the federal courts dismissed this defense quite some time ago (*Robinson v. Jacksonville Shipyards, Inc.,* 1991). Simply stated, the university's sexual harassment policy will apply to this student in this type of setting.

There are several other university policies with which you will want to be familiar that are also designed to protect you while on campus or as a student in your internship. If you are like we were and like all too many students continue to be, you will not even bother to find the policies, let alone read them. After all, you are far more interested in criminal justice and social work and in learning the applications in the field than in reading a bunch of university policies written by lawyers, professors, and administrators.

Perhaps, then, a more modest proposal is in order: locate the university policies, which are likely to be in your student handbook, field education of internship manual, or university bulletin, and simply read the title and purpose. If you understand these elements of the policies, you will at least know where to begin to find the policies that protect you as a student and an intern and those that may give rise to a contradiction between the university and the agency. The following form is provided for this purpose.

We suggest that you use this information as you learn the policies of the agency in order to recognize conflicts and to better understand the agency policies by way of comparisons. Additionally, early in your field internship it will be helpful to discuss the university policies and those of the agency with your field instructor or supervisor. Four policies that we think are likely to be relevant to you and your internship are the sexual harassment policy, the academic honesty and integrity policy, the unsatisfactory student performance policy, and the student conduct code, with particular attention given to the policy on drugs and alcohol.

■ ■ ■

Identify four university policies that affect you in the field internship. What are the titles of each?

1.

2.

3.

4.

What is the purpose of each of these four policies?

1.

2.

3.

4.

Now record the essence of your discussion with your field instructor about the compatibility and apparent and relative incompatibility between the university policy and your internship. (Remember to discuss the comparison of the agency and university policies with what you actually do in practice as an intern.)

THE INTERNSHIP CONTRACT OR EDUCATIONAL CONTRACT

Once you have familiarized yourself with the ropes of your internship agency or program, you will soon start to develop some form of learning contract. This might be called an educational agreement, a learning agreement, or an educational or learning plan. The terms vary from school to school and author to author, but the guiding principle remains: the learning contract, as we prefer to use the term, is the individualized course of learning and experience agreed on between you and your field supervisor and agency. To say "whatever" simply will not work, and few academic programs would permit such a casual approach to establishing a successful field experience. We doubt that you would be satisfied, either.

The learning contract should be comprehensive and explicit and based on your personal strengths, limitations, and needs. This is the reason we had you complete the PAI earlier in this chapter. We suggest that you use it with your supervisor to develop your individualized contract.

As the discussion suggests, the learning contract must be in writing. It must be signed by you and your field instructor, and in some criminal justice and social work programs, the field liaison from the university will need to sign it as well. The learning contract should delineate the particular goals and objectives for your individualized learning and needs. Remember, the goal is what you want to accomplish, the objective is the outcome needed to reach the goal, and the plan describes how you will reach the outcome.

Although your learning contract is individualized, there are a number of common goals for the social work and the criminal justice intern. The need to be familiar with the agency's policy—the focus of this chapter—may in fact be built into the learning agreement in the form of the first goal and objective. If this were the case for your agency, your learning contract would have a first clause that appears like this:

Goal 1: The student will become familiar with the policies and procedures of the agency.

Objective 1: The student will have mastery of the purpose and procedures delineated in the three most relevant policies.

Plan 1: The student will complete the appropriate exercises in this chapter and discuss them thoroughly with his or her supervisor.

There will, of course, be some rather mundane aspects of your learning contract, including such things as the number of hours per week you will be in the field—often specified by the university program—where you will be located and whether you will have a desk or an office; and the times during which you will be supervised. Although these may seem unimportant, it is critical for you to specify them in the learning contract.

Aside from office-keeping topics such as those just discussed, we are certain your school and agency will have several more areas, such as the need for transportation, whether the student must carry malpractice insurance, confidentiality codes, professional dress codes, expectations for making up absences, and so forth. In other words, as you work with your field instructor, be prepared to be told of additional expectations and make sure you ask about any of particular concern to you.

Another topic that is common to most learning contracts is professional growth and development, which includes the goals of becoming a professional worker in the social welfare or criminal justice system, developing professional parlance and lexicon, and developing professional communication styles, including writing and verbal communication and possibly even PowerPoint presentations (for a quick guide to writing and doing presentations see Szuchman & Thomlison, 2007). Some other important common clauses in your contract will concern the acquisition of professional knowledge, skills, and procedures, which may include how to do an intake and screening to determine the mental health condition of juvenile offenders or incarcerated adults, how to do a home visit with a teen mom, or . . . well, just about any and every professional activity imaginable. The most critical aspect, then, is for this to be individualized: what are the limitations you wish to improve, the professional educational needs to be met, and the professional strengths to build on? As professional goals are individualized to your personal limits, needs, and strengths, you will need to develop specific objectives for each one, much as we did earlier in the chapter.

One common characteristic of the internship, regardless of whether it is in the administration of justice or in social work, is that it is time-limited. It will end after a summer or a semester or two. Therefore, you will need to include goals related to termination. You must know how to terminate with clients, which is considerably different with different client populations, settings, and programs. Termination with an offender is much different from termination with a client in clinical social work. Similarly, termination with a child in protective services is different from termination with the parents of the child in protective services. You will need to include the goal of learning how to terminate with your particular client population and program setting.

In spite of these noticeable differences from population to population and setting to setting, all types of terminations have at least one thing in common: even though these are professional relationships, they carry concomitant emotions. Terminating with your supervisor and your field agency is no exception. It is an emotional experience to review the progress made and needs unmet and to come to finality in the relationship. Sometimes it is hard to say good-bye; with some other clients, it may not come soon enough. For this reason, you simply must be aware of your own sentimentalities and beliefs about ending relationships. We address this topic further in chapter 15. Consider the following list as you delineate and enumerate your goals, objectives, and plans for your internship. While completing the following items, it is important to realize that it should be a work in progress, one that will not be finished in one sitting. You may, for example, need to first establish a number of goals with your supervisor and then work out the objectives and the plans. The following form, however, should get you started on developing a workable learning contract.

Develop one goal for the early phase of your internship and one goal for a more advanced professional skill. Define these goals in observable terms, which should include quantitative and qualitative definitions; they are your objectives. Now, determine how you will accomplish each of these goals in terms of activities you will do to meet the objective and obtain the goal; this is your plan.

My initial goal is to be able to/attain mastery of: _____

_____.

The way I will define this goal in observable terms is: _____

_____

I will reach this goal by the following activities or tasks:_____

_____

_____

My goal for an advanced skill is: _____

_____

The way I will define this goal in observable terms is: _____

_____

I will reach this goal by the following activities or tasks:_____

_____

_____

Once you have completed the prototype for an initial and a more advanced goal, discuss each with your supervisor. Based on that discussion, revise the two goals and develop the other ones that will become your learning contract.

Some important goals for the more advanced period of your internship might include developing advanced interviewing skills, improving assessment and intervention skills, learning motivational interviewing, and developing procedures for systematic observations of clients' change.

INTERNSHIPS AT CRIMINAL JUSTICE AGENCIES

The plan outlined in this chapter will enable you to gain the most from your criminal justice internship experience by affording you hands-on experience at the various federal, state, and local criminal justice agencies. In addition to developing marketable skills, you will also establish valuable networks to further a potential career in criminal justice. Internships at criminal justice agencies, especially within law enforcement, carry additional considerations that you should be mindful of as you conduct your assignments. For example, many police departments permit students to ride along in patrol vehicles to see firsthand the daily operations and tasks of police officers. The police officer can explain to the intern how seemingly innocuous situations in an environment may pique his or her interest as potential crime situations. A deviation from the routine activities of a neighborhood may go unnoticed by an intern but raise the suspicions of the officer. Therefore, if you are permitted to accompany an officer, let your curiosity about the environment raise questions that will help you understand the officer's thought process during patrol. Interns accompany officers on nondangerous patrols, but nevertheless they can experience the professional environment from a different perspective than that of the much-joked-about "donut eating." Another typical intern assignment in law enforcement agencies is to assist detectives in their daily investigative tasks. An intern may enter subpoenaed telephone records, financial records, or address records into an Excel database, an exercise that forms an integral part of a detective's investigation and that often becomes vital to the prosecution at trial time, especially in cases of white-collar crime. Thus interns should not take such an assignment lightly. Similarly, interns should be aware that such information is confidential, that they usually have been granted special permission to view such records, and that they may face prosecution for any unauthorized disclosure. If interns feel that they may be in a conflict of interest because they know the target of the investigation, they should immediately relay that information to their field supervisor and seek reassignment to another investigation.

As criminal justice interns, you may be interacting with defendants, witnesses, and victims, and as such it is important that you be guided by your field intern officer as to what role you will assume. For example, if you are witnessing a statement made by an alleged offender to a detective that is later recanted, you may be called on as a witness to testify to your recollection of what the offender said. It is equally important that your daily activities, your observations, and your interactions with those coming in contact with the criminal justice system should not be put down in any written form without prior approval of your field intern coordinator. A review of your written research by the field coordinator will not only ensure accuracy but will also shield you from making any unauthorized disclosures. Your internship as a student-participant will permit discussion with police officers or other criminal justice practitioners as they perform their duties, enabling you to ask questions concerning their actions and thought processes. This hands-on experience will be invaluable to you if you should later choose a career in public service.

THE INITIAL PLACEMENT

Thomas Alexander Washington

Case Description

Valexis was a 22-year-old African American heterosexual female social work intern who was assigned to an agency that provides comprehensive services to HIV-positive gay men. Notwithstanding the fact that she had a close relationship with her gay brother, Valexis had a paucity of knowledge about the gay community, the services available in the agency, and the specific needs of the population the agency served. Nevertheless, she had a desire and the motivation to work with this population.

Each intern received training and mentoring from a licensed clinical social worker (i.e., field instructor). The grant-funded agency had been in existence for 5 years and had maintained an outstanding record of providing great services and excellent client relations. The agency offered quality care services, such as case management, testing for tuberculosis and sexually transmitted diseases, home care referrals, mental health counseling, adult day treatment, and HIV treatment education.

In a conversation with the field instructor, Valexis asked, "When will I have an opportunity to work with a real client?" The field instructor responded, "You will need to become familiar with the agency first, then I will allow you to observe me conduct an assessment with a client. But, again, it is important for you to first learn the ropes of this agency." Valexis rolled her eyes slightly as she was given the policy and procedures manuals for the agency. Additionally, she was given a brochure that explained the different services provided at the agency.

After getting this information, Valexis was given the opportunity to interact with clients as they came into the social service department seeking assistance. Her first task was to assess the client's basic problem and to refer the client to the appropriate licensed social worker for a psychosocial assessment. The agency had social workers who specialized in specific areas within the agency. Valexis was given this assignment to help her get acquainted with the client population and familiarize her with the services available to clients. The intake coordinator observed Valexis on this task.

Assessment/Screening and Problem Identification

The first client Valexis encountered was an HIV-positive Latino gay injection-drug-using preoperational transsexual woman who presented with a drug abuse problem. Unfamiliar with drug abuse treatment services internal and external to the agency, Valexis was at a loss in assisting this client. Furthermore, Valexis was not sure of services for women at this agency.

The intern glanced at the brochure to identify drug treatment services and at the internal agency referral list to determine which social worker to refer this client to. After several glances, she still had no idea as to whom to direct the client. Valexis's anxiety grew to panic. She remembered that the field instructor encouraged the interns to ask for assistance when they felt at a loss. Hence, Valexis asked the intake coordinator to whom she should refer the client. The intake coordinator first instructed Valexis to inform the client to take a seat, stated "I will be with her shortly," and gestured her toward the magazines and newspapers. Next, the intern instructor asked Valexis to once again look at the services manual to identify the appropriate service for this client.

Intervention Selection

Valexis noticed this time that "drug treatment" was listed under the mental health services section on the agency's list. However, Valexis was still confused about the services for women in this agency. After all, the agency's mission was to serve HIV-positive gay men. Therefore, Valexis asked the intake coordinator about services for women, acknowledging that the client of interest was a preoperational transsexual. The field instructor responded, "Our agency is culturally sensitive and the staff works hard to create an environment that is conducive for gay men to define themselves, regardless of which gender they identify with cognitively and socially." With that stated, Valexis referred the client to the mental health services social worker.

Evaluation

To evaluate how well she had learned the agency and its components, Valexis was given a survey at 6 weeks and then again at 12 weeks after beginning the internship. The evaluation included questions regarding the agency's (1) mission, (2) objectives, (3) policies and procedures, (4) available programs, (5) level of supervision for interns, (6) orientation for interns, (7) available resources for interns, (8) reaction to diversity, and (9) working climate. Additionally, the survey included questions regarding the efficiency of the workshops provided to interns, the intern's perception of the clients' experiences, and whether the internship provided the experience needed to develop the intern's skills as a competent social worker. Finally, the survey included a section that asked the intern to provide suggestions that could improve an intern's experience in the agency, particularly the experience of adequately learning about the agency. Simultaneously, Valexis's field instructors were given an evaluation form to complete regarding her knowledge, skills, and abilities and her adjustment to the agency.

Discussion

In the fast-paced and demanding environment in which Valexis (and most interns) gained her first practice experience, it was helpful for her to use the following model: (1) being introduced to the field instructor and staff; (2) reading the agency's mission statement and policy and procedures manual; (3) reading the information regarding the general and specific services available for the population; (4) reading articles about the client population served at the agency; (5) completing tasks that introduced her to the agency with supervision; (6) performing specific tasks and utilizing generalist skills with supervision; (7) expressing any concerns and asking questions; (8) evaluating the effectiveness of the training of interns and the process used by interns to learn the ropes of the agency; (9) being evaluated on her knowledge, skills, abilities, and practice skills.

This model allows the intern to get acquainted with the agency, the client population, and the services available to clients. With this model, Valexis was able to build rapport with her field instructor, become familiar with the agency and its services, gain practice experience, and ultimately to feel competent and assured that she could perform as a professional social worker by the end of her internship.

▪ ▪ ▪

Activities

1. List and describe two ways in which the intern connected with the agency.

2. In your opinion, what methods were most helpful for the intern in learning the agency?

3. Do you think that this model for getting acquainted with your agency can be effective for all types of agencies? Please explain your response.

4. Where there any barriers presented in the case study that could have served as challenges for the intern in learning her agency? If yes, please list the barrier and think of a way that the field instructor could have assisted the intern.

5. In an agency that emphasizes "best practice," is it important to have a model that may assist interns in learning the ropes of the agency?

3 ETHICS, VALUES, AND LEGAL ISSUES FOR INTERNSHIPS

KEVIN CORCORAN *and* BARBARA THOMLISON
With BRIAN C. RENAUER

> *This chapter exposes you to the complex world of law, ethics, and values as they are likely to apply to your internship. Relevant issues include confidentiality, informed consent and the duty to report, the dual relationship and sexual harassment, and finally the federal law called the Health Insurance Portability and Accountability Act (HIPAA). The chapter ends with exercises that cover each issue and a case study of an intern who asserted confidentiality over a reportable matter.*

In the classroom, topics of values, ethics, and the law are often esoteric, philosophical, pedantic, distant, attenuated, and daunting. If all that were not enough, unfortunately sometimes the topics are also boring. In your internship, however, values, ethics, and the law are quite different. The dusty and distant topics actually come to life and play an active role. In your internship you will find that issues of values, ethics, and the law are exciting and something you will encounter fairly regularly.

We consider the more common values, ethics, and legal issues in social work and criminal justice. We do not mean to suggest to the criminal justice student that this discussion will cover the legal issue of the administration of justice but that the chapter is more narrowly tailored to the practice you will find in your internship and profession. The social work student needs to understand that we are not addressing the National Association of Social Workers (NASW) Code of Ethics (1999) so much as ethical issues that are commonly faced by social workers. In part the reason is that we base much of our coverage on the law of practice, which is distinguishable from a profession's code of conduct. We do, wholeheartedly in fact, hope that you examine the Code of Ethics in depth as a student and a practitioner. More so, we hope you adhere to it.

We consider the legal and ethical issues of confidentiality, informed consent, the duty to report, and the duty to protect. These topics, although distinguishable, are, in fact, highly interrelated. We also consider the dual relationship (which is actually an ethical issue of a conflict of interest), sexuality and sexual harassment, negligence practice—which is commonly referred to as malpractice—and the new role for social workers that was introduced by the federal government with the HIPAA. We do not mean to suggest that this coverage is thorough, as the material is massive and often quite complex. We do hope, however, to give you an initial understanding of how values, ethics, and law come to play in a daily routine in an internship and how to recognize and manage the dilemmas that may emerge when values, ethics, and law conflict with your field experience.

First, however, we must comment once again on the topic of what "evidence" is. The reason is the contrast between what is considered "evidence" in the social and behavioral sciences and what it is in the law. In law, evidence is what is obtained and submitted to aver truth, and, most critically, that which is judicially acceptable within the rules of the courts (*Black's Law Dictionary*, 1979). The rules of evidence are such that scientific studies may or may not be admissible evidence. Similarly, evidence designed to illustrate cause, such as that multisystemic therapy causes improvement in antisocial youths, is different in the eyes of the law. *Cause* in the legal view includes *proximal* causes, which in lay terms means something that is *approximately* the cause or *next to* the cause. Thus, as far as evidence-based internships are concerned, this chapter includes a whole new definition.

WHAT ARE VALUES, ETHICS, AND THE LAW?

Most professional disciplines have a set of ethics, standards, or codes of conduct. Regardless of the term used, they are designed to govern those who practice the profession. The NASW Code of Ethics governs social work practice, whereas criminal justice workers are expected to comply with the Law Enforcement Code of Ethics.

These codes of conduct are the ethical obligations of the professional. They may be based on a particular professional value, such as the right to self-determination in social work or the social contract in criminal justice. Ethics may also be predicated on a law, either by statute, as we will see with HIPAA, or case law, as seen in the duty imposed by *Tarasoff v. the Board of Regents of the University of California* (1976). The value or the ethic may also be a legal matter. An example of this is informed consent, which is based on the democratic value of individual autonomy and delineated in the United States Constitution. Laws, in contrast, must square with the Constitution and are often quite complicated in their delineation, such as the duty to report child abuse, which is law in every state and jurisdiction. Ethics, in contrast, are standards comprehensible to everyone in the profession.

There are many similarities between the primary codes of conduct for social workers and for criminal justice workers. Of course, there are also critical distinctions between these codes. The peculiarity of these codes of conduct is that they are intended to govern the professions, but there is often very little enforcement on the professionals. What we mean is that policing of professionals is restricted to those who choose to be members of a professional organization, which is the case with the NASW. Thus the NASW may sanction us, the authors, for misconduct because we are both members of the professional organization, but the Law Enforcement Code of Ethics has no jurisdiction for violation of the same ethic. If we were not members and we engaged in misconduct, we could scoff at NASW, just as we could at the Law Enforcement Code of Ethics if we were not employed in a law enforcement or allied agency. That is, although the ethical standard of a profession *should* apply to all professionals in the discipline, the enforcement of a code of ethics is limited to the reach of those in the professional membership or the purview of employment or the internship. For example, the Law Enforcement Code of Ethics requires criminal justice workers to report miscarriages of justice. But who is to enforce this rule? And on whom is this rule to be executed? Certainly a local police department can impose this standard on sworn officers, civilian employees, and interns, but does it apply to the student who may be placed in a residential program for juvenile offenders? If you say "yes" or "it should," the question again is, Who will enforce it? Certainly not the local police department, as it would with its own officers. Because there is no singular national organization for criminal justice, there is even less oversight or redress for those who transgress the Law Enforcement Code of Ethics except by internal means of employment or internship policies.

What about the social work student placed in the same residential program? Shouldn't he or she adhere to the same standards as a criminal justice student? If so, does that mean we expect the NASW to enforce the Law Enforcement Code?

As this discussion evidences, the peculiarity of professional ethics and values is understandable. Therefore, we are of the opinion that the *professional's* values and ethics must be integrated into your very definition of yourself as a social worker or criminal justice worker. Adherence to the values and ethics is your personal challenge and professional obligation, whereas the enforcement of sanctions for transgression is a distinguishable matter.

As we noted earlier, there are many similarities in the ethics and values of different professions, and some are clearly distinguishable by professions. In this sense, then, we believe you must go beyond the professional parochialism of whether you are a social work student or a criminal justice student. You will likely be expected by your field instructor and faculty to adhere to the professional ethics of your discipline, even if you are not a member of a professional organization. If you are a social work student with an internship in a police department's employee assistance program, for example, you will need to adhere to the obligations of the NASW Code of Ethics and the Law Enforcement Code of Ethics. Similarly, a criminal justice intern working with adjudicated youths in a family service center will find that he or she is expected to follow the NASW Code of Ethics and the Law Enforcement Code. Both professions must adhere to a minimum standard of values and ethics and legal requirements, which we consider subsequently.

CONFIDENTIALITY

Confidentiality is the sine qua non of almost every profession that works with people regarding private matters (Weiner & Wettstein, 1993). This includes social workers with clients and law enforcement professionals' use of informants. It is considered the cornerstone of therapeutic trust and is an essential feature in almost all mental health membership organizations (Winslade & Ross, 1985). This is especially so for counseling relationships in social work. But it contrasts sharply with law enforcement, in which much is public information and is no longer considered private, with exceptions such as the confidential informant mentioned before.

The importance of confidentiality cannot be overstated. It is not only the hallmark in establishing trust with a client or informant but it also facilitates client self-disclosure of private matters and promotes the client's privacy interests, thus allowing personal control by the client of private information (Smith & Meyer, 1987). Moreover, confidentiality promotes the public interest by encouraging people in need of services to seek those services, which in turn is good for society: needs do not go unmet, people don't continue to be distressed, and productivity is not thwarted. In essence, it is good for society for troubled people to get better, and it is good for society for wrongdoers to be pursued by the law. Without a confidential relationship, clients and informants might fail to disclose sensitive and private information or might not seek services at all (Corcoran & Winslade, 1994).

It is the very notion of privacy that gives rises to confidentiality (Corcoran & Winslade, 1994). In fact, the U. S. Constitution provides a right to privacy by way of the First, Third, Fourth, Fifth, and Ninth Amendments. Together these amendments create a zone of privacy (*Griswold v. Connecticut,* 1965). Moreover, this is a fundamental right, which means it has rather rigorous protection from government intrusion. Government may not intrude in a fundamental or constitutionally enumerated right unless two conditions are met: (1) there is a compelling state interest in government intrusion; (2) the intrusion is narrowly tailored to address that interest. In the parlance of Constitutional law, this is known as "strict scrutiny."

Your privacy interests, however, are not actually "private" once there is disclosure to a social worker, criminal justice worker, or most other human service professionals. Privacy, in fact, concerns one's self, namely, one's autonomy. Confidentiality, in contrast, is distinguishable in that it concerns another's knowledge of information that was once private. If one of us, the authors, for example, thought about murdering the other author because of events during the course of writing this book, it is private information. Once this is disclosed to a social worker in psychotherapy, though, it is not a private matter any more. In order to protect the client's privacy interest, the law considers this disclosure to be "informational privacy." Society tries to protect certain relationships in which informational privacy exists, for example, relationships between spouses, penitents and clergy, lawyers and clients, and social workers, counselors, or others who provide mental health services (*Jaffee v. Redmond,* 1996). In this sense, the confidential relationship is "privileged" in the eyes of the law. A privileged relationship is simply one in which the professional cannot be compelled to testify in legal proceedings and may impose a standard for redress if breached.

Because confidentiality is predicated on privacy, it is afforded some Constitutional protections, but not as much protection as is provided for actual private matters. That is to say, the law provides more protection for privacy interests than for confidential information. Confidentiality, for example, is the Constitutional basis for reproductive rights established in *Roe v. Wade* (1973). Confidential information is protected by prohibiting disclosure of what was once a private matter that has been disclosed to another party. In contrast to privacy, in which the state must have a compelling interest to intrude, confidential information is less protected in that the state only has to have a "rational basis" for the intrusion that outweighs the individual's interest. In the parlance of the law, this is known as the "rational basis test."

The contrast between strict scrutiny and the rational basis test is illustrated in *Whalen v. Roe* (1977), in which the Supreme Court ruled that the State of New York could require disclosure of the identity of a patient receiving certain medications. Writing for the majority, Justice William Brennan argued that the intrusion was permissible because the state had a rational basis for the information (e.g., in part, due to public health and the never-ending "war on drugs") that outweighed the individual's right to informational privacy. It is interesting to note that Brennan also based the ruling on the predicate that the information obtained by the state would be secured and dissemination restricted. Without these safeguards, the intrusion would affect the individual's constitutionally protected right to privacy.

Confidentiality is established by other means, as well. Confidentiality is promised to clients through contract law, by which the client has an implied or explicit contract under which social workers and criminal justice workers agree not to disclose the information that was once private (*Roe v. Doe,* 1977). Confidentiality is also based on the fiduciary relationship, which is the relationship in which one party (i.e., the service provider) has power over another party (i.e., a client) such that the second party has no option but to trust the first party (*MacDonald v. Clinger,* 1982; *Horak v. Beris,* 1992). In *MacDonald* a concurring opinion asserts that the fiduciary is not necessary for confidentiality because it is a standard of care; that is, unlawful disclosure by a service provider falls below the standard of care and is thus considered negligence or malpractice. We say more about malpractice a little later in this chapter. For now suffice it to say that the laws in some states allow redress for unlawful disclosure of confidential information. This liability loop includes unlawful disclosure by an individual (*Humphers v. First Instate Bank of Oregon,* 1985), such as the professional social worker, or by an employer (*Horne v. Patton,* 1973), such as your field agency.

Not everything your clients tell you, however, is confidential. There are legal exemptions from the obligation to keep client information confidential. The most pertinent example for your internship is the exemption from confidentiality for educational purposes. In the student-teacher role, as in consulting with a specialist, the confidential information must be disclosed in order for you to acquire the necessary supervision, know-how, and skills to actually help the client and learn to be a professional. Imagine, if you can, what it would be like to have to say to your supervisor, "Sorry, I can't discuss that. It's confidential." You certainly couldn't get much feedback or learning with such a strict and unworkable interpretation of confidentiality.

You have probably experienced this exception to confidentiality yourself as a client or patient. As health care consumers, we all see this just about every time we are in any teaching hospital; the proctor will say to an entourage of residents "Come see the case of premature [.....] in Room 12. You'll never see another case like it. . . ." As this suggests, we could hardly teach a new generation of criminal justice workers or social workers without this type of exemption to confidentiality. The need to discuss your cases with your supervisor challenges the obligation to keep the information confidential. You must balance your individual need to become a professional criminal justice worker or social worker with the client's right to confidentiality. Much of the right to confidentiality is based on the legal notion of a "reasonable expectation." It is not reasonable, for example, to expect privacy in a public place, such as a waiting room of a clinic or your classrooms. Similarly, it is not reasonable to expect confidentiality when the provider is a student intern whose purpose is to learn professional skills, thus necessitating disclosure to your field instructor or faculty advisor.

But this does not mean that you are freed from this ethical duty of confidentiality. One way to balance your need to learn with your client's right to privacy is to tell your clients that you are, in fact, a student intern, that your internship is supervised, and that you simply must discuss the client's case with proper authorities, such as your supervisor or a faculty member. Not only is honesty the first policy here, but it also helps to establish trust in you and eliminates any erroneous notion of an expectation of privacy. Additionally, you should inform the client that even though you will discuss the case with your supervisor and faculty members, it will remain relatively private because the supervisor and faculty members are is also ethically—and possibly legally—bound to keep the information confidential. This is similar to the *Whalen* case, in which the state had access to confidential information because the state was obligated to also protect the disclosed information. In a sense, by discussing your client's confidential information with a supervisor, your obligation "follows through" to the supervisor.

Another exemption from confidentiality is criminal intent. You are exempt from keeping information confidential when the client discloses the intent to commit a crime—but not just any crime. The best known example is the mandatory reporting of child abuse, which has been enacted in every state. However, if at the end of a session your client says, "My! Look at the lateness of the hour. I'll have to speed to get home in time to watch the season finale of *Desperate Housewives*," you certainly would not be compelled to call the highway patrol. But what about the youngster in detention who says that he or she intends to "pop that bastard when I get out of here!" What about the welfare recipient who acknowledges that assets have been hidden in order to qualify for Section 8 housing? Or the mental health client who intends to defraud an insurance company by overstating his or her depression but who does not meet the criteria for dysthymia?

These examples illustrate two elements of the exemption from confidentiality when faced with the intention or commission of a crime. First of all, you must believe that the client is sincere about committing the crime, and, second, the crime must be more than trivial. As this suggests, then, the threshold is your professional judgment and what the reasonable and prudent practitioner would do in the same situation. Consider the youth in detention. What does it mean to "pop"? Is it a whack on the back of the head? A poke in the nose? Or is it perhaps a drive-by shooting? Because you are new to social work and criminal justice, your professional judgment is still developing; this is the reason that you are an intern. Therefore, it is important to be conservative when considering whether the intent to commit a crime is sincere and the crime sufficient enough to report. (One of us still remembers with burning embarrassment contacting the police when a client stated she was going to kill her estranged husband; it later turned out that the client had told this to every previous clinician and that the police were comically familiar with the client.)

The situation, however, gets even more complex. You may not be required to report the intent or commission of a crime if it has already been reported. Imagine that your client was referred to you because of child abuse; in the course of your work, he or she tells you about the incident of abuse that resulted in the referral. Would you have a duty to protect and thus have to report this to the authorities? The answer is "yes . . . , but maybe not." There is a duty to protect, but in some states and in many circumstances, once the duty is fulfilled, it is fulfilled. To require additional reporting may make collecting evidence easier for the prosecutor but certainly would decrease the likelihood of working on the issues of anger and child rearing. Public policy is better served if both the duty to protect is fulfilled and the reason for the protection is addressed. After all, the duty to protect does not require you to become a witness for the prosecution (Leong, Spencer, & Silva, 1992).

As this discussion suggests, even the exemption for nondisclosure is rather complex and probably confusing. In this sense, you are best off discussing the matter in supervision. These examples and the unique ones you will encounter make for valuable classroom discussions as well. In discussions with your supervisor, you will find that there are many other times when you are exempt from nondisclosure. There are many, including reporting information to insurance companies, revealing information from a court-ordered assessment (which are generally not confidential), and in the case of a client suing for malpractice. In these circumstances the client cannot claim that the relationship was confidential and that you may not disclose the information. Imagine a court counselor assessing a juvenile's mental status, only to say to the judge or other justice authorities that the information was confidential and that the client wished for it not to be disclosed! The actual client here is not the youngster but the court that ordered the evaluation.

These limits to confidentiality exempt disclosure from being considered wrongful. They do not necessarily mean that you must disclose information, however. All of this discussion has likely left you with confusion and uncertainty of just what to do about the confidential relationships in your internship. The topic, like most legally derived issues, is multidimensional and turns on the facts of the cases. Even two seemingly similar circumstances may be quite different and may require different actions. There is no simple suggestion for handling this complex topic, save for continuous examination and exploration in supervision, in the classroom, and in your future professional practice.

INFORMED CONSENT

Informed consent is closely related to confidentiality in that your clients must consent to the confidential condition of the relationship. In this respect, informed consent actually precedes confidentiality.

Informed consent is not simply having the client agree to certain terms or conditions of the professional relationship. The operative word is *informed*. In order for consent to actually be consent, at a minimum the client must be informed about three things: (1) the procedures to be used, (2) the risks involved in the procedures, and (3) the alternative procedures and their concomitant risks. This must also occur before the implementation of the intervention.

This should sound like a formidable task for any professional. It is especially so for social work and criminal justice, as they are broad disciplines with many available procedures or interventions. How can one know not only the intervention that seems most appropriate but also *all* the alternatives and all the risks of each one? This should seem especially daunting for the student in his or her first internship.

Because of the huge size of this demand, you will find informed consent to be one of the first topics for supervision. It will be helpful for you to discuss the intervention of choice and other interventions that might have been used. Supervision, then, should focus on *what* procedure to use and how to implement it, but it should also examine *why* it is the intervention of choice over others. Only after you have a grasp on this will you be in the position to obtain the *informed consent* of your client.

Keep in mind, too, that this process of inquiry never ends. As research in criminal justice and social work continuously improve the available interventions and often develop new ones, your career will constantly demand that you learn about the effectiveness or lack of effectiveness of an intervention. Of course, we hope the content of this manual facilitates your mastery in acquiring knowledge of evidence-based interventions.

Another element of informed consent is the timing at which permission is obtained. As mentioned earlier, the three elements of informed consent must occur before the intervention begins in order for the consent to be informed. Consent obtained after the fact may seem like consent, but in the eyes of the law it is not considered to be informed (*Roe v. Doe,* 1977). The reason for this is clearly the effect the relationship might have on your client's ability to consent or refuse to consent. In particular, your relationship may give rise to undue influence on your client; as we mentioned in the previous section, the relationship is likely one of trust. *Undue influence* is quite a broad concept, referring to "constraints, machination, or urgency of persuasion" that induces or prevents something that otherwise would happen differently if one were left to act freely (*Black's Law Dictionary,* 1979, p. 1370). This influence may be intentional, or it may not. The very fact that you have a confidential and trusting relationship on some level may prohibit your client from saying "no." The client probably likes you and trusts you, so he or she is not perfectly objective and free to agree or not. This is even more apparent in many criminal justice settings, in which a worker may hold power over the client, such as a youth in detention or an adult on parole.

Consider the example of a student with a unique case, such as a gay 13-year-old struggling with his identity and orientation who just happens to be incarcerated. We would all agree that the circumstances and the setting would warrant some form of intervention. The intern and the youngster decide to implement a program of coping, personal safety, and identity development. Assume further that the student did a remarkable job and wanted to discuss the case at a professional conference or perhaps even to write it up as a case study for publication. The student then goes to the supervisor to ask how to get permission to do this, only to be told that it cannot be done, that it's too late. Why? The reason is that the consent would be given after the fact, and, therefore, it would not be "informed" consent. The absolute finality of this may seem rigid. If you think of it from the client's perspective, it is not. After all, it is hard to imagine that the youth who has been helped would really be able to say "no" once there is a trusting and caring relationship.

In most social work and criminal justice settings, the ideals of informed consent are lacking. A youth in a foster home, for example, probably did not consent to the placement in any "informed" manner, especially if the child is young or not intellectually capable of understanding; that is, the youngster may not have the capacity to consent due to age or comprehension. Similarly, criminal justice settings rarely gain consent once a youth is adjudicated or even simply arrested. In many professional relationships in which informed consent is seminal, consent may not be truly "informed" as the client may feel pressured or even coerced into seeking professional help. This is often the case in family therapy. Time and again, when you ask a teenager why she is seeking counseling, you will hear, "my parents made me." It also occurs frequently with couples. Bill and Betty Bicker-more may consent to marital therapy only because Bill was told that if he did not stop drinking Betty would divorce him.

Informed consent is questionable even in many counseling relationships be-cause the intervention may be based on insight and self-disclosure of unknown information. On occasion, a client will not remember an event that later comes back to him or her by way of insight. How does a person consent to something he or she does not know will happen? Additionally, some clients' levels of distress are so high at the beginning of treatment that their capacity to consent may be dimin-ished because they are unable to refuse services.

This may suggest to you that trying to manage even the simplest professional relationship is difficult, confusing, and even elusive. It is difficult, confusing, and elusive to the point of chaos because one has to know more than is possible to know (i.e., all the available procedures and risks) and must do so in advance with a person who is probably not truly consenting.

There are, of course, ways to make informed consent more manageable and, frankly, more realistic to criminal justice and social work relationships. We are of the opinion that some of the best of suggestions appear in the American Psy-chiatric Association's (1987) *Guidelines on Confidentiality*. These guidelines point out that the consent must be given prior to starting treatment and given freely, or as freely as possible in light of pressure from others or from the client's cir-cumstances (e.g., such as requiring therapy as a condition of enrollment in a program). Most important, the APA suggests that informed consent be considered a dynamic *process* more than a static *product*. As such, the consent of the client should be obtained continuously throughout the counseling relationship and not just at the beginning.

Additionally, just as consent can be given, it can be taken away. In many criminal justice settings, once consent is obtained, such as to a search of one's person or property, it may not necessarily be able to be withdrawn. In most social work and criminal justice settings, however, the clients not only have the legal right to con-sent but also have the power to withdraw the consent. By continuously reassessing and reaffirming the client's consent at various points in the relationship, not only are you considering the best interest of the client in terms of giving permission, but you have also created the environment for your client to withdraw consent.

Before closing this discussion on informed consent, we ask you to consider these questions: Do you think your clients know that you will be discussing their cases with your field supervisor? Do you think they know that you are likely going to write a term paper or give a classroom presentation about them, even if you disguise their identity? These questions may appear to be more germane to confidentiality than to informed consent. They illustrate that there are limits to confidentiality. Before you can reasonably expect a confidential relationship, you must discuss these limits with your client at the time he or she is consenting to have you work with him or her. As a student, you simply must learn to be a professional, and this requires that you work with your supervisor and classroom instructors. Therefore, we think it is critical for you to inform your clients that you will discuss their cases and get their consent in order to learn from the internship experience. But remember, this must be done before the professional relationship begins.

MANDATORY REPORTING

Even when you have successfully obtained informed consent for a confidential relationship, it does not mean that there are not situations in which you may disclose confidential information or situations in which you must. Remember that we mentioned earlier that confidentiality will emerge if your client has a "reasonable expectation" that the information will stay private. However, there are times when an expectation is not reasonable and the confidential information may demand disclosure.

The most common example of this is the mandatory reporting laws regarding child abuse, as mentioned earlier. This is fairly unique in law, as it imposes an obligation for affirmed behavior rather than, as most laws do, prohibiting behaviors; that is, mandatory reports require that you do something, whereas most laws forbid you from doing something.

This exception to confidentiality is predicated on the duty to protect third parties. The duty to protect may be statutory, as with child abuse, or it may be derived from case law. The most well-known example is *Tarasoff v. Board of Regents of the University of California* (1976). In this case a therapy patient threatened to kill Tatiana Tarasoff, the object of his unrequited love, and actually did kill her. The therapist, an employee of the university, advanced a number of defenses for not disclosing this information in a reasonable and prudent manner, including the defense that the relationship was confidential and, therefore, private. The courts held that "privacy stops when public peril begins" and that there was a duty to protect a third party when the therapist knew—or should have known—that someone was in imminent danger. The duty to protect is known as the Tarasoff Rule.

Oftentimes in the behavioral and social sciences, people incorrectly refer to this as a "duty to warn." In the case itself, the justices sometimes used the words "duty to warn" and at other times "duty to protect." It is confusing because a warning may be sufficient to protect someone; but a warning alone may not be enough. The duty to protect is a higher duty, and when the court spoke of both, it subsumed the duty to warn under the duty to protect. In other words, the court established the higher duty as the duty to protect, which includes the duty to warn.

As you are seeing with many areas of your internship, however, the Tarasoff Rule is not actually all that clear and comprehensible. There are limits to the duty to protect. Some say it applies only to very narrow circumstances that meet several conditions. This argument says that the Tarasoff Rule applies only when the responsible party is employed by the state, *and* has a special relationship with the client, *and* when the danger is actually reasonably foreseeable, *and* the professional did not do what the reasonable and prudent practitioner would do in the *exact* same situation. Each of these conditions has specific definitions in law and must be particular to the client's circumstances. Therefore, defending against violating the Tarasoff Rule may be a fairly easy affirmative defense. Additionally, the last standard, as we shall see in the following discussion on malpractice, is the standard for negligence. Many would not consider it to be a terribly high standard and, therefore, not likely to assure much return with or without Tarasoff. Moreover, Tarasoff's authority is restricted to California and to other states that have adopted the rule either by legislation or by case law. These states are called Tarasoff States. Some states, such as Oregon, have not adopted Tarasoff, only because the duty to protect was established before the Tarasoff case.

The duty to protect is not always as simple as it might seem, even with all the restrictions previously suggested. For example, what is meant by "foreseeable"? Additionally, in some states and in many circumstances the duty to protect and report may not need to be reported more than once. Because of this, we trust that you will always question the understanding of your duty to report and discuss this issue frequently with your field instructor, classroom instructors, and professional colleagues once you finish your education. In fact, we cannot stress enough the importance of immediately reporting any suspicion of abuse.

THE DUAL RELATIONSHIP AND CONFLICT OF INTEREST

The ethical issue prohibiting—or greatly restricting—the dual relationship is similar to the ethics of obtaining informed consent. To be considered "informed," consent must occur prior to the initiation of the activity because of the danger of an undue influence on the client's autonomous decision making. Undue influence is also the basis for prohibiting dual relationships because of the effect you may have on your client. A dual relationship essentially means that you are seeing a client for services and concomitantly using the client commercially.

In social work and criminal justice, the dual relationship is particularly critical because of the actual and perceived power you have over a client. The most obvious example is in criminal justice, in which the power over a client may extend to the most basic American rights: liberty and freedom. There is little doubt that one who holds the key to the detention center—does indeed have power and, therefore, influence that may be undue over the client. As we discussed regarding the power-trust relationship of the fiduciary, the client has no alternative but to trust you.

Let us consider another example from criminal justice of a dual relationship. Criminal justice workers and social workers who work in corrections know that close to release the inmate begins some form of a "parole plan," which is also called a "release plan." A successful parole plan has many elements, including housing, substance abuse treatment, transportation, employment, changing criminal thinking, and restricting friendships with other wrongdoers. Let's assume that the inmate, on release, starts working for X Construction and Painting (XCP), a work-release program. As a parole officer, you might consider having the crew paint your house for a number of seemingly good reasons. By using the XCP, you might actually help the client in his rehabilitation. Moreover, you know you will get a better price and that the workers will do a job "above and beyond" your expectations. And yet, these good intentions are the very reasons for prohibiting this type of dual relationship. Suppose, for example, you ordered a yellow paint that was a shade different from the one the crew applied to the house. Would any parolee be able to refuse to repaint the house? It would be nearly impossible, and the apprehension of adverse repercussions unavoidable. Therefore, the undue influence puts the client at risk of exploitation of your power and his trust. As this example illustrates, undue influence exists even when the intent is altruistic.

We can also see this type of conflict in activities that might be trivial on the surface. Assume that your internship is in a group home for teenage women who are "aging out" of the foster care system. The young women want to have a car wash in order to raise money for a group activity, such as a field trip to a very popular "clothing optional" beach. They charge $10 for a car and $15 for SUVs and other trucks. If your SUV needs washing, would you be prohibited because of a dual relationship? Doesn't it seem a bit trivial to refuse to participate in this event and instead spend your money at Big K's Car Wash down the street, even if Big K were slightly less costly? Isn't the convenience alone worth the price?

It may seem to be folly to raise the dual relationship shield in this circumstance. But suppose one youth tells you, "We'll give you an extra waxing and a half-price discount. Call it a professional discount." Who would not immediately have a more favorable impression of this youth? (Or, perhaps, an unfavorable one if you thought she was being manipulative.) Either way, even this seemingly harmless example might well present deep difficulties.

If you still think there is no potential for undue influence, we'll make this example a little more provocative. Say the young women secretly decided to wear bikini bottoms and t-shirts while washing the cars and that they have the customers stay in the cars. They "accidentally" get the t-shirts wet, revealing the words "tips welcomed." Your initial altruistic support for the youths' fund raising would now be inappropriate. Clearly, as this case illustrates, the dual relationship is complex and should be seen as a continuum of potential conflict.

This type of power-trust dynamic is found in nearly every professional relationship in the human services in which there is direct human contact. This does not mean that all professional relationships, such as research, education, and training, impose a fiduciary duty. In social work we see this when doing counseling with adults (*Horak v. Biris*) and case management with youngsters (*Simmons v. United States of America*, 1986). Because social workers and criminal justice workers have the power to implement interventions, often under the color of the authority of the state, and because they have a knowledge base that the client lacks, the client simply must trust that he or she will proceed with the client's best interest in mind. Your moral and professional compass must point toward your client's best interest.

Similarly, in clinical settings, regardless of whether you are an intern in social work or in criminal justice, the power you have over your clients is even greater than in more indirect human services, such as discharge planning or administration. In the counseling relationship, not only does the professional have knowledge and skills that are unknown and generally unavailable to the client, but these skills are also so powerful that he or she can actually reach and touch the client's unconscious. Even the courts, which generally shy away from social science theories, have averred that the talents of a therapist allow unlawful touch by reaching into one's unconscious (*Rowe v. Bennett*). The knowledge and skills, if used properly, enable your clients to discover new things about themselves through insight and, ideally, change the clients' daily lives. How much more power is imaginable? By the time you graduate from your program, you will have the ability to affect how a person lives day after day.

These examples should convince you that your power could be abused fairly easily and even unintentionally. For these reasons, some professional organizations, such as the NASW, strictly prohibit the dual relationship. However, it is not always simple to avoid the dual relationship. Persuasive examples abound in small towns and rural areas. For example, assume that a clinician lives in a small town and is building a house that requires a well. There are no other mental health providers within 50 miles and only one well driller in the town. If the quarrelsome well driller and his argumentative wife needed clinical services, they would either be referred to another professional in a nearby town or go without treatment. This essentially means that the couple will get no services, as it is cumbersome to drive for over an hour, especially alone with a disputatious spouse, to access the services. In the alternative situation, the clinician will not get water from the well he needs drilled. To avoid the dual relationship, one party is going to lose: either the well driller and his wife will receive no therapy and will likely continue in their distress or the clinician will have no water. Either alternative is unfair to one of the parties and violates the public policy of getting services to those in need, as well as the basic need for water. As this example suggests, although the reason for restricting the dual relationship is for the good of society, its rigid adherence may also run against the public policy.

We assume, as was the case with the ethics issues discussed earlier, that you are likely shaking your head, wondering how the straightforward class content about values and ethics became so complicated when you reached their applications in your internship. Like confidentiality, informed consent, and mandatory reporting, the nuances of avoiding the dual relationship require consistent self-monitoring and feedback in supervision. We hope the learning activities in this chapter actually help you see how to address and resolve ethical dilemmas in your internship and in your professional practice.

SEXUALITY AND SEXUAL HARASSMENT

As you start this section, do not think that, unlike the preceding issues, the ethics of sexuality and sexual harassment will be simply cut and dried. The professional ethical, and often legal, prohibition against having sex with a client is quite clear and forbidden. As such, sex with a client—regardless of how you define sex—is clearly unethical and, in some states, unlawful.

This does not mean, however, that the topic of sex will not be relevant to many of your clients. As a person who works with people, you will deal with sexuality issues more than any other professional with the exception of the clergy. It will not always be relevant—for instance, with a family applying for various social services. It will, however, be relevant to many counseling concerns, as with victims and offenders in the criminal justice system and, of course, with many couples who are distressed by their sex lives. Therefore, regardless of whether your internship is in criminal justice or in a social work setting, it is important for you to be comfortable talking about and dealing with sex. If you are not comfortable, you need to work on this in supervision or select an area of practice in which sex is not likely to be relevant, such as public welfare or research (actually, there are not too many areas in which sex is not somewhat relevant).

Sexuality also comes into play between professionals. This may range from the "office affair" to sexual harassment in the workplace. We are of the opinion that the office affair is likely to cause harm and may complicate, if not compromise, the professional relationship and the learning experience for interns. It is probably best and easiest to keep the professional realm separate from your social and intimate world. Yet we understand that students are people, that people meet people, date, fall in love, and have intimate relationships; this often happens in social environments such as school and work. Your professional development does not mean that you must choose between being a professional human service worker and having a fulfilling, intimate love life. Do, however, use your professional judgment to guide your decisions before giving the lead to your heart or desires.

When your client's sexuality is relevant, a good and clinically useful question to ask is, "How old were you when you first had sex, and with whom"? This question allows the client to define what is meant by "sex," and because it is a nonthreatening question, the answers are typically completely honest. Even when the question gives your client pause, it tells you something important. You are likely not only to hear answers that provide valuable private information, such as about abuse or assault, but you may also hear about activities that you consider surprising if not shocking. It is of critical importance that you remain nonjudgmental.

Once you have opened this door, what do you do with the information that comes into the professional relationship? First and foremost, the questions must be asked in the best interest of the client, not out of your personal curiosity. Second, the answers should be relevant to the purpose of the professional relationship; if not, a proper referral is in order. Oftentimes, though, learning about a person's sexuality greatly facilitates your understanding of the dynamics in his or her life and of his or her sense of self, as well as of common behaviors that may result from sexuality, such as the sexual acting-out behaviors of youths or persons with a borderline personality disorder. Your client's sexuality may even be the focus of the intervention, whether in social work or criminal justice. As such, it must be enumerated in the client's treatment plan, including what is to be done after the professional relationship is terminated.

Needless to say, these issues will require serious and sincere discussion in supervision. Thus our assertion that you simply must be, or become, comfortable knowing about, talking about, and dealing with sex. If you are not comfortable at the beginning of your internship, we wager that either you will be comfortable at the end of your internship or you will be reconsidering your professional goals in criminal justice or social work.

Another area of sexuality that you will deal with in criminal justice and social work is sexual harassment. Sexual harassment is prohibited by federal law. It is defined in two ways: (1) as a quid pro quo relationship in which the commodity exchanged is sexual behavior for something else, such as a raise, a promotion, or a grade in a class; (2) as a hostile work environment that affects one's performance and well-being. In the event that you experience either, you should immediately seek help from your supervisor or faculty liaison (assuming that neither of them is the one harassing you). Alternatively, every college and university will have a sexual harassment officer available to help you. Do not hesitate to contact this person in the event of sexual harassment.

NEGLIGENCE AND MALPRACTICE

Another pertinent issue in your field placement and in your professional career is the duty to provide a professional standard of care. Failure to do so may result in a lawsuit based on the tort claim of negligence. This is commonly called *malpractice*.

For reasons seemingly peculiar to our profession, many professionals in the human services fear being sued for malpractice. These is especially true of counseling and clinical social workers in various private or not-for-profit agencies, more so than of criminal justice workers, who are often employed in state programs and are indemnified by a state's defense of eminent domain. In contrast to the apprehension felt by many professionals, instances of malpractice are quite rare, especially by interns. In part, the reason is that the interventions are not necessarily intrusive, as is the case with surgery or in prescribing medications. Additionally, in many state jurisdictions the emotional duress associated with malpractice must be accompanied by physical symptoms, even those as commonplace as headaches or stomach pains; without physical symptoms, the courts may rule against the plaintiffs, even if the negligence was obvious.

Chief among the reasons for the lack of threat from malpractice suits are that social workers and criminal justice workers must provide services at or above the "standard of care." Additionally, both disciplines typically are closely supervised, and negligence is less likely. This last point is probably the best reason for the lack of malpractice lawsuits, in that the best malpractice insurance is providing effective services and using good "bedside manners." This is the most important-point: worries about malpractice suits can be allayed by simply providing good services at the standard of care.

What is the standard of care? you might well ask. As with other issues in this discussion of values, ethics, and the law, the answer is, unfortunately, nebulous and not always clear. The answer, then, is "it depends," which is the typical answer to legal questions. There is no singular standard of care, and much of the liability rests in what you are doing and how you present yourself while doing it. If you are implementing a behavioral intervention for school-phobic youths in a school-based internship, then the standard of care is to do as good a job as the reasonable and prudent practitioner in the exact same situation would do. This does not mean that you must be effective; in this sense, there is no legal right to "effective" treatment (Corcoran, 1998), only a legal redress for practice below the standard of care. This should make sense: if no established way to address a client's problem exists, as with some personality disorders, then one clinician cannot be expected to be any more effective than another. This means that your legal obligation is to provide services that are just as good, or just as poor, as those of other professionals and to do the best job possible in the best interest of the client.

Using a client-centered approach with the school-phobic youths would not be effective or appropriate, as only exposure therapies are the treatment of choice for such problems (see Rygh & Sanderson, 2004). You might fail with such an approach, but this would not constitute malpractice. It might be unwise, inappropriate, and ineffective, but with a negligence claim in torts, the law requires that the unwise, inappropriate, and ineffective therapy fall below what the reasonable and prudent practitioner would do in the exact same circumstance and be the proximate cause of some damage.

So for a practitioner to be sued for malpractice there needs to have been some damage done to the client. If you use client-centered therapy, you may learn some critical techniques, such as reflective listening, and the youngster may respond favorably because of interpersonal attraction, but the phobia will not change; the treatment won't work. However, there may be little, if any, damage to the client beyond wasting the client's time and parental or state resources. You may suffer some embarrassment when your supervisor and class instructors furrow their brows and ask critically why you would use this outdated approach.

The standard of care is also a national standard and not a local one (Furrow, Greaney, Johnson, Jost, & Schwartz, 2004). If the typical practitioner in your region of the country always uses family-of-origin work and genograms for each and every client, no matter what the presenting problem, you might very well be negligent if you do the same thing as others in your area. In other words, the mentality that "one therapy fits all clients" is likely to be below the national standard of care, even if every social worker and criminal justice worker in Oregon or Florida believes in it. The ethical obligation of the human service worker is to use the best intervention. The standard of care may sound like a steep and high hill to climb. It is not. There are a number of reasons for this. First of all, in spite of the impressive efforts to develop evidence-based interventions (see, e.g., Roberts & Yeager, 2004), there are still many client problems for which we do not have bona fide interventions. With the exception of multisystemic therapy (MST; Henggeler, Schoenwald, et al., 1998), which is terribly costly and difficult to use in most settings, nothing has been shown to work with antisocial personality disorder. Yet the intervention may not be available in your internship, even though you are working with such conduct disorders. A good example of the use of MST is the case study reported by Jennifer Powers in Chapter 15 of this volume. Negligence may involve more than simply what intervention you use (or use poorly). It is also determined, in part, by how you present yourself. If you are a clinical social worker and present yourself as an expert in marriage and family therapy, then under the laws of malpractice you will be held to the standard of care of a marriage and family therapist. In other words, if you hold yourself out as someone you are not, the courts will say that the client has a right to expect that level of expertise (*Horak v. Biris,* 1985).

As an intern you can see how important this aspect of negligent practice might be. You are a student, and your clients have a right to know this and should not be misled to believe that you are more than that. If you present yourself as a family psychotherapist, then your clients have the right to expect you to be a family psychotherapist. If you present yourself as a sworn officer in a law enforcement internship, not only is this probably the unlawful impersonation of an officer, but also your clients will be able to hold you to the standard of the Law Enforcement Code. And, finally, if you present yourself as a clinical social worker in a residential internship, then you are a clinical social worker. In all three examples, in the eyes of the law and the hearts and minds of your clients, you are what you present yourself to be, and you are held to that standard even if you are not qualified to do so.

In terms of malpractice, this is important, because the standard of care is higher for someone who is an expert or a specialist than it is for the typical practitioner. Malpractice by an expert may occur even if the level of care was higher than would be expected of a typical practitioner if it is also lower than the standard for the specialization.

Clearly, then, it is important to not oversell yourself and your circumstances to clients in your internship—and afterward, as well. This is not such a difficult condition. You simply need to be honest.

As an ethical and legal issue, negligence is closely connected to informed consent. Negligent practice constitutes a nonconsensual relationship. If you present yourself as a professional and not an intern, then your clients, in fact, have consented to receive services from a professional. They did not consent to see an intern. Therefore, the relationship with the intern is nonconsensual and could result in a tort suit of malpractice. Similarly, if you said to the school-phobic youth and her parents that you would use an evidence-based intervention and only a few client-centered techniques, then the tort action would include the assertion that they did not consent to the sole use of a client-centered approach but to a particular evidence-based intervention.

In spite of all this discussion about malpractice, we believe it is easily the most avoidable concern you will have in your internship and in your professional practice. The easiest way to avoid the problem is to be honest, to select the intervention based on the best available evidence and relevance to your client, and to implement it as it is designed, with fidelity to the intervention. Additionally, your supervisor will help to prevent you from slipping below the standard of care and professional conduct (i.e., your "bedside manner"). In summary, do the best job you can, do it with the best intervention available, and be honest and professional. And in spite of these preventive suggestions, pay your malpractice insurance premiums on time! Like all insurance policies, the malpractice policy is there because you probably won't ever need it. Nevertheless, you should pay for it, anyway.

THE ROLE OF HIPAA IN HUMAN SERVICES

We discuss one final legal concern here, although you should remember that there are more than those covered in this chapter. This is the impact of the recently implemented federal law known as the Health Insurance Portability and Accountability Act, or HIPAA (PL 104-191). HIPAA is a federal statute, and as such it applies to all states and jurisdiction in the United States. Much of HIPAA concerns the portability of insurance from one employment setting to another, requiring coverage of preexisting conditions and for all health conditions and encouraging medical savings accounts. It also addresses the need to simplify the insurance claim process by implementing a single form, as currently nearly 400 different forms are in use (Seifert, 2003).

Moreover, HIPAA addresses the privacy interests of consumers of health care, including many social work and criminal justice services by which a client's identity may be determined. HIPAA establishes a minimum protection of a client's medical records. It defines *medical records* as any recording of any kind that identifies the individual's past, present, or future conditions for which he or she receives medical, behavioral, and many social services. This would include written records, electronic records, and oral communications. It even includes records pertaining to information obtained from research (Corcoran, Gorin, & Moniz, 2005), if the research participant's identity is determinable. Thus HIPAA is designed to protect the privacy interests of your clients and consumers, and it specifically prohibits disclosure of any identifiable information without written consent from the consumer. HIPAA also allows patients access to their records, regardless of whether the record is from a private insurance company or whether the patient is uninsured or covered by Medicare and Medicaid programs (Hester, 2003).

There are, of course, exemptions from these protections. Some examples include public health threats, terrorist threats, and some issues of law enforcement. Most important, it is not unlawful disclosure if the client agrees to the release of information. This provision allows you to seek outside advice from specialists and other experts. The release of information is lawful if three conditions are met: (1) the client agrees in writing, (2) the disclosure is in the best interest of the client in bettering treatment, and (3) only the minimally necessary information is disclosed.

HIPAA's impact on your internship will be far reaching. The minimal-necessity standard, by way of illustration, is likely to occur regularly and is critical in your internship and eventual professional practice. It includes not only disclosing as little information as is relevant but also disclosing only to those individuals and organizations that "need to know." As you probably already know, few clients present a single problem. Most have complexities and conditions that affect a range of daily living, distress, or disability. For example, it is not necessary to share all the prurient details of a client's sex life if the condition under consideration can be summarized as "sexually acting out." Similarly, because HIPAA protects even oral records, you probably will restrict your use of cell phones, which use public airwaves; the Internet, and even the intercom systems in various agencies. For example, it would likely be a violation for a receptionist to holler down the hallway, "Captain Kirk is here for his Viagra prescription."

Compliance is critical because HIPAA imposes criminal, as well as civil, sanctions for violations. The penalties for wrongful disclosure are fairly lenient—only $100 per violation, far less than those for many traffic violations—but the maximum fine is $25,000 per year. The sanctions for knowingly obtaining individually identifiable information—as might be done by pharmaceutical companies, managed care organizations, commercial marketers, and the like—can range from $50,000 and 1 year imprisonment to $100,000 and 5 years in imprisonment for obtaining information under false pretenses to $250,000 and 10 years imprisonment for selling, transferring, or using unlawfully disclosed information for commercial advantage, personal gain, or malicious harm.

Although this may sound threatening, it is unknown how well HIPAA will be implemented. Just as with the issue of confidentiality, it is unclear who is to enforce this law. The law assigns power of enforcement to the Office of Civil Rights, which provides available information at its website (http://www.hhs.gov/ocr/hipaa). As Hester (2003) notes, one the largest unanswered questions about HIPAA is the extent to which the Office of Civil Rights will monitor compliance and enforce sanctions. Clearly, this could depend on who is in the executive office and on the difficulty in monitoring and enforcing.

To summarize, the HIPAA will require obtaining written permission for release of information and allowing your client fairly complete access to all the records you keep and those of your supervisor. It will also influence how and with whom you communicate, including by cell phone. It will also affect your internship because it is relatively new. Although it was enacted in 1996, it did not take effect until April of 2003. As such, many agencies and internship settings are struggling with how to comply with HIPAA, you will probably struggle with it, too.

EMERGING VALUES AND ETHICS

From the recently enacted HIPAA to stalwart values of social work and criminal justice, the landscape of ethics is changing. The change is not so simple as the deletion of old ethical standards; it requires a redefinition to make the ethics more comprehensible and enforceable. Managed care, which first began in medicine and psychotherapy, has now influenced most social services. Managed care also has had an impact on ethics, especially as it reflects a conflict of interest between providing complete care for the client and maintaining financial stability (Corcoran & Vandiver, 1996).

We do believe, however, that much of this can be summarized as duties that are emerging in the human services. The emerging duty is to protect the interest of the client over the pecuniary interest of a funding source, whether it is a state tax-supported program or a health care insurance company.

Secondary to the duty to protect the client's interest is the duty of honest disclosure. For social work, this might include disclosing who might have access to the confidential information, and in criminal justice it might mean honest disclosure of a plea bargain or a release plan for incarcerated offenders.

Once you have put your client's interest first, and done so with honest disclosure of all the relevant information, you will find you have a duty to provide complete care. This is, in fact, a fairly well-established duty in medicine (Furrow et al., 2004) and psychotherapy (Slobogin, Reisner, & Arti, 2003). It is harder to implement in criminal justice. For example, a youth serving a 30-day detention may have the right to expect complete care; and yet once the detention sentence is served, the intervention is likely to stop. This is also a problem in some social work settings. Consider the school setting, for example; it is not possible to give complete care to the student who walks out the schoolyard for the summer. If a youngster needs 12 sessions of counseling, for example, does that mean we cannot take on his or her case for the last 3 months of the academic year? From the program perspective, the answer is a resounding "no." But as an intern, you might very well not take on any new cases as you approach the end of the practicum. Some cases are appropriate at the last stages of the internship, especially those cases that require only an assessment, diagnosis, and referral. The question we think is wise to ask is "Can I provide what this client needs in the time I have"? If the answer is no, it gives rise to the second question you should ask, "What referral source is available that can provide the complete care for this client"?

These duties are borne by the provider of services, regardless of whether the provider is a social worker or a criminal justice worker. There are also emerging duties for those who pay for services, whether the taxpayer, a third-party insurance company, or an individual consumer. Because there is an inherent conflict between protecting the client's interest and the interests of those providing the pecuniary resources, the conflict cannot be resolved simply, despite the provider's seminal duty to protect the client's interest. There is also a duty to pay for services in a speedy manner. Many states have statutes that require insurance companies to provide reimbursement within 30 days or so. Clients and even state tax-based funding sources can be delayed in making payments, something that will adversely affect your professional practice. Although you must provide complete care, it cannot be done for free. Human services, like all resources, cost money. Someone or some entity is going to pay for the services. In order for the conflict of interest to be addressed, the party that pays for services must do so willingly and expeditiously.

Another emerging duty for agencies and funding sources is to provide coordinate care. A social worker practicing in a managed care company or a hospital's discharge planning program, for example, must not simply refer the client to one place for one problem without considering biological factors that might require medical attention. The care must be coordinated and not haphazard. That is, this duty of coordinated care is similar to the provider's duty to put the client's interest first, not to protect profits by denying care or providing simply the cheapest care.

As a result of the duty to pay for the services that are based on coordinated care, agencies and their funding bodies have the duty to provide quality professionals to deliver the services. You may think this is a given. It is not. Oftentimes agencies will hire the young graduate because he or she gets a lower salary than a seasoned professional. Similarly, many agencies are hiring workers as independent contractors. This may sound as though it would allow more autonomy in the job, but what it really translates into is no benefits, including insurance, sick days, family emergency leaves, and vacation time. For the agency, it is a cheaper way of doing business.

In summary, the recent trends have changed funding procedures and led to restriction of services in social work and criminal justice. This has been done, in part, by managed care in the private and public sectors and by statutes (e.g., HIPAA) and case law (e.g., the Tarasoff rule). The results have shaken some of the very values and ethics of criminal justice and social work. They have also produced three emerging ethical duties for you as an intern and in your future profession. There are: (1) the duty to protect the client's interest; (2) the duty to provide full and honest disclosure; and (3) the duty to provide complete care.

These duties are balanced by three emerging ones for agencies, funders, and other entities that enable you to provide services. The emerging duties for these bodies are: (1) the duty to pay for bona fide services in a timely fashion; (2) the duty to provide coordinated care for the client's interest; and (3) the duty to provide quality social workers and criminal justice workers.

UNINTENDED CONFIDENTIALITY AND MANDATORY REPORTING

Elizabeth Mayfield Arnold

Case Description

Amber was a 15-year-old African American female client who presented for outpatient counseling at a mental health clinic in a mid-sized city in a southeastern state. Amber was in the 10th grade and had lived in this city all of her life. Sara was a 23-year-old white graduate student intern who was completing her field placement at the clinic. Besides her foundation placement at a domestic violence shelter, Sara had no other formal professional experience. Sara also grew up in this city but attended a different high school than did Amber. Going into this placement, Sara told her supervisor, Karen, that she wanted to work with "high-risk youth." Sara stated that she felt that one of her strengths was that she was close in age to the clients with whom she would be working. Because of this, she believed that she would be able to relate easily to clients.

Assessment/Screening and Problem Identification

Amber was referred to Sara by Sara's supervisor, Karen. When Amber called for an appointment, she indicated that she needed some help with "stress and friend issues." She also stated to the intake counselor, "I want to feel better about myself and my life." Sara arranged to meet with Amber to do the initial assessment with the understanding that she would videotape the session for supervisory purposes. Written consent to videotape the session was obtained from Amber and her mother. In addition, per agency policy, Sara had Amber fill out the agency intake and history form and a standardized depression inventory used in the clinic. Amber completed the forms prior to meeting with Sara and gave them to Sara at the beginning of the session.

Sara began the session by attempting to build rapport with Amber with the goal of then proceeding to talk with Amber about why she was seeking services at the clinic. Amber was verbally open and cooperative with the interview process. She began by telling Sara where she went to school. Sara then asked Amber where she had grown up. Amber replied, "I'm from here, too, but I went to a different high school. However, I know people who went to your school." Amber then proceeded to tell Sara about some of the other teens that she "hangs out with." Amber began to talk more in detail about two of her friends, Crystal and Jennifer, who were "into" things that were "scary." Sara listened as Amber told her that Crystal and Jennifer were "into boys," specifically "older guys." Sara elicited more information and asked, "What do you mean by 'scary' and 'older guys'?" Amber replied, "You know, they are doing crazy things, stupid things—like having sex with older guys who work at the restaurant next to the school. They hang out with them after school when they are supposed to be at dance practice." She went on to say that these guys were known to be troublemakers and had "lots of girlfriends." Amber said that she was afraid that Jennifer, who was 14 years old, had caught a sexually transmitted disease from Ronald, the 21-year-old assistant manager of the restaurant. Not only was Amber worried about Jennifer, but Amber's mother also thought that both Crystal and Jennifer were "bad news" and did not want her hanging out with them. Because she could not see these two friends, Amber reported feeling down and irritable. Her mother had noticed the changes in her mood and suggested that Amber seek professional help. According to her mother, Amber had said to her, "I don't have anyone that I can count on without Crystal and Jennifer. I'll be a loser with no friends!" Sara reviewed Amber's intake forms as they talked and noted that Amber had checked off the following symptoms from a list provided on the intake form: sadness, irritability, sleep problems, loss of appetite, guilty feelings, and problems concentrating. Sara discussed each symptom to gain additional information from Amber. Sara also examined Amber's completed depression inventory and noticed that her scores were elevated (in the range of indicating moderate to severe depression). As they neared the end the session, Sara suggested that they focus in future sessions on Amber's "apparent depression" and the identification of specific treatment goals. Sara reviewed the agency's policies related to scheduling appointments, after-hours crisis procedures, confidentiality, and fees. At that point, Amber asked, "So, everything that I tell you is confidential except if I'm going to hurt myself, hurt someone else, or if I'm being abused?" Sara replied, "Yes, that is correct." Sara noted as they wrapped up the session that there was a great deal of information that they would need to cover in the next session. Sara felt that she was working hard on building rapport and thus ran out of time to ask more questions about Amber's history. She made some notes to herself about things that would need to be addressed during the next session.

Intervention Selection

After meeting with Amber, Sara reviewed her notes in preparation for the case review with Karen. She went through her notes, the intake forms, and the depression inventory. She then reviewed her textbook on mental health practice and began to think about what type of intervention might be most appropriate to use with Amber. Later that day Karen and Sara met to go over the case. Karen suggested that they start by watching the video together prior to discussing the case. After watching the video, Karen asked Sara to give her an overview of the case and the "presenting problem." Sara said that the presenting problem was clearly "depression" related to Amber's not being able to hang out with her friends. Sara indicated that she felt that Amber's symptoms of depression and her elevated depression score clearly reflected the impact that the loss of social support from her friends had had on Amber's mood and functioning. From her reading and classes, Sara had decided that she wanted to use cognitive-behavioral therapy (CBT) with Amber, as she felt that it was a good fit with the client's needs. Specifically, she noted the negative statements that Amber had made to her mother about not being able to spend time with Crystal and Jennifer.

Karen also brought up another issue with Sara—Amber's revelation that her friend was allegedly having a sexual relationship with a male significantly older than she. Karen reminded Sara that, according to the law in the state they reside in, sexual behavior between Jennifer and this individual would be a mandatory reportable offense. Sara expressed regret that she had not known this and had told Amber that their conversation would be confidential but for the exceptions that she had reviewed. Karen and Amber then discussed how they would handle this situation. It was decided that Sara would need to address this with Amber and then decide how to proceed from there, given that she did not know Jennifer's last name.

Intervention/Treatment

With Karen's input, Sara developed some ideas about how to implement CBT with Amber. She made notes for herself in preparation for her next session. Her plan was to review the rationale of CBT and then help Amber identify some of the situations in which she tended to have negative and self-defeating thoughts. The following week, Sara met with Amber as scheduled. Sara discussed the use of CBT with Amber and decided, based on Amber's responses, that it would be a good fit. Together they identified the following goals: (1) to reduce Amber's depressive symptoms, as indicated by her weekly scores on the depression inventory; and (2) to help Amber reduce the number of her negative self-statements, as documented with a thought record to be completed by Amber each day.

Despite her discomfort, Sara also brought up the issue of Jennifer's sexual involvement with Ronald. Sara explained the state law to Amber and told her that Jennifer's sexual relationship with Ronald was a mandatory reportable offense. Amber was clearly upset with this news and responded, "I thought that they were having sex but I found out that they weren't. Besides, you don't have Jennifer's last name, and because of my own confidentiality with my friends, I can't give that to you." Sara validated Amber's feelings about the incident and told her that she would have to explore whether she still had a legal obligation to make a child protective services report with the information that she already had. They agreed to discuss the issue further at their next session. After the session, Sara talked with Karen about the session and the issue related to Jennifer. Karen suggested that Sara call the child protective services office to see whether or not this would need to be reported. Sara did this and was told that, based on the recanting of the information about the sexual relationship and because she did not have Jennifer's last name, the event would not be reportable. However, she was instructed to call back if she obtained additional information about the case that would be relevant. Karen and Sara discussed how Sara could again raise the issue with Amber to make sure that they had adequately addressed the impact of this situation on their professional relationship. Furthermore, Karen cautioned Sara about trying to bond too much with Amber based on personal experiences.

Evaluation

At the next session, Sara told Amber that she would not be making a child protective services report regarding Jennifer. When Sara asked Amber how she felt about the situation, Amber said, "It's fine. I'm not upset about it. I guess I just thought that since you grew up here and were about my age that you would understand this stuff." Although Amber did not seem angry, Sara sensed that this incident might hurt their rapport and that Amber might trust her less because of it. However, Sara continued to work with Amber weekly for the next 10 weeks, and in Sara's opinion they worked through the initial incident. Amber was cooperative and kept all of her scheduled appointments. Each week when Amber arrived at the clinic, she completed the depression inventory. Amber also brought in her daily thought record to each session for review. After the initial assessment, Amber's depression scores gradually went down, indicating a decrease in her depressive symptoms. Additionally, the number of negative daily thoughts went down from six per day to one or two per day.

Discussion

Amber's depression appeared to improve during the time period that she worked with Sara. However, there were a couple of issues that needed to be explored further with Amber. First, Sara needed to be clear about whether Amber's lack of social support was truly the "cause" of the depression. It is possible that Sara's assessment was inaccurate or that other factors might have been contributing to Amber's depression that would also need to be addressed. Sara also needed to be careful about the techniques that she used to build rapport. At some points during the initial session, it appeared that Sara was trying to build a therapeutic relationship based on personal commonalities. Because of this, Amber told Sara some things that she might not otherwise have chosen to share that ended up affecting their relationship. In part, however, Sara's lack of knowledge of the state law and Karen's not making sure that she was aware of this also affected Amber's treatment. In addition, Sara needed to assess whether the intervention was culturally relevant and whether Amber completely understood the theoretical rationale for the intervention. If a client does not believe, for example, that thoughts are connected to feelings and behavior, he or she may go along with the treatment but never completely benefit from the intervention. Furthermore, it was important that Sara stress with Amber that these were "skills" that she could use the rest of her life when she encountered stressful situations—not tools specific only to the current situation.

■ ■ ■

Activities

Answer the following questions as they relate to this case and record your answers in the space provided.

1. What were the other issues that Sara did not address during the first session that needed to be addressed that day?

2. What were the other issues that needed to be addressed in future sessions?

3. Based on the description of this case, do you think CBT was the intervention of choice? Why or why not?

4. How and when should confidentiality issues be addressed with clients?

5. Was Sara's approach to building rapport with Amber appropriate? Why or why not?

6. Once child protective services stated that they would not be able to take the case of Jennifer's alleged sexual relationship with Ronald due to Amber's recanting and the lack of sufficient information, should Sara have let it go or pursued it further with Amber?

7. From the outcomes measured, do you think that Amber is ready to terminate treatment? Why or why not?

8. What else could Karen have done in this case as Sara's supervisor?

9. Should Sara have told Amber that she was an intern? Why or why not?

This chapter covers many topics of law, ethics, and values. There are, of course, many exercises, as a consequence of the number of topics. You surely should not expect to get them all done in a single setting. Many also require the participation of your supervisor and classroom instructors. We hope that you complete some of the exercises with your supervisor and instructors, but remember that they have a learning agenda as well and this may not be possible. Additionally, for those exercises in which you solicit opinions and information about the case and work within your agency, remember to be diplomatic. You are to solicit information for your learning, and it is important not to put the supervisor, instructor, or others on the defensive.

Federal and state laws, known as statutes, have a direct impact on your internship. So do local ordinances. This may be a federally mandated program, such as Medicaid and Medicare, or education programs for children with emotional and behavioral disorders. Local ordinances may affect your internship, such as mandatory arrests and community corrections or services for the homeless. An important part of the laws or ordinances is funding. This exercise is designed to help you understand which laws and ordinances affect your agency and how they are associated with funding.

Enabling Statues

What federal, state, and local laws provide for what particular services available through your agency?

Federal:

State:

Local:

What is the source of the funding from these laws?

Ask your field instructor for copies of the forms and procedures for procuring the funding. Examine these materials thoroughly. Does the process seem overwhelming? __ Yes   __ No

List five questions about this process to discuss with your field instructor in supervision and for discussion in the classroom. Bear in mind that the day may very well come when you are in charge of an agency or program and will have to solicit the funding.

1. _____

2. _____

3. _____

4. _____

5. _____

Confidentiality

Your internship might require various referrals or consultations. Solicit a copy of whatever release of information form your agency uses.
Read the form and fill it out as if you were the client.

In the following space, describe how well the form fulfills the requirements of HIPAA.

Consider the typical client you will be working with at your internship. Do you think the form is appropriate for him or her? __ Yes   __ No

Is your client's reading level and comprehension level sufficient to truly understand the release of information? __ Yes   __ No

If no, what can you do to fulfill your duty to the client and the requirement of HIPAA?

Discuss this with your supervisor and consider whether or not it would be a learning opportunity for you to revise the form. If so, record here what steps you will take to revise it.

Did you include client involvement in the revision? __ Yes   __ No

How so, or why not?

Informed Consent

Assume that in your internship you are working with a youngster in a counseling setting. It could easily be a youth in the juvenile justice setting, a family services agency, or an employee assistance program. As a result of the insight-oriented counseling, repressed memories of child sexual abuse by a clergy member came forth, which made the client extremely anxious and agitated. Although the client consented to treatment during the intake interview, he or she certainly did not consent to the treatment dredging up such horrible memories.

What will you do to ensure that the client's consent is informed?

Ask your field instructor for his or her opinion about this case, and record his or her recommendations here.

Compare your initial approach with your field instructor's. How has your opinion changed?

What about your classmates? In your classroom discussion, how have their opinions differed from yours and how has your thinking changed now?

Mandatory Reporting

Assume that in your internship one of your clients has been arrested for child abuse. It could be an adult or a youth, and the issue is relevant to both social work and criminal justice. Because you are concerned about your client, you and he discuss the circumstance in detail. Your client tells you, "I just lost my temper and whooped the tar out of her. Although she was trying to act tough and was dissing me I took my belt to her. I really didn't means for her to start bleeding, but she deserved a good beating." Being diligent in your notes for supervision, your record these statements verbatim.

The next time you are at the agency, you are served with a subpoena ordering that you turn over the records. This is called a *subpoena duces tecum*. We will not ask you what the first thing is that you should do. We know that you know that the first order of business is to immediately sit down and discuss this with your supervisor.

With that discussion in mind, are you required to turn over the documents?
__ Yes   __ No

If so, why? Or if not, why not?

What about the fact that your client has already been arrested? What is the opinion of your supervisor about the fact that the purpose of the mandatory reporting has been fulfilled?

Ask your supervisor whether his or her supervisor has the same opinion.

If you must relinquish the records, how will it affect your client's relationship with you?

What will you do to minimize the adverse impact of relinquishing the records, or how can you use the ethic of nondisclosure to facilitate your client's service goals?

Conflict of Interest and the Dual Relationship

Your internship is 30 miles outside of town at a halfway house for paroled felons who need drug or alcohol treatment. Your town and the area have excellent public transportation, including a free van to and from the state capitol building, which is only three blocks from the halfway house. You decide that by taking the van you will save money and will be able to use the time for your classroom reading.

The first client assigned to you is Viktor Droopoff, who was just released to the halfway house. As a condition of his parole and admission to the program, Viktor has agreed to drink no alcohol and use no drugs, including tobacco and the caffeine in coffee and chocolate. At your first meeting with Viktor, you find him quite charming. He is polite, cooperative, engaging, and very grateful to you for being willing to work with him. You are pleased with yourself and believe you will actually be able to help this man. (You are, in fact, likely to have been manipulated at this time.)

The next day of your internship you walk to the van for the 30-minute ride from town to the agency. You enter the bus and see that the driver is none other than Viktor.

Is there conflict of interest in this case? __ Yes   __ No

Will you be able to continue to take the van, or must you pay the cost of driving and parking and lose out on the 30 minutes of reading time?

Now, let's do a reality check. What are the opinions of your field instructor and/or classroom instructor?

How do your opinions and those of your field and classroom instructors differ, or are they in agreement?

Let's "kick it up a notch." Assume that as you approached the van you saw Viktor smoking a cigarette, drinking a cup of coffee, and eating a chocolate donut. Now what do you do?

Considering your previous answer, how will that affect your professional relationship with Viktor and other clients at the halfway house?

Sexuality and Sexual Harassment

Assume that you and a classmate are placed at a single residency occupancy for persons with severe and chronic mental illnesses. Your classmate is a rather shy young woman from a small town, a very close religious family with whom she attended Sunday services and prayer meetings regularly. She has led a rather sheltered life. The big city is fairly overwhelming to her. At the agency, you and she are in the lounge and see a men's magazine on the table opened to a page with a sexually explicit picture of a couple having intercourse. Your classmate is shocked and gasps, "oh my!" You, in contrast, say "looks like an awkward and uncomfortable position."

During a discussion in the classroom, your professor utters excitedly, "That's sexual harassment! You must leave the agency immediately and not return." Ask yourself the following questions:

In your opinion, is the magazine creating a "hostile work environment"?
__ Yes __ No

Why do you believe it is or is not?

What about the perspective of your intimidated classmate? Is it sexual harassment for her? __ Yes   __ No

If your answers were not the same, how do you square these distinguishable conclusions?

Now, consider facilitating a classroom discussion on this case. How have the opinions of your classmate changed or confirmed your beliefs?

If you were the field supervisor—a likely possibility in your professional career—what would tell your intern students?

What about the clients you have been working with so far? How is your opinion on whether to stay or leave the placement going to affect them?

What would you do if either of the students followed the classroom instructor and simply did not return to the agency?

Negligence and Malpractice

Assume that you are placed in a setting in which you are providing counseling services for an adjudicated youth. Your client is an enrolled member of a managed care plan run by the state departments of mental health and juvenile justice. The program limits services depending on the medical necessity and severity of distress or disability, a common practice in managed mental health care. After 10 sessions the managed care program refuses to authorize any more treatment.

Is this a case of malpractice or negligence? __ Yes   __ No

Why is it, or why is it not?

Has your answer considered that you may be abandoning your client? And what is your duty to the client to provide "complete care"?

What can you do, and what are you legally expected to do, for your client and the managed care provider?

If you decide that services should be continued and then the managed care organization says, "We are not saying you are not authorized to provide services; we are just saying we will not reimburse the agency for the additional services provided," how can you fulfill the duty for complete care in light of the managed care organization's refusal to pay for services?

After you have answered these questions, we suggest that you discuss the case with your supervisor and/or classroom faculty and classmates. What are their opinions?

Do you think this is a common situation? __ Yes or __ No

If you answered "no," you are incorrect, and thus we encourage you to discuss it in more detail both with your field instructor and in the classroom. Although it is, indeed, a distasteful situation, you will likely encounter it more often than you wish.

Medical Records and HIPAA

The exercise is similar to the preceding ones on confidentiality and informed consent. This should not surprise you, as you will remember that all three topics have a strong nexus. In this exercise, assume that you are working with an emotionally and behaviorally disturbed 14-year-old named Cindy Lou. She was referred by the school counselor for bullying after school. The two of you are using a variety of interventions, as is often the real-life circumstance, including sand-tray therapy, therapeutic equestrian riding, and Flieschman, Horne, and Author's (2002) self-help workbook for families with an aggressive and acting-out youth. Cindy Lou tells you that she assaulted the neighbor boy, age 9, by penetrating his rectum with a pencil and says "next time I won't use the eraser end first. The little bastard!" You know this is beyond your abilities and discuss with your supervisor the need for a referral.

In addition to the release of information form you considered in the earlier exercises, what information will you disclose to the specialist or the referral agency?

What about the neighbor child's parents? Can they sue you for a failure to protect? That is, do you think you have a duty to protect the neighbor boy? __ Yes or __ No

Why do you believe this is so or why not?

Share these answers with your supervisor, and ask what he or she thinks are the most appropriate answers. Record your instructor's opinions.

How do your answers and the instructor's differ?

4 EVIDENCE-BASED PRACTICES FOR SUPERVISION

BARBARA THOMLISON *and* KEVIN CORCORAN

In this chapter you will learn about learning styles and sources of expertise. We review the following topics: what is good supervision, including supportive supervisory relationships; critical reflection and thinking; and competency-based and educational focus for best student practices. We provide you with guidelines for conduct in supervision, best available supervision formats, coaching and mentoring, setting educational goals, and practical considerations for learning.

Supervised practice is an essential component of the education and training of social workers, criminal justice workers, psychologists, counselors, psychiatrists, pastors, teachers, and other professional helpers. As an intern, you will learn more about practice and working with people from intern supervision than from most books that you read. Consensus among the helping disciplines is that the supervised practicum experience enhances the interns' skills, knowledge, and behavior and contributes to protecting the public. This chapter reviews the best practices associated with how students learn in the field and the evidence for effective supervision. Due to the breadth of learning that occurs in the practicum and the diversity of practice opportunities and challenges students and supervisors encounter, this is a difficult task. Despite the complexity involved, it is helpful to begin your practicum by understanding how you approach learning, how you learn best, and what your preferred learning approach to practice is.

GUIDELINES FOR ASSESSING HOW YOU LEARN

The education and training of professionals is uniquely challenging. Students are expected to master theory and develop skills for the application of theory to various practice situations and populations. Field supervisors are expected to enable students to apply what they have learned in the classroom to learning experiences in the internship setting. They are expected to help students develop practice-based skills and to socialize students to the profession. To realize these expectations requires field supervisors and students to understand how learning takes place. What makes learning easier for you? Do you prefer to read about something new, think about it, and then apply it? Or would you rather learn by doing?

The process by which you move from novice to expert is facilitated by the knowledge that supervisors have about how to practice. They assist you in critically appraising the realities of each practice exemplar of planned and unplanned practice they encounter. So where do you start? What do you learn, and what is to be learned? This is a highly individualized process, and it involves drawing on a variety of ways of sensing—hearing, thinking, feeling, doing, writing, describing, reading, and reacting. Your learning style may or may not be the same as that of another student. This is the reason that different students approach a task in different but equally effective ways, none of which is either right or wrong.

LEARNING STYLES

Learners in the practicum can be students, clients, and supervisors. This chapter focuses on students, but the learning assessment framework can be applied to supervisors, as well. Adult preferred learning is interactive (Meyers & Jones, 1993) or critical reflection. Giving students real-world scenarios from which to construct knowledge is the best learning situation. They are then actively involved in thought-provoking work. There are a number of tools for identifying the learning styles of students, but these tools need to be valid, reliable, and relevant. One common valid and reliable tool for understanding your approach to learning is the Kolb Learning Styles Inventory (LSI; Kolb & Kolb, 2005),which describes the way you learn and how you deal with ideas in day-to-day situations, that is, learning from experience rather than being taught. This is helpful for practicum learning. The latest version of the LSI can be downloaded or taken for a fee at http://www.learningfromexperience.com/images/uploads/Tech_spec_LSI.pdf. There are four kinds of knowledge: convergent and divergent knowledge and assimilation and accommodation knowledge.

Convergent

The learner with this preferred approach likes to learn by doing but finds it difficult when the situation is ambiguous and there is no one right response. You like to try things first, and practicality and usefulness are key issues to your understanding. Your strengths are that you make decisions quickly, prefer one right answer, and are able to detect the essential aspects of a case or piece of practice. You also prefer to work alone as you learn. It is recommended that you use the following tools for learning:

1. Design a problem-solving protocol in your notebook.
2. Review your notes to see patterns and understand the method or approach to tasks and practice.
3. Write or record ways to improve tasks and case management in your day-to-day practice.
4. Access case studies or simulations to prepare for practice (Reimer, Thomlison, & Bradshaw, 1999, pg. 116).

Divergent

Students with this preferred approach to learning also like concrete experiences and prefer supervisors with good organizational skills. They focus on detail, enjoy brainstorming, and like to know how things work. If you have this learning style, you have more difficulty with abstract interpretations and creativity. You like to start with examples first and then receive the theory. You need time to express your feelings and see things from different perspectives. Discussion and interactions with a supervisor and others are important to your learning. You are good at generating ideas. The following tools for learning are recommended:

1. Use free forms of writing to record ideas.
2. Ask yourself "why" questions as you search to understand the importance of a task or concept.
3. Review materials, cases, and ideas with peers.
4. Share personal reactions and opinions with your supervisor and peers to clarify issues about cases and the practice process (Reimer et al., 1999, pg. 116).

Accommodation

If this is your preferred learning approach, you like to learn and think through self-discovery. Given a situation or problem, you will do best when you can create something new with it. You learn from mistakes and are identified as a problem solver or risk taker. Students with this learning style accommodate or adapt what they have learned from one situation to another, often improving on it. As a learner, you are also a good teacher. You will use your supervisor as a resource as you prefer less direct guidance. It is recommended that you use the following tools for learning:

1. Explain issues or problem solving to other students.
2. Write an explanation for solving an issue or task in social work or criminal justice practice or in a client situation.
3. Write a one-page description of future problems or issues in a particular area of practice.
4. Approach learning in an open-ended manner (Reimer, Thomlison, & Bradshaw, 1999, pg. 117).

Assimilation

Assimilators prefer to reflect and observe first. Gaining a conceptual understanding first and learning from an expert through reading, listening, and lectures are ways you approach your learning. You prefer well-organized situations, detail, and good directions, and you like to analyze pieces of information. The following tools for learning are recommended.

1. Mapping techniques and graphic tools are helpful to your learning.
2. Use of summaries and highlights builds on your strengths.
3. Write only after thinking or reflecting.

The various methods of learning must therefore address the needs of different learners. One size does not fit all, and individuals combine the preceding styles of acquiring knowledge and thinking. Although these are only suggestions to aid your learning and development, you will need to draw on all methods more or less to enhance learning.

A thorough understanding and awareness of your learning style will help your supervisor support what you do best and understand your strengths and skills, as well as your needs and knowledge gaps.

SOURCES OF EXPERTISE

Research on supervision indicates that there is an accumulating body of empirical knowledge that primarily focuses on effective supervision. For the most part, this evidence for supervision acts as a framework for defining the various competencies. These competencies are derived from preferred or best practices, from standards of practice associated with discipline-specific guidelines, and from those approaches identified by existing research as defining the distinguishing characteristics of a "good" or "bad" supervisor, of effective supervision, and of approaches to supervision. This evidence leads to the determination that there is no one prescribed or ideal approach to "good" supervision; various supervisory styles and behaviors can be appropriate (O'Connor, 2000). For this chapter, a summary of the approaches to the issue of how interns learn from supervision is drawn from (1) best practice guidelines from practicum and internship field manuals from the Carnegie I Research Extensive Universities, (2) expert consensus guidelines from the empirical literature and Internet sites; and (3) the best available evidence (Association of State and Provincial Psychology Boards [ASPPB] Task Force on Supervision Guidelines, 2003; Corcoran & Vandiver, 2004; Munson, 2000; McNeece & Thyer, 2004; O'Connor, 2000; Thomlison, 2002).

Supervision is an important learning context that teaches students to access multiple sources of practice knowledge and attain understanding about the primary work with clients. Do not forget that the practicum or internship is a course with goals and objectives to be met and that it represents a substantial amount of time and effort during your educational program. The instructional method is supervision. Supervised learning imparts an educational focus to your assignments and practice tasks. Different methods of supervision must reflect different learners (their learning styles and needs), strategies, and outcomes that can be assessed. This process requires supervisors to teach students to identify, critically appraise, and apply practice-relevant research findings to their practice over the course of the internship (Howard, McMillen, & Pollio, 2003; Sackett, Strauss, Richardson, Rosenberg, & Haynes, 2000). A member of the staff from the agency internship site who is approved by your college or university will supervise you, and a faculty member from your college or university will be assigned to that site to monitor your progress during the internship. The assigned agency supervisor will not only be an experienced professional but also will be familiar with the rules and expectations that govern the agency and the conduct of professional practice for that setting.

The relationship you develop with your supervisor is critical and affects your learning and development. You should thoughtfully weigh what you share with your supervisor; personal information is usually inappropriate and may reflect negatively on you. Essentially, you will discuss problems, concerns, issues, and any other matters concerning your observations, assignments, and experiences related to your learning. Use good judgment in your communication and demonstrate motivation to learn. Asking good questions about clients' behaviors and about interventions will go a long way in maintaining professionalism and demonstrating your interest and desire to learn. Your relationship with your agency supervisor should be professional, respectful, and productive toward your learning goals. Your supervisor is the person who will challenge your practice decisions and will use these opportunities to provide teaching moments to assist you in personal and professional development and critical thinking skills.

Ideally, your supervisor is someone who places value and emphasis on a scientific orientation to professional practice. Similarly, the internship site ideally is a setting that emphasizes a science-informed theory and practice intervention approach. Evidence-based practice settings are more likely to inform your learning process and lead to evidence-based decisions for practice accountability. Of course, this necessarily depends on a good supervisor and his or her good relationship with the person being supervised—you, the student. This fact leads us to ask, then, What are the elements of good supervision? Who can be an effective supervisor? In addition, what are the best evidence supervision guidelines?

WHAT IS GOOD SUPERVISION?

Research on the factors that contribute to high-quality supervision is principally derived from studies with small samples and findings that are supported by program evaluation designs that use no group comparisons or use comparisons of supervisors and those supervised (Baird, 2004, Howard & Jenson, 1999; Munson, 2000; Sowers-Hoag & Thyer, 1995; Thomlison, 2002). Studies rely on self-report methodology, and, therefore, findings as to what makes for good supervision need to be tentatively interpreted. Research (Falender & Shafranske, 2004; Henderson, Cawyer, & Watkins, 1999; O'Connor, 2000) suggests that multiple factors contribute to effective supervision within the context of three elements: (1) a supportive supervisory relationship, (2) critical reflection and thinking, and (3) established competency-based practices or strategies for learning in the practicum. According to the best available evidence, good supervision has the following qualities.

Supportive Supervisory Relationship

The quality of the supervisory relationship is related to successful supervision. Studies view a positive and supportive supervisory relationship as the primary *process* by which novice practitioners and interns learn to practice effectively. In order for a positive learning experience to occur, the supervisory relationship must proceed within a framework consisting of beginning, middle, and end phases of a supportive and interactive relationship. Personal qualities of the supervisor, the approach to supervision, and the student's perception of good supervision can be important to a supportive relationship (Kadushin, 1992; Henderson et al., 1999; Henggeler, Schoenwald, Liao, Letourneau, & Edwards, 2002; Munson, 1993; Shulman, 1982, 1993). Following are some critical points.

1. Students' perceptions of the quality of the supervision is the most important factor in satisfaction with their placement (Fortune & Abramson, 1993).
2. A good supervisor is a respected individual who is accomplished and competent in a professional practice area, such as clinical practice.
3. A good supervisor clearly separates supervision from psychotherapy and does not provide counseling as part of supervision (Falender & Shafranske, 2004).
4. Personal abilities such as empathy and genuineness must be high and used in the process of supervision to convey understanding of the student's difficulties, struggles, and sense of accomplishment (Henderson et al., 1999; Henggeler et al., 2002; Shulman, 1982, 1993; Stein & Lambert (1995).
5. Ideal supervisors recognize the personal strengths and abilities of students and know how to impart attitudes, behaviors, and practices to specific skill learning, such as family therapy, functional assessments, or other skills (Stein & Lambert, 1995).
6. Students prefer supervisors who are flexible, amicable, and approachable and who model the qualities of genuineness and congruence (Baird, 2004; Kaiser, 1997; Munson, 1989)
7. Supervisors who emphasize students' strengths rather than their deficiencies encourage them to reach for positive alternatives to unwanted practice behaviors.(Baird, 2004; Falender & Shafranske, 2004)
8. Interns who reported their theoretical orientations as behavioral tended to prefer task-oriented supervisors, whereas interns with a psychodynamic orientation preferred supervisors who were warm, supportive, and friendly (Lochner & Melchert, 1997)

Critical Reflection and Thinking

Supervisors who use critical reflection and thinking processes turn novice learners into informed learners. Through the supportive supervisory relationship and open communication, these supervisors encourage students to actively explore alternative ways of thinking about practice and practice situations. Each time you reflect on your practice behavior, you are exploring the values, beliefs, and expectations essential to good practice and professional outcomes. When you challenge yourself to examine alternative ways of thinking and practicing, the potential for new ideas and creative thoughts can emerge. You may even need to challenge yourself in complex and high-risk practice situations with new and different questions. Supervisors assess and evaluate your work, help you ask critical thinking questions to ensure ethical value-based practice, and help you acquire knowledge. Knowing about your thinking will assist you in determining what has been most helpful to your learning and what has been least helpful.

1. Supervisors who require you to engage in critical thinking challenge your intellectual knowledge and your interpersonal and technical skills. It means that you will critically appraise the effect of values, beliefs, and expectations on your developing professional behaviors.
2. Learning through critical reflection is a continuous process of self-exploration and change, reasoning, and acquiring decision-making skills to effectively learn competent and safe practice.
3. Demonstrating interest in student educational needs and the learning process were supervisor qualities that were assessed as more important than the supervisor's experience.
4. Supervisors who have various theoretical and knowledge bases and the ability to explain how they are applied to practice situations are more effective (Henderson et al., 1999; Nelson, 1978).
5. Supervisors need skills in analyzing the events of therapy (Henderson et al., 1999).
6. Clinical understanding and technical competence proceeds along a developmental continuum from global to concrete to more differentiated and integrated levels, indicating that practice learning progresses over time when reflective activities are engaged in (Platt, 1992).

Competency-Based Practices and Educational Focus

Good supervision is a form of socialization to the profession. In other words, the role of the supervisor is to assist you in developing practice skills, learning job functions, and increasing self-awareness for professional competence. The outcome of supervision is ensuring your competency in client service and your appropriate and ethical practice during the internship. The purpose is to develop a beginning level of practice competence defined as "the habitual and judicious use of communication, knowledge, technical skills, clinical reasoning, emotions, values, and reflection in daily practice for the benefit of the individual and the community being served" (Epstein & Hundert, 2002, p. 226).

1. Essential elements of supervisor tasks and responsibilities are instruction, modeling, monitored practice, and feedback (Kadushin, 1992; O'Connor, 2000).
2. Supervisors who demonstrate mastery of knowledge and practice are effective.
3. Supervisors who assist in helping students to view alternate positions about practice cases, projects, or other assignments are effective.
4. Students prefer regular feedback with constructive criticism and encouragement toward the agreed-on learning goals (Henderson et al., 1999).
5. Ideal supervisors recognize personal strengths and abilities of students and know how to facilitate the application of attitudes, behaviors, and practices to specific skill learning, such as family therapy, functional assessments, or other specific skills (Stein & Lambert, 1995).
6. Students prefer a supervisor who is flexible, who is currently in practice, and who allows maximum autonomy in students (Henderson et al., 1999).
7. Research suggests that interns tend to practice with individuals and families by replicating the styles of their supervisors, shaping practice outcomes at multiple levels (Kniskern & Gurman, 1979).
8. Students who are taught specific skills in a structured and systematic competency-based approach function in the practicum at a higher practice level than students who are not taught using this approach (Kadushin, 1992; Sowers-Hoag & Thyer, 1995; Tourse, McInnes-Dittrich & Platt, 1999).
9. Supervisors who provide clear, frequent, timely, and relevant feedback about performance that balances student strengths with vulnerabilities also function at a higher level. Confident supervisors also ask for feedback.

EVIDENCE-BASED PRACTICES FOR STUDENTS

The single most important quality of highly effective learners is that they are seen as always ready to get help and seek support. Students enter the practicum with classroom learning (thinking skills) and a background of life experiences (daily activities of living skills). Your supervisor wants you to draw on these resources as a source of expertise. By acknowledging what you know and what you do not know and understanding that there are many situations with no right answers, you will develop greater competence. Asking for assistance and advice when needed from your supervisor is the best strategy for analyzing the many situations you will encounter in practice. The best students get and seek help using multiple sources of expertise in the internship site, including your supervisor and others, such as peers, consultants, and even your clients.

Most of the research on supervisors and students has not yet been linked to practice, educational, or treatment outcomes. Furthermore, Goodyear and Bernard (1998) concluded that if a supervisor likes a student, that student is more likely to receive a positive evaluation. Students who liked their supervisors also tended to give them higher satisfaction ratings.

GUIDELINES FOR CONDUCT IN SUPERVISION

Supervised practice is guided by a strong emphasis on ethics and integrity. The power influences of supervisor-student relationships places special importance on the character and integrity of supervisors to ensure fairness, confidentiality, and actions in accordance with the highest standards of professional integrity and impartiality (Canadian Association of Social Workers [CASW], 1996; National Association of Social Workers [NASW], 1999). Most settings have established general policies and protocols to address ethical and integrity issues to protect the well-being of those persons receiving services and of students, practitioners, and the profession.

Professional relationships are not to be exploited for personal gain. Examples of malpractice that constitute violations of a professional, ethical, and legal nature include, but are not limited to, the following: violating personal boundaries; discrimination; harassment; breaching confidentiality with minors; and having sexual relationships with clients and supervisors. Unwanted contacts, actions, comments, and behaviors may potentially come not only from supervisors but also from peers, colleagues, and others. If such problems or issues arise for you or for someone who is receiving services, recognize that these are contrary to the code of conduct in the internship site, as well as to professional and other codes of legal ethics. Corruption and misconduct relate to behaviors that are prohibited by the internship site, such as becoming involved in any illegal activities, misuse of power, misuse of technology to access confidential information, accepting gifts or bribes, and many other examples. You have a right to file a complaint or grievance and to demand that the behavior be stopped. Most agencies have guidelines for this procedure. It is necessary that the tasks and processes or context of supervision follow ethical, as well as commonsense, practices.

BEST SUPERVISION FORMATS

Supervision can occur under many different formats. The most common supervision format is the individual case consultation method, a meeting between intern and supervisor, which is used by 85% of supervisors. Supervision in a group format was the second most used format, but it was ranked low in effectiveness by both supervisors and students (Goodyear & Nelson, 1997). Written verbatim transcripts of student work with clients were ranked the lowest in terms of helpfulness. Graduate students prefer more emphasis on demonstration of techniques and use of videotape and observation and less emphasis on discussion. The Association for Counselor Education and Supervision's (1995) "Ethical Guidelines for Counseling Supervisors" defines audio recording and videotaping of sessions as a standard of care. Other professional associations have not identified such practice guidelines.

Individual Supervision

This format features regularly scheduled meetings between student and supervisor for case consultation and information. Students discuss elements of the case experience and analyze the reasons that things happened as they did to discover causes, usefulness, and applicability of what was learned from the meeting with the client. Through discussion, the supervisor teaches the student concepts of the case to generalize knowledge and skills acquired in specific situations so that they can be applied in other practice situations. The tasks of the supervisor are to model critical thinking skills and to examine the student's work, encouraging openness and honesty about practice through the sharing of feelings, thoughts, and struggles. Responses to authority, power, and relationship issues may also be discussed between supervisor and student.

Team or Peer Supervision

Team or peer supervision meetings bring together individuals with the same or different professional orientations to provide specific assistance related to case or practice issues. Collaboration is an underlying theme in team meetings. Teams provide exposure to a wide range of problem-solving techniques and the opportunity to compare practice experiences and generate different observations and suggestions for interventions among the team members. Team discussion develops a menu of different perspectives and understandings of the case. Case presentations and role plays may also occur among the team members in an effort to teach interventions and broaden understanding (Thomlison, 1999).

Group Supervision

Group supervision with several students is used to develop practice expertise and skills and to obtain moral support, self-confidence, and awareness. Students may rotate case presentations, but everyone participates in the case issues and discussion. Although students report that this method of supervision ranks lower in effectiveness, it offers a context in which members share conflicts, problems, and dilemmas from their practice and receive assistance from their peers.

Live Supervision

Live supervision is most often used in interdisciplinary or clinical and family therapy settings as a technique for training or developing clinical skills. Your supervisor and other team members watch and listen from behind the observation window or watch closed-circuit taping, or they will sit in with you during an actual interview. Videotaping usually occurs for later review. This supervision format involves active working together, monitoring, or suggesting various interventions during the actual interview, which is usually with a family. Immediate corrective feedback on performance is given through a variety of communication devices, such as telephone, bug-in-the-ear, notes, or other interventions. This method provides greater opportunity for enhancing competence and personal development because students are more likely to use this immediate feedback in the practice context (Thomlison, 1995, 2002).

Coaching and Mentoring

Coaching and mentoring are highly rated (Johnson, 2002). Coaching and mentoring relationships assist students by exposing them to learning on the job by having someone work with them or provide a role model for them. In this way, the student is exposed to another colleague, usually with expert skills, to show her or him firsthand on-the-job and on-the-spot practice skills. Mentors serve multiple roles: teacher, advisor, consultant, role model. The negative side is that mentors receive no preparation, training, support, or supervision, so there is the potential for negative results due to the power imbalance and exploitation potential (Johnson & Nelson, 1999). Your role may be that of a participant-observer, or your coach or mentor may walk through a situation in a step-by-step manner, offering advice, knowledge, or support. Coaches and mentors provide firsthand advice, instruction, and direction by instructing you through a situation. Coaches and mentors are considered to have special wisdom, expertise, or ability, and they serve as expert role models. The use of these collaborative learning and teaching roles has evolved in many different settings and organizations. Your coach or mentor may not be in the same setting that you are in but will usually be someone in the same profession.

SETTING EDUCATIONAL GOALS

Goals of supervision depend on your learning outcomes, the educational outcomes or demands of your professional program, the opportunities within the internship site, and to some degree the orientation of your supervisor. The method of attaining your educational goals is through the supervisory relationship and a learning contract. The learning contract is used to construct an individual learning plan based on an assessment of your current competencies compared with the level of competencies you want to achieve.

Developed between student and supervisor, the learning contract consists of the agreed-on learning goals in a written contract or learning plan that identifies the objectives used to attaining the goals (Goodyear & Bernard, 1998). Goals are usually articulated as knowledge and skill acquisition, professional development, and the demonstration of values, attitudes, and ethical behavior for specific disciplines.

A study (Nelson, 1978) of interns reported the following reasons for supervision: (1) to gain therapeutic competence; (2) to develop professional confidence and independence; (3) to improve self-awareness; and (4) to acquire theoretical and practice knowledge. Your learning plan may be similar and may include skill development, professional growth, self-awareness, and application of skills and theory to a variety of practice situations, as well as meeting the service requirements of the setting. The learning contract with your supervisor should clearly articulate who will do what, to what extent, under what conditions, and when. The learning contract is the foundation for the supervision relationship, and it is thus a type of accountability contract that is explicitly discussed and reviewed periodically so that both you and your supervisor understand what is expected from the process. Other factors that affect the learning contract include managing the elements of authority, trust, and sharing (Goodyear & Bernard, 1998; Kaiser, 1997). Your educational program may have a specific learning contract for you to use. Exemplars of criteria that may be found in a learning plan include:

1. The learner's personal objectives
2. The learner's professional objectives
3. The potential work assignments or projects or learning opportunities to address the objectives
4. The timeline for achieving the objectives
5. Evidence of the accomplishment of the objectives

PRACTICAL CONSIDERATIONS FOR LEARNING

You will need to tend to practical matters in supervision. When and how often will you interact with your supervisor? What do you need to be preparing in advance? What portion of supervision time is to be spent on case discussion, specific topics, specific skills, review of cases, issues, and self-evaluation? How are your learning objectives to be demonstrated and evaluated? Are you expected to take the lead or will your supervisor? Clarifying the practical matters of supervision helps you manage and shape the results of your learning.

Clarify basic work requirements and discuss knowledge about the population served, treatment approaches, types of investigations to be completed, types of mapping programs and technology skills needed, presentation of aspects of your work from such products as case notes, reviews, records, and reports, and documentation requirements. Finally, discuss your impressions, reactions, and experiences.

Furthermore, you need to know about specific indications for supervision use. Immediate supervision or consultation should be obtained when there are sudden unexpected changes in those being served. This may include deterioration in behaviors or mental status; problems that emerge after a contact that were not apparent initially; or when danger or issues of safety and protection arise, particularly in cases of family violence, child maltreatment, threats, and other safety concerns. Certain other conflicts or stressful situations for individuals, families, or organizations may also precipitate a request for immediate guidance from supervisors or consultants. Students need to realize that such situations require early or even immediate attention. Specific issues should not be reserved until the next supervision or consultation conference in such instances. To start off in the right direction, experts suggest the following:

1. Use honest, clear communication skills and interactions.
2. Be flexible in attitude and manner.
3. Expect that the internship is going to be a new learning experience.
4. Be open about what you need and want to learn.
5. Don't forget that you are there to learn, so ask questions and seek assistance.
6. Build on what you know.

GUIDELINES FOR SUPERVISION

The following guidelines, derived from key authors (Baird, 2004; Gordon, McBride, & Hage, 2001; Kaiser, 1997; Munson, 1989, 2000; Reimer et al., 1999; Thomlison, 2000; Schulman, 1993), form the essential elements of supervision.

1. *Modeling*. Your supervisor should model impeccable professional behavior for you. Observe her or his professional behavior and management of different situations, from direct practice situations to conflict resolution. Make sure your supervisor has the appropriate credentials to supervise you. Learning from other disciplines is valuable, but it is not the same as learning from your own discipline. Your supervisor will also assist you with learning and will support you, provide practice behaviors that reflect organizational skills, and model elements of authority, trust, and sharing.
2. *Planning*. Supervisors balance assignments or workload. Workload should be manageable and provide a balance of difficult and familiar assignments, combining challenge (in terms of learning new skills) with relevancy for the student's level of competence.
3. *Feedback*. You can expect your supervisor to provide regular, clear, frequent, timely, and relevant feedback about performance that balances your strengths and vulnerabilities. Feedback on performance is most useful when it occurs as soon as possible after the practice situation, because it sets the stage for change opportunities. Interns should ask for feedback and comments as a primary function of learning. Confident supervisors also ask for feedback and comments.
4. *Expectations*. Supervisors build competencies, but they need you to discuss your learning needs. They will expect you to approach them for assistance

as needed apart from formal interview or meeting times. Obtain information about your supervisor's preferred means of communication—telephone numbers, e-mail, emergency contact plans, and any relevant expectations for when your supervisor is not present.

METHODS FOR ASSESSING PROGRESS

Depending on the type of setting, more than one approach to assessing progress may be used. Daily and periodic assessment will occur, including written work, review of videotapes or audiotapes, and, of course, periodic progress reports. In terms of effectiveness, supervisors and students ranked videotapes and live supervision as the first and second choices (out of 17 possible rankings) of favored supervision formats for assessing progress (Goodyear & Nelson, 1997).

Documenting Information

Documentation tools assist students in their efforts to strive for clarity, precision, and accuracy, as well as depth and breadth of learning, in the practicum. Documentation requires paying attention to the process of reasoning or critical thinking in your writings.

Recording Information

Through awareness of your experiences with taping of clients or through role-play exercises, you learn to understand your reactions, yourself, and specific situations of practice. As you become aware of and are able to understand where you have gaps in learning, your practice skills are likely to improve. Videotaping role plays helps reduce apprehension before you see a client and allows you to practice skills and gain confidence. Remember, if you are taping clients using either audiotaping or videotaping, you must seek consent to tape in order to protect your client.

A common technique for recording information is by audio recording or videotaping. As noted earlier, students and supervisors view technical methods such as taping to be superior to other forms of collecting information, such as case notes or journal writing. Videotaping requires access to equipment, and therefore it is often not convenient to videotape a client in certain settings. Videotaping a client or a role-play simulation provides a full recording of an actual exchange, which has certain learning advantages. Recordings are used as a mirror to reflect your practice and communication skills. In viewing the tape, your supervisor will highlight verbal and nonverbal elements of interaction that will assist you in developing and assessing content and process of interviews. Videotaping an intervention or a skill performed in a clinical or simulated setting is another approach to learning that lets you analyze the sequence, efficiency of steps, and precision of technique, as well as your interaction with the client, during the meeting or session. Self-awareness is another additional benefit of videotaping. Some things to look for in reviewing a video recording include:

- Body language and behavior
- Language used and tone of voice
- Speech patterns
- Degree of comfort in executing a skill or interaction

The advantage of an audio recording is that the recorder is portable and can be taken with you to different locations. Although it certainly does not provide the visual aspects of analysis, it does allow you to capture your interactions or contacts exactly as they occurred. Many internship settings and programs have opportunities for students to access both technologies for learning.

An alternative to working with videotapes of clients is to enact, simulate, or role-play with another student to portray a situation or interaction about some aspect of your practice or case assignments. Rehearsing a practice skill or intervention is helpful before trying the technique with clients.

Guidelines for Recording

The following are basic guidelines that pertain to audiotaping and videotaping either a client or a role-play situation:

- Practice using the equipment before you need to use it.
- Keep taping equipment visible.
- It is natural to feel somewhat anxious about taping for the first time.
- Present the notion of being taped in a relaxed manner to the client.
- Clients readily give consent for taping, but you should always ask for written permission. Some agencies require that the client repeat permission to be recorded at the beginning of the recording. Do not use clients' names.
- Fully explain to the client exactly who will be viewing the tape if someone other than yourself will be looking at it (e.g., your instructor), the purpose of reviewing the tape, and how long the tape will be kept. Include this information in a written consent form.

- You do not have to tape the full interaction with a client if it is preferable to keep the taping short.
- Making a tape available for clients to view or listen to is often a clinically helpful tool in work with a client.
- If you taped an actual client, store the tape in a safe location.
- Indicate a time frame for erasing or destroying the recording (Reimer et al., 1999, pg. 145).

Writing

It is prudent advice for every student to clearly and accurately document your work and experiences during the internship and practicum. Managing your practice through documentation is no longer an option but a risk-management strategy (Falender & Shafranske, 2004; Falvey, 2002). Your instructor will expect your writing to reflect the scientific approach and scholarly quality of the journal articles you are reading. You may believe that good writing comes naturally for some people, but even for the experienced writer, it is hard work. The development of quality writing skills is not only desirable but may also be critical when legal and managed care issues arise. At all levels of social work education and professional practice, writing skills are intrinsic to competency skills.

Journal Writing

Journaling is a useful analytical tool to help you document the events and experiences in your life as an intern. Journaling is somewhat different from keeping a diary. As a journal writer, you will primarily focus on the significance of activities or events related to your learning and practice. The journal chronicles meaningful contacts with clients and others.

A journal is a safe place to raise issues and express yourself, deal with your fears and concerns, and log life's ups and downs. Journal writing needs to be organized and directed, but it is the process of writing that is important. The process of critical thinking forms the basis for writing, searching for details of events, and formulating themes and communicating results. Above all, your journal should be relevant to you and enhance your learning needs.

What information do you put in the journal? A journal is an analytical tool for recording facts, events, and processes. There should be a record of observations and experiences and of the impact of these events on you and your practice. It is a form of feedback about what you see and hear in your environment. Different processes come into play with written words than with spoken words.

Begin writing with a question about the internship, with your interaction with a client, or with the best or worst thing that happened in an interview; it does not really matter. What does matter is that you begin to put your thoughts, ideas, and feelings on paper. Committing your thoughts to paper requires particular qualities such as humility, integrity, perseverance, empathy, and self-discipline. As you are writing, you are thinking about the elements present in a client problem or situation. You are making connections between the elements and the issue or problem at hand. Through journaling you can clarify your thinking and form a baseline against which to measure changes in your experiences, thereby obtaining evidence to inform practice. For example, you can question yourself about many things. Are you having difficulty communicating with certain types of clients? Do you feel anxious and uncomfortable working with sexual perpetrators or with individuals with suicidal thoughts? Do you feel uncomfortable approaching your supervisor? Are you proud of your collaborative skills with other health care providers? Review your journal entries regularly for themes, ideas, and patterns. Here are some guidelines for writing and analysis (Reimer et al., 1999):

1. Think in terms of opposites.
2. Explore different views from different perspectives.
3. Focus on finding and solving problems.
4. Emphasize understanding.
5. Reflect on the language you use.
6. Recognize affective influences.
7. Recognize attitudes and values associated with cognitive biases.
8. Reflect on self-awareness by asking, What do I believe? Why do I believe that?
9. Identify recurrent patterns of interaction.
10. Keep your journal in a safe or private place, and keep your journal entries neat.
11. Always include one positive statement about your abilities and strengths.
12. Use language that is nonjudgmental, nonderogatory, and clear.
13. Make entries daily or at least after each clinical encounter, and ask good questions; for example, Is this the best intervention for mothers with a diagnosis of depression?
14. Use different colored pens for various entries.
15. A two-column format provides space to return to the entry for later reflections and additions.

Journaling aids in self-assessing and self-improving. From this self-discovery process, you will uncover thinking and learning styles, attitudes, and strategies associated with your developing skills, ethics and values for informed practice. Ultimately, you are writing to evidence your accomplishments and learning experiences, but each time you engage in critical thinking, you are also helping your clients in valuable ways. It informs your practice decisions and your directives for safety, ethical, and legal choices for clients.

REFLECTING ON PRACTICE IN SUPERVISION

Learning is a unique mixture of personal knowledge, past concrete situations, individual preferences, and cognitive characteristics and paradigms. From conversations with your supervisor, you will learn that you have certain patterns, themes, and practice behaviors that are developing. As an intern you will share belief systems about yourself, cases, and assignments. Often these matters will center on worries stated as, "I don't know what to do with this person," or "How do I go about doing it?" or "I am afraid my client will know I don't know what to do" or "I don't like my client." This also translates into "I don't know what to do if my supervisor realizes I am not helping this person" or "I am afraid my supervisor will know I don't know what to do with my client." If you are concerned about competence or poor evaluations, share these thoughts with your supervisor. From the outset, your supervisor will create a safe, supportive supervisory environment to nurture your development and address your concerns about professional competence (Thomlison et al., 1996).

The content and activities discussed during supervision vary, but supervision is essentially the place for interns to tell their stories or experiences during practice, which include explanations and reactions to practice. Different supervision activities promote cognitive, affective, and operative learning. Content is presented in written and verbal formats. Tapes, didactic discussions, role plays, journals or logs, simulations, case discussion of reports, process recordings, direct observations of work, and working jointly are also activities that may form the content of supervision. These activities, experiences, and expectations are clarified as a shared meaning of practice develops between supervisor and intern. For a more complete discussion of documentation, clinical notes, and records, see Rogers and Thomlison (2000) and Baird (2004) (Szuchman & Thomlison, 2007).

SUMMARY

This chapter focused on understanding how to develop your knowledge, skills, and professional resources in the context of your supervision experience. Guidelines for maximizing quality supervision follow.

- Supervision continues to be a primary forum for learning and maintaining practice skills and competencies.
- Be open to learning, ask questions, and regularly seek consultation and collaboration with others in the learning environment.
- There is a wide range of learning styles; therefore, recognize your learning preferences.
- Supervision promotes competence, develops professional confidence and independence, improves self-awareness, and helps you acquire theoretical and practical knowledge.
- Internships are potentially stressful experiences for various reasons, so seeking and accepting support in the supervisory relationship is essential.
- Identify your personal resources or attributes and build on the following competencies: increasing your evidence-based knowledge, keeping a positive and flexible attitude toward learning, practicing necessary skills for moving from a novice to an expert, motivating yourself for various experiences and capabilities.
- Know the appropriate lines of communication, policies, and procedures for locating resources.
- Document your activities, thoughts, ideas, and decisions.

THE PATIENT IN THE NEXT DESK

Kim Strom-Gottfried and Nikki D. Mowbray

Case Description

James was a second-year intern whose field placement was in an acute adult admissions unit of the state psychiatric hospital. When James arrived this morning, he heard the treatment team discussing the case of Margaret, a 29-year-old female who had a history of major depression and was admitted two nights earlier after going to a local emergency room with suicidal thoughts. James's field instructor, Alice, had been assigned to be Margaret's social worker. Alice asked James to review the chart before they met with Margaret to complete her biopsychosocial assessment.

When reviewing the record, James found out that Margaret was also a graduate student at the same school he attended. When he saw her last name and picture in the chart, he realized that the patient was his classmate, Maggie, who had not been in class that week. James remembered that the professor mentioned that Maggie would be out this week and possibly next week due to a death in the family.

James was uncertain about what to do next. Should he tell Alice? If so, would he have to give up his work on the case? Would he have to excuse himself from all activities on the unit that Maggie might attend (such as group therapy and psychoeducational sessions)? How should he approach Maggie in the milieu (or should be approach her at all)? Did he have an obligation to inform the school or her field placement that she was experiencing grave difficulties? How would James relate to Maggie when she returned to class?

Assessment/Screening and Problem Identification

In order to work through this dilemma, James would likely engage in supervision and consultation. These techniques are well-respected ways to evaluate a situation. However, professionals should also learn to use ethical decision-making models to organize the facts of a case and weigh the possible options and consequences. Using Reamer's (2006) decision-making model, James was able to create a clearer picture of what the issues were in this case and was better able to define his possible options. Reamer's model required James to consider several steps.

1. What are the major issues or values?

Several values and ethical standards are invoked in this case, among them preserving Maggie's dignity and worth, in spite of her current impairment; avoiding potentially harmful dual relationships; protecting client confidentiality; and ensuring the competent delivery of services. We examine these principles more thoroughly later.

2. Which individuals, groups, or organizations are likely to be affected?

Several individuals and entities have a stake in James's decision, though not all are equally affected by his decision. The stakeholders include James himself, Maggie (his classmate and patient), Alice (James's field advisor and Maggie's assigned social worker), the hospital treatment team, the academic program, Maggie's field placement agency, Dr. Brown (Maggie and James's professor in the class they have together), and potentially Maggie's future clients if she is not competent to provide professional services. The hospital itself may have policies that dictate the worker's role when called on to care for a friend or acquaintance, so James should take the institution into account. Seems rather complicated, doesn't it?

3. What viable courses of action exist? What participants are involved, and what are the potential risks and benefits for each?

Action	Participants	Risks	Benefits
Tell no one; treat Maggie	James, Maggie		Dual relationship
Decline to treat Maggie	James, Maggie, Alice		No dual relationship
Tell the school	James, school	Patient confidentiality	
Tell Maggie's placement	James, agency staff	Patient confidentiality	Protects her clients
Encourage Maggie to tell	James, Maggie	Maggie might not agree	Protects her patient rights

Explore the reasons for and against each viable course of action.

- *Tell no one:* This will ensure Maggie's confidentiality but might create a dual relationship, as James adds his therapeutic role to the colleague role he already shares with her.
- *Decline to treat Maggie:* Will eliminate dual relationship but will require collaboration and agreement from Alice and the treatment team. It may affect James's learning opportunities for the week, but his needs should not take precedence over those of the client.
- *Tell the school:* Will likely make James feel better by warning them of Maggie's potential need for support or assistance with her competence, but it violates her confidentiality.
- *Tell Maggie's placement agency:* Will likely make James feel better by possibly protecting her clients but will violate Maggie's confidentiality.
- *Encourage Maggie to tell* the school and her agency about her current hospitalization: Could help Maggie get the support and supervision she will need and protects her own patient rights, but Maggie might feel coerced and might not agree to share. This would also require James to reveal his role on the unit to her, and it raises questions about whether it is James's role to counsel Maggie on her school and placement decisions.

4. Consult with colleagues or appropriate experts

James has many resources at his disposal here, first and foremost his field instructor, Alice. The treatment team may also be a resource in helping him negotiate this complex situation and assist in taking over his responsibilities so that he isn't inadvertently exposed to information about Maggie's care. James's faculty advisor and field director may also be possible advisors, though he would need to maintain Maggie's confidentiality while asking about policies by which students are put in the role of providing services to their classmates.

Intervention/Treatment

After examining his situation through the perspectives of the decision-making model, James concluded that he needed to tell Alice and seek her advice. As a result of his ethical decision making, James had determined that it would have been inappropriate to serve on Maggie's treatment team, that it would have constituted a complicated and potentially harmful dual relationship. If he was not involved with her care, he also had to avoid seeking or reading information on her case. Beyond that, he had to take care not to share information he already knew with anyone outside the hospital, including her placement agency or the school of social work. It was up to the school and the placement to evaluate her competence, and there was no compelling reason for him to divulge her hospitalization to them.

If Maggie had concerns about her continued relationship with James, what he knew and what he might have shared, Alice might have facilitated a conversation between the two in which Maggie would be reassured of James's dedication to patient privacy and in which any concerns about returning to their classmate relationship were addressed.

Evaluation

Interns evaluate the adequacy of their ethical decision making by considering the process they used in reaching a decision, the consequences of the decision for those involved, whether anything unexpected occurred, and how the decision might generalize to future dilemmas. As James discusses these elements with Alice, and as the case unfolds, he will be able to determine whether his appraisals and choices were on target. Others in his setting, including Maggie, may also give feedback to help him evaluate the appropriateness of his decision.

As Maggie returns to school and her field work, the long-term effects of his decision will become clear. If Maggie demonstrates performance problems, perhaps James will reevaluate his decision not to divulge her condition to the school or her placement, though her rights to privacy would still likely outweigh any benefit that might occur from his breaching her confidentiality.

If he and Maggie are able to successfully work together as classmates when she returns to school, this outcome may reinforce his decision to keep a clear boundary in not serving on her treatment team.

Discussion

Ethical dilemmas, by their very nature, represent a conflict: between competing choices, between the needs or interests of two groups or individuals, or between an individual's values and those of his or her profession or work setting. The first step in addressing a dilemma is recognizing that it exists, and James was wise to step back and consider carefully the issues in this case before following up on Alice's directions. James used an established model for examining his options and the ethical standards involved. He appropriately decided to seek consultation from his supervisor on the matter. His decision to recuse himself from the case put the interests of the client, Maggie, first in protecting her confidentiality and preserving their existing relationship as classmates.

▪ ▪ ▪

Activities

The following activities can be conducted individually in a journal or as part of a small-group discussion. Space is provided for notes.

1. Imagine that you were James. What if a classmate (or friend, neighbor, or family member) of yours appeared for service at your field placement setting? What difficulties might you foresee?

2. How would your relationship with this person be affected by his or her seeking service in your agency?

3. What concerns and interests would you weigh in trying to resolve this dilemma? Would you resolve it the same way he did?

4. Would you be comfortable raising the issue with your field supervisor? Are there any circumstances under which you think it would be appropriate to continue as part of the treatment team?

5. Now put yourself in the client's shoes. What concerns would you have about seeking mental health treatment or other services at an agency where your classmate, friend, neighbor, or family member is placed?

6. What precautions are important to safeguard your privacy and make you comfortable accepting services here?

7. Consider other dilemmas you have experienced in your field placement. Try using the ethical decision-making model as a structured way to examine and weigh your options. What are the advantages and disadvantages of a structured ethical decision-making process?

Revealing Your Learning Preferences

This exercise is about identifying your preferences and strengths, as well as reflecting on the thinking processes you use to identify these. Answer the following questions about your preferences and strengths. The purpose of this exercise is to increase your self-awareness and your ability to articulate your strengths and preferences. Many of the questions are phrased in "either/or" terms, but you may feel that you have some of both—if so, write about that.

1. Task-related preferences

a. How much variety do you need in your work? Explain.

b. Do you like to take complex situations, examine the parts, and show how the parts are interrelated? *Or* do you like to take an overview of many events and see how they fit together? Give an example.

c. What kinds of problems get your creative or determined juices flowing (e.g., people problems, ideas, problems relating to things)? Give an example.

   d. What are your work habits? Are you spontaneous, fairly disorganized, heedless of details? Or do you like to work in a methodical way? Explain.

2. Self-related preferences

   a. Do you prefer to work alone or in a group?

   b. How competitive are you? Rate yourself on a scale from 1 to 10. How might this be a help or a hindrance in the internship?

   c. Do you tend to work to deadlines, or do you like to plan and work far ahead?

   d. How much praise do you need to keep yourself going? What do you do if no praise is forthcoming?

   e. In making a decision, do you obtain large amounts of information or advice and ponder carefully all of the alternatives? *Or* do you follow your "inner sense" and make an instinctive decision? Describe your decision-making process.

3. Summarize your strengths

   a. What are your important strengths? Don't limit yourself to one area of your life (e.g., think of your educational life, your social life).

   b. What was the process you used to determine your strengths? For example, did you start by naming various categories or various roles? How could you use your strengths as strategies for effective learning?

The Learning Plan

Use the sample learning plan or contract from your professional program to develop your goals and objectives for the internship.

1. Describe the knowledge, skill/performance objectives, professional competencies, and values necessary for your professional development.

2. Determine what types of projects and assignments you need to achieve these objectives.

3. What types of documentation will be used to assess your progress?

4. How will you know when you have achieved these objectives?

5. Review your learning plan with your supervisor. How often should you review your plan with your supervisor?

Checklist for Evidence-Based Practices for Supervision

The checklist is designed to assist both students and supervisors in assessing their status with reference to supervision practices. The purpose is to use the checklist as a tool for identifying or enhancing awareness of qualities of supervision competency. Circle the number that best represents your current supervision context.

Critically reflect on items that you rate below three to assess how you can improve that dimension for improved learning.

Supportive Supervisory Relationship

1. My supervisor provides quality supervision.

   Not at All   1   2   3   4   5   Very Much

2. My supervisor is a respected individual.

   Not at All   1   2   3   4   5   Very Much

3. My supervisor is an accomplished individual in my discipline.

   Not at All   1   2   3   4   5   Very Much

4. My supervisor is competent in his or her professional practice area.

   Not at All   1   2   3   4   5   Very Much

5. My supervisor clearly separates supervision from counseling.

   Not at All   1   2   3   4   5   Very Much

6. My supervisor conveys understanding when I have difficulties.

   Not at All   1   2   3   4   5   Very Much

7. My supervisor conveys understanding when I have accomplishments.

   Not at All   1   2   3   4   5   Very Much

8. My supervisor recognizes my personal strengths and abilities.

   Not at All   1   2   3   4   5   Very Much

9. My supervisor is flexible, amicable, and approachable

   Not at All   1   2   3   4   5   Very Much

10. My supervisor models the qualities of genuineness and congruence.

    Not at All   1   2   3   4   5   Very Much

11. My supervisor emphasizes my strengths rather than my deficiencies.

    Not at All   1   2   3   4   5   Very Much

Critical Reflection and Thinking

1. My supervisor enhances my critical thinking skills.

   Not at All   1   2   3   4   5   Very Much

2. My supervisor helps me to improve my communication skills.

   Not at All   1   2   3   4   5   Very Much

3. My supervisor helps me increase my scientific reasoning skills in practice.

Not at All   1   2   3   4   5   Very Much

4. My supervisor has competent skills in analyzing events.

Not at All   1   2   3   4   5   Very Much

Competency-Based Practices and Educational Focus

1. My supervisor helps me view alternate positions about whether practice cases, projects, or other assignments were effective.

Not at All   1   2   3   4   5   Very Much

2. My supervisor provides clear, frequent, timely, and relevant feedback about my performance that balances my strengths and vulnerabilities.

Not at All   1   2   3   4   5   Very Much

3. My supervisor also asks for feedback.

Not at All   1   2   3   4   5   Very Much

4. My supervisor recognizes my strengths and abilities.

Not at All   1   2   3   4   5   Very Much

5. My supervisor is flexible and allows maximum autonomy in my assignments.

Not at All   1   2   3   4   5   Very Much

6. My supervisor provides clear, frequent, timely, and relevant feedback about my performance

Not at All   1   2   3   4   5   Very Much

7. My supervisor provides balanced feedback about my strengths and shortcomings.

Not at All   1   2   3   4   5   Very Much

Part II Evidence-Based Practice Skills and Interventions for Internships

5 EVIDENCE-BASED SKILLS FOR INTERVIEWING

BARBARA THOMLISON *and* KEVIN CORCORAN

*In this chapter you will learn about qualities and characteristics
that influence your interactions with others. You will review essential
skills of communication to assist you in engaging others in interaction, in
asking questions, in using critical thinking skills to improve thinking
and actions, and in the basics of interviewing. The focus is on
understanding yourself and improving interactions with others. This
chapter emphasizes the importance of self-knowledge for self-learning.
The chapter ends with exercises on self-assessment and asking for
help and a case study.*

You will undoubtedly draw on both personal and professional skills and resources in the conduct of your work during the internship. You will incorporate
many influences into practice. As a practitioner, you come to the internship with
your own beliefs, values, understandings, and preferences about many issues that
contribute to client situations. The focus of this chapter is on personal influences
that shape the outcomes of your conduct and, ultimately, your practice. Underlying all effective practice are the ability to communicate clearly and the skills
to understand the communications of the interviewee. Human service workers
conduct many different types of interviews and assess all sources of information.
The range of skills can be overwhelming. You might be required to interview
children, youths, and adults or all of these, and even other professionals. The
purpose of the interviews will vary, but they must be done with sensitivity and
compassion and with a keen eye for details and chronological synchronicity. For
example, an interview with a child who has allegedly been maltreated is affected
by interviewer and interviewee characteristics—physical, cognitive, and affective
factors; by message components—language, nonverbal cues, and sensory cues;
and by interview climate—physical, social, temporal, and psychological factors.
For the most part, your task is to control for as many of these factors as possible in
order to obtain an unbiased and untainted interview. However, it will be impossible to control for all of these factors, and you will necessarily call on essential
skills of communication in response to clients' affective, cognitive, and behavioral
reactions. There are many excellent books on communication skills, and we intend

here to highlight several *essential* skills necessary to developing competencies. We highlighted (1) essential skills for engaging your clients to work with you and (2) skills for mutual exploration of the work you will do with the client.

PRINCIPLES AND ASSUMPTIONS

Practitioners in various settings will have in common a set of skills with which to approach practice. Those in clinical and social service settings will need more than to be a compassionate practitioner with good intentions. If your internship is in a clinical or social service setting, you will need to use a range of interpersonal processes and skills. If you are doing an internship in a criminal justice setting, then you may emphasize the use of investigative, analytical, research, synthesizing, and action-taking skills.

Communication skills are the foundation of just about all that you will do in the internship. What skills do you use for new situations you encounter? You may be observing and not directly involved in assignments. What skills are tapped into at this time? You may be doing a lot of thinking about what you are observing. It can be overwhelming, and you may not think that you are making a contribution or that you know what skills to use. Although you may be learning directly through the assignments, you are learning as an observer an important skill that leads to reflection and critical thinking. This contributes to knowledge development. Above all, take the opportunity to ask questions. No one expects you to know everything about the internship site, its cases, its clients, and the role of the staff in the setting. Certainly no one expects students to come with a complete repertoire of advanced skills in interviewing, assessment, synthesizing, researching, and more. As a student, you will come with essential skills for ready learning in the internship. As a professional, you have to acquire strong communication skills, written and oral. There are several basic principles for success.

- Draw on critical thinking skills.
- Reflect on the work practices in the internship setting; it is more than a matter of acquiring knowledge and a set of technical skills, although these are important.
- You will learn from action and problem solving in the work environment of the internships.
- What you learn in the internship is viewed as a creation of knowledge as it is shared with other people through discussing and sharing ideas, problems, and solutions.

- Keep your attitude and expectations open and flexible, not critical.
- Develop a learning plan.
- Keep focused. Get your personal life and priorities in order (e.g., you may need to make changes in part-time work hours, babysitting arrangements, or extracurricular activities because of the demands of the internship).
- The internship will be about not only acquiring new knowledge but also acquiring many competencies to learn. (Learning and Teaching Support Network [LTSN], 2001)

ENGAGEMENT

Getting started involves engaging the client in the process of change. This is paramount and necessary and requires the practitioner to achieve a positive and trusting relationship with the client as they begin to assess and contribute to the "work." It is an alliance and connection between two systems, not just individuals. Therefore, the first encounters are very important and will determine the nature and process of what evolves therein. Engagement is a foundation skill for developing a relationship with the client. Through this process of engagement, information should result that helps us decide what intervention is needed to generate particular results. Failure to adequately engage and retain clients in interventions is a serious problem. Little research is available to guide practice. The processes of client engagement and participation vary, but some practitioners use specific strategies such as contracts, rewards, and culturally specific content for alliance building with clients to develop readiness to change (Rollnick & Miller, 1995). Risk factors for intervention dropout include language barriers and cultural mismatch, as well as client preferences for interventions, perceptions of intervention relevance, beliefs, and values. Engagement is further complicated by the fact that individuals are often engaging with multiple systems, and efforts to involve another service may confound intervention with you. Within this context, you will engage the client and work for a recognized and agreed-on purpose. Empathic listening underpins this process.

ASKING QUESTIONS

If you are a good listener, you are more likely to ask good questions. Clarification and probing questions are two effective types of questions. Clarification questions are structured and thought of as closed questions with brief, "yes," "no," or "maybe" answers. Probing questions are open-ended, encourage deeper responses, and permit comments to be expanded. Good probing questions are broad and cannot be answered with "yes" or "no." Do not interrupt speakers or make critical comments or judgments. This may be difficult, as you will work with many people who differ from you in numerous ways. Some you may find more difficult to work with than others; hence the temptation to sometimes want to disagree and offer suggestions. However, this will not be helpful.

EMPATHIC LISTENING (ATTENTIVE AND CRITICAL LISTENING SKILLS)

Great listening does not come easy. It is hard work. In fact, this may be one of the most important skills to cultivate for practice, because you will do more listening than any other activity, and if you wish to excel in your work it is recommended that you practice this skill in every situation, even outside the internship. Empathic listening is also called *active* listening or *reflective* listening and is a way of responding to another person that improves mutual understanding and trust. Listening is an active behavior rather than a passive skill. Attentive and critical listening are two skills that are not easy to acquire but are tantamount to a successful interview and to building trust and respect. If you do not have these skills in your listening interactions, then you should take every opportunity to practice them, as the payoffs will be great.

Attentive listening involves thinking and acting in ways that connect you with the interviewee. The goal of attentive listening is to understand and remember what you are hearing. Because you often need to connect in a relational way with the person, you have as a goal to give a positive impression, to advance the relationship, and to demonstrate that you care and are concerned and connected to their points. The quality of information exchanged, your experience as a listener, the experience of the person you are listening to, and your relationship with the listener will all determine the outcome.

Critical thinking involves evaluating and assessing what you are hearing. Critical listening emphasizes critical thinking skills. This is related to asking good clarification questions, but listening critically provides the basis for good probing questions. Critical thinking skills include:

1. Questioning and challenging
2. Recognizing difference between facts and opinions

3. Forming opinions and supporting claims (determining what you think and what contributes to it)
4. Putting ideas into a broader context

Critical listening involves acting as a sounding board for the person speaking. The listener helps the person speaking by only listening, not giving any advice. Guidelines for improving your listening skills include:

1. Reviewing and paraphrasing—restating what you believe to be the essence of the speaker's comments
2. Reflecting feelings
3. Reflecting meanings
4. Summarizing

SELF-DISCLOSURE

Through your interactions with your client and even your supervisor, you may give statements that reveal something personal about yourself; this is called self-disclosure. Intentional self-disclosure may be helpful, but usually self-disclosure should be avoided and certainly used infrequently. Interns often think it increases client-worker similarity, models appropriate behavior, fosters the engagement process, and even normalizes the experience of helping or the client's experience. Reassurance and self-disclosure may be confused with each other, but reassurance is more helpful, if it is sincere, than self-disclosure (Hill, Mahalik, & Thompson, 1989). Although there is little research to guide us in this matter, a review of best practices (Hill & Knox, 2001) recommends the following practice guidelines.

1. Disclose only very infrequently.
2. The most appropriate content involves professional background; the least appropriate topic is sexual practices and beliefs.
3. Practitioners use disclosure to validate reality, normalize experiences, and model alternative ways to think or act.
4. Disclosure can remove the focus from the client or confuse the client.
5. The degree of self-disclosure to use is always difficult to gauge, but for the most part it is not recommended, and judicious application is necessary.

SELF-AWARENESS

Use Your Mind

- Listen with your mind completely engaged. Listen for accuracy or inaccuracy. Focus.
- Do not become preoccupied with what you are going to say next or what question to ask, because you will miss what the interviewee is saying and how he or she is saying it. Also, effective listening is hampered when you prematurely evaluate and judge everything the person is saying.
- Do not start to formulate impressions or judgments before you finish the interview. Obviously, impressions will come to you, but do not allow them to bias your interview without the proper line of questioning for supporting evidence.
- Both you as the interviewer and the client as the interviewee will be forming initial impressions of each other. The ebb and flow of the interaction will continually modify the impressions both of you have.
- Be aware of your impressions, but do not mold them as truth.
- Don't multitask if you are supposed to be listening. If you are thinking about something else, you will miss nonverbal cues and information and lower the commitment level of your client.

Listening to Yourself

Being an effective listener also means listening to yourself.

- Become attuned to your thoughts, feelings, and actions and learn how to deal with them appropriately during the interview.
- Learn from everything you do.

Body Language

Your body language conveys meaning to the interviewee.

- Use positive body language; make frequent eye contact.
- Avoid negative body language, such as frowning and looking away. You may unknowingly bite your nails, crack your knuckles, twirl your hair, tap your pen, rock in your chair, play with your hands, or any other nervous habit that may distract, annoy, or alter the client and the interview.
- Supportive and accepting body language will put the client at ease and convey a message of understanding and trust.

- As human service workers, it is our duty to embrace the different cultural nuances that clients display. Be cognizant of your body language and what it may convey to persons of different backgrounds as you conduct the interview. You may have to alter your stance, posture, eye contact, and so forth depending on what background or culture the interviewee comes from.
- Your posture or body position should not be distracting.

Listen to the Whole Message

You need to tune in not only to the words of someone speaking but also to his or her body language and tone of voice in order to hear the whole message. Listen to both the verbal and nonverbal parts of the message. Empathy is the ability to project yourself "into" the other person in such a way that you understand that person's feelings: "I understand what you are saying, and I am not judging you." In this way you will elicit openness and be able to share the other's ideas, thoughts, and concerns. You are acquiring information from others in a nonjudgmental and empathic way.

One of your major resources is yourself and your sincerity or genuineness in various interactions. Don't be afraid to laugh with clients at times. The genuineness that you bring to situations is part of shared human experience. There will be other times when it is not appropriate to show your feelings; part of your learning is to know which is which.

ADVOCACY SKILLS

Assertiveness is such an important skill for professionals that many programs have built assertiveness training into their curricula. The ability to be assertive rather than passive or aggressive is a useful skill for anyone. What makes assertiveness so important in the helping professions is the link with being an advocate for the clients with whom we work. How assertive are you? Can you intervene in such a way that your client's needs are met?

APPROACHING YOUR FIRST INTERVIEW

Identifying and sorting through all the potential factors that affect the outcomes of your work is a complex undertaking. Research has not been entirely helpful in this regard, but certain characteristics are emphasized at various times. Warm, accepting qualities that are necessary in interviews in which the primary purpose is therapeutic are not the same qualities required in an interview whose primary purpose is to gain a disclosure from a perpetrator; in this case an investigative, aggressive, directive, and dominant approach is necessary (Cournoyer, 2000). Core qualities of professionals are qualities that facilitate problem solving A productive interview features the following basic qualities:

- The parties respect each other.
- Clear expectations are communicated about purpose and about how to contribute to the process.
- The professional is sincere, warm, and genuine and expresses empathy for the client's experiences.
- The meeting is goal directed and structured, and in-session and out-of-session tasks are clearly developed.

You are learning to become competent, but your skill set is just developing and is greatly affected by whether or not you have had certain opportunities. Even your supervisor may need to rely in part on your judgment as to whether or not you are competent to handle a particular procedure or situation alone. It is therefore your responsibility to seek out supervision if:

- You have not done something before.
- You do not feel confident that you are ready to do it without supervision.
- You have never worked with this type of client (e.g., an aggressive adult in a domestic dispute, a child, a suicidal adolescent).
- You are having problems with a particular type of process or procedure

In general, as an intern you need certain qualities to engage with the client.

- Empathy: Understanding how someone feels
- Communication: Ability to communicate understanding through active listening
- Openness: Willingness to discuss sensitive subjects without being judgmental
- Encouragement: Ability to give hope and confidence
- Composure: Remaining calm regardless of the situation or client's behavior
- Respect: For clients' well-being
- Genuineness: Relating to children, adults, and staff members in real and honest ways
- Specificity: Being concrete and focusing on specific concerns of the client.

The foundation of essential skills is possessing facilitative or social skills. Social skills are critical to promoting positive interactions with others. Of course, depending on the clients being served, some skills may need to be added and others deleted. In general, you will: (1) create an atmosphere for positive interactions to occur. (2) Ask questions to get to know the client; you will start the conversation or interview. (3) Ask probing questions to get deeper and more detailed responses if necessary. (4) Express support but moderate your own feelings. (5) Understand the boundaries between the helper and the client, even though you are very interested in and like your client. (6) Give feedback so the client understands that you understand. (7) Identify how the client feels (empathy), yet invite the client to say more; follow good listening rules and don't interrupt. (8) Make responsible, data-driven decisions with the client, but don't be afraid to ask for assistance from your supervisor.

To avoid criticism that often arises about helpers and law enforcement personnel:

- Be careful to be responsible but not become overzealous in your work.
- Know your roles and responsibilities.
- Remain accountable to the public.

CHECKLIST OF SKILLS

Test yourself on the principles that apply to developing essential skills:

- I listen to understand.
- I do not prepare a response while listening.
- I listen without interrupting.
- I listen respectfully and nonjudgmentally.
- I use paraphrasing responses, restating the client's position.
- I listen for the key ideas.
- I listen for the facts.
- I listen without interrupting.
- I pay attention to eye contact and focus on the speaker.
- I use positive body language.
- I listen for meta meanings: listening to tone of voice and body language.
- I try to draw out the client's thinking and not provide answers.
- I listen supportively.
- I listen to myself.

SUMMARY

This chapter focuses on enhancing awareness of yourself and the meaning, values, and interrelationships you are discovering in your learning experiences as an intern. Reflection promotes inner or emotional awareness. It is a cognitive process. Talking to your supervisor and documenting your thoughts in a daily log or journal motivates you to reflect rather than ruminate. Reflecting on your writing enables you to draw on inherent resources. Interviewing skills provide the foundation for all practice perspectives. Using the suggested techniques delineated in this chapter interns can improve their abilities and skills to become competent practitioners.

IN THE NICK OF TIME

David W. Springer and Stephen J. Tripodi

Case Description

Disruptive behavior disorders among adolescents are on the rise (Loeber, Farrington, & Waschbusch, 1998). In a recent epidemiological study that examined psychiatric disorders in juvenile delinquents (Teplin, Abram, McClelland, Dulcan, & Mericle, 2002), the most common disorders were substance use disorders and disruptive behavior disorders (conduct disorder [CD] and oppositional defiant disorder [ODD]), with more than 40% of males and females meeting criteria for a disruptive behavior disorder. Sometimes referred to as externalizing disorders, such presenting problems are some of the most common encountered by criminal justice and social work interns and other helping professionals who treat juvenile delinquents. The term *dual diagnosis* is frequently used to refer to adolescents with at least one Axis I diagnosis in the *DSM-IV-TR* (American Psychiatric Association, 2000) and a substance abuse problem. This case presents an exemplar of an intern who treated a court-referred dually diagnosed adolescent, Nick, and his family.

Nick was a 15-year-old European American male, recently arrested and taken to a local juvenile assessment center for truancy, possession of marijuana, and possession of a deadly weapon (a knife). This was Nick's second arrest in 6 months—he had been adjudicated through the juvenile court 6 months earlier for breaking into a neighbor's house and vandalizing their property. Because this was Nick's second arrest within 6 months, the judge extended his probation and required Nick to receive counseling, assuring him that if he was arrested again he would be sentenced to a secured facility or residential treatment.

Nick lived with his mother, five brothers, and one sister. Nick never met his biological father and was physically abused by his stepfather, who was killed in a drunken driving accident. Nick had consistently been getting into trouble since the age of 12 years. He ran away from home twice, each time for 1 week, when he was 12 and 13. Several of Nick's close friends had been arrested for truancy, robbery, assault, and drug possession, including his good friend Ernie, who was arrested while holding marijuana for Nick. Nick often disrespected his mother by cursing at her and disobeying her rules. He showed little remorse for this behavior. Nick's IQ fell within the normal range, and his medical history was uncomplicated.

Assessment and Diagnosis

The first active phase of treatment is a thorough assessment, and a biopsychosocial history often serves as the cornerstone of a solid treatment plan (Springer, 2002). During their initial session together, the intern conducted a complete biopsychosocial assessment with Nick and his family. (For a more detailed exposition of the biopsychosocial interview, see, e.g., Austrian, 2002; Springer, 2002).

Incorporated into the biopsychosocial assessment was the time-line follow-back procedure (Sobell & Sobell, 1992), which was used to assess Nick's substance abuse history (his primary drugs of choice were alcohol and marijuana). This procedure, a structured interview technique that samples a specific period of time, may offer the most sensitive assessment for adolescent substance abusers (Leccese & Waldron, 1994). A monthly calendar and memory anchor points were used to help Nick reconstruct daily use during the past month. Nick was also referred for psychological assessment as part of the juvenile court's assessment process. After ruling out medical causes, and based on the collective results of the biopsychosocial assessment, the time-line follow-back, and psychological testing, the intern used the *DSM-IV-TR* (APA, 2000) to diagnose Nick as follows:

Axis I.   312.82 Conduct Disorder, Adolescent-Onset Type, Moderate
           Alcohol Abuse
           305.20 Cannabis Abuse
Axis II.   V71.09 No diagnosis
Axis III. None
Axis IV.   V61.20 Parent-Child Relational Problem; V62.3 Academic
           Problems; Involvement with juvenile justice system

Once the initial assessment had been conducted, the intern began working collaboratively with Nick and his mother to decide the best course of action. Through a search of the literature and key databases (cf. Fonagy, Target,

Cottrell, Phillips, & Kurtz, 2002; Kazdin, 2002; Kazdin & Weisz, 2003; Lipsey & Wilson, 1998; Springer, 2005; Springer, McNeece, & Arnold, 2003; http://www.effectivechildtherapy.com; http://www.gainsctr.com/html/default.asp; http://www.ojjdp.ncjrs.org; http://www.nida.nih.gov; http://www.samhsa.gov), the intern was able to determine that expert consensus exists that treatments with the strongest evidence base (as demonstrated in randomized controlled clinical trials) for treating children and adolescents with conduct disorder include parent management training (PMT), multisystemic therapy (MST), cognitive problem-solving skills training (PSST), and functional family therapy (FFT; Baer & Nietzel, 1991; Brestan & Eyberg, 1998; Durlak, Furhman, & Lampman, 1991; Fonagy & Kurtz, 2002; Hanish, Tolan, & Guerra, 1996; Henggeler, Schoenwald, et al., 1998; Kazdin, 2002).

Intervention Selection

The intern shared as much as he knew about all of these approaches with Nick and his mother, and the collaborative decision making took place as follows. Given that Nick was 15 years old, that the outcome findings on PMT with adolescents were equivocal, and that his pattern of behavior was rather entrenched, the intern and his mother decided against PMT as a primary treatment option for Nick. However, given that Nick's 6-year-old brother, Noah, had been diagnosed with oppositional defiant disorder, the intern and mother agreed that the mother would benefit from PMT. Although MST is probably the most effective treatment available for treating high-risk juvenile offenders like Nick, MST was not being used in the community. Nick's treatment package included both PSST and FFT, as well as group therapy. To help Nick's mother parent Noah, PMT was also part of the treatment package.

Problem-Solving Skills Training

PSST (Spivak & Schure, 1974) is a cognitively-based intervention that has been used to treat aggressive and antisocial youths (Kazdin, 1994). The problem-solving process involves helping clients learn how to produce a variety of potentially effective responses when faced with problem situations. Regardless of the specific problem-solving model used, the primary focus is on addressing the thought process to help adolescents address deficiencies and distortions in their approaches to interpersonal situations (Kazdin, 1994). A variety of techniques are used, including didactic teaching, practice, modeling, role playing, feedback, social reinforcement, and therapeutic games (Kronenberger & Meyer, 2001). The problem-solving approach typically includes five steps for the practitioner and client to address: (1) defining the problem; (2) brainstorming; (3) evaluating the alternatives; (4) choosing and implementing an alternative; and (5) evaluating the implemented option (Corcoran & Springer, 2005; Kazdin, 1994).

Parent Management Training

PMT is a summary term that describes a therapeutic strategy in which parents are trained to use skills to manage their child's problem behavior (Kazdin, 1997), such as giving effective commands, setting up reinforcement systems, and using punishment, including taking away privileges and assigning extra chores. Although PMT programs may differ in focus and therapeutic strategies used, they all share the common goal of enhancing parental control over children's behavior (Barkley, 1987; Cavell, 2000; Eyberg, 1988; Forehand & McMahon, 1981; Patterson, Reid, Jones, & Conger, 1975; Webster-Stratton & Reid, 2003). To date, parent management training is the best treatment for youths with oppositional defiant disorder, such as Nick's brother Noah.

Functional Family Therapy

FFT (Alexander & Parsons, 1973, 1982), grounded in learning theory, is an integrative approach that relies on systems, behavioral, and cognitive views of functioning. Clinical problems are conceptualized in terms of the function that they serve for the family system and for the individual client. The goal of treatment "is the achievement of a change in patterns of interaction and communication, in a manner that engenders adaptive family functioning" (Fonagy & Kurtz, 2002, p. 158).

Nick's Treatment

The intern used FFT techniques to enable Nick and his family to reduce substance use and maintain behavioral and cognitive changes. During the early phase of FFT, the intern and Nick's family concentrated on establishing rapport, reducing negativity, minimizing hopelessness, and increasing motivation for change (http://www.fftinc.com). This was vital, as Nick's mother lacked hope that behavior change was possible and Nick lacked motivation to improve his behavior and reduce his substance use. To accomplish the early phase goals, the intern focused on interpersonal skills; specifically, validation, positive interpretation, reframing, and sequencing. Additionally, the intern was regularly available to provide these services. As the family was able to agree on the presenting problem, as risk and protective factors were identified, and as adequate rapport was established, the therapy sessions evolved to the middle phase.

The intern and Nick's family agreed that the goals of the middle phase were to implement the individualized treatment plan that they collaboratively developed, to change the behavior that Nick presented with at the beginning of treatment, and to improve relational skills such as communication and parenting (http://www.ffinc.com). During the middle phase, the therapy sessions became more structured, and the intern implemented the treatment plan. The intern evaluated the family during this stage by assessing the quality of relational skills—such as communication and parenting—and by measuring the family's compliance with the individualized treatment plan.

The goal of the last stage in FFT, also known as the generalization stage, is to maintain change and prevent relapses. The intern implemented effective relapse prevention techniques (e.g., role playing and discussing how to cope with emotions without using drugs and how to socialize and have fun while staying sober) when Nick's substance use significantly declined (Tripodi, Kim, & DiNitto, 2006). The intern became more of a family case manager during the late phase, helping the family find resources such as Alcoholics Anonymous (AA), Narcotics Anonymous (NA), Al-Anon, Alateen, and the National Alliance for the Mentally Ill (NAMI). The intern concluded the FFT sessions when the family was able to identify community resources and prove maintenance of change.

During individual sessions (with Nick) and family sessions, techniques commonly used in PSST (e.g., role playing, feedback, and in vivo practice) were used to help Nick generate alternative solutions to interpersonal problems that triggered his alcohol and drug use. PSST was used to help Nick think of alternatives to getting into fights at school, as Nick reported that he often fought with other students because they provoked him. The intern engaged Nick in multiple role plays, repeatedly practicing how he might respond to perceived provocation. The intern effusively praised Nick's quick recall of the self-statements and his efforts to use a "stop and think" technique that he modeled and prompted. Additionally, they practiced how to respond to mistakes and failure without exploding at others or destroying property. Nick's mother was instructed to praise and reward his efforts to avoid conflicts and to employ the problem-solving steps in everyday situations at home. As treatment progressed, Nick was encouraged to use the steps in increasingly more difficult and clinically relevant real-life situations (Kazdin, 2003).

Evaluation of Treatment

As the termination of treatment approached, the intern introduced longer intervals between sessions, treating the final sessions as once-a-month maintenance sessions during which the family reported on how things were going.

Nick and his family made considerable progress in their treatment goals, as evidenced across several areas of functioning (e.g., improved grades in school, producing clean urinalyses as part of his probation, not being rearrested). However, on two separate occasions, Nick did report drinking a few beers at a weekend party. Using a harm-reduction approach to substance abuse treatment (e.g., McNeece, Bullington, Arnold, & Springer, 2002), the intern encouraged the family to view this as a normal part of the treatment process. The intern also encouraged Nick's mother to remain consistent in rewarding positive behavior and substance-free periods, no matter how long or short, and to follow through on consequences for negative behavior, particularly when the substance use escalated (Tripodi et al., in press). He worked with Nick on identifying what contributed to his drinking (such as hanging out with certain friends) and, using PSST, discussed with him what he could do differently next time.

Nick's treatment progress was also monitored using the Child and Adolescent Functional Assessment Scale (CAFAS; Hodges, 2000), a standardized scale that is used to measure the degree of impairment in youths. It is a clinician-rated measure that covers eight areas of functioning: school/work; home; community; behavior toward others; moods/emotions; self-harmful behavior; substance use; and thinking. The CAFAS was completed by the intern at intake and termination, and the scores from the CAFAS demonstrated an overall improvement in Nick's level of functioning. Standardized scales such as the CAFAS should be used to guide treatment planning, to monitor client functioning, and to evaluate the effectiveness of interventions (Springer, 2002; for further discussion, see chapter 13, this volume).

Discussion

Despite the promising treatment effects produced by the interventions reviewed here, existing treatments need to be refined and new ones developed. More research is needed so that we can determine with greater confidence the long-term impact of evidence-based treatments on conduct-disordered and substance-abusing youths, and it is unclear what part of the therapeutic process produces change. In the meantime, practitioners can use the existing evidence-based practices to guide their work with this challenging population.

■ ■ ■

Activities

1. Consider the case of multisystemic therapy (see chapter 10, this volume). In the absence of MST, consider how the intern appropriated an MST model.

2. Where do you think this client will be in 5 years? In 10 years?

3. What type of employment would you see as likely for this client?

4. There were many components to the intern's intervention. List them.

5. Which one do you think contributes the most to the client's well-being? Why?

The purpose of this activity is to enhance your awareness of what it is like to receive and seek help. Your thoughts, feelings, and experiences about asking for and receiving help from others influence how you will relate to clients who need your help.

Consider three types of help-seeking situations. Record your reflections of these experiences.

Scenario 1: Reflect on a recent situation in which you asked for and received help.

1. Describe the scenario.

2. What were your *feelings* about asking for help?

3. What were your *thoughts* about asking for help?

4. What actions were taken in seeking help?

5. What would you do differently the next time?

Scenario 2: Reflect on a recent situation in which you asked for help and
          the person did not give help:

1. Describe the scenario.

2. What were your feelings about asking for help and not receiving it?

3. Did you receive no help or just not the help that was useful for you?
   Explain.

4. What were your thoughts about asking for help and not receiving it?

5. What actions were taken in seeking help? What did you do after not receiving help from this person?

6. What would you do differently the next time?

Scenario 3: Reflect on a recent situation in which you needed help but did not
          ask or did not ask directly for help.

1. Describe the scenario.

2. What were your feelings about not asking for help?

3. What were your thoughts about not asking for help?

4. What actions were taken instead of seeking help?

5. What would you do differently the next time?

6. For reflection or discussion with someone:

Look at the similarities and differences between your thoughts and feelings in the foregoing situations.

Reexamine the actions you took as well. Do you tend to ask directly in some situations but not in others? What is different about these situations? Do you subtly expect people who know you to "read your mind" and anticipate your needs and meanings?

Examining the interrelationship between your thoughts, feelings, and actions is based on cognitive-behavioral theory. What does this mean for your way of approaching clients and others and engaging in a professional relationship?

7. Read the following list of relationship skills and assess your skill level in each area with ratings ranging from 1 = *not at all* to 10 = *all the time.* Identify more than one example of demonstrating the skill at a high level. This is only a partial list; please add other skills to these skills. How might you strengthen your skill level in these areas?

Skill	*Rating*
1. Offered empathetic responses	
2. Listened well	
3. Asked helpful questions	

4. Comforted when appropriate

5. Offered encouragement

6. Accepted compliments or praise

7. Conveyed respect

8. Offered suggestions

9. Considered client's feelings

10. Accomplished purpose

EVIDENCE-BASED SKILLS FOR ASSESSMENT

KEVIN CORCORAN *and* BARBARA THOMLISON

In this chapter you will learn the importance of having evidence about your client's condition or conditions. This requires accurate assessments and diagnoses, and we illustrate how to make them. We show you how to conduct a mental status examination and how to make accurate diagnoses using the Patient Health Questionnaire and the DSM.

By now you have settled into your internship and have actual clients you work with on a regular basis with ongoing supervision. We trust you are using at least one evidence-based practice or intervention focused on a client issue or challenging behavior. You have to admit, even though privately, that you have learned a lot so far in your internship and that you are moving rapidly in your professional development.

With this in mind, we now turn our attention to some additional advanced skills: assessment and diagnosis. These observational skills require a degree of mastery of the interpersonal skills covered in chapter 5. This is necessary because, if you cannot interview a client, you will not be able to assess and diagnose the conditions, as the necessary information comes chiefly from interviewing the client and relevant others. We illustrate the ins and outs of conducting a mental status examination and how to use two major diagnostic systems, the Patient Health Questionnaire and *DSM*.

HOW TO CONDUCT A MENTAL STATUS EXAMINATION

A mental status examination is a snapshot of the psychosocial functioning of a client. It will likely guide your complete assessment and potential diagnosis. Familiarity with a client's mental status is important in numerous settings, from a youth confined to detention to the client seeking clinical services. From case management to probation and parole, many clients will present with mental health issues; some quite serious, others less so. What are often needed are quick assessment tools for ascertaining a client's general mental functioning and clinical symptoms.

The assessment of general mental functioning is accomplished with a brief and structured interview in which you will solicit information on mental health, mental functioning, and social environment in order to ascertain a general impression of how well or how poorly your client functions in his or her daily life. The mental status exam is typically conducted at an intake or after an initial referral. The better mental status exams are those that are standardized or based on a semistructured interview schedule. Standardized mental status exams are necessary, as it is very easy to forget to assess a particular area of your client's behavior. The standardized forms essentially focus your attention in an interview in order not to overlook or forget important domains of human behavior.

Some allow quantification of the client's functioning (e.g., Doverspite, 1990), although most simply allow a qualitative impression. One benefit of a quantitative mental status exam is that it gives you a number as a reference point that you can compare with other numbers throughout the course of your service delivery and as a follow-up after services have ended. The comparison of the scores on a mental status exam allows you to determine whether the client's functioning has improved, deteriorated, or remained stable. We discuss this type of case evaluation in detail in chapter 13.

Even with standardized tools, mental status exams are assessments made by you, the interviewer. The determining factor is not the "exam" itself but your ability to isolate problems, symptoms, and strengths by way of your interviewing and observation skills. For example, a youngster at a group home may say she does not have a drug problem, even though she uses marijuana daily. It is your job to observe the condition of the client and base your observations on your understanding of how most people function successfully and unsuccessfully.

Figure 6.1 displays one semistructured mental status exam that covers the domains of presentation of self in the environment, behavior symptoms, cognitive symptoms—including hallucinations, delusions, and orientation—and symptoms of affect or mood disturbances. The instrument is very easy to use, but you should familiarize yourself with it in advance of your first intake interview. You may be able to assess some items simply by looking at your client, such as bizarre clothing or particular motor skills. You may simply want to ask the client about other symptoms or any other questions. An example of this is hallucinations, as you cannot actually observe the hallucinations (or at least not without serious concern for your own mental status). What the exam is attempting to ascertain is whether your client seems to be different from the typical person in society. Deviation from the norm may very well illustrate mental health, behavior, or social problems.

Below are 32 questions designed to help you complete the OMHRC (Figure 6.3), should you not be familiar with the youth and need to conduct an interview. Record your observations on the OMHRC by checking the bold **O** if the youth has this problem or the lighter O if you suspect this youth has the problem.

1. Have you recently thought about killing yourself? You know, maybe committing suicide?
2. Have you ever tried to commit suicide?
3. Have you wanted to kill someone? I mean, really wanted to kill somebody?
4. Have you heard voices when no one was around or had visual hallucinations, while not on drugs or alcohol?
5. Do you believe something to be true when almost everybody else says it is not true, like someone is out to get you or you can influence how others think or act?
6. Have you felt out of touch with reality, like you were living in a dream-world or felt "crazy," while not on drugs or alcohol?
7. Have you intentionally harmed or injured an animal, like hitting or kicking a dog or cat when you were mad?
8. Have you ever started a fire that was dangerous? You know, like it could have done harm or damaged something?
9. Have you ever sexually assaulted another person or taken sexual advantage of another?
10. Do you use drugs or alcohol?
11. Have you had frequent sex with people or used sex to start a relationship?
12. Have you ever physically hurt yourself, like cutting yourself or putting a cigarette out on your skin?
13. Have you ever been sexually abused or forced into a sexual activity?
14. Have you seen traumatic things or horrible events, such as severe violence including domestic violence?
15. Have you threatened or intentionally harmed another person?
16. When you get mad, do you have explosive outbursts or throw fits?
17. Have you destroyed someone else's property, such as vandalism?
18. Have you ran away from home or your residence in the past 6 months?
19. Do you feel depressed more times than not?
20. Do you feel a sense of deep loss or grief for no reason at all?
21. Do you feel out of control of your emotions?
22. Are you frequently confused or easily distracted?
23. Do you feel overactive or hyperactive, like you can't sit still or concentrate?
24. Do you have thoughts you can't get out of your mind or behaviors you just can't seem to stop?
25. On a typical day, do you have extreme moods or do your moods change dramatically?
26. Are your feelings usually appropriate for the situation? For example, do your feelings seem quite different from others in the same situation?
27. Do you feel withdrawn or isolated from other people?
28. Have you had any problems sleeping, including nightmares?
29. Have you lost or gained a noticeable amount of weight in the past 6 months?
30. Do you feel anxious or worried most of the time?
31. Would you say you are an angry type of person, or do your argue a lot?
32. In your opinion, do you think you should see a mental health counselor for a personal problem?

Figure 6.1 OMHRC Semi-Structured Interview

In additional to tests of general mental functioning, many social work and criminal justice settings need instruments to quickly determine the mental health needs of a client, consumer, inmate, or other recipient of services. In criminal justice you will need to determine the risk assessment for suicide and other major mental health symptoms. In youth services and family treatment, the youth is often focus of clinical attention, thus warranting an assessment of the young person's mental health symptoms.

A brief and convenient assessment tool is the Oregon Mental Health Referral Checklist (OMHRC; Corcoran, 2005; also available in Fischer & Corcoran, 2007a), which is designed to measure observations by a youth, his or her parents, and a social service agent, such as a probation officer, social worker, or court counselor. Students in various mental health agencies will also find the tools useful and efficient methods of determining the presence or absence of mental health problems common to youths in most settings. The three parallel forms are reproduced in figures 6.2 to 6.4. The instruments are in the public domain; therefore, they may be reproduced for nonprofit use *ad libitum*. Figure 6.1 reproduces a semistructured interview schedule that you may follow when conducting an assessment interview. It, too, is in the public domain and may be used without cost or written permission from the author. Feel free to use it in your internship and eventual practice.

The OMHRC has good data to support its psychometric soundness. It was developed from a pool of 84 symptoms considered by a panel of experts to be "typical" or "characteristic" of youths in the juvenile justice system with mental health needs. The expert panel consisted of 15 administrators and providers in mental health and juvenile justice, including one board-certified child psychiatrist. Sixteen items were eliminated because they seemed to be unobservable by someone making an assessment; for example, traumatic brain injury resulting from a closed head wound, which can be assessed but not seen by a social worker or juvenile justice worker. Other symptoms were eliminated because they were not mental health problems, such as hearing and vision problems.

The 68 items that survived this screening were then analyzed using statistical procedures known as concept mapping (Trochim, 1989). The statistics describe an idea or a topic and then display the elements of the idea or topic on a three-dimensional map. There are three general steps in the concept mapping process.

First, a group of experts brainstorms a set of statements or elements of a concept, which in the case of the OMHRC were mental health symptoms descriptive of youths in the juvenile justice system. Second, the participants categorize or sort the statements or elements into distinguishable groups and rate each on some relevant scale. In the case of the OMHRC, the rating scale was

OMHR CHECKLIST—PARENT VERSION

Youth's name: _____   What is today's date? _____

Youth's age: _____ Sex M F   Race: _____

What agency gave
you this form? _____

Who is your contact
person at that agency? _____

What is your relationship with
the youth? (please specify) _____

> I *know* or am *fairly certain* this item describes this youth.

> This item is *probably descriptive* of this youth.

INSTRUCTIONS
Below are 32 behaviors you may have observed with this child. Please check the **black** circle for each item which you **know** or are **fairly certain** describes this youth. Unless told otherwise, consider the youth **within the past 6 months.** If you have your suspicions or a hunch that an item describes this child, then please check the **gray** circle.

○ ○ He/she seems actively suicidal/suicide risk.
○ ○ Has this youth ever made a suicide attempt?
○ ○ The child expresses a desire to kill another person(s).

○ ○ He/she appears to have hallucinations (acts as if sees or hears things when not on drugs or alcohol).
○ ○ The child expresses bizarre ideas/strong beliefs that are not true (e.g., someone is out to get him/her).
○ ○ While not on drugs or alcohol, this child seems out of touch with reality/incoherent.

○ ○ Has intentionally harmed or injured an animal.
○ ○ Has intentionally set a fire.
○ ○ Sexually assaulted another or has taken sexual advantage of another in the past 6 months.
○ ○ Has used drugs or alcohol in the past 6 months.
○ ○ Sexually acts out, such as frequent sex with people or uses sex to start a relationship.

○ ○ Physically harmed him/herself (such as cutting self with razor or burning self with cigarette).
○ ○ Has this child ever been sexually abused or forced into a sexual activity?
○ ○ Has he/she ever witnessed a traumatic event or severe violence (e.g. domestic violence)?

○ ○ He/she threatens others or has intentionally harmed others in the past 6 months.
○ ○ Has explosive outbursts/throws fits.
○ ○ Intentionally destroyed property.
○ ○ Frequently runs away from home.

○ ○ Has seemed depressed most of the time in the past 6 months.
○ ○ Expresses grief/loss for no reason.
○ ○ Has seemed out of control of his or her emotions in the past 6 months.

○ ○ Seems frequently confused.
○ ○ He or she is overactive or hyperactive.
○ ○ Has had repetitive thoughts or repetitive behaviors.

○ ○ He/she has had dramatic mood swings.
○ ○ His/her moods have been inappropriate (e.g. extreme or different from others in the same situation).
○ ○ This child has been detached or withdrawn.

(continued)

Figure 6.2 OMHR Checklist: Parent Version

○ ○   He/she is having difficulty sleeping (too much or too little).
○ ○   I've observed noticeable weight gain or weight loss.
○ ○   He/she has been very anxious/nervous or worries most of the time.

○ ○   He/she is angry or has argued excessively during the past 6 months.

○ ○   In your opinion, does this youth need to see a mental health counselor?

Please return this to the juvenile justice counselor or mental health counselor, unless told otherwise.

Figure 6.2 (*Continued*)

a 5-point Likert scale that triages the symptoms according to the immediacy of need for a referral for mental health treatment, with 1 considered to be no need for a referral and 5 an immediate need.

The third step is to analyze the sorted elements or concepts using two-dimensional multidimensional scaling. This statistic essentially examines how often the items or elements are sorted into the same category by the panel of experts and then displays them on a two-dimensional space where symptoms that are more similar are clustered closer together and dissimilar items are further apart. The average rating, in this case triage rating, are then calculated for each symptom, and a three-dimensional map is produced that displays the average rating for all symptoms in the cluster of similar symptoms and an average rating for each symptom.

From these procedures a 38-item prototype was developed as a staff and parent version to assess the mental health needs of youths. This prototype was then used by a sample of juvenile justice workers to evaluate the symptoms of 146 youths who were adjudicated and sentenced to community service and by 52 parents who evaluated their children. Additionally, the instrument was evaluated on a sample of 83 incarcerated youths. The results produced the best measure by using 31 symptoms and suggest that the OMHRC is a stable assessment; the internal-consistency reliability coefficients were .91, .71, and .92 for the parent, staff, and youth versions, respectively. These numbers suggest that juvenile justice workers are less consistent in their observations than are either parents or the youths themselves and that youths and parents are quite consistent in observing mental health symptoms.

The three forms were moderately correlated, with parent and staff scores correlating .51, whereas the parent and youth versions correlated .69. These coefficients suggest that the parallel forms are fairly equivalent to each other, with the youth and parent versions having observed 47% of symptoms in common; this statistic is called *shared variance*.

OMHR CHECKLIST—STAFF VERSION

Youth's Name _____   Today's Date _____

Age _____ Sex   M   F   Race _____

Initiating Agency _____   Contact person _____

_____   Phone # _____

Case # _____

INSTRUCTIONS

Below are 32 problems or symptoms descriptive of youth who might need a mental health referral. Please check the **black** circle for each item which you **know** or are **fairly certain** describes this youth. If you have a suspicion or hunch that an item is probably descriptive, then please check the **gray** circle.

I *know* or am *fairly certain* this item describes this youth.

This item is *probably descriptive* of this youth.

Notes you wish to share about your observations:

Actively suicidal/suicide risk	○	○	_____
Any prior suicide attempts	○	○	_____
The child has desire to kill another person(s)	○	○	_____
Appears to have hallucinations	○	○	_____
Expresses bizarre ideas or delusional	○	○	_____
Out of touch with reality/incoherent while not on drugs or alcohol	○	○	_____
Intentionally harms or injures animals	○	○	_____
Fire setter	○	○	_____
Sexually offends	○	○	_____
Substance abuse	○	○	_____
Sexually acts out	○	○	_____
Physically harms self	○	○	_____
Ever sexually abused	○	○	_____
Ever witnessed traumatic event or severe violence (e.g. domestic violence)	○	○	_____
Threatens others or intentionally harms others	○	○	_____
Explosive outbursts/throws fits	○	○	_____
Destroys property	○	○	_____
Frequently runs away	○	○	_____
Depressed	○	○	_____
Expresses grief/loss	○	○	_____
Feels out of control	○	○	_____
Frequently confused	○	○	_____
Overactive or hyperactive	○	○	_____
Repetitive thoughts or repetitive behavior	○	○	_____

(continued)

Figure 6.3 OMHR Checklist: Staff Version

Dramatic mood swings	○	○	_____
Inappropriate moods	○	○	_____
Detached or withdrawn	○	○	_____
Difficulty sleeping	○	○	_____
Noticeable weight gain/loss	○	○	_____
Anxious	○	○	_____
Angry or argues excessively	○	○	_____
Does this youth need a mental health counselor?	○	○	_____

Sent to: _____   Date Sent: _____
            Name of HMO/MH Agency
Phone #: _____

Figure 6.3 (*Continued*)

There is also pretty good evidence to suggest that the OMHRC is an accurate assessment of the mental health needs of youths. For examples, youths who have been told by someone they trust that they might have a mental health or emotional problem had parents who observed 19.4 symptoms. Those who had not been told that they might have a problem were observed by their parents as showing 12.6 symptoms. Similar differences were noted when the juvenile justice workers completed the OMHRC. This is called *known-groups validity*. More symptoms were observed by the youths who had been told of an emotional or mental health problem, and more symptoms were reported by those youths who had ever been in treatment, those who reported that they believed they needed to see a mental health provider, and those who had histories of suicide attempts.

Finally, scores on the OMHRC also correlated with internal and external behavior problems, as defined by Achenbach's (1997) Child Behavior Checklist (CBCL). This was especially so for the youth version, on which the number of symptoms correlated .67 and .65, respectively, with scores on internal and external problems. What these coefficients suggest is that over 40% of the symptoms observed in one measure are also ascertained by the other. In other words, scores on the new instrument, the OMHRC, were similar to scores on a well-established instrument, indicating that the former is accurate relative to the latter.

There is one other added feature of the OMHRC; namely, it is hierarchical. Remember that the panel of experts rated each symptom on a 5-point measure of the need for a mental health referral. As a consequence of these averages, the symptoms are presented in descending order of triage ratings. That is, the first symptoms are the most severe and have the highest need for referral, and the latter ones

OMHR CHECKLIST—YOUTH VERSION

What is your name? _____   What is today's date?

How old are you? _____ Sex   M   F   What is your race? _____

What agency gave
you this form? _____   Who do you typically
see at that agency? _____

What is your
medical card #? _____   What is your case #? _____

This statement describes me.

This statement describes me
a little.

INSTRUCTIONS

Below are 32 statements that might describe you. Please check the **black** circle for each item which describes you. Unless told otherwise, consider whether each item describes you **within the past 6 months**. If the phrase only describes you **a little**, please check the **gray** circle.

○ ○ I have made a plan to commit suicide.
○ ○ I have attempted suicide at least once in my life.
○ ○ I feel like killing somebody.

○ ○ I have had hallucinations (seen or heard things that weren't there when not on drugs or alcohol).
○ ○ I have a strong belief that something is true when most people say it isn't (e.g., someone is out to get me).
○ ○ While not on drugs or alcohol, have you lost touch with reality (felt "crazy")?

○ ○ Have you intentionally harmed or injured an animal?
○ ○ Have you started a fire that was dangerous or could have done harm or damage?
○ ○ Have you sexually assaulted another or taken sexual advantage of another in the past 6 months?
○ ○ I have used drugs or alcohol in the past 6 months.
○ ○ Have you had frequent sex with people, or used sex to start a relationship?

○ ○ I have physically harmed myself (such as cutting yourself, or putting a cigarette out on your skin).
○ ○ Have you ever been abused sexually or forced into a sexual activity?
○ ○ Have you seen horrible/traumatic things or severe violence, including domestic violence?

○ ○ I have threatened or intentionally harmed others.
○ ○ I have explosive outbursts or sometimes throw fits.
○ ○ I have intentionally destroyed someone else's belongings/property (e.g., vandalism).
○ ○ Have you run away from your home or residence in the past 6 months?

○ ○ I feel depressed most of the time.
○ ○ I feel a sense of grief or deep loss for no reason at all.
○ ○ I feel out of control of my emotions.

○ ○ I frequently feel confused or get distracted easily and get off task.
○ ○ I feel overactive or hyperactive.
○ ○ I have thoughts I can't get out of my mind or behavior I can't stop.

○ ○ On a typical day my moods are extreme and change dramatically (e.g., going quickly from happy to sad).
○ ○ My moods seem extreme or different from others in the same situation.

(continued)

Figure 6.4 OMHR Checklist: Youth Version

○	○	I feel withdrawn or isolated from others.
○	○	I have difficulty sleeping, including nightmares.
○	○	I have lost/gained a noticeable amount of weight in the past 6 months.
○	○	I feel anxious or worried most of the time.
○	○	I feel angry much of the time or argue a lot.
○	○	Do you need to see a mental health counselor?

Please return this to the juvenile justice counselor or mental health counselor, unless told otherwise.

Figure 6.4 (*Continued*)

reflect less need for referral. We do not want to overstate this delineation, however. We are not suggesting that symptoms at the end of the instrument mean that the respondent does not have a mental health condition that warrants services. He or she very well might. Moreover, a number of symptoms with lower ratings may warrant services simply because of the complexity of the client's conditions. Many of the symptoms, however, in and of themselves, may indicate a need for services, such as suicidal behaviors, homicidal desires, hallucinations, delusions, being out of touch with reality, torturing animals, and in fact just about all of the symptoms on the OMHRC. Therefore, we see once again that, just like the mental status exam, the OMHRC actually requires your professional judgment. As we are fond of saying, any assessment tool is a supplement in your work and not a substitute for your thoughtful and professional opinions and knowledge.

There are, of course, many other assessment tools for observing a client's mental health symptoms. We would be remiss not to reference some of these. Following is a list of five very good instruments for observing mental health symptoms in youths. All five of these instruments are evaluated and reprinted in Fischer and Corcoran (2007a & 2007b).

1. Sheila Eyberg's Child Behavior Inventory, which assesses conduct problems and behaviors in youngsters.
2. The Behavior Rating Index for Children by Arlene Stiffman, John Orme, and associates, which ascertains the presence of 13 behavior problems.
3. The "How I Feel" Scale by Walden, Harris, and Catron, which assesses the emotionality of youngsters between the ages of 8 and 12 years.
4. The Positive and Negative Affect Scale for Children by Kiernan, et al., which measures depression and anxiety in youths.

5. Charles Glisson and associates' Short Form Assessment for Children, a single-page, 48-item instrument that measures the mental health and psychosocial functioning of children between the ages of 5 and 18 years.

Although not necessarily a mental health measure, we also recommend to you Eleanor Dibble and Donald Cohen's (also found in Fischer & Corcoran, 2007a) Childhood Personality Scale, which assesses general personality and competency.

For adults, we recommend the following five instruments, many of which may be useful for children as well. With the exception of the Symptom Checklist Revised, all of these instruments are evaluated and reprinted in Fischer and Corcoran (2007b).

1. The Symptom Questionnaire by Robert Kellner. This is a marvelous single-page checklist that assesses four aspects of mental health pathology, namely, anxiety, depression, somatic complaints, and hostility. Concomitantly it measures four parallel conditions of well-being: relaxation, contentment, somatic well-being or health, and friendliness.
2. The Scales for the Assessment of Negative and Positive Symptoms, by Nancy Andreasen, are two exceptional instruments to ascertain symptoms of psychopathology, particularly schizophrenia, that respond to medication and those that demand more social services.
3. The Symptoms Checklist Revised (Derogatis, Lipman, & Covi, 1973; Derogatis, 1975) is a 90-item instrument that measures mental health symptoms of psychopathology or perhaps general neurosis. It is a well-established instrument that has been translated into 20 different languages.
4. Mark Bauer and his associates have developed a very useful instrument called the Internal State Scale, which assesses the severity of manic and depressive symptoms. This short, 16-item instrument has also been translated into French, German, and Spanish.
5. And finally, as an alternative to measuring symptoms, O'Hare and his associates (O'Hare, 2005) have developed an instrument to ascertain psychosocial well-being called the Psychosocial Well-Being Scale, along with other useful tools. This instrument measures a number of areas of well-being, including cognitive and emotional states of well-being, impulse control, use of alcohol and other drugs, coping, health, leisure, social networks, and work satisfaction.

As with the preceding child instruments, we would also like to recommend a general measure of health and mental health. A widely used measure of mental and physical health status is the Health Survey, which has also been called the Medical Outcomes Survey. This is a marvelous instrument that comes in two short forms, one called the SF-36 and the other the SF-12, where SF stands for "short form." The Health Survey provides two composite measures, one of physical health and the other of mental health. Additionally, each of these composite measures includes a number of narrowband assessments. The physical health composite scores include physical function, physical role, body pain, and general health. The mental health composite score includes vitality, social functioning, emotional role, and general mental health. The instrument is widely used in health and mental health settings, has been translated into several languages, and is available on the web (http://www.outcomes-trust.org), as well as reprinted in Fischer and Corcoran (2007b).

These instruments, whether the children's measures or the adult measures, are all what are we refer to as broadband scales, and many include subscales that serve as narrowband measures. Broadband measures are more general categories and are distinguishable from narrowband instruments, which measure particular problems, such as depression, substance use, and just about every human behavior there is to imagine. There are many outlets for locating these instruments, and in chapter 13 we present a list of many of these resources. As you will learn shortly, you will find narrowband measures helpful in isolating the presenting problem in a manner that allows you to observe change in your client over the course of your intervention. As you might well imagine, and as we suggested pertaining to quantitative mental status exams, we think your assessment is best when it is repeated over the course of the intervention in order to determine whether your client is improving, staying the same, or getting worse. All of this, though, is predicated on reaching an accurate diagnosis of your client.

FORMING A DIAGNOSTIC IMPRESSION

The result of your mental status interview and assessment of symptoms is the emerging diagnostic impression. Note that we have used the word *impression* and not *conclusion* or even *diagnosis*. We do this first because of the possibility that your impression may change as your understanding of the client increases and second because we want you to be humble in your use of the knowledge you have of social work and criminal justice. You could be slightly inaccurate or even wrong, and we want you to be open and flexible in how you see any client. It is easier to change an impression than it is a conclusion.

Diagnosing clients, needless to say, has been criticized from many angles, from labeling (Szasz, 1974) to the symptomization of common complaints into mental health conditions (Kutchins & Kirk, 1997). These limitations notwithstanding, a diagnosis serves many purposes. Chief among them is culminating and communicating a constellation of symptoms that result in a condition that is distinguishable from other conditions. Moreover, different mental health conditions necessitate different interventions. The antisocial youth would surely need something quite different from the school-phobic youngster, or the youth who is depressed due to a major loss, such as parental divorce or major illness in the family, would need something quite different from the youth whose depression is more biologically based, such as major depression or a bipolar disorder.

A diagnosis does more, though. The value of a diagnostic categorization includes a nomenclature of lists of categories of consensual terms within the profession that describe observations on clinical conditions. The conventional nomenclature for mental disorders, as well as other reasons for seeking clinical services, is the *Diagnostic and Statistical Manual of Mental Disorders* (*DSM*; American Psychiatric Association Press, 2000). The DSM claims to be primarily atheoretical about the origins of most mental disorders and is simply descriptive of behavioral signs, symptoms, and manifestations of mental health conditions. For some conditions, etiology is well established, such as the organic disorders, drug induced psychosis, posttraumatic stress disorder, and others.

A mental disorder is defined as a predominant disturbance that is a clinically significant behavioral or psychological syndrome that is associated with distress, disability or the risk of death, pain, or an important loss of freedom, such as a conviction for driving under the influence of drug or alcohol associated with substance abuse disorders or incarceration resulting from an antisocial personality disorder. A distressful symptom is considered one that is painful to the client, and a disability refers to impairment in functioning.

Moreover, the symptom must not be a result of a culturally appropriate circumstance, such as grief over the loss of a loved one. The symptoms should not arise from a conflict between an individual and society, such as seeing communists as mentally ill or the racist as paranoid. Finally, the symptom may not be part of a mental disorder if it is "deviant" behavior, whether political, religious, or sexual.

This definition of a mental disorder is no more than that: a definition of a mental disorder. It is not intended to be a classification of a person who happens to have symptoms that reflect a disorder, such that one might say someone is "a schizophrenic." The more appropriate view is to see a person as someone with schizophrenia, just as a person who is HIV positive is not "an AIDS patient" but a person living with AIDS. This is more than just political correctness. It is, in fact, an effort to keep your focus on the person you are working with rather than seeing just a number of symptoms that you are trying to reduce. The person living with schizophrenia is simply much more than "a schizophrenic." It is important to see the human being and not just "an inmate," "a parolee," an "offender," and so on.

The *DSM* also includes what are called V-codes. V-codes are used when the focus of treatment is not attributable to a mental health condition. Some of the specific V-codes are relational problems, such as parent-child conflicts and couple conflicts; problems related to abuse or neglect, including physical and sexual abuse of a child or adult; and a broad category of "additional conditions" that include 12 nonmental disorders that may be the reason for treatment, such as antisocial behavior, borderline intelligence, academic or occupational problems, acculturation problems, bereavement, and phase of life problems, such as entering school, getting married, divorced, or remarried, and retirement.

Clearly, many of these are problems that you are likely to work with in your internship and professional practice. That is, many of your clients will have problems that simply are not mental disorders but that still warrant social work and criminal justice services. The teen incarcerated for sexually abusing the younger neighbor child with a pencil certainly needs significant services in order to achieve the rehabilitative ideal; the teen could even receive the diagnosis with the code of V61.21 ("physical abuse of child"). This conduct could be but is not necessarily the result of a mental disorder. This is illustrated in the case of a young man with paranoid schizophrenia who was arrested for assaulting and performing oral sex on a child. Due to his paranoia, however, he was in fact literally trying to cannibalize the youth, and the legal offense would have been more appropriately called attempted murder, with a "guilty but mentally ill" verdict. As this discussion suggests, and the examples hopefully illustrate, this is all the more reason to keep your focus on the individual client and not the condition.

Let's now look more closely at how to actually use the *DSM* in your internship. The *DSM* is a multiaxial system in which assessments are summarized for five different biological, psychological, and social areas. Each is called an *axis*.

Axis 1 is used for classifying the clinical disorders and other conditions that are the focus of treatment—including the V-codes. If your client has more than one mental health condition and reason for clinical attention, then all are recorded on Axis I. One rule of the *DSM*, which is designed to facilitate efficient communication, is that in cases of more than one diagnosis or reason for clinical services, the primary diagnosis must appear first. Axis II is used for personality disorders and mental retardation. Axis III is used for general medical conditions, which incorporates another nomenclature, the International Classification of Diseases (ICD). Axis III is also used to highlight health conditions that may affect mental health, such as complications of pregnancy and delivery or endocrine and nutritional diseases. Axis IV is used to record psychosocial and environmental problems that are stressful. These include problems within the client's primary support group and problems related to social environment, education, occupation, housing, finances, accessing health care, and the legal system. The primary focus is to record those psychosocial stressors that may cause the mental health condition or may exacerbate the symptoms. Finally, Axis V is used to record your global assessment of the client's psychological, social, and occupational or school functioning.

Axis V is accompanied by a rating scale ranging from 1 to 100, divided into 10-point units, with each symptom considered as to severity and functioning. It is called the general assessment of functioning, or GAF. The assessment of your client's functioning should be made for his or her current or presenting circumstances. The GAF rating may provide added understanding of your client by estimating the highest level of functioning over the past few months. The actual GAF score is recorded on Axis V and should include a parenthetical statement of the time frame of the assessment, such as "current," "highest level in past 12 months," or "at discharge."

As evident from the breadth of the scope of areas under consideration in the *DSM* multiaxial system, comorbidity is likely. It is more likely that a client has one or more problems (see chapter 3 for further discussion). Because the diagnostic system has five axes and allows for multiple diagnoses, comorbid conditions are far less likely to be overlooked.

This system of diagnosis may seem complicated, especially when you consider that there are so many diagnostic categories. Additionally, some categories require an assessment of the severity of the disorder, such as in conduct disorders and oppositional defiant disorder. It is, in fact, difficult, if not impossible, to master the entire *DSM* in a single internship. You will find that you will become familiar with the conditions that are more common to your agency, such as conduct disorders and affective disorders in juvenile justice and social work.

It might help, however, to realize that there are basically 11 major or general categories of mental health conditions commonly seen in social work and criminal justice settings. They are:

1. Substance-related disorders
2. Psychotic and schizophrenic disorders
3. Disturbances in mood, including depressive and bipolar disorders

4. Anxiety disorders
5. Somatoform disorders, such as somatization—once called *hysteria*
6. Dissociative disorders, such as amnesia and multiple personality disorder
7. Sexual and gender disorders, including sexual dysfunctions and paraphilias (e.g., fetishism)
8. Eating disorders
9. Impulse-control disorders
10. Adjustment disorders
11. Personality disorders, such as borderline personality disorder.

There are other major or general categories, including a vast category of disorders usually first diagnosed when the person is an infant, child, or adolescent. These include conditions commonly seen in criminal justice and social work, such as an attention-deficit disorder or oppositional defiant disorder. There are also large categories for delirium and dementia and fairly narrow categories for sleep disorders and what are called factitious disorders. Unless you are in a placement that particularly focuses on children or on a particular problem such as sleep, the 11 major categories delineated here will probably include most of the mental health conditions you will see in your internship.

With time, practice, and a range of experiences, you will soon become facile with your diagnoses and more accurate, as well. We suggest you start by determining which general category your clients' symptoms reflect, such as depression or a psychosis, and then examine each subclass to see which is more descriptive of your clients' conditions. The Mental Status Exam in Figure 6.1 is designed to facilitate this determination.

With each new time you use the *DSM*, you will find your diagnostic abilities improving. So start using the *DSM* and practice as much as you can, but don't try it on your family members and friends—that will just anger them.

The *DSM* also has six "decision trees." Decision trees guide your differential diagnostic impressions by delineating the presence or absence of symptoms and time frames that define a mental health condition. The six decision trees are: mental disorders due to general medical conditions, substance-induced disorders, psychotic disorders, mood disorders, anxiety disorders, and somatoform disorders. With the aid of these helpful tools, you will be able to reach a sound and accurate diagnostic impression of the vast majority of the mental disorders in the *DSM*. We must warn you, though, that at first the enterprise of differential diagnosis will seem foreboding.

Another way to master the *DSM* and to further your assessment skills is with the use of a self-report instrument called the Patient Health Questionnaire (PHQ; Spitzer, Kroenke, & Williams, 1999). This four-page instrument is designed to screen for major mental health disorders and is also available as a brief two-page instrument. The PHQ is available in English and Spanish. It is designed to facilitate the recognition of somatoform disorders, major depression and other depressive syndromes, panic disorders and other anxiety disorders, eating disorders, alcohol abuse and functional impairment, psychosocial stressors, and women's health, such as menstruation, pregnancy, and childbirth. The PHQ is accompanied by algorithms that are designed for expedient scoring and interpretation. In addition, the instrument is extremely quick for clients to complete, taking about 3–5 minutes.

Moreover, the instrument is good, and you will find it helpful as you formulate your diagnostic impressions. We say it is good because several good research studies evidence that it is a consistent instrument (i.e., reliable) and an accurate instrument (i.e., valid). Copies of the PHQ are available from one of its authors, Robert Spitzer, MD, Biometrics Research Department, New York State Psychiatric Institute and Department of Psychiatry, Columbia University, New York, NY. A 9-item version for depression is available on the Web (http://www.pfizer.com /phq-9).

DIAGNOSIS AND THE CRIMINAL JUSTICE SYSTEM

With all this discussion of mental disorders, the *DSM*, and the PHQ, it is necessary to consider their interaction with the criminal justice system. This is so critical that a section is devoted to it in the *DSM*, and we think both social workers and criminal justice students need to understand that there are "significant risks that diagnostic information will be misused or misunderstood" (APA, 2000, pp. xxxii-xxxiii).

In general, the information about your client's mental health or deficits is distinguishable from what is necessary to establish mental illness for purpose of prosecution, as mitigating circumstances in a crime, or for involuntary commitment. In other words, the clinical and legal definitions often present different standards. For example, in most states, mental incompetence requires both a mental health condition *and* dangerousness to self or others; some states, such as New Jersey, widen the scope to include dangerousness to self, others, *or* property. However, in practicality, not simply any mental disorder is legally considered a mental disorder; the neighbor kid with an anxiety disorder who happens to throw a rock through your window in New Jersey is not going to be involuntarily committed to a psychiatric facility, even if you wish he would be. Attempting to kill President Reagan and having a diagnosis of schizophrenia, in contrast, may mitigate sentencing with a conviction of "guilty but mentally ill."

As these examples illustrate, what does distinguish the forensic utility of mental disorders is the degree of impairment that accompanies the mental disorder. The degree of impairment or disability varies widely between the numerous disorders. At issue is the degree of control the wrongdoer with a mental disorder has, which determines whether the criminal activity includes *mens rea*, or degree of culpability and therefore responsibility. For example (and don't try this yourself), if a college youth said "fuck you" to a law enforcement officers, the act would not be freedom of speech as protected by the First Amendment but is "conduct" that is considered to be "fighting words" and is unlawful. The person with Tourette syndrome, however, has a neurological condition, and most reasonable-minded prosecutors and judges would take this into consideration. Similarly, it won't do you much good to say to a judge, when busted for possession of marijuana, that "its not my fault; I have the mental disorder of cannabis dependency, which is *DSM* disorder number 304.30!" (Again, don't try this one either!)

In general, then, the use of the *DSM* and diagnoses for mental health purposes may not fit very well for some social work and criminal justice students. It is likely that, regardless of the discipline and the intern setting, a diagnosis may be warranted. We are suggesting, however, that you realize that the two systems in our society have different purposes, goals, and standards. The role of a diagnosis in forensics may be appropriate, and yet it may not reflect the standards of crime, responsibility, and punishment.

THE HOMECOMING

Patricia B. Higgins and Shannon C. Wright

Case Description

Anne was a 55-year-old woman diagnosed with paranoid schizophrenia more than 30 years ago. Three years ago she transferred to Northwestern State Hospital from out of state to be closer to her family members. She had been hospitalized continuously in state psychiatric facilities for 25 years. At Northwestern State Hospital she received treatment on a 24-bed co-ed inpatient unit. Her daily experiences included auditory hallucinations and fearfulness about the motives of everyone around her. Her pervasive suspiciousness incorporated her family members, other patients, and staff members. Although she struggled to manage these symptoms, she maintained many social skills, including music, poetry, and writing. She enjoyed conversation and new adventures (something as simple as dining in a new restaurant) and had a great sense of humor. She was a book lover, and one of her most valued possessions in her hospital room was her bookcase, loaded with poetry and classics. Anne responded well to treatment with a new atypical antipsychotic medication and 20 hours a week of active psychosocial treatment. Anne's hospital treatment team believed she had met discharge criteria and informed her that it was "time to leave the hospital." Anne was assigned to work with a graduate intern during the 8 months prior to her discharge from the hospital. The intern's work with Anne focused on the transition from the hospital to community living.

At Northwestern State Hospital, the social worker has the primary responsibility for bringing together the hospital treatment team, community providers, and involved family members to facilitate discharge. Rarely do all these parties agree completely about the best strategy for implementing a discharge plan. In Anne's case, this dynamic was particularly pronounced. Anne had no desire to the leave the hospital . . . ever. Her family, who were loving and supportive, had doubts about Anne's return to the community after so many years of institutionalization. They feared for Anne's safety, afraid that she might "fall through the cracks" in the community, and worried that Anne would resent them if they supported the discharge plan. Community providers also had their doubts about Anne's discharge because she had not lived in the community in decades and there was no way to predict whether the services available were adequate to support her outside of the hospital structure.

Problem Identification

Disorders such as schizophrenia most often emerge between the ages of 15 and 35, during the years when independent living skills are developed. For those with schizophrenia, the process of learning to live independently and pursue intimate relationships is interrupted. In the recovery process, the person with schizophrenia must learn the skills to manage day-to-day life, as well as the experiences that go along with the disorder (impaired thinking processes, hallucinations, delusions and paranoia, etc.). Anne had not lived on her own in more than 25 years and could not cook reliably, was unable to manage her medications, had no transportation and was not licensed to drive, and could not manage money without assistance.

Advocacy in Anne's discharge was a complicated issue. Her wish was to remain in the hospital indefinitely. The intern struggled with the issue of client autonomy, with not advocating for what Anne really wanted (to stay in the hospital forever) but instead promoting Anne's discharge to the community. The intern faced immense pressure from the treatment team and the hospital administration to discharge Anne. The state mental health system dictated that Anne should live in the least restrictive environment possible and that it was the duty of the hospital to see that this happened. The intern determined that the family would need encouragement to support this goal and education about community providers and potential living arrangements. The intern recognized that community care providers needed to be convinced as well. Despite their commitment to Anne's right to live outside the hospital, community-based providers feared that someone like Anne might not succeed. They had to be challenged to think creatively in crafting a truly individualized discharge plan that both addressed Anne's needs and built on her considerable strengths. In addition, Anne needed a residential facility that could address her daily needs and provide some supervision.

Intervention Selection

The intern understood that a successful outcome (i.e., discharge) depended first and foremost on developing a trusting relationship with Anne. The intern hoped that, within the context of a therapeutic relationship, Anne might begin to share in the belief that she was ready to leave the hospital. The intern knew that Anne's experiences of paranoia and suspiciousness would make this challenging and that interventions would require creativity. In addition to individual time with the intern, Anne attended psychoeducational groups 5 days per week, designed to teach her the skills necessary to live in the community. The intern identified "community exposure" as an additional intervention. In order to provide this, the intern would have to create opportunities for Anne to "practice" her coping strategies and skills outside the hospital environment.

The intern learned that Anne's situation was not unique at Northwestern State Hospital and that, in fact, there were several people receiving treatment at the hospital who did not want to leave their hospital "home." The intern wanted to address Anne's issues and provide peer support for her in this discharge transition. The intern developed a "women's issues" group to subtly address these issues and provide a support network for Anne and the other participants.

Additionally, the intern's interventions had to address resistance on the part of Anne's family and community providers. Her family's fears would have to be explored and quelled in order to gain their support in the discharge process. The intern needed to develop a trusting relationship with them in order to do so. In addition, the intern identified the need to include Anne's family whenever possible when discussing the plans or when visiting potential community living alternatives so that they might gain firsthand knowledge of the supports available to Anne. By providing opportunities for Anne's family to see facilities themselves and to interact with the community mental health staff, the intern hoped that they would come to believe that Anne might succeed outside the hospital. At the same time, community providers would need to become acquainted with Anne and her family so that they too would become invested in pursuing the goal of Anne's discharge. The intern believed that, with time, those in the community would get to experience many of Anne's unique and wonderful qualities and see for themselves the terrific family support she enjoyed. The intern hoped that then the community staff would become more invested and committed to the pursuit of Anne's discharge despite the challenges.

Intervention/Treatment

Facilitating Anne's discharge to the community required interventions with different systems: with Anne individually, with her family, and with multiple community-based agencies and mental health providers. First, the intern had to form a working relationship with Anne. This required frequent meetings that usually lasted no longer than 5–10 minutes due to Anne's initial suspiciousness of the intern. Much of the time spent together was designed to develop trust and to dispel any paranoid ideas that Anne had about the intern. Conversations sometimes centered on books and poetry and sometimes on future plans. Over time Anne began to believe that the intern was not out to harm her and wanted nothing of her. Anne's paranoia was reduced to a persistent but vague suspiciousness. Several months into their work together, Anne told the intern, "You don't treat me like a patient; you treat me like a person." However, during the course of their work together, there were many times when the intern became the focus of Anne's paranoia. This resulted in bizarre and sometimes insulting suspicions and accusations about the intern's motives and angry verbal attacks on the intern's character.

The next intervention was to get Anne out into the community. The intern devoted 4 to 8 hours of work each week with Anne outside of the hospital setting. They ate at interesting restaurants, explored bookstores, visited a clubhouse program, and window-shopped a variety of residential settings, such as apartments, supervised apartments, and assisted living facilities. Over time, Anne began to see herself differently, as a person who could mingle in the community without being overwhelmed by fear and suspiciousness. When paranoid feelings arose, she was able to "reality test" her fears with the intern and was able to internalize the reassurance. Anne began to enjoy spending more and more time outside of the hospital setting.

The psychosocial rehabilitation group developed by the intern met once a week for 16 weeks. The intern helped group members focus on visualizing a living situation outside of the hospital in which members would feel comfortable. Over the course of the 16 weeks, Anne was empowered by other group members. She shared with them that she was "ready for discharge," and they began to cheer her on, applauding her adventures into the community. In this setting Anne could tolerate comments and questions from peers when she verbalized her fears and anxiety about leaving the hospital.

The intern was sometimes a cheerleader, sometimes a coach. Anne had to be convinced of her ability to live a different life, a life that she could barely fathom after so much time within hospital walls. Her family had to be educated about community services and reassured about the wisdom of the discharge plan. Frequent telephone contacts with Anne's family to include them in all stages of planning helped to assuage some of their fears and concerns. Eventually, Anne's family also developed a trusting relationship with the intern and treatment team, which helped them to support the plan. However, community providers had reservations about pursuing Anne's discharge. Whereas these mental health professionals certainly believed in deinstitutionalization, the intern worried that Anne was viewed as one of those cases for whom discharge was a long shot at best. In order to convince them otherwise, the intern took every opportunity to share Anne's strengths, her improving behavior on the ward, and her progress during community outings. Many times, the intern had to "push" the community providers to continue working on the case when they asserted that they had no more options to explore on Anne's behalf. Simultaneously, this felt scary to the intern at times; working so closely with Anne had convinced the intern that Anne could succeed if given a chance.

Finally, a potential placement was identified. The community facility impressed both the treatment team and the community providers with its knowledgeable staff, supervision, and lovely physical environment. However, staff members had little experience in serving people with serious mental illnesses. The student intern offered to provide education for the staff about schizophrenia and paranoia. The facility staff eagerly accepted the offer, and the educational in-service program was well attended. In addition, the intern worked with the community providers to develop a crisis plan to address episodic paranoid thinking and occasional verbal aggression toward others. The intern made certain that the facility staff, Anne's family, and all involved providers from the community mental health clinic had access to the plan in hopes that any eventual problems would be addressed effectively.

Evaluation

Throughout the discharge planning process, the intern struggled with feelings of guilt over "forcing" Anne to leave her hospital home. These feelings were most intense on Anne's day of discharge from the hospital. On the drive to her new community home, Anne asked the intern, "Are you happy now? Does this get you a good grade in school?" In an effort to reassure Anne, the intern told her, "You are ready to leave that hospital. You are doing so much better than the folks back there," to which Anne responded, "Be careful! I was just a patient there five minutes ago." Many such interactions occurred during the termination phase, and the intern had to rely on supervision to process the conflicting emotions and feelings that arose throughout. The intern came to understand that many of Anne's angry outbursts were her way of separating herself from the hospital staff, with whom she had become so close. The intern worked in supervision not to personalize Anne's verbal attacks. The intern was able to understand that, after so many years in the hospital, Anne was struggling with her own feelings of loss, her fears about returning to the community, and how to say goodbye to a structure and routine that had been home for most of her adult life. Over time Anne began to talk about how she would decorate her room, about the activities available to her at the community clubhouse (psychosocial rehabilitation program), and about the opportunities she would have to spend time with her family.

Discussion

Anne was discharged to a community facility that provided the services necessary to address her daily living needs. The intern referred her to the local community-based assertive community treatment (ACT) program. This team began working with Anne prior to her actual discharge. ACT staff met with Anne daily to establish a new community support network and assist Anne in managing her symptoms, which were especially difficult during this transition. Anne's family remained very involved. They visited her frequently, helped her decorate her new space, and engaged her in activities around the community. They were instrumental in "modeling" some of the benefits of living outside the hospital: regular access to events that interested Anne, increased autonomy, and more frequent contact with her loved ones. A month after her discharge, Anne and her family organized a lunch and invited hospital staff and some of Anne's new community providers to celebrate her success.

■ ■ ■

Activities

1. What emotions may occur in the termination process? What was Anne's emotional reaction to the termination process? How do you deal with a client's anger?

2. What ethical issues arise when discharging a patient from a psychiatric hospital who does not want to leave? Should Anne have been allowed to stay in the hospital?

3. Discuss the importance of client autonomy and decision making in this case.

4. What interventions were most beneficial to Anne?

5. Discuss the advocacy role in this case.

Now let's put your assessment and diagnostic skills to work. Consider the previous case. As best possible, complete the Semistructured Mental Status Exam from the information provided in the case. Many domains you simply will not be able to assess or observe from the case, such as areas in which the client was unkempt. Review the symptoms identified from the MSE and describe the signs, symptoms, and manifestations in the following multiaxial diagnosis.

Axis I: Clinical disorder or other conditions that are focus of treatment

_____

_____

_____

(Be certain that the "primary diagnosis" is in the first line and so stated)

Axis II: Personality disorders or development disabilities

_____

_____

Axis III: General medical conditions

_____

_____

Axis IV: Psychosocial and environmental problems/stressors

_____

_____

From these assessments, what additional information would you solicit from the client at the intake interview?

Discuss your diagnostic impression with your field instructor. Has your diagnosis changed? Yes or no? If X symptom were not evident, do you think you would have a different diagnostic impression? Yes or no?

   Why:

7 OMHRC Exercise

This exercise is best completed by groups of two students: one student to be the interviewer and another to assume the role of a youth confined to a youth detention facility. Your task is to conduct an assessment interview using the interview schedule found in Figure 6.4. The student assuming the role of the youth confined to detention should assume numerous characteristics or symptoms of serious mental health conditions.

   Conduct the assessment or diagnostic interview and complete a staff version of the OMHRC. What is the most serious symptom? What is the least serious symptom? (Remember, the symptoms are organized in descending order from most to least serious, as defined by triage ratings.)

   Most serious symptom: _____

   Least serious symptom: _____

How will you begin to intervene in the most serious symptom?

_____

_____

Share the preceding suggestion of your intervention with your field instructor and discuss why you believe the intervention will be effective.

Are there any treatment manuals available that will facilitate your use of this particular intervention? Locate and identify at least two manuals and list them here.

1. _____

2. _____

Let's turn to more practical matters. We have shown you a number of assessment methods. Some methods and some problem identifications are more or less suited to different settings. With this in mind, we suggest that you not hesitate to adopt the assessment procedure to your internship setting that best fits the client population served and the types of programs—long-term, short-term, group, or individual format. If your clients, for example, are not in a controlled setting or under the legal system, then some assessments are superfluous. If you are in a setting that serves various clients who are seriously and persistently mentally ill, then please don't think all the preceding is something to apply to your intern assessment experiences. Similarly, if your entire client caseload has some risk of social transgressions, then we hope you are able to routinely use an instrument for a risk assessment (see chapter 12 for a discussion of evidence-based practices for risk assessment). In summary, then (we hope you agree), assessments are designed for the very client who sits with you and whom you intend to help. The primary purpose of the selected assessment and diagnostic instruments is to facilitate consistent and accurate observations of the client.

7

MOTIVATIONAL INTERVIEWING SKILLS

CHRISTOPHER RICE

In this chapter you will learn about motivational interviewing, which is identified as one evidence-based therapeutic intervention that works for substance abuse and other health-related problems. Specifically, you will learn: how motivational interventions work; the principles of the transtheoretical model of change; the interconnections among the theoretical foundations of motivational interventions; the purported mechanisms that lead to behavior change; how the assessment and feedback components of motivational interventions promote self-regulations of behavior; the types of problem behaviors that motivational intervention is effective with; the best tools for assessment; how you can organize data to provide personalized feedback to clients; and the therapeutic style that complements the delivery of motivational interventions. The chapter ends with role-play exercises using motivational interviewing, an evidence based intervention discussed in this chapter. Finally, you will find evidence-based resources for substance abuse problems and for special topics such as criminal justice or mental health and co-occurring disorders, along with directions for accessing Treatment Improvement Protocols (TIP), which is a series of guidelines for practice from the Center for Substance Abuse. A case study provides you with opportunity for further assessment and intervention planning practice.

In general, when you consider intervention with people who have overly learned habituated behaviors, such as those found with substance addictions, you begin from a practical position. To consider intervention at all is to assert that the behavior can change, and the question simply reduces to What intervention works? Motivational interviewing is brief evidence-based intervention that works for problems involving alcohol, drugs, diet and exercise, and other health-related problem behaviors (Burke, Dunn, Atkins, & Phelps, 2004). Motivational interviewing is an intervention found to be effective, and for this reason, we believe it to be an important and relevant skill that is useful in many client situations.

Motivational intervention is one of the "best practice" interventions for changing addictive behavior not only because of the convergence of the interconnections among the theoretical foundation areas but also because of a more important consideration: the scientific evidence supports such a claim.

DEFINITION

Motivational interviewing is a directive, client-centered counseling style for eliciting behavior change by helping clients to explore and resolve ambivalence. The goal of motivational interviewing is to explore ambivalence and to encourage clients to express their concerns and individual reasons for change (Rollnick & Miller, 1995). You elicit from clients their reasons for concern and their arguments for change. The goal is not to change clients' behavior but to allow clients to argue for their own change. Two concepts in motivational interviewing are ambivalence and readiness to change. Used primarily with clients who have problems with drugs or alcohol, the principles and method are generalizable to other behaviors.

THEORETICAL UNDERPINNINGS OF MOTIVATIONAL INTERVIEWING

There is no single, widely accepted theory of human behavior that explains how people change health-related behaviors. Under these conditions it is helpful to consider the one theoretical model that explicitly recognizes a number of the leading psychotherapy systems—that is, the psychodynamic, behaviorism, and cognitive theories—as offering both corresponding and supplemental elements that can be fruitfully integrated into a model of how people change. This perspective is called the *transtheoretical model of change.*

Transtheoretical Model of Change

The transtheoretical model of change (TTM) combines the use of insight, conditioning and counterconditioning, and learning methods into a single system of therapeutic change (Prochaska & DiClemente, 1986). TTM is intended to provide a comprehensive description of behavior change, based on several assumptions underlying the model. TTM assumes that there are behavior change processes that are common to but independent of the type of intervention and that no single system of therapy is inherently superior. The model also assumes that change processes generalize over different types of behavior and that the model is useful in identifying the common elements in the sequence of behavior change. Another feature of TTM is that it is adaptable to new theoretical developments.

TTM proposes that behavior change can be viewed as: (1) a movement through specific stages of change that is cyclical rather than linear; (2) a common set of processes of change; and (3) an integrating process of change within the stages of change. TTM has gained wide acceptance as a useful approach to behavior change in general and health-related behaviors in particular.

Stages of Change

A basic concept of TTM is the stages-of-change model (SCM; Prochaska & Di-Clemente, 1984). SCM posits that a common sequence is apparent in a wide range of health-related behaviors, such as smoking cessation, losing weight, and reducing use of substances. The stages in the sequence of change are identified as: (1) *precontemplation,* in which the person is unaware of risk and has not thought about change; (2) *contemplation,* in which the person is aware of their risk relative to a behavior and makes a commitment to change; (3) *determination/preparation,* in which the person makes a clear decision and commitment to change; (4) *action,* in which the person begins to make changes to eliminate the risk behavior by setting goals and changing habits; and (5) *maintenance,* in which the person develops methods for reinforcing change, coping with slips, and preventing relapses. A possible sixth stage is *relapse,* in which the previous efforts fail, a relapse occurs, and the individual begins another cycle.

TTM suggests that the process of change is another important construct. These processes are thought to be common across a range of behaviors. Table 7.1 provides a representation of the change processes associated with the movement through the stages.

Use of standardized measures for assessment of biopsychosocial functioning and feedback of that information are techniques that are suited to helping people move from the precontemplation into the preparation stage.

Self-Regulation Theory

Although it would be comforting if TTM were the only theoretical foundation from which to approach motivation-based change of addictive behavior, the historical development of motivation-based intervention also has strong roots in self-regulation theory. In order to have a full appreciation of the pragmatics of increasing a person's motivation to change behavior, it is helpful for you to understand the concepts of self-regulation.

All living organisms self-regulate, and in the most fundamental sense, self-regulation is an evolutionary process of optimal adjustment whereby the organism

Table 7.1 Stages by Processes of Change

	Stages-of-Change Model			
Pre-contemplation	*Contemplation*	*Preparation*	*Action*	*Maintenance*
Consciousness raising				
Dramatic relief				
Environmental reevaluation				
	Self-reevaluation			
		Self-liberation		
			Reinforcement management	
				Helping relationships
			Counterconditioning	
			Stimulus control	

Note: Adapted from Prochaska, DiClemente, and Norcross (1992)

is able to maximize gain from the environment (Mithaug, 1993). For human behavior change, self-regulation theory (Kanfer, 1970, 1979, 1986) provides a conceptual framework for understanding how people: (1) adopt new behavior and (2) keep or modify present behavior. One practical application of self-regulation theory is the development of motivational intervention (Miller & Brown, 1991). Within motivational intervention, self-regulation is viewed as a sequence: (1) information about the person's present function is received from the environment; (2) the information is compared with personal goals, norms, and expectations; (3) a discrepancy is detected (or not detected) between the person's current and desired state; (4) a discrepancy instigates ambivalence; (5) a state of ambivalence is uncomfortable, and the person attempts to reduce the ambivalence; (6) a strategy for resolving the discrepancy is developed; and (7) a change in behavior is implemented.

STIMULATING MOTIVATION FOR CHANGE

Consistent with self-regulation of behavior, the assessment and feedback components of motivational interventions are designed to promote the self-regulation of behaviors (Miller, Toscova, Miller, & Sanchez, 2000). The feedback component of motivational intervention is thought to increase motivation to reduce alcohol use by creating a discrepancy between a person's desired goals and the consequences or potential consequences of current behavior that conflict with or impede achievement of those goals (Miller & Rollnick, 2002). The discrepancy results in an ambiguity about changing behavior. The assessment feedback is intended to amplify the ambiguity that often accompanies recognition of the discrepancy between desired goals and current behaviors. This amplification of discrepancy is thought to stimulate motivation to resolve the ambiguity through regulation of the behavioral impediment to goal achievement (Miller, 1999).

Efficacy of Motivational Interventions

The sources of evidence that supports motivational interventions are extensive and beyond the scope of this book. What is important for you as a student to know is that the efficacy of motivational interventions with alcohol-abusing clients is well supported by the treatment outcomes research literature (see Bein, Miller, & Tonigan, 1993; Burke, Arkowitz, & Dunn, 2002; Dunn, DeRoo, & Rivara, 2001; Noonan & Moyers, 1997; Wilk, Jensen, & Havighurst, 1997, for reviews; see Project MATCH Research Group, 1997, 1998, for recent treatment efficacy studies). Motivational intervention is one of only two treatments (the other is relapse prevention) for alcoholism to receive a rating of "efficacious" treatment according to the standards (evidence of efficacy against a placebo from at least two randomized clinical trials with adequate statistical power done by different investigators or research teams) set by the APA Division 12 Task Force (McCrady, 2000).

Motivational intervention has been used as a treatment approach with clients in treatment for cocaine abuse (Alterman et al., 1996), chronic marijuana use (Roffman, Stephens, & Simpson, 1989; Stephens, Roffman, & Curtin, 2000), and opiate abuse (Saunders, Wilkinson, & Phillips, 1995; van Bilsen & Whitehead, 1994; van Bilsen & van Emst, 1986). Findings are less impressive due to methodological weaknesses, including lack of random assignment and high attrition rates. However, motivational intervention applications are successful in the alcoholism treatment field, and these present a strong case that exposure to motivational intervention does result in reduction of alcohol use.

Assessment of Function

As a student you are familiar with assessment and its purpose. Assessment plays a pivotal role in motivational intervention. Assessment provides a foundation for motivational intervention by collecting information not only about a person's substance use but also about his or her medical health and a broad range of psychological and social functioning. Assessment can assist further in the following seven ways:

1. Many people do not think of themselves as having a substance abuse problem and often view their use as a source of enjoyment. Assessment is one method of obtaining objective information that can help a person evaluate the role that substance use plays in his or her life. A simple examination of objective information about the relative normalcy of his or her substance use pattern is sometimes sufficient to create discrepancy.

2. Assessment can identify the following about a client's substance use: level of dependence, use patterns, medical and physical implications of use, psychological and social consequences attributed to use, and the positive attributes or incentives a client ascribes to continued use.

3. Assessment can provide clients with a personalized assessment feedback on the risks associated with their use and how their use compares with use norms in the general population, as well as in subgroups similar to the clients'.

4. Assessment provides comparative information that can help the client to recognize *discrepancies* between his or her behavior and his or her expectations. Recognition of discrepancy allows you to recognize and amplify the person's ambiguity about changing use behaviors.

5. Assessment can help to identify areas of concern and where change might be considered.

6. Assessment can assist you in helping the client to evaluate his or her motivation to change his or her substance use.

7. Assessment can help you build rapport with your client.

As noted, assessment is critical to the process of change and therefore must be conducted with great care and integrity. To be most effective as feedback and to ensure the greatest degree of credibility to the client, the assessment instruments used should have sound psychometric properties known as reliability and validity. I have identified and selected these sources in the following section.

SELECTING ASSESSMENT TOOLS

As a student you are probably aware that there are many assessment tools. The most common assessment tools (Miller, Zweben, DiClemente, & Rychtarik, 1992) for determining whether the client has an addiction problem are listed here.

Screening and Assessment Tools for Adults

The Addiction Severity Index (ASI) is a good tool to administer at intake and during the assessment process. The ASI has been widely used for adult treatment and research since its development in 1980 (McLellan, Luborsky, Woody, & O'Brien, 1980). The ASI, as well as information related to assessment instruments, can be located on the Treatment Research Institute website, http://www.tresearch.org/resources/instruments.htm This widely used instrument is considered reliable and valid and has normative reference data available (Appleby, Dyson, Altman, & Luchins, 1997; McLellan, Kushner et al., 1992).

Screening and Assessment Tools for Adolescents

Assessment tools for adolescents can be found in the government publication series titled *Treatment Improvement Protocol (TIP), TIP 3* (http://www.treatment.org/Externals/tips.html; McLellan & Dembo, 1993). Another excellent resource, published by the Northwest Frontier Addiction Technology Transfer Center (NFATTC), from the Best Practice Resources Series is "Substance Abuse Screening and Assessment Instruments for Adolescents" (Winters, 1999).

Screening and Assessment Tools for Co-Occurring Problems

Assessment for clients with co-occurring psychological disorders and substance abuse are available from *TIP 9* (Ries, 1994). Allen and Columbus (1995) and Miller (1999) provide a good sample of references for additional screening and assessment instruments.

Screening and Assessment Tools for Use in Criminal Justice Settings

Assessments for clients with alcohol and other drug abuse among adults in criminal justice settings can be found at *TIP 9* (Ries, 1994). For assessment of substance abuse treatment and domestic violence, see *TIP 25* and *TIP 35*.

PERSONALIZED FEEDBACK REPORT

Now that you have completed the assessment, you must consider organizing the information so that the client receives meaningful feedback. Feedback presents an objective feature of the addictive behavior in a nonjudgmental manner. Where possible, the objectivity of the information is reinforced through the presentation of normative standards, or what the average person in the population looks like on a particular measure. Often the differences between the client and the general population are in stark contrast to one another. These contrasts can be a point of discrepancy between the client's self-image and his or her actual behavior. The information presented to the client is placed in a personalized feedback report (PFR). An example is presented in Figure 7.1.

The PFR is a summary of data collected during the assessment protocol. It is designed to provide objective information to the client about the effects of his or her alcohol and other drug (AOD) use. In prompting the client's reaction to the feedback, the counselor uses motivational interviewing techniques to amplify discrepancy and to reinforce the client's motivation to change his or her AOD use. A new perspective can arise when clients understand that ambivalence about their own ability to change AOD use is a common concern. The PFR has provided an objective look of their AOD use in comparison with normative patterns, or use among the general population. Furthermore, their levels of risk for undesirable consequences, in comparison with the AOD use of others of their age and gender, is noted, and this is often enough to tip the balance in favor of change.

In addition, the client receives a narrative explanation of the results of the PFR, "Understanding Your Personal Feedback Report" (UYPFR). The UYPFR used in this chapter is an adaptation of the one developed for Project MATCH (Miller et al., 1992). Two specific areas of feedback include the narrative comparison with others who do not drink and the ASI scores.

1. For clients who predominately use alcohol, an additional handout is provided, "Alcohol and You," which is a pamphlet developed by William R. Miller that helps clients to assess whether they are drinking too much, the health risks, the correlation of drinking with social and psychological problems, and how much is too much. This document is published also in Miller et al. (1992).

2. The ASI provides a composite score that is the sum of response values within a problem area measured on the ASI. The ASI composite score ranges have been ordered into low-, medium-, and high-risk levels based on the distribution of composite scores in normative samples of clients seeking treatment for AOD problems (McLellan, Kushner, et al., 1992). The composite scores in the PFR are used as criteria against which the client's own ASI composite scores are compared. See Figure 7.1.

Name: _____   Date _____

1. YOUR DRINKING _____

    Number of standard drinks per week: _____ drinks

    Your drinking relative to American adults (same sex): _____ percentile

2. LEVEL OF INTOXICATION _____
    Estimated Blood Alcohol Concentration (BAC) peaks:

      in a typical week: _____ mg %

      on a heavier day of drinking: _____ mg %

3. RISK FACTORS _____
Tolerance Level:
___ Low (0–60) ___ Medium (61–120) ___ High (121–180) ___ Very High (181+)
Other Drug Risk:
_____ Low   _____ Medium   _____ High

Family Risk: _____
      LOW: 0–1 MEDIUM: 2–3 HIGH: 4–6 VERY HIGH: 7+

Age at onset: _____ years
Under 25 = Higher Risk   25–39 = Medium Risk   40+ = Lower Risk

Medical Composite:

	Low Risk	Medium Risk	High Risk
Alcohol Abusers			
Male	<0.255	0.255–0.582	>0.582
Female	<0.120	0.120–0.356	>0.356
Opiate Abusers			
Male	<0.220	0.220–0.550	>0.550
Female	<0.313	0.313–0.667	>0.667
Cocaine Abusers			
Male	<0.267	0.267–0.600	>0.600
Female	<0.186	0.186–0.481	>0.481
Multiple Abusers			
Male	<0.226	0.226–0.414	>0.414
Female	<0.138	0.138–0.432	>0.432
			(continued)

Figure 7.1 Example of a Personal Feedback Report

Employment Composite:

	Low Risk	Medium Risk	High Risk
Alcohol Abusers			
Male	<0.702	0.702–0.971	>0.971
Female	<0.392	0.392–0.677	>0.677
Opiate Abusers			
Male	<0.820	0.820–0.900	>0.900
Female	<0.803	0.803–0.900	>0.900
Cocaine Abusers			
Male	<0.697	0.697–0.900	>0.900
Female	<0.483	0.483–0.700	>0.700
Multiple Abusers			
Male	<0.608	0.608–0.900	>0.900
Female	<0.448	0.448–0.700	>0.700

Legal Composite:

	Low Risk	Medium Risk	High Risk
Alcohol Abusers			
Male	<0.074	0.074–0.248	>0.248
Female	<0.050	0.050–0.184	>0.184
Opiate Abusers			
Male	<0.152	0.152–0.352	>0.352
Female	<0.103	0.103–0.317	>0.317
Cocaine Abusers			
Male	<0.089	0.089–0.235	>0.235
Female	<0.041	0.041–0.167	>0.167
Multiple Abusers			
Male	<0.046	0.046–0.145	>0.145
Female	<0.074	0.074–0.127	>0.127

Psychiatric Composite:

	Low Risk	Medium Risk	High Risk
Alcohol Abusers			
Male	<0.236	0.236–0.448	>0.448
Female	<0.242	0.242–0.464	>0.464
Opiate Abusers			
Male	<0.155	0.155–0.368	>0.368
Female	<0.379	0.379–0.575	>0.575

Figure 7.1 (*Continued*)

	Low Risk	Medium Risk	High Risk
Cocaine Abusers			
Male	<0.245	0.245–0.468	>0.468
Female	<0.258	0.258–0.471	>0.471
Multiple Abusers			
Male	<0.243	0.243–0.460	>0.460
Female	<0.225	0.225–0.442	>0.442

Alcohol Composite:

	Low Risk	Medium Risk	High Risk
Alcohol Abusers			
Male	<0.643	0.643–0.869	>0.869
Female	<0.631	0.631–0.808	>0.808
Opiate Abusers			
Male	<0.266	0.266–0.521	>0.521
Female	<0.098	0.98–0.272	>0.272
Cocaine Abusers			
Male	<0.257	0.257–0.520	>0.520
Female	<0.241	0.241–0.563	>0.563
Multiple Abusers			
Male	<0.289	0.289–0.458	>0.458
Female	<0.308	0.308–0.595	>0.595

Drug Composite:

	Low Risk	Medium Risk	High Risk
Alcohol Abusers			
Male	<0.031	0.031–0.098	>0.098
Female	<0.023	0.023–0.084	>0.084
Opiate Abusers			
Male	<0.265	0.265–0.396	>0.396
Female	<0.314	0.314–0.461	>0.461
Cocaine Abusers			
Male	<0.245	0.245–0.327	>0.327
Female	<0.256	0.256–0.320	>0.320
Multiple Abusers			
Male	<0.284	0.284–0.495	>0.495
Female	<0.155	0.155–0.258	>0.258

Figure 7.1 (*Continued*)

ASSESSING READINESS TO CHANGE

As mentioned in the foregoing sections, with the use of motivational interviewing, your goal early in any intervention is to determine the level of motivation your client has to change a long-maintained harmful behavior. By change, of course, we mean some behavior change in how the client feels, acts, or thinks. In helping your client evaluate his or her motivation to change, you are able to reinforce that motivation and provide positive reinforcement to the client for actually changing a behavior in terms of increasing or decreasing the intensity, frequency, or duration of some affect, cognition, or physical action.

Now I show you some straightforward ways of assessing the stage of change using the transtheoretical model of Prochaska and DiClemente (1984). To review, this model asserts that change in behavior results from progress through five stages of change: precontemplative, contemplative, preparation, action, and maintenance. These stages represent temporal, motivational, and stability dimensions of change (Prochaska, DiClemente, & Norcross, 1992), with *experiential* processes of change found with earlier stages and *behavioral* processes being used in the action and maintenance stages. Making an accurate assessment of a client's actual phase and then using strategies to advance him or her to the next phase is the key to changing your client's behaviors using this model. The transtheoretical model is, in fact, a very powerful model, predicting change in cigarette smoking, cocaine use, domestic violence, and weight control and psychological distress (Prochaska & DiClemente, 1986), as well as high-fat diets, adolescent delinquent behaviors, the practice of safer sex, condom use, sunscreen use, radon gas exposure, exercise acquisition, mammography screening, and preventive practices with smokers (Prochaska, Velicer, Rossi, & Goldstein, 1994). As this wide range suggests, the readiness-to-change model is very adaptable to many common problems we see in social work and criminal justice settings.

Table 7.1 illustrates the readiness-to-change model with the five stages of change. The precontemplation stage is the period in which your client has no intentions of taking action to change a problem or acquire a behavior in the foreseeable future, which typically lasts about 6 months or so. Even though you may have clients in treatment or in a program, they may still be precontemplative, such as the youth whose parents force him or her to see a social worker or the youth adjudicated to a residential program; he or she may be there but may have no intentions of cooperating and are likely to see no reason to. Because the client has no intent to change and does not believe there is a reason to, your first step is threefold: (1) help the client identify points of discrepancy between his or her goals and the consequences attributed to the behavior; (2) amplify any resulting discrepancy; and (3) reinforce any indication that the client has to change the behavior. Remember that the client is the agent of change and that your role as counselor or helper is to identify, amplify, and reinforce. Direction and confrontation are not recommended, as these are much less likely to promote client change.

Clearly, the stages of change are progressive and require different skills depending on the stage. At each stage of change, your client is reflecting a behavioral intent to change, and the preparation through the maintenance stages represent actual behaviors manifesting a change. For example, nicotine withdrawal requires something quite different in the action stage of quitting smoking from the resistance to temptations and avoiding behavioral cues that are more appropriate at the maintenance stage, although the contemplation stage requires the cognitive decision to quit smoking. As discussed earlier in this chapter, one of your initial goals is to help move clients along in the change process by motivating them toward progressive stages and providing the appropriate services depending on your client's stage in the change process. By knowing your client's stage in the change process, you can focus your intervention to the needs of that particular stage and plan to help your client advance to the next stage, then to prepare your future work toward the needs of the upcoming stage.

Let's consider an example faced all too frequently in criminal justice and social work settings alike, namely, domestic violence. Review Table 7.1, the stages-of-change process, and then consider our problem of domestic violence. Assume that you have an 18-year-old mother who is in a violent domestic relationship with her partner. Data suggest, in fact, that this situation is likely to occur for one out of four teenage mothers, with the domestic violence occurring within the preceding 6 months (Sussex & Corcoran, 2005), with rates as high as 57% (Hickman, Jaycox, & Aronoff, 2004) or perhaps as low as 16% (Covington, Justason, & Wright, 2001; Martin, Clark, Lynch, Kupper, & Cilenti, 1999). A woman appears to be most at risk of violence during the preparation stage, especially if she takes out a restraining order. At this stage the need for a safety action plan would be more urgent than if she were in the precontemplative stage or had left the relationship 6 months previously—and yet, 6 months may be far too short a reprieve for many clients who are exiting violent relationships with intimate partners, especially young moms whose sense of self and other strengths are still developing and who have the responsibility of raising a baby.

In such circumstances, and when clinical and professional judgment compels, the time frame for using the readiness-to-change model may need to be extended to a year. In other cases, such as anxiety disorders and especially simple phobias, the time frame will likely need to be narrowed; weeks and months may suffice with anxiety conditions. In sharp contrast, using a readiness-to-change model with persons with persistent and long-term mental illness will likely necessitate a wide time frame and would include developing advance directives in and during the maintenance stage for providing the requested care during probable periods of psychotic episodes.

In the precontemplation stage, your client's cognitions are not focused on changing his or her behavior, and your task is to help identify points of discrepancy. Now, let's look at another example: a client who is in treatment for "driving under the influence" (DUI) and who might insist that he or she doesn't need treatment because he or she is not an alcoholic. You could reflect agreement that he or she is not an alcoholic but ask how it was that he or she came to be in treatment for DUI. Raising awareness by pointing out discrepancy helps to stimulate ambiguity, and because ambiguity is an uncomfortable state, your client's cognitions are directed toward ways to resolve the ambiguity. The client goes from precontemplation into a state of contemplation: "What would it be like if I changed my behavior?" The contemplation stage is characterized by self-evaluation. The client is wrestling with the ambiguity that results from becoming aware of the discrepancy between the positive and negative consequences of the addictive behavior. Here the intervention task is to both amplify the discrepancy and motivate the client's expressions of intention to change his or her behavior.

Although the precontemplation and contemplation stages largely involve cognitive tasks, elements of behavior mixed with cognitive tasks characterize the preparation stage. In the preparation stage, your task is to reinforce the client's motivation to change and to promote the transition to action by motivating the client to create a plan for action. A principle to keep in mind is promoting client self-efficacy. In promoting the self-liberation that characterizes this stage of change, the action plan should contain behaviors that, first, resolve ambiguity and, second, the client thinks he or she can actually accomplish. To illustrate, although "going cold turkey" and quitting a two-pack-a-day cigarette habit resolves ambiguity, the client's level of confidence about being successful might be low because prior similar attempts ended in relapse. It would be your task to ensure that your client chooses an action goal that he or she has strong confidence in achieving.

In the action stage, the task is not only to avoid the cues that stimulated the old behavior but also to focus on establishing new behavioral habits. Helping the client identify the positive consequences of the new behavior results in a reinforcing of motivation and helps the client to affirm his or her confidence that the change plan is working. It is also helpful in the action stage to encourage the client to connect with resources that will provide additional positive reinforcement for the changed behavior and help the client establish a support system that will enhance the maintenance of the new behavior. By the maintenance stage, the new behavior is firmly established, and the task for the client is to strengthen his or her support system. It is prudent to adopt a long-term perspective when reviewing your client's plans for maintaining his or her new behaviors.

MOTIVATIONAL INTERVIEWING EXAMPLE

The example that follows illustrates several of the tools inherent in a motivational interviewing style. The example comes from the alcohol treatment field, but principles that are illustrated are common to the treatment of any well-maintained behavior. As in any motivational intervention, your goal as the counselor or helper is to help the client identify areas of discrepancy, to amplify the ambiguity about changing long-standing behavior, to reinforce the client's motivation and commitment to change, and to encourage the client to build a plan for action.

JT is a 48-year-old customer representative for a multinational pharmaceutical company. He has held this job for the past 15 years. JT has been married for 20 years and has three children, a son 17 years old and two daughters 19 and 15 years old. Initial assessment indicated that JT averaged 31 standard drinks per week, with peak blood alcohol levels reaching 15 on two weekends over the 3 months prior to interview. When compared with the national norm for weekly alcohol consumption, JT's drinking places him at the 91st percentile for men.

During the feedback session, when you inform JT that he drinks more than 91% of men in the population, he reacts with surprise, stating that during the preceding 6 months or so he has reduced his weekly drinking in response to his wife's insistence. "Maybe that 91st percentile thing was true 6 months ago, but not now since I've cut back," JT might say.

This is a good point at which you can employ simple reflection. State that you noticed the surprise in JT's voice about the discrepancy between what he considered a reduced level of drinking and his position against the national norms. JT reacted to your statement by questioning the accuracy of the data. Often clients respond with "Is that right? How do you know that's where I fit? It seems high because I don't drink any more than my friends." Your response is to acknowledge the skepticism and then offer a clarification that explains that the source of the national norms are data collected in standardized national surveys funded by the federal government and to remind JT that the data on his drinking were obtained from his self-report during the initial assessment. It's important that you help JT understand the objective nature of the feedback. If he perceives that the feedback is simply your opinion, then it is easier for him to dismiss the information as nagging or confrontation.

At this point you might redirect JT by reflecting on his positive changes to reduce his drinking. Here you can reflect that JT's wife must be concerned about him and that he, out of concern for her, responded. JT's surprise is understandable because, although he has cut back, his drinking remains well above what is average in the population. JT might then respond that he feels that he drinks no more than any of his friends do and certainly no more than his golf buddies. You might simply use a clarifying reflection here, asking JT, "Help me understand how your golf buddies drink a lot." JT provides a narrative that details how his golf buddies often meet one or twice during the week to watch sports at a local bar after work. On the weekend after golf, they spend late afternoons and early evenings at the golf club bar relaxing. Having this information, you could redirect JT now and reflect on the importance that these friends have to JT. JT would likely provide further elaboration on the nature of these relationships.

What is important at this point is that you now have an opportunity to identify discrepancy based on JT's social relationships. JT's golf buddies form a source of reinforcement of drinking behavior that is in stark contrast to what is tolerable to his wife. Because JT has reduced his drinking in response to his wife's concern, he appears to value that spousal relationship. You can view this as a discrepancy between JT's level of activity with his golf buddies and his wife's discomfort with his drinking-related behavior. To bring this part of the feedback session to closure, you can use a summarization technique that ends with a reflection of both sides of this discrepancy.

To use a summary technique, you state that you are going to review the points just discussed so that you can be sure that you understand JT correctly. You then review the level of JT's drinking compared with the national norms; JT's surprise that he was in the 91st percentile after reducing his drinking; the wife's concern for JT; JT's positive response to this concern; and the importance that JT places on his friendship with his golfing buddies. Having summarized the feedback and characterized JT's responses, you can then use a double-sided reflection. On the one hand are the positive aspects of not further changing his drinking (he maintains his friendships) and the negative aspects of not changing (his wife becomes more concerned about his drinking); on the other hand are the positive aspects of changing (he improves his relationship with his wife) and the reduction in negative aspects that change provides (saving the costs of drinking, getting fewer complaints from his wife, and having more time for his family). JT can react to this statement, and you attend to any ambiguity JT makes about changing his drinking further, reflecting that it is normal to "be of two minds" about something that he's been doing for a long time. You can further amplify the decisional balance by listing a menu of things JT might consider changing.

SUMMARY

This chapter provided a brief overview of motivational interviewing, an intervention that has sufficient scientific evidence to conclude that it is an efficacious therapeutic intervention for alcohol abuse and alcohol dependence. Individuals with alcohol dependence who are exposed to motivational interviewing are, on average, likely to show a reduction in their drinking behavior. Although this type of evidence is critical, it is not the only factor to consider before a recommendation of "best practice" can be made. For instance, the level of training that is required of the therapist and the acceptance of the intervention by clients is important. Therefore, it is advised that you practice this intervention with supervision from an expert in the field of addictions.

ERNIE SEEKS TREATMENT

Mandy Davis

Ernie Lidquest was a 12th-grader attending an alternative high school after being caught by the school resource officer smoking marijuana in the school parking lot. His records indicate that he had had problems with marijuana use as a junior high school student as well. All students at the school were assessed in the school health center by a multidisciplinary team to determine what services may be needed to support the students' return to their home schools. The treatment team, Ernie, and his mother determined that his cannabis use was the primary cause of Ernie's problems in school.

The team assigned Ernie's case to Sophie, a second-year intern serving on the treatment team. The team asked Sophie to document and evaluate her work with Ernie and report back to the team about Ernie's progress. Sophie was anxious about working with Ernie, and now she had to evaluate her work. She had just learned about single-case design in class and thought this was an appropriate time to practice what she had learned. Sophie went through her class material and thought it most efficient to apply the direct observations instruments (DOI) model of a simple design determined by the course of the intervention, an observation system used systematically, and a graph of the observations in order to interpret the outcomes (see chapter 13). With this plan in hand Sophie set up her first appointment with Ernie.

Assessment and Screening and Problem Identification

Sophie knew from her class that evaluating practice began with identifying the problem and deciding on measurable goals, and she was learning the skills of motivational interviewing and the readiness-to-change model. During their first meeting Sophie asked Ernie what he wanted to accomplish during their time together, and Ernie said, "I want to get out of this dump of a school and go back to where my friends are." When asked what needed to happen for Ernie to return to his home school, he stated that he needed to "stop getting in trouble." "But what do you actually have to do?" Sophie asked. "Not what do you have to *not* do, but what do you have to do?" With this type of questioning, Sophie and Ernie continued to narrow down the target behavior and goal. Together they decided that Ernie's use of marijuana was the primary problem and that the goal was to abstain from use. Sophie and Ernie worked together to identify observable behaviors that would change if, in fact, progress was being made: Ernie would smoke marijuana less frequently, he would decrease the amount of marijuana he smoked, and he would increase the duration of abstinence from marijuana. Sophie also assessed Ernie's strength and the risk and protective factors of his social environment, noting a proclivity for math appreciation, a high achievement motivation, and good ACT and SAT scores. However, he had an attention span that lasted about 12 weeks.

Intervention and Treatment

Sophie employed a cognitive-behavioral intervention model that included antecedent control, positive punishment, cognitive restructuring, and positive reinforcement to decrease the use of marijuana and increase the duration of abstinence from marijuana. She continued to use motivational interviewing skills in her sessions with Ernie.

Measurement

In order to evaluate her work, Sophie needed a way to measure Ernie's use of marijuana. Ernie said, "I usually roll one up and smoke at least once a day and sometimes more when my mother is on my case." Sophie and Ernie agreed that they needed to measure how many days Ernie went without using marijuana and how much Ernie used when he was not abstinent. Because Ernie smoked joints, they agreed to count the number of joints Ernie smoked within a week as a measure of the amount of marijuana he was using. Because Ernie's use of marijuana is an observable behavior, they decided that measures would be taken through direct observation recorded by Ernie.

Sophie developed a weekly calendar for Ernie, and for each day he marked off how many, if any, joints he smoked that day. Sophie collected the calendars at their weekly sessions. Sophie also collected the same information for the 4 weeks prior to implementing the CBT intervention. This meant that Sophie asked Ernie to report how many joints he smoked per day on weekly calendars representing weeks prior to the intervention. Two of these weeks occurred before Ernie entered the alternative high school, and 2 weeks occurred during the intake and assessment phase of treatment. Sophie and Ernie met for 12 weekly sessions to complete the intervention, and each week a calendar was completed. For 2 weeks following the end of treatment, Ernie completed a weekly calendar and turned it in to Sophie.

Findings

Each week Sophie plotted the number of joints smoked and the number of days Ernie abstained from marijuana (see Figure 7.2).

Though Sophie had initially been anxious about evaluating her work, she realized that using the single-case design method increased her confidence in her skills and in presenting her work to the team. She presented the graph to the treatment team and concluded that, because Ernie had increased the number of

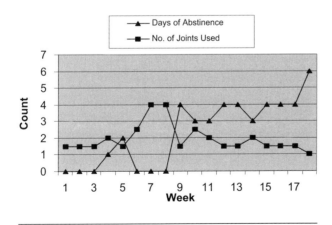

Figure 7.2 Ernie's Weekly Progress

days he abstained from using marijuana, the intervention had been successful in meeting the goals of reducing the amount and frequency of use and the duration of abstinence. The treatment team applauded Sophie on her method of evaluating her practice but did not agree completely with her conclusions.

■ ■ ■

Activities

1. Looking at the graph in Figure 7.2, why do you think the treatment team did not completely agree with Sophie's conclusions?

2. If we concluded that Ernie did in fact decrease his use of marijuana and increase days of abstinence, can we say the intervention was the cause of this progress?

3. Why or why not? How could the evaluation be changed to better understand the impact of the intervention on the desired outcomes?

4. What are the strengths and limitations of how the behavior was measured? (Here is a hint about the case: Ernie started using a rolling paper that was extra long.)

5. How might evaluating your practice affect you and your client?

6. Think about a case you are involved in and identify:

   a. the problem/target behavior.

   b. the goal(s).

   c. treatment/intervention.

d. how the desired change will be measured.

e. how the actual organization of the intervention can determine your evaluation design.

Role-Play Exercise

In order to learn more about motivational interviewing, it is important to practice the skills, and this exercise requires you to engage in a role play. If you are in a classroom, then students should work together in groups of three, assigning roles as follows: a client, an interviewer, and an observer. Based on the following vignette, the information in this chapter, role-play an interview based on the following case.

Andres is a 48-year-old auto salesman. He has held this job for the past 12 years. He has been married for 20 years and has one child, a son, 17 years old. Andres drinks most nights after work at home. On most weekends he generally drinks more, up to 8–10 drinks each evening. He denies any prior problems with alcohol. He doesn't think he has an alcohol problem. He is surprised that you are concerned about his drinking. He says he drinks less than his friends do. He says that his dad is an alcoholic and that he knows all about alcohol problems. Sometimes he worries that his son may become an alcoholic.

Role-Play Task

Take turns among the participants and role-play (1) screening, (2) assessment, (3) brief intervention, and (4) motivational interviewing techniques. The person in the role of counselor or therapist should add additional information based on his or her own experiences with individuals. The client is meant to display a moderate amount of resistance.

1. How well did the interviewer do in demonstrating motivational interventions?

2. What observations can be made about the interaction between the client and interviewer?

3. Switch roles to practice motivational interviewing in different roles.

4. You may wish to present a different problem, such as that of a client in your own internship.

EVIDENCE-BASED RESOURCES

The National Institute on Alcohol Abuse and Alcoholism (NIAAA) site (http://pubs.niaaa.nih.gov/publications/Social/Module6Motivation&Treatment/Module6.pdf) summarizes the strategies for improving alcohol treatment adherence. These skills and techniques, listed here, can assist you with your interview style and in addressing culturally competent and appropriate issues:

1. Asking open-ended questions
2. Conducting empathetic assessments
3. Discovering the client's beliefs
4. Using reflective listening (rather than asking for more information). (Center on Alcoholism, Substance Abuse, and Addictions, 2006)

Motivational interviewing techniques also include strategies for motivating individuals toward making changes in their alcohol use practices:

1. Normalizing client uncertainties
2. Amplifying client doubts
3. Deploying discrepancy (fostering cognitive dissonance)
4. Supporting self-efficacy
5. Reviewing past treatment experiences
6. Providing relevant feedback (learning the results of their own tests motivates people)
7. Summarizing and reviewing potential sources of nonadherence
8. Negotiating proximal goals (i.e., opportunity to achieve "quick successes")
9. Discovering potential roadblocks

10. Displaying optimism
11. Involving supportive significant others

Following are ways to maintain respect for clients while mobilizing their resources:

1. Expressing empathy by accurate listening that clarifies the client's experience, feelings, and interpretations.
2. Amplifying discrepancy between current behavior and broader goal by weighing pros and cons.
3. Avoiding arguments
4. Rolling with resistance.
5. Supporting self-efficacy.

ASSESSMENT INSTRUMENTS

1. Go to the website http://pubs.niaaa.nih.gov/publications/Assesing%20 Alcohol/intro.htm and click on *publications*, on *reports/manuals/guides/ briefs*, and on *Alcoholism Treatment Assessment Instruments*.
2. Go to http://casaa.unm.edu/michange.html. Under special topics such as "criminal justice or mental health, co-occurring disorders," you can access *Treatment Improvement Protocol (TIP) Series 3* resources and treatment protocols according to your interests.
3. Motivational change for alcohol treatment: http://pathprogram.samhsa.gov/ pdf/Motivational_Interviewing_Mat_2_11_03.pdf
4. Evidence-based treatment for homeless individuals with co-occurring mental health and substance abuse disorders: http://www.motivational interview.org/
5. Motivational interviewing resources for practitioners and researchers: http:// www.health.org/catalog/catalog.htm
6. *TIP 35: Enhancing Motivation for Change in Substance Abuse Treatment,* BKD 342, available from the National Clearinghouse for Alcohol and Drug Information (NCADI): http://www.treatment.org.
7. A complete curriculum of slides for alcohol assessment (see Module 04), treatment, and motivational interviewing (see Module 06) and curriculum for special populations: http://www.niaaa.nih.gov/publications/Social/ ContentsList.html

CRIMINAL JUSTICE RESOURCES

Center for Substance Abuse Publications contain many different protocols for use with clients.

- *TAP (Technical Assistance Publication) 23: Substance Abuse Treatment for Women Offenders: Guide to Promising Practices*
- *TAP 19: Counselor's Manual for Relapse Prevention with Chemically Dependent Criminal Offenders*
- *TIP 30: Continuity of Offender Treatment for Substance Use Disorders from Institution to Community*
- *TIP 23: Treatment Drug Courts: Integrating Substance Abuse Treatment With Legal Case Processing*
- *TIP 21: Combining Alcohol and Other Drug Abuse Treatment With Diversion for Juveniles in the Justice System*
- *TIP 17: Planning for Alcohol and Other Drug Abuse Treatment for Adults in the Criminal Justice System*
- *TIP 12: Combining Substance Abuse Treatment with Intermediate Sanctions for Adults in the Criminal Justice System*
- *TIP 7: Screening and Assessment for Alcohol and Other Drug Abuse Among Adults in the Criminal Justice System*
- *TIE (Treatment Improvement Exchange) Communique: Forging Links to Treat the Substance-Abusing Offender* (Spring 1993)

Hard copies of CSAT TIPs can be ordered from the National Clearinghouse for Drug and Alcohol Information (NCADI) by accessing its electronic catalog or by calling 1-800-729-6686.

National Institute of Justice

Publications from the National Institute of Justice that are relevant to your internships include the following (see http://www.ncjrs.gov/App/QA/ServicesList .aspx):

- *But They All Come Back: Rethinking Prisoner Reentry* (May 2000)
- *The Rebirth of Rehabilitation: Promise and Perils of Drug Courts* (May 2000)
- *Evaluation of DC Superior Court Drug Intervention Programs* (April 2000) *First-time Study Describes Substance Abuse Treatment in*
- Correctional Facilities (SAMHSA, April 27, 2000)

- National Symposium on Alcohol and Crime: Recommendations to the Office of Justice Programs (http://www.ojp.usdoj.gov/aac/)
- Forty-seven Jurisdictions Receive Funds for Drug Courts (OJP http://www.whitehousedrugpolicy.gov/enforce/drugcourt.html

Other Criminal Justice Resources

Other helpful resources for criminal justice settings, clients, and professionals are listed below:

1. Department of Justice National Criminal Justice Reference Service (http://www.ncjrs.gov/)
2. University of Washington Alcohol and Drug Abuse Institute Library: (http://lib.adai.washington.edu/ADAILibInfoFeb06.pdf)
3. Alcohol, Drugs, and Tobacco websites (http://www.oas.samhsa.gov/drugs.cfm)
4. Bureau of Justice Statistics (http://www.ojp.usdoj.gov/bjs/)
5. Department of Justice Drug Courts Program Office (http://www.ncjrs.gov/pdffiles1/ojp/fs000265.pdf)
6. HIV Education Prison Project (HEPP) News (http://www.idcronline.org/)
7. Justice Information Center (http://www.ncjrs.gov/)

8 IDENTIFYING EVIDENCE-BASED PRACTICE INTERVENTIONS FOR CO-OCCURRING CONDITIONS

BARBARA THOMLISON, ROBIN JACOBS, *and* JENNIFER BECKER

In this chapter we show you how to search the Internet for information on evidence-based practices. We show you a six-step process: (1) Defining the clinical problem: preliminary search questions and evidence-based assessment tools. (2) Constructing good questions: descriptive questions, risk factors, assessment questions, effectiveness questions, and prevention questions. (3) Selecting a search strategy: model programs, systematic reviews, other levels of evidence, restricting and broadening your search, outcome studies, journal articles, and conferences. (4) Appraising the evidence. (5) Integrating clinical state and circumstances: research evidence, client preference, and actions. (6) Evaluating: Bringing research into practice. We also provide you with an evidence-based practice resource guide and annotated bibliography.

In chapter 1 you learned about evidence-based practice and sources for finding best practices to help your clients. This chapter extends that learning to specific situations and exemplar problems that you are likely to encounter during the internship. Specifically, this chapter provides guidelines for executing an Internet search to locate evidence-based practices for a specific problem you need information about.

Before conducting your Internet search, it is important to understand the evidence-based-practice model. Evidence-based practice is more than just applying researched interventions with your client. According to Mullen, Shlonsky, Bledsoe, and Bellamy (2005), employing the best-practice model requires the "synergistic combination of best evidence, client values and expectations, and the practitioner's clinical expertise" (p. 65). The integration of these three elements is illustrated in a model developed by Haynes, Devereaux, and Guyatt (2002), found in Figure 8.1 This evidence-based practice model shows how professional expertise is used to integrate: (1) the client's clinical state and individual circumstances;

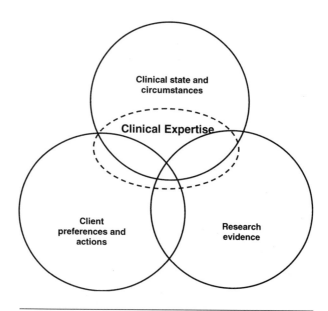

Figure 8.1 Evidence-Based Practice Model. *Source:* Mullen,
Shlonsky, Beldsoe, & Bellamy (2005, p. 65);
Haynes, Devereaux, & Guyatt (2002).

(2) the client's preferences, needs and values; and (3) the evidence from the
research. In this chapter you will not only learn the steps to finding empirical
literature and best practices but also how to apply research to your professional
decision making in identifying best practices for your client's specific needs.

Several researchers have suggested variations to the model shown in Figure 8.2
for systematically executing the search protocol while simultaneously integrating
the elements of the evidence-based practice model (Gibbs, 2003; Rosenberg &
Donald, 1995; Sackett, Rosenberg, Gray, Haynes, & Richardson, 1996; Sackett
et al., 2000). Following the step-by-step strategy detailed here, you can obtain
information about the prevalence and nature of the problem, about empirical
research, and about the efficacy of clinically tested interventions. Your knowledge
of the empirical literature will then inform professional decision making in
identifying the best practice for your client.

CASE SCENARIO

Alec is a 15-year-old Latino who has been referred to the Juvenile Assessment
Center after being arrested for aggravated assault on school personnel. He
threw a book at a guidance counselor, injuring her face. This is Alec's second

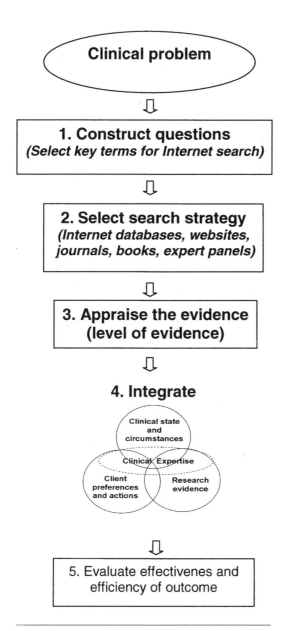

Figure 8.2 Steps to Finding Best Practice for
Clinical Problem

arrest for assault in the past 3 months. His first arrest was for physically assaulting another male adolescent in his neighborhood. Over the past 2 years,
Alec has had problems with truancy and excessive school suspensions, de-
struction of school property, frequent fighting, verbal aggression toward teachers, and stealing. He is in the eighth grade after having been retained in the

seventh grade. He is currently enrolled in the school's dropout prevention program. Alec has been diagnosed with attention- deficit/hyperactivity disorder (ADHD). Although he was once prescribed stimulant medication to treat ADHD, he has declined to take it for more than 1 year.

As reported by his mother and as evidenced by school records, Alec's defiant and aggressive behaviors have been escalating since he entered middle school. Alec's mother, who immigrated from Venezuela just before Alec's birth, states that she is very concerned about her son's behaviors. He repeatedly violates rules at home, refuses to do chores, comes home after curfew, steals money from her purse, and spends most of his time with older delinquent peers. He is physically aggressive toward his younger brother and verbally aggressive toward his mother. Currently, Alec's mother works two jobs and is solely responsible for the care of Alec and his 11-year-old brother. Alec has no contact with his father, who lives in Venezuela.

The preceding case scenario describes a Latino adolescent with conduct disorder, as evidenced by persistent aggression, rule violations, stealing, and truancy. He has been diagnosed with ADHD and, although he has previously taken medication for it, he has declined to take it for more than 1 year. The client's mother is supportive, but she works two jobs and is rarely home. With the objective of identifying best-practice interventions for this client, an Internet search protocol is described next.

STEP 1: DEFINE THE CLINICAL PROBLEM

Preliminary Search Questions

Before conducting your search, identify the nature of the clinical problem to be researched. Consider the following questions: Who is the client? What presenting problems and symptoms does the client identify? How does the problem affect overall functioning? What are the major cultural, socioeconomic, environmental, and family factors? Formulate preliminary search terms and enter them into the search engine most likely to produce relevant and reliable results.

In the case scenario of Alec, the problem may be identified as a Latino adolescent who demonstrates physical and verbal aggression, stealing, truancy, defiance of authority, frequent fighting, and school suspensions. To gather preliminary information about the clinical problem, the following search terms were entered into the Google (http://www.google.com) search engine: *adolescent aggression truancy stealing.* The first result was a link to a document on the National Criminal Justice Reference Service website (http://www.ncjrs.org/html/ojjdp/jjbul9712-2/jjb1297b.html). This article provides a theoretical overview, as well as results of an empirical study, of adolescent behavior problems, juvenile delinquency, and developmental pathways to disruptive behaviors in youths. This article is helpful in more clearly defining Alec's clinical problem as conduct disorder. Other useful websites for exploring clinical problems include: Psychology Net (http://www.psychologynet.org), the National Institute of Mental Health (http://www.nimh.nih.gov), and the Centers for Disease Control (http://www.cdc.gov).

Evidence-Based Assessment Tools

Another way to integrate evidence-based practice into your profession is to use evidence-based assessment tools to measure the presence and/or severity of a client's problem. The client; client's parent, spouse, or other family member; client's teacher; or the practitioner typically completes such research-developed, standardized assessment tools. Measurements vary in length and format, but most are relatively short scales, which can be scored by the practitioner to determine the presence or absence of symptoms (behaviors, moods, and feelings) related to the presenting problem.

For example, the Conners's Rating Scale (Conners, 1997) measures attention-deficit and hyperactivity disorders and related symptoms in children. This may also be a useful tool for determining whether Alec meets the diagnostic criteria for ADHD. Before using any standardized measure, be sure you are familiar with it before you administer it and that it is appropriate to be used with your client. (We cover this more fully in chapter 13.) Check with your supervisor to learn which standardized measures are commonly utilized in your practice setting. To research available measurements for specific problems, see the *Mental Measurements Yearbook* (http://www.unl.edu/buros/bimm/html/subarts.html), which provides a wealth of searchable measures used in the social sciences and which is updated every 6 months.

Standardized measures are also used to evaluate the outcomes of interventions by measuring client's symptomatology before and/or after their participation in the intervention. It is important to note that standardized measures demonstrate varying degrees of validity and reliability. An instrument is valid to the extent that it measures what it is designed to measure and accurately performs the function(s) it is purported to perform. Reliability has to do with the quality of measurement. In its everyday sense, reliability is the "consistency" or "repeatability" of your measures. In scientific investigations, the use of valid and reliable testing instruments improves the methodology of the study, thus making the results more accurate. For a useful Internet resource guide to research methods in the social sciences, visit the University of Miami Library website (http://www.library.miami .edu/netguides/psymeth.html).

STEP 2: CONSTRUCT GOOD QUESTIONS

Once you have clearly defined the clinical problem, prepare questions about the problem and corresponding interventions, as well as the outcomes of different treatment options. This provides a framework for the evidence-based literature search. Good questions are action-oriented, clear, and concise. Formulate questions about: (1) symptoms of conduct disorder and ADHD; (2) client factors (e.g., age, gender, and ethnicity); (3) family factors (e.g., socioeconomic status, family constellation, family dynamics); (4) environmental factors (e.g., school environment, peer influence, available resources); (5) interventions (e.g., family, individual, and group interventions, mental health and juvenile justice settings). Gibbs (2003) identifies five types of questions practitioners should gather information on: descriptive, risk factors, assessment, effectiveness, and prevention.

Descriptive questions:
1. What are the prevalence, incidence, and age of onset of conduct disorder? Of ADHD?
2. What sociocultural and socioeconomic factors are related?
3. What are the causes of or factors that contribute to the onset of conduct disorder? of ADHD?
4. How do symptoms of conduct disorder and ADHD affect social, emotional, and academic functioning in adolescents?

Risk-factor questions:
1. What risk factors are associated with the onset and persistence of conduct disorder? Of ADHD?
2. Does the empirical literature identify individual, family, social, and environmental protective factors that significantly reduce risk of conduct disorder? Of ADHD?

Assessment questions:
1. What are the diagnostic criteria for conduct disorder? For ADHD?
2. Which rapid assessment tools can be used to accurately diagnose Alec with these disorders? Which are the most reliable and valid?
3. Who should complete these measures for the most reliable and valid results?

4. Are there other presenting symptoms that should be further explored, such as learning problems or depressive symptoms?

Effectiveness questions:

1. For Latino adolescent males, which interventions demonstrate the best evidence for reducing conduct disorder behaviors, specifically physical and verbal aggression, truancy, and stealing?
2. What is the best available evidence about family, individual and group interventions? Have empirical studies been conducted to compare these different types of interventions?
3. Are specific interventions more efficacious for Latino youths?
4. What are the best practice interventions designed to treat ADHD in adolescents?
5. Have psychotropic medications been found to effectively treat ADHD? Is the efficacy of medication treatment increased when combined with other interventions?

Prevention questions:

1. What factors are associated with the probability that Alec's behaviors may continue to increase in severity?
2. What protective factors (individual, family, social, and environmental) might prevent his negative behaviors from recurring?
3. What education and support will Alec's mother, school personnel, and others in the community need to support Alec's reduction of conduct disorder behaviors and problems associated with ADHD?

STEP 3: SELECT A SEARCH STRATEGY

With so many resources available on the Internet, it is important to develop a search strategy that will produce the most accurate, evidence-based answers to the questions you have formulated. You must not only devise appropriate search terms but also identify the databases and reference sources that will produce the most accurate, timely information.

Model Programs

Prioritize resources that provide information on the current best practices in the field. Several government agencies and research groups have systematically reviewed the available evidence and developed a classification system to identify best practices, based on levels of empirical evidence. First, explore resources that identify model programs and best practices, such as the Office of Juvenile Justice Delinquency Prevention (OJJDP; http://www.ojjdp.gov), the Substance Abuse and Mental Health Services Administration (SAMHSA; http://www.samhsa.gov), the Administration for Children and Families (ADF; http://nccanch.acf.hhs.gov/profess/promising/index.cfm), and the Society of Clinical Child and Adolescent Psychology (SCCAP; http://www.effectivechildtherapy.com).

For example, go to the OJJDP website and, from the Programs menu, select Model Programs. You are given the option to enter several criteria to find a model program that would be most readily aligned with Alec's needs. Enter his age, ethnicity, community setting, and other variables to search for best practices identified by OJJDP. Or utilize the website's search tool, entering terms such as *conduct disorder, Latino youth, Hispanic males, ADHD, model programs.*

Systematic Reviews

You may also choose to search for systematic reviews, as well as meta-analyses, conducted by researchers to synthesize the available evidence and report the findings of several outcome studies that address the same problem. These reviews offer a thorough synthesis of the intervention literature, giving you the opportunity to evaluate the outcomes of several studies and gather information on which types of interventions are most effective for a specific population. On-line resources that publish systematic reviews and meta-analyses with a strict evidence-based protocol include the Cochrane Collaboration (http://www.cochrane.org), the Campbell Collaboration (http://www.campbellcollaboration.org), and the Campbell Crime and Justice Coordinating Group (http://www.aic.gov.au/campbellcj). For example, on the latter website, users may click on the Systematic Reviews menu to browse titles of recently published materials. Several reviews of juvenile delinquency programs are available on this site.

You can also search for systematic reviews using academic databases, which should be available through your university library's subscription, such as: Psyc-INFO, Sociological Abstracts, Social Work Abstracts, Criminal Justice Abstracts, Criminology: A SAGE Full-Text Collection, MEDLINE, and PubMed. The most useful way to search these databases is using retrieval systems, such as Cambridge Scientific Abstracts (http://www.csa.com), Ovid (http://www.ovid.com), and Proquest (http://www.proquest.umi.com). Not only are these retrieval systems designed to produce more accurate searches, but they also allow you to search several databases simultaneously.

In researching interventions for Alec's presenting problem, using Cambridge Scientific Abstracts retrieval system, the following databases were selected: Psyc-INFO, Sociological Abstracts, and Criminology. The terms were first entered to be searched for anywhere in the document; they were then entered to be searched for only as keywords. Note how this seemingly minor change dramatically narrowed the search. The search results are listed in Table 8.1.

Outcome Studies

You may also want to explore primary research by searching for the findings from clinically tested interventions, known as outcome studies. To locate outcome studies, you will need to search many online databases. It is highly recommended that you access only reputable clearinghouses or academic databases, such as those listed earlier, to ensure that the outcome studies use sound methodology and data analysis strategies. Utilize the levels of evidence in Table 8.2 to evaluate the research methods and empirical data reported in outcome studies. In addition to academic databases, the following websites are good resources for reports of empirical studies: National Criminal Justice Reference Service (http://www.ncjrs.org), the Cochrane Collaborative, and the Campbell Collaborative.

Other Levels of Evidence

You may not be able to find systematic reviews or clinical trials of interventions that address the problem you are researching. In fact, many social and clinical problems have not been rigorously researched. In this case, you may rely on lesser degrees of scientific evidence, such as quasi-experimental designs (studies with no control group), expert consensus guidelines, pilot studies, surveys, and qualitative

Table 8.1 Search Results Using Cambridge Scientific Abstracts Retrieval System and PsycINFO, Sociological Abstracts, and Criminology Databases

		Results	
Search #	Search Terms	Anywhere	Keyword
1	conduct disorder	7,338	3,382
2	conduct disorder AND attention-deficit/ hyperactivity disorder	1,789	574
3	conduct disorder AND systematic review OR meta-analysis	1,314	13
4	conduct disorder AND attention-deficit/ hyperactivity disorder AND systematic review OR meta-analysis	468	4
5	Conduct disorder AND Latino OR Hispanic AND systematic review OR meta-analysis	147	0

Table 8.2 Levels of Evidence

Level 1. Meta-analyses/systematic reviews
- Positive evidence from more than one meta-analysis of randomized clinical trial.
- Positive evidence from more than two randomized clinical trials.

Level 2. Randomized controlled trials (RCT)
- Positive evidence from at least one RCT with placebo or comparison condition.
- Positive evidence from more than two quasi experimental studies.

Level 3. Comparative studies or observational study
- Positive evidence from comparative studies, correlation studies, and case-control and cohort studies. Pre-experimental group studies (no control groups; posttest only).
- Surveys and expert consensus reports.

Level 4. Qualitative studies
- Anecdotal case reports, case studies, single-subject designs

Source: Thomlison & Jacobs, 2006.

studies. Although the results of these studies are not as readily generalizable to all clients, they may have a sound theoretical basis and present some promising intervention strategies. To search for these types of studies, broaden your search of the academic databases. For example, use search terms such as *intervention strategies* or *qualitative studies*. A useful site through which to find expert consensus guidelines is http://www.psychguides.com.

Restricting and Broadening Your Search

Searching for empirical studies can be challenging. It is important to formulate good search terms, using Boolean operators (such as AND, OR, and NOT) to refine your search. Use AND and NOT to *restrict* your search and OR to *broaden* it. The term OR is useful when several terms have similar meanings. For instance, using Cambridge Scientific Abstracts to retrieve articles from the PsycInfo database, use the Advanced Search option, enter *outcome studies OR clinical trials AND conduct disorder AND Hispanic OR Latino.* Using the retrieval system Cambridge Scientific Abstracts to search PsychInfo, this search produced 11 publications, 6 of which were peer-reviewed journal articles. You may broaden the search by looking for terms anywhere in the document or restrict the search by identifying the search terms as keywords or as terms in the article's title or abstract. Some retrieval systems offer the option of selecting publication type, by which you may further restrict your search to clinical trials, literature reviews, peer-reviewed journals, and so forth.

Journal Articles and Conference Presentations

Editors of professional journals employ varying degrees of rigor in selecting and editing articles for publication. Prioritize searching among articles published in peer-reviewed or refereed journals to obtain data on best practices. You can investigate the publication's guidelines by visiting the websites of the publishers, such as Sage Publications (http://www.sagepublications.com) and Haworth Press (http://www.haworthpress.com). It is a good idea to become familiar with the peer-reviewed journals in your field. The journals mentioned in chapter 1 have excellent records for publishing evidence-based practices and reviews.

Researchers often present findings of their research at academic conferences. Given that journal publication is a lengthy process, conference presentations may provide more current information that has not yet been disseminated. If you locate a link to a conference presentation, be sure to check the professional organization that sponsored the conference and the date of presentation. You should also become familiar with professional organizations associated with your field, such as the National Association of Social Workers, the Society for Social Work Research, the American Society of Criminology, and the American Psychological Association.

STEP 4: APPRAISE THE EVIDENCE

Once you have located research about the problem, critically appraise the empirical evidence using the following five elements (Thomlison & Jacobs, 2006):

1. Theoretical basis: Is it sound, novel, reasonable?
2. Clinical or anecdotal literature: Is it substantial or limited?
3. General acceptance or use in clinical practice: Is it widely used or pilot tested?
4. Risk: Is it possible that the risks outweigh the benefits?
5. Level of empirical support: What is the level of scientific rigor applied to the intervention research? Empirical studies range from high levels of empirical support (e.g., positive evidence from randomized controlled trials) to lower degrees of support (e.g., positive outcomes of a single case study)

depending on the research methodology employed and the validity and reliability of the results.

See the following list for levels of evidence and example search strategies:

Level 1: Meta-Analyses/Systematic Reviews
- Positive evidence from more than one meta-analysis of randomized clinical trials
- Positive evidence from more than two randomized clinical trials
- Example search terms: *systematic OR quantitative OR evidence OR trial AND review OR meta-analysis AND conduct disorder*

Level 2: Randomized Controlled Trials (RCT)
- Positive evidence from at least one RCT with placebo or comparison condition
- Positive evidence from more than two quasi-experimental studies
- Example search terms: *randomized clinical controlled trial OR controlled clinical trial OR clinical trial AND conduct disorder*

Level 3: Comparative Studies or Observational Studies
- Positive evidence from comparative studies, correlation studies, case-control, cohort studies, preexperimental group studies (no control group, posttest only)
- Surveys and consensus reports
- Example search terms: *comparative study OR cases OR review AND conduct disorder*

Level 4: Qualitative Studies and Single-Subject Design
- Positive evidence from anecdotal case report, qualitative study, case study, or single-subject design
- Example search terms: *case study OR qualitative study OR single subject AND conduct disorder*

Once you have reviewed the research and appraised the available evidence, you may have identified the best practice intervention with which to address the clinical problem. However, your client will rarely match the clients in a research study exactly. For instance, Alec might live in a different type of community than the research participants or have unique life experiences. Alec and his mother might have their own unique belief systems, values, cultural norms, and family dynamics, as well as preferences and expectations for treatment. Before selecting the intervention, the practitioner must not only appraise the available evidence but also integrate the client's state and circumstances, preferences, and willingness to engage in treatment.

STEP 5: INTEGRATE

We do not live in a perfect world in which every best practice matches every client. Therefore, the practitioner must integrate relevant scientific information, strengths, needs, and preferences of the client and assess the "goodness of fit" of the intervention, using professional knowledge and skills (Howard, McMillen, & Pollio, 2003; Thomlison & Jacobs, in press). Using the evidence-based practice model in Figure 8.1, apply not only your own clinical expertise but also that of your supervisor and professional colleagues to integrate: (1) clinical state and circumstances; (2) client preferences, values, and actions; and (3) research evidence (Haynes et al., 2002).

Clinical State and Circumstances

Begin by assessing the client's strengths and personal goals and the outcomes he or she expects from treatment. Evaluate the appropriateness of the intervention, considering the client's specific problem and current situation and socioeconomic, cultural, and other contextual factors. Provide the client with information about the clinical problem, available resources, and interventions. The geographic location and type of setting of the agency where the intervention is available, as well as the duration of treatment and associated expenses, might affect the client's decision to participate. Discuss the potential risks, benefits, and costs thoroughly with the client, as well as any other individuals who may participate, to help him, her, or them make an informed decision.

Research Evidence

As stated earlier, appraise the level of scientific evidence to support the intervention. Consider how closely the study's population matches the client's clinical problem, as well as individual, family, and sociocultural characteristics. Remember, not all interventions can be applied across cultures, settings, and communities.

Client Preferences, Values, and Actions

It is of the utmost importance for the practitioner to carefully consider the client's cultural norms, values, beliefs, and expectations before selecting an intervention. Issues such as socioeconomic status, language barriers, religious beliefs, and other sociocultural factors may affect the client's desire to engage in certain types of treatment. Based on cultural values and norms, as well as prior negative experiences, the client may be mistrusting of mental health professionals. This mistrust could cause the client to be uncomfortable in a clinical setting or hesitant to accept medication treatments. Explore with the client his or her personal preferences and expectations for treatment, including (1) setting; (2) practitioner characteristics; (3) treatment modalities; (4) length of treatment; and (5) desired outcomes. The client's right to self-determination should always be highly regarded by the practitioner.

For example, Alec's mother may state that she does not wish to attend a parent support and education group for delinquent youths, despite information from the practitioner about its effectiveness. After further inquiry, however, the practitioner learns that Alec's mother is not resistant to treatment but is uncomfortable in a group setting because she is not confident in her English-speaking skills. Moreover, she cannot afford child care for her youngest son during group meetings. The practitioner can then explore intervention alternatives or solutions to these barriers with Alec's mother.

STEP 6: EVALUATE

Once you have identified and located the most appropriate evidence-based practice for your client, it is essential to follow up regularly with the agency or practitioners who provide treatment, as well as with your client. Assessment of clients' clinical problems, preferences, and needs is an ongoing process. Practitioners who provide best-available practice interventions should use valid, reliable, and culturally sensitive measurement tools to: (1) assess the nature and severity of the client's problem at intake; (2) monitor the client's progress and improvements or relapses of the problem throughout the course of the intervention; and (3) evaluate the maintenance of progress or recurrence of the problem at follow-up intervals following completion of treatment. The frequency of evaluation depends on the length of treatment and measurements used, but it should be specified prior to implementation of the intervention. Ongoing evaluation of client outcomes provides a means to accurately assess the effectiveness of the intervention.

In addition to measuring the client's clinical treatment progress, the practitioner should solicit feedback from clients regularly to ensure that their needs are effectively being met by the intervention. Clients' needs and preferences change over time and are largely dependent on changes in circumstances, unanticipated events, and the client's responses to intervention strategies and treatment providers. Some helpful questions to ask clients include:

1. How has the intervention worked?
2. Are you comfortable in the treatment setting?
3. Are your treatment goals consistent with the treatment provider's perceptions of your needs?
4. What are the costs and benefits to you as the client?
5. What is your assessment of your treatment progress?
6. What are the most beneficial aspects of the intervention?
7. What improvements would make the intervention more effective for you?

Feedback from the client's family members, spouse, teachers, and others should also be sought whenever appropriate.

It is the practitioner's responsibility to initiate a "feedback loop" in which the input of the client, the treatment provider, the practitioner, and other relevant persons contribute to a comprehensive evaluation of the appropriateness and efficacy of the intervention on an ongoing basis. If at any time the intervention no longer meets the needs and preferences of the client or is presenting an unforeseen risk, the practitioner should facilitate collaborative decision making about alternatives for the client. Adjustments are made to the intervention.

BRINGING RESEARCH TO PRACTICE

In the social sciences, evidence-based practice comes together with the successful integration of empirical data, client needs, and practitioner expertise. The practitioner plays an important role in bringing research into practice through: (1) the use of evidence-based assessment tools and clinical assessment skills, (2) critical appraisal of the available interventions, (3) unbiased evaluation of the client's strengths, needs, preferences, and expected outcomes; and (4) sound professional judgment. Bringing research into practice is a process that ensures that clients receive the best available intervention to most readily meet their individual needs. It is important to note that professional judgment and ethics should always include a commitment to staying apprised of the most current research in your field, as well as respect for the client's right to self-determination.

RESOURCE GUIDE AND ANNOTATED BIBLIOGRAPHY

The following websites are helpful resources in searching for evidence-based practice in the social services. This list is in no way exhaustive but is meant to serve as a guide.

Government-Sponsored Sites

1. Administration for Children and Families: National Clearinghouse of Child Abuse and Neglect Gateways to Information: Strengthening Families and Protecting Children: http://www.nccanch.afc.hhs.gov

   This website is a service of the Children's Bureau, Administration for Children and Families, U.S. Department of Health and Human Services. It provides practical, timely, and essential information on programs, research, legislation, and statistics related to the safety, permanency, and well-being of children and families.

2. Centers for Disease Control and Prevention (CDC): http://www.cdc.gov

   This site provides information on health topics, data and statistics, and current health concerns and provides many links to research reports and specialty websites on health and mental health issues.

3. Office of Juvenile Justice Delinquency Prevention (OJJDP) Model Programs Guide: http://www.ojjdp.gov

   This website profiles more than 175 prevention and intervention programs that can be searched by program category, target population, risk and protective factors, effectiveness rating, and other parameters.

4. National Criminal Justice Reference Service Library (NCJRS): http://www.ojjdp.gov/publications/ncjrslibrary.html; http://www.ncjrs.org

   Administered through OJJDP, these websites offer justice and substance abuse information to support research, policy, and program development worldwide. The abstracts database provides criminal and substance abuse information, in addition to information related to juvenile justice. The database contains summaries of more than 170,000 publications.

5. National Institute on Drug Abuse (NIDA): Clinical Trials Network: http://www.nida.nih.gov/CTN/Index.htm

   This U.S. institute website provides information about drug-abuse-related research studies and contact information for regional research "nodes" that are currently carrying out studies and training related to research-based practice.

6. National Institute of Mental Health (NIMH): http://www.nimh.nih.gov

   This federal institute website provides information on current biomedical research, the brain, mental health, and behavior, and related clinical studies, as well as information about current government-funded research projects.

7. Substance Abuse and Mental Health Services Administration (SAMHSA) and Center for Substance Abuse Prevention (CSAP): Model Programs and National Registry of Effective Programs: http://www.samhsa.gov/index .aspx; http://modelprograms.samhsa.gov/template.cfm?page=default

    These websites provide information about substance abuse and mental health programs tested in communities, schools, social service organizations, and workplaces in the United States. Nominated programs are reviewed by research teams who rate the programs primarily on methodological quality but also consider other factors, such as theoretical development and community involvement. Programs are rated in increasing order of quality as either *promising, effective,* or *model.*

Nonprofit Organizations, Research Groups, and Other Helpful Sites

1. American Academy of Child and Adolescent Psychiatry: http://www .aacap.org

    This site provides information on the treatment of developmental, behavioral, and mental disorders in children and adolescents, current research, practice guidelines, and much more.

2. Campbell Collaboration Library and Database: http://www.campbell collaboration.org

    This website posts a searchable database of randomized controlled clinical trials and systematic reviews of social, psychological, educational, and criminological research. All research presented on the website has met rigorous methodological standards. The site is designed to provide researchers, policy makers, and practitioners with critical reviews of current research.

3. Campbell Crime and Justice Coordinating Group: http://www.aic.gov .au/campbellcj

    Hosted by the Australian Institute of Criminology, this group is an international network that prepares updates and disseminates systematic reviews of high-quality research conducted worldwide on effective methods for reducing crime and delinquency or improving justice.

4. Centre for Reviews and Dissemination: Database of Abstracts of Reviews of Effects (DARE) at the University of York: http://www.york.ac.uk/inst/ crd/darefaq.htm

    This site contains summaries of systematic reviews that have met strict quality criteria. Each summary provides a critical commentary on the quality of the review. The database covers a broad range of health and social care topics.

5. Cochrane Collaboration : http://www.cochrane.org

   This is an international not-for-profit organization that provides up-to-date information about the effects of health care. This group produces and disseminates systematic reviews of health care interventions and promotes the search for evidence in the form of clinical trials and other studies of interventions.

6. Expert Consensus Guideline Series: http://www.psychguides.com

   This website provides practical clinical recommendations based on wide surveys of expert opinion. Users can search expert consensus-based practice guidelines.

7. *Mental Measurements Yearbook:* http://www.unl.edu/buros/bimm/html/subarts.html

   Developed through the Buros Institute of Mental Measurements, this site provides the most up-to-date information about clinical assessment and measurement tools used in research with human participants.

8. Psychology Net: http://psychologynet.org

   This site provides information on clinical diagnostic criteria (DSM-IV diagnoses), diagnostic tools, and other information related to psychological disorders.

9. Society of Child and Adolescent Psychology and Network on Youth Mental Health, http://www.effectivechildtherapy.com

   This site provides up-to-date information about evidence-based mental health practice for children and adolescents. Treatments listed here have been evaluated scientifically for efficacy and are updated as new treatment research is completed.

10. University of Miami Library—Research Methods in the Social Sciences: An Internet Resource Guide: http://www.library.miami.edu/netguides/psymeth.html

    This is a very helpful Internet resource guide that provides links to websites related to scientific research methods, instruments, and outcomes in the social sciences.

Academic Databases

The following databases should be available through your university library subscription. You can also access them directly or search them using a retrieval system listed in the next section.

1. Criminal Justice Abstracts: http://www.sagepub.com/journal.aspx?pid=253
   This database contains hundreds of in-depth abstracts of current books, book chapters, journal articles, government reports, and dissertations published worldwide related to the field of criminal justice.

2. PubMed Clinical Queries Database: http://www.ncbi.nlm.nih.gov/entrez/query/static/clinical.shtml
   Provided by the National Institute of Health (NIH), this site contains over 14 million literature citations, including options to search clinical trials and systematic reviews.

3. PsycINFO: http://www.psycinfo.com
   This electronic bibliographic database provides thousands of abstracts and citations to the scholarly literature in the behavioral sciences and mental health.

4. Social Work Abstracts: http://www.naswpress.org/publications/journals/abstracts/swabintro.html
   This collection is hosted by the National Association for Social Workers and includes abstracts from more than 400 international and domestic academic journals. You can access empirical research on social welfare, crime, psychology, child welfare, mental health, health care, substance abuse, and public health.

Resource Retrieval Services

The following data retrieval systems let you search several databases simultaneously while also linking you to full-text articles and electronic resources.

1. Cambridge Scientific Abstracts: http://www.csa.com
   This search retrieval system specializes in publishing and distributing 100 bibliographic and full-text databases and journals in four primary editorial areas: natural sciences, social sciences, arts and humanities, and technology.

2. Ovid: http://www.ovid.com
   This system provides platforms (Ovid and SilverPlatter) to access 1,200 journals, more than 160 books, and more than 300 databases, with specialized services for browsing, searching, and retrieving research.

3. ProQuest: http://www.proquest.com
   This service allows you to access thousands of current periodicals and newspapers, many updated daily and containing full-text articles from 1986.

ASSERTIVE COMMUNITY TREATMENT FOR A PERSON WITH SEVERE AND PERSISTENT MENTAL ILLNESS

Victoria Stanhope and Phyllis Solomon

Case Description

John was a single 39-year-old African American man suffering from severe mental illness. He had a psychiatric diagnosis of schizoaffective disorder and alcohol dependence. He also had Type II diabetes. John was homeless, with virtually no support in the community. He had a brother who lived in the vicinity, but the brother felt "burned out" by John's behavior and was reluctant to assist him. John also had a 12-year-old son whom he occasionally visited. John was not receiving welfare or medical assistance. He survived by going to food programs and staying in shelters when the weather was severe. Occasionally he got work as a casual laborer on construction sites. John's contact with the criminal system had been minimal. He had developed good survival skills on the street, managing to keep to himself and stay away from trouble.

He first presented to the city community mental health system 9 years ago when he was hospitalized after a psychotic episode. Since that time John has had multiple hospitalizations and several stays in inpatient rehabilitation treatment programs for his alcohol dependence. On discharge from inpatient hospitalization, John was often referred to outpatient services, including partial hospitalization, supported housing, and case management, but he consistently dropped out of these services after a few weeks. He had a prolonged history of homelessness, staying intermittently in the shelters but spending the majority of his time living on the streets. John was a classic example of a "revolving door" consumer, who comes into the system through acute psychiatric hospitalization only to return to life back on the streets without treatment.

Assessment/Screening and Problem Identification

Initially, John was referred to intensive case-management services during his most recent hospitalization on an acute psychiatric facility. Intensive case management involves many of the tasks of traditional case management, such as assessment, service planning, linking to services, monitoring service provision, and advocacy, but it increases the intensity of service provision by lowering staff-consumer ratios, emphasizing assertive outreach and service provision in the community, and providing assistance with activities of daily living (Bond, Drake, Mueser, & Latimer, 2001). An intensive case manager (ICM) is expected to make at least two contacts a month with the consumer.

After several meetings with the student intern, John eventually agreed to services, and the ICM completed an intake interview while John was still in the hospital. He had already had a psychiatric evaluation, a psychosocial assessment, a Global Assessment of Functioning (Jones, Thornicroft, Coffey, & Dunn, 1995), and a medical examination as part of his inpatient treatment. The case manager completed opening paperwork, which included the Medical Outcomes Study Survey (SF-12; Salyers, Bosworth, Swanson, Lamb-Pagone, & Osher, 2000), and initiated a treatment plan with John. The immediate goals of the treatment plan were for John to attend outpatient services, to seek treatment for his diabetes, and to apply for welfare and medical assistance. The case manager also attended a treatment meeting in the hospital with John's psychiatrist, nurse, and social worker as part of the discharge planning. The treatment team referred John to a group home facility and a partial hospitalization program.

However, shortly after discharge, John left the group home and stopped attending the partial hospitalization program, as well as other outpatient services. The ICM attempted to stay in contact with John but soon lost track of him. Periodically, the ICM would check the shelters, contact John's brother, and search in the parts of town that John was known to frequent. However, with a caseload of more than 20 other consumers, many in crisis situations, it was difficult for the ICM to take the time necessary to find John. At team meetings, the ICM discussed the difficulties of John's case and frustration with not being able to engage him in services.

Intervention Selection

The ICM supervisor reviewed John's case with the ICM, and they discussed the possibility of closing his case, as the ICM had been unable to reestablish contact with him. As they discussed the case, it became clear that John's case required more assertive outreach efforts than was possible for an ICM, given the size of ICM caseloads. The ICM supervisor, therefore, recommended that the ICM refer John to a more intensive type of treatment: assertive community treatment (ACT).

The ACT model is based on the key principles of multidisciplinary staffing, integration of services, team approach, low staff-consumer ratios, locus of contact in the community, medication management, focus on everyday problems in living, rapid access, assertive outreach, individualized services, and time-unlimited services (Bond et al., 2001). The multidisciplinary ACT team consisted of 10 staff members, including a psychiatrist, nurse, social worker, case manager, consumer case manager (Dixon, Krauss, & Lehman, 1994), vocational rehabilitation specialist, and substance abuse counselor. The team shares the caseload, with a staff-consumer ratio of 1 to 10, and provides coverage 7 days a week, 24 hours a day. As opposed to linking consumers to services, the team provides an array of individualized services, including treatment, rehabilitation, substance abuse treatment, social services, assistance with daily activities, and family services. The services are delivered in vivo, with case managers spending up to 80% of their time in the community with consumers. Medication management is a priority for the model, with an emphasis on effective use of medications, including appropriate diagnosis, choice of medication, and managing of side effects. The 24/7 availability of a multidisciplinary model is also designed to allow rapid response to consumer crises and flexibility in service provision.

ACT has been the subject of extensive research studies since its inception in the 1970s (Bond et al., 2001). These research studies consistently demonstrated that ACT was successful in reducing hospitalization and led to ACT being identified as one of the few evidence-based practices for persons with severe mental illness (U.S. Department of Health and Human Services, 2003). As a result, the federal government (see www.mentalhealthpractices.org) and advocacy groups such as the National Alliance for the Mentally Ill (see http://www.nami.org), have been disseminating information on ACT to policy makers, providers, and consumers. These efforts led to mental health funds being made available at the local level to encourage agencies to implement the ACT model. The agency serving John had successfully applied for these funds and had established three ACT teams as part of its case management program.

Intervention/Treatment

On receiving the referral, the first task for the ACT team was to locate John and attempt to engage him in services by building a relationship with him. The small caseload allowed the team members to be more persistent in finding John, and when they located him, a team member visited him almost every day to build rapport and establish trust. In addition to assisting John by providing food and clean clothes, the team was also able to offer him a subsidized apartment, a resource they often used to engage homeless consumers in services. Once John had initially agreed to work with the ACT team, they began collaborating with John to develop a treatment plan. Together, they came up with goals that both parties could agree on and specified concrete tasks to be completed by John and the team. The most difficult part of the negotiation was getting John to agree to the team becoming his representative payee, which meant that they would receive his benefits directly and monitor his finances. Being John's representative payee enabled the team to ensure that his rent was paid and also to restrict the money he had available for alcohol. However, this arrangement caused tension between the team and John.

Once John's basic needs were met, he became more open to receiving mental health services, primarily because they would be provided by members of the team, which included a psychiatrist, a nurse, and a social worker, people he had come to know and trust. The flexibility and immediacy of the services meant that there was less opportunity for John to miss an appointment or "fall through the cracks." The team carefully monitored his medication, visiting with him every day to ensure that he had taken his medication and to monitor possible side effects. The team also helped John set up appointments with a diabetes specialist and monitored his treatment regimen. The consumer case manager on the team began to work with John on his alcohol addiction and offered to accompany John to a community 12-step meeting. Although John did start to attend meetings, he suffered several relapses in his drinking, on one occasion even abandoning his apartment to return to the streets. The team worked with the landlord to prevent John's eviction and, after a time, were able to persuade him back into housing. Gradually John stabilized, and he was able to maintain longer periods of sobriety. With help from the team, John began to rebuild his relationships with his brother and his son, and he took great pride in inviting them to his apartment, which reinforced him in maintaining his apartment.

Evaluation

Six months after John had entered the program, the team met with John to review his case. On reviewing his treatment plan, the team assessed his progress in the following domains: mental health, substance abuse, physical health, housing, financial, vocational, and social support. In each of these domains, John had made significant progress: he was engaged with the team and taking his medication; he was maintaining periods of sobriety and had attended some 12-step meetings; he was treating his diabetes; he had maintained his housing; he was receiving public assistance; and he was in contact with his family. John's progress was also measured by the Global Assessment Functioning scale and the Medical Outcomes Study (SF-12), both of which reflected his improvement in the preceding 6 months. John and the team collaborated on his treatment plan for the following 6 months, the goals of which included John's taking more responsibility for his own care, consistently attending 12-step programs, and beginning to attend vocational rehabilitation services.

Discussion

The evidence on ACT has established the intervention's effectiveness in reducing hospitalization, whereas the research findings on other outcomes, such as quality of life, functioning, and symptom reduction, have been less definitive (Marshall & Lockwood, 1998). As the case study shows, the intensity of the model promotes engagement in services using a high level of control and monitoring of the consumer, which can be effective in the short term for consumers such as John, who are hard to engage. However, ACT has been criticized by the consumer movement for being too "paternalistic" and even "coercive" (Diamond, 1996). ACT does not set a time limit for the program, and consumers can receive this intensity of services indefinitely. The challenge for the model in John's case is to convert these short-term gains into long-term stability—to adjust the intensity of the model in order that John can take a more active role in his recovery.

■ ■ ■

Activities

Discussion questions for classroom, supervision, or peer supervision:

1. What factors led to John's engagement in services?

2. To what extent is ACT a consumer-centered model of care?

3. What are the advantages and disadvantages of consumers receiving ACT services indefinitely?

4. For what type of clients would you recommend ACT services?

5. Where do you see John in 20 years?

IDENTIFYING EVIDENCE-BASED PRACTICES FOR MENTAL HEALTH

DAN COLEMAN

As discussed in chapter 1, the most rigorous means of conducting evidence-based practice is by use of a treatment manual that has demonstrated efficacy in randomized controlled experiments. In many areas of practice, treatment manuals with varying degrees of research support are available. In a few practice areas there may be no manualized treatments, no systematic reviews of research evidence, and perhaps even little research of any kind. In these circumstances the practitioner will have to look for expert consensus guidelines and search for whatever literature may be available to marshal the best evidence available to guide treatment.

This chapter focuses on those areas of practice that have been subject to systematic reviews of the research literature. Manualized treatments exist in these areas, and the quality of the research evidence has been weighed in a systematic manner. The APA Division 12 (Clinical) systematic review task force labels research-supported treatments as "empirically supported treatments," which we are generally calling "evidence-based practices." In order to help you understand the process, this chapter discusses considerations in choosing an evidence-based intervention and training in that treatment. Case examples of clinicians training in such interventions illustrate this step-by-step process. The final sections list resources for finding systematic reviews that focus on your area of practice and provide ways to identify treatment manuals in your internship.

CONSIDERATIONS IN CHOOSING EMPIRICALLY SUPPORTED TREATMENTS

If asked to identify their theoretical orientations, most mental health clinicians would identify two or more theories that influence their work (Jensen, Bergin, & Greaves, 1990). Students are still in the process of forming an orientation and so are less likely to clearly identify one as their own. Theoretical orientation guides the way the clinician understands the client's difficulties and the process of helping, and each theory has associated techniques and a style of relating to the client. Norcross (1985) states that theoretical orientation serves "descriptive, explanatory, developmental and generative functions in clinical practice" (p. 14). Research on psychotherapy theories has shown that differences in theoretical orientation persist over time, even as eclecticism becomes more common (Coleman, 2004; Larson, 1980; Poznanski & McLennan,1995).

Theoretical orientation serves as a useful organizing metaphor for the series of training and practice experiences that are reflected in a clinician's areas of expertise. To say "I'm psychodynamic" or "I'm a Bowenian family therapist" reflects the accumulated effects of education, work experience, and postgraduate training. It is helpful, then, for interns to use their core and developing theoretical orientation, or core area of strengths, as a foundation for planning training in an empirically supported treatment. Choosing a treatment that accords with core theoretical orientation will ease the learning process and tap into your already well-developed skills. Some may need to "unlearn" techniques that do not fit with a given empirically supported intervention.

As noted before, it is important for supervisors and interns to remember that it is normal to be unsure of your own theoretical orientation. There are many experiences in the internship and in the classroom that may help you explore and clarify your theoretical orientation. An additional resource is the Theoretical Evaluation Self-Test (TEST), a scale of therapist theoretical orientation that gives immediate feedback on the test taker's theoretical orientation. It appears as the first exercise at the end of this chapter. It is also available in an interactive Web version or as a downloadable version that can be printed out (http://www.web .pdx.edu/~dcoleman/test.html).

The preliminary validation evidence for TEST is that it has been shown to help graduate students better understand the principal elements of the most prevalent theoretical orientations (Coleman, 2003, 2004). It may be helpful to discuss the results of the test with a supervisor or fellow trainees.

Although the early lists of evidence-based practices were dominated by behavioral and cognitive-behavioral treatments, theoretical diversity increasingly appears in the later catalogues. For some disorders, such as depression, a great variety of theoretical orientations exist, whereas with other disorders, such as most anxiety disorders, only behavioral and cognitive-behavioral treatments appear in the Division 12 list. This may reflect the fact that clinical trials of other approaches have not been done, that some other treatments have not had good results, or that the task force has not comprehensively reviewed the literature in that area (Chambless & Ollendick, 2001). I mention this in order to alert you to a limitation. I fear to say that, as an intern likely overwhelmed with new materials, you cannot conclude that a treatment has no empirical support just because it does not appear in a systematic review. That is, regardless of what list you locate of available evidence-based interventions, you cannot infer that other efficacious interventions aren't available somewhere else.

As a clinician and clinical supervisor in community mental health agencies for more than 12 years, I have observed the work of many people, both experienced practitioners and trainees. Although almost none used evidence-based practice in the form of manualized treatment, my impression was that most of the practitioners were effective most of the time. For a given clinician, effectiveness likely flows from the well-developed skills and understanding that can be captured in the clinician's theoretical orientation. It is logical, then, for clinicians to choose training in empirically supported treatments that match their core theoretical orientation. In this way a strong research-practice bridge is built: from the strengths of the practitioner to strengths in the research. Training and use of empirically supported treatments increase the likelihood that we will provide effective treatment to our clients. The next part focuses on some of the considerations in planning training in an empirically supported intervention.

In some areas of social service practice, such as services to delinquent youth or medical social work, theoretical orientation may be less immediately useful. Manualized interventions are less likely to exist. However, there is probably some outcome research that examines different interventions or techniques, and groups such as the Campbell Collaboration (http://www.campbellcollaboration.org) and the Cochrane Library (http://www.cochrane.org) may have done a systematic review of the research literature. Many of the considerations in choosing among the research-supported interventions and in training and implementing the interventions remain the same. For example, the practitioner will want to consider how a research-supported intervention matches his or her usual approach to practice, whether the clinical sample was similar to the particular client, how acceptable the treatment is to the client, and how likely the client is to comply with the intervention.

Students who work in corrections with adolescents or adults must consider several issues. One is whether the focus of the intervention is on the client's antisocial behavior itself or on co-occurring mental health or substance abuse disorders. Most of the research on interventions for antisocial behavior itself is focused on the program level rather than on treatments that could be implemented by a single practitioner. However, the description of successful programs provides much useful information to clinicians working with similar populations. Recent meta-analyses of adult and juvenile corrections programs found that most programs reduced recidivism and that cognitive-behavioral, behavioral, and interpersonal-skills interventions were part of successful programs (Lipsey & Wilson, 1998; Redondo, Sanchez-Meca, & Garrido, 1999). Lipsey and Wilson's (1998) meta-analysis of 83 residential treatment programs for juvenile offenders provides descriptions of some model programs.

For youths with antisocial behavior problems, multisystemic therapy (MST) is a set of interventions that has been operationalized in a manual and that has good clinical trial performance (Henggeler et al, 1998); see the case study by Jennifer Powers in chapter 15 in this volume. MST would be challenging for one or two clinicians to independently implement, as it is an intensive package of several treatments, but its robust research performance with complex, multiproblem youths and families suggest it is worth consideration.

For the treatment of mental health or substance abuse problems in corrections-involved youths or adults, the manualized treatments specific to these disorders may be appropriate. The adjustments needed to fit the treatment to specific clients should be researched and discussed with your supervisor and other experienced professionals.

COMPLEXITIES OF TRAINING

There are several areas of ambiguity about training in an evidence-based treatment in your internship and after graduation. Some therapy manuals have been published as widely available books that detail such methods as interpersonal therapy (IPT; Klerman, Weissman, Rounsaville, & Chevron, 1999); cognitive-behavioral therapy (CBT; Beck, 1995); and dialectical behavior therapy (DBT; Linehan, 1993), among others. The presence of these books on the shelves of university bookstores suggests that training is as simple as purchasing the book, reading it, and applying it in practice. This is somewhat true, and it is hoped that you are among those acquiring new skills with self-directed learning. To facilitate this learning, a self-guided pathway is described in Table 9.1.

It is unknown at what rate clinicians and interns who undergo this type of self-directed learning actually achieve a reasonable level of adherence (or fidelity) to the manualized interventions. In other words, it is unknown whether they are actually practicing the therapy described in the manual. This is an important area of focus for dissemination research. Whatever the results of future research, we know that interns and clinicians will independently buy and read these texts and attempt to apply what they learn to their mental health practices. Most authors

Table 9.1 Steps for Increasing the Research Support of Practice[1]

Step	Task
Step 1.	Select an empirically supported treatment (EST) that accords with your core theoretical orientation and that is directed toward a frequently encountered clinical problem.
Step 2.	Develop a program of training in the EST. *Self-guided:* Engage in self-study and self-supervision using EST manual; use appropriate pre- and postmeasures. *Intermediate:* Add as many elements of formal training as feasible: supervision, taping of sessions, adherence measures, and so on. *Formal training:* Follow training protocol of original studies of EST, typically involving didactic learning, supervised practice, taping of sessions, and observer ratings of treatment adherence.

[1]See the exercise at the end of the chapter to help you with this process.

who discuss this use of treatment manuals are optimistic that a clinician engaged in self-guided training can learn to deliver the treatment as intended (Luborsky, 1993; Mufson, Dorta, Moreau, & Weissman, 2004).

At the opposite end of the spectrum from self-guided study and self-supervision is training that follows the protocol used to direct the clinician in the clinical trials of the evidence-based intervention. Table 9.1 shows what is involved in formal training programs in these types of evidence-based interventions. The training for clinical trials typically includes didactic learning, individual and/or group super-supervision, video or audio recording of sessions for review in supervision, and some structured adherence rating. Naturally, clinical trials also include measures of treatment outcome.

Between the self-guided and formal training pathways, there is an intermediate level. At this level, the training program in the empirically supported treatment is constructed with as many of the formal training ingredients as possible to increase confidence that the therapist is replicating the manualized treatment. In other words, you enhance the successful mastery of these interventions by combining as many experiences as possible, including discussion in supervision, classroom work, and practice in implementing the intervention with a real client.

Different research groups have noted the benefits and limitations of training in this type of evidence-based practice. Some of these limitations may apply to you. Binder (1993) summarized observations from several groups that some trainees would apply techniques too rigidly, neglecting the therapeutic relationship. The IPT research group encountered trainees who presented in supervision as having mastered IPT but whose videotaped sessions were low in adherence to the IPT protocol (Klerman et al., 1999). That is, how competent the intern considers himself or herself was distinguishable from how well they actually did the intervention. Both the "rigid" trainees and those who "only talk a good game" would fare poorly in self-guided training without the assistance of expert supervision and taped sessions. Current research does not inform us about what proportion of trainees would be successful in self-guided training, nor what the characteristics are of those who need more rigorous training models.

The research does, however, give rise to two critical questions you should ask yourself as you learn to master a manualized intervention. First, remembering that manuals are to serve as a guide, are you so tightly adhering to the manual that you are forgetting the importance of fitting the intervention to your client's needs?

Second, how well are you doing? I mean how successful are you with the intervention? It is hoped that the answer is that you are not doing that well. If, for example, you feel that you are excellent—or even good—after one or two tries, then perhaps your evaluation is similar to those of the trainees in IPT mentioned previously.

In summary, then, two lessons are gleaned from this research. First, applying the components of a manualized intervention takes fidelity balanced against flexibility; that is, fitting it to the client's circumstances while maintaining the original intent. Second, mastering a manualized intervention is not necessarily easy, and you should expect that it will take a considerable amount of time to succeed. With many interventions, this process of gaining mastery will extend long after your internship. Be reassured, however, that you can provide effective treatment while you continue to develop your mastery of a treatment. Using standardized measures at regular intervals will help you track symptom response and prompt you to take corrective action when necessary, as covered in chapter 13 in this volume.

Research on training has also evidenced positive outcomes, as well as the two limitations mentioned earlier. Rounsaville, Chevron, Weissman, Prusoff, and Frank (1986) reported on training in IPT for the National Institute of Mental Health (NIMH) Treatment of Depression Collaborative Research Program (TDCRP) and for another study of recurrent depression. Both inexperienced and experienced therapists showed statistically significant gains in adherence to the therapy protocol over the course of training, but gains were larger for the younger and inexperienced trainees. Rounsaville and colleagues suggest that the small training effect for older, experienced therapists showed a "ceiling effect" due to starting with all highly competent therapists and thus leaving little room for improvement.

Crits-Cristoph et al. (1998) studied training in three treatments for cocaine dependence and found better training effects in cognitive therapy (CT) than in a psychodynamic therapy (supportive-expressive therapy) between the first and the fourth supervised case. Several authors have speculated that, due to the more discrete nature of CT and cognitive-behavioral therapy (CBT), better training effects are easier to achieve (Crits-Christoph et al., 1998; Rounsaville et al., 1986; Shaw et al., 1999). However, the effect size found in the CT study was commensurate with that found in the recurrent-depression IPT study (see chapter 1 of this volume for a refresher on effect sizes). It is possible that training in psychodynamic therapy, such as supportive expressive therapy or Strupp's time-limited dynamic psychotherapy (TLDP) is a more complex and challenging task than training in either IPT, CT, or CBT (Bein et al., 2000).

There is some debate as to whether training in a manualized intervention is good for a novice practitioner who is still gaining a foundation of basic skills (Calhoun, Moras, Pilkonis, & Rehm, 1998). This hesitation, of course, applies to interns in social work or criminal justice, regardless of whether you are at the undergraduate or graduate level. It is arguable that training in an evidence-based intervention with a well-articulated manual is a natural match for training students, as long as it occurs in the context of training in basic skills (Moras, 1993). The dangers of neglecting the therapeutic relationship and the complexities of developing more advanced competencies, such as timing and sequencing of interventions, illustrate the basic tension in internships in which evidence-based interventions are available.

The challenge is to develop the intern's capacity for warmth, empathy, and genuineness while he or she learns to apply specific techniques such as systematic reinforcement, cognitive restructuring, or supporting adaptive defenses. Training in evidence-based interventions requires a sustained focus on good basic practice that facilitates the therapeutic alliance, as well as developing competence in specific techniques. This simply means that you must therapeutically bond or connect with your client while developing skills and techniques from a manual.

Most clinical trials have used experienced therapists, not students or interns, so this is another area of limited research evidence. However, when less experienced practitioners have been used, they have showed large gains in adherence to the treatment manual and in therapeutic competence (Rounsaville et al., 1986). As an intern and fairly young in your career, this is to your advantage. As you study, learn, and try out the interventions, greater gains are possible.

I used treatment manuals for IPT, CBT, and a psychodynamic therapy (see Table 9.2) in an advanced clinical practice class focusing on treatment of major

Table 9.2 Empirically Supported Treatments for Depression

Therapy	Manual
Cognitive-behavioral therapy (CBT)*	Beck, Rush, Shaaw, & Emery (1979)
Interpersonal therapy (IPT)*	Klerman et al. (1999)
Brief dynamic therapy (BDT)**	Mann (1973)

*Rated well established by APA Division 12 Task Force.
**Rated "probably efficacious" by APA Division 12 Task Force.

depression. Students could choose which manual they wanted to read. The overwhelming favorite was the IPT manual, followed by the CBT manual. Although not required, many students chose to discuss the manual with their supervisors and to implement the treatment with a client, writing this process up in a paper. At the cost of considerable effort by interns and the field instructors, the students developed sophisticated clinical applications of IPT and CBT.

Overall, the class was excited to learn research-supported treatments and appreciated the detailed "how-to" nature of the manuals. This experience has made me highly optimistic about the use of manuals in graduate education. It put to rest, in part, the concern noted earlier about younger inexperienced social workers and criminal justice interns simply applying a new technique without concern for the therapeutic relationship. However, it may be premature to introduce treatment manuals until students and interns have learned the basic interpersonal, interviewing, and assessment skills in the first part of the internship. Therefore, I suggest that you wait patiently in your internship to develop manualized skills until you have learned the ropes of the agency, become comfortable with interviewing clients, and have assessed with your supervisor your readiness for a particular evidence-based and manualized intervention.

It is likely that a reasonable percentage of interns could gain competence and mastery in self-guided training (probably including students reading this book). Creative dissemination and training methods, such as telephone or computer consultations following review of taped sessions, could provide some oversight and guidance in the training process. The Beck Institute includes telephone supervision in some of their training programs in CBT (http://www.beckinstitute.com). There is a clear need for research into what types of training reliably produce therapists who are competent and effective in an empirically supported treatment

(EST), but in the meantime you and your supervisor must consider yourselves a "single case study" and proceed with thoughtful and cautious use.

SELECTING AND DEVELOPING EVIDENCE-BASED INTERVENTIONS STEP BY STEP

Table 9.1 summarizes the steps in choosing and designing training in an evidence-based intervention. Step 1 suggests building on the clinician's strengths in choosing an intervention that accords with his or her core theoretical orientation. In some situations in which a clinician has received training in two or more theoretical approaches, he or she will have a broader range of choices of evidence-based treatments that are related to his or her areas of strength. As noted, students may have at best a hazy idea of their theoretical orientations and may find comparing multiple theories confusing. For advanced practitioners, it may be a more meaningful challenge to train in an evidence-based intervention outside of their core theoretical orientation. As noted, step 2 summarizes the levels of training: self-guided, intermediate, and formal training. Because the only research evidence we have is on formal training, student interns are encouraged to emulate this model as much as possible. To further clarify, the next section presents some examples of clinicians proceeding with this process of training in an evidence-based intervention.

EXAMPLES: THERAPY FOR DEPRESSION

Major depression is the most common presenting problem in community mental health practice (Maxmen & Ward, 1995). In all likelihood you will work with clients with major depression in your internship. As noted earlier, there is some variety in the evidence-based interventions that are manualized and available for addressing depression. For these reasons, depression was selected as the focus for three illustrative examples. Later, resources are provided for finding similar information about treatments for other disorders and in other areas of practice.

In these examples, we assume that the practitioner is a graduate intern early in his or her program with a good foundation of basic practice skills from classroom and field experiences. Given this assumption and a focus on depression, the next step is selecting an evidence-based intervention for training. Table 9.2 presents three evidence-based interventions for depression. Cognitive-behavioral therapy

(CBT) and interpersonal therapy (IPT) are both listed as "well-established" treatments by the APA's Division 12 Task Force. Brief dynamic therapy (BDT) is listed as "probably efficacious" for general adult depression and as "well established" for geriatric depression (Chambless et al., 1998). At least two clinical trials of BDT used Mann's (1973) book *Time-Limited Psychotherapy* as the foundation for a manual for treatment of depressed caregivers (Gallagher-Thompson & Steffen, 1994).

As discussed earlier, it is recommended that interns initially select an intervention that is near their core theoretical orientation, perhaps later seeking training in an intervention further from their preferred theoretical approach. You will still be forming your theoretical orientation, and a process of reflection and discussion with faculty members, supervisors, and fellow students can help you make an informed choice of a manual. Three examples are discussed here: one of the self-guided approach and two that follow the intermediate approach.

Intern Alice follows the self-guided approach. She works in a rural town in a very small mental health agency, mostly with depressed clients with diffuse concerns about meaning, identity, and intimate relationships. There are few other mental health treatment resources in the area, with the exception of a behavioral medicine clinic at the local hospital that provides focused cognitive-behavioral and pharmacological interventions. The agency has a reciprocal referral arrangement with the behavioral medicine clinic, trying to match clients with appropriate treatments. Alice has enjoyed classroom material on psychodynamic therapy, and her supervisor is a psychodynamic clinician. Given her orientation and the type of client she tends to work with, Alice chooses BDT.

Intern Burt views himself as eclectic. He likes the humanistic-relational perspective and an ecological family systems approach to treatment. His supervision has focused on these approaches to treatment. His internship is in a busy urban community mental health center in the outpatient adult mental health department. Burt chooses to train in IPT. He is attracted to IPT in part because it has been studied for the treatment of eating disorders, as well (Chambless & Ollendick, 2001). He plans to train in the IPT approach to eating disorders after he has trained in the IPT protocol for depression.

Intern Cathy is in a field placement at a suburban managed care organization (MCO) that operates from a cognitive-behavioral perspective. Her supervision and trainings with the MCO all have focused on CBT. As is often the case, these trainings have focused on techniques and haven't pulled together a whole guide to treatment such as what is found in a treatment manual. Cathy will clearly want to train in the cognitive-behavioral interventions for depression. For future training, Cathy will be able to choose among cognitive-behavioral interventions for a wide range of problems.

Once a type of therapy is chosen, the intern must then design a training program, ideally together with his or her supervisor. Recall that we will have the greatest confidence that the training will result in the desired result if the intern follows the formal training protocol. In each example, I discuss how each clinician included as many formal training elements as possible.

Recall that Alice has decided to train in BDT for depression. Due to a limited part-time schedule, she has chosen to train independently. Her supervisor has agreed to read the manual, and they will discuss the EST in supervision. Using an online bookseller, she purchases the manual from the clinical trial of BDT, Mann's (1973) book *Time-Limited Psychotherapy*. Because she is not near a university library, she orders the research report of the clinical trial of BDT through inter-library loan at her local library (Gallagher-Thompson & Steffen, 1994). Following the clinical trial, she begins to use the Beck Depression Inventory (BDI; Beck, Ward, Mendelson, Mack, & Erbaugh, 1961) with her depressed clients at intake. She administers the BDI again at the 10th session and at termination. Alice studies the treatment manual and keeps notes on questions or concerns. Once she is satisfied that she understands the approach represented in the manual, she selects a new client with depression as a case in which to implement BDT.

To try to increase her ability to self-correct, Alice seeks permission from the client to videotape the sessions. She reviews the videotapes and consults the manual to shape her in-session behavior. Her plan is to continue videotaping with several clients until she is comfortable with the protocol, and then to videotape only occasionally to maintain adherence to the intervention; that is, to ensure fidelity.

Intern Burt has chosen IPT. He introduces the idea of training in IPT to the supervision group at the agency where he works, and the group agrees, all purchasing the IPT manual. The members of the supervision group begin using the BDI with all of their depressed clients. The BDI was one of the outcome measures used in the NIMH Collaborative Study of Depression, a clinical trial including IPT and CBT (Elkin, Parloff, Hadley, & Autry, 1985). The BDI is administered at intake and at 8-week intervals. The group is discussing the feasibility of selecting cases to video- or audiotape to bring to their supervision group.

Intern Cathy has chosen CBT. She opts to attend a training program at the Beck Institute (http://www.beckinstitute.org, or see Table 9.2) designed for long-distance trainees. The program includes in-residence training at the institute for several weekends and telephone supervision of selected audiotaped cases. Her supervisor continues to provide primary supervision on her cases. She also begins to use the BDI as an assessment and outcome measure with her depressed clients.

These three examples suggest possible pathways that include some components of the best standard training in the specific evidence-based interventions. There are many possible permutations that would be shaped by the intern's theoretical orientation, experience, and available resources for training. Hopefully research on training will soon provide some answers about the most important components in producing therapists competent in a specific therapy. For now, however, it is prudent to include as many of the formal training components as possible, to increase confidence that the training process will be successful.

These examples have centered on treatment of depression, so if your internship includes a lot of depressed clients, some of your work has been done for you! However, if your internship focuses on a different mental health problem, or if you practice in another area, you will need to find the information you need. The first steps are finding systematic reviews of the literature and tracking down the citations of clinical trials or other studies to find the citation for the treatment manual used (if one was used). So getting the information entails a little detective work.

FINDING EVIDENCE-BASED INTERVENTIONS IN MENTAL HEALTH

Unfortunately, there is no one clearinghouse for information on systematic reviews. There are a few central places to look, however, and Table 9.3 provides details on resources discussed in this section. The findings of the APA Division 12 task force have been summarized in journal articles, and several websites have some information on their work. Also focused on psychotherapy are two books that undertook systematic reviews, *What Works for Whom* (2nd ed., Roth & Fonagy, 2005) and *A Guide to Treatments That Work* (3rd ed., Nathan & Gorman, 2007). Like Chambless and Ollendick (2001), both the Roth and Fonagy and Nathan and Gorman books also provide a table that lists the research ratings of different treatments by the Division 12 group.

The weakness of the Chambless and Ollendick (2001) table is that it doesn't provide references to manuals. Table 9.4 collects information on all the mental health manuals known to me, and to my knowledge is the largest list currently available. Web addresses and further information on the books and the Chambless and Ollendick (2001) article are listed in Table 9.3, and LeCroy (2007) reprints a number of manuals for children and adolescents.

Table 9.3 Resources on Empirically Supported Treatments (ESTs)

World Wide Web Resources

1. For an interactive Web version of a scale of therapist theoretical orientation and a downloadable paper version: http://http://www.web.pdx.edu/~dcoleman/ test.html

2. An APA Division 12 website provides a link to a repository of Task Force on ESTs documents, including updated lists and references for treatment manuals: http://pantheon.yale.edu/~tat22/

3. Dr. John Grohol's Mental Health Page is a resource for information on treatment manuals: http://psychcentral.com/txmanul.htm

4. For information on training in cognitive-behavioral ESTs: http://http://www .beckinstitute.org

5. New Harbinger Home Page. New Harbinger Publications publishes a series of treatment manuals. Unclear research support for all manuals. http://www .newharbinger.com

6. *Treatments That Work*, series published by Oxford University Press, formerly published by Graywind Publications Incorporated. A series of treatment manuals. Unclear research support for all manuals. http://http://www.oup.co .uk/academic/medicine/psychiatry/ttw/

7. The EMDR Institute has information about efficacy research and training in eye movement desensitization and reprocessing (EMDR): http://www.emdr.com

8. The Cochrane Collaboration is an international cooperative effort to draft systematic reviews of research literature that focuses on medicine and health care, but it includes some mental health reviews. Unfortunately, free access to the reviews is no longer provided. Many university libraries now purchase access. http://www.cochrane.org

9. The Campbell Collaboration is an international cooperative effort to draft systematic reviews of research literature that focuses on education and social welfare: http://www.campbellcollaboration.org

Useful Books and Journal Articles

Chambless, D. L., & Ollendick, T. H. (2001). Empirically supported psychological interventions: Controversies and evidence. *Annual Review of Psychology, 52,* 685–716.

Roth, A., & Fonagy, P. (2005). *What works for whom?* (2nd ed.). New York: Guilford Press.

Nathan, P. E., & Gorman, J. M. (Eds.). (2007). *A guide to treatments that work* (3rd ed.). London: Oxford University Press.

Table 9.4 Selected Treatment Manuals and APA Division 12 Research Ratings

Manual Citation	Rating
Treatment of Depression	
Beck, A. T., Rush, A. J., Shaw, B. F., & Emery, G. (1979). *Cognitive therapy of depression.* New York: Guilford Press.	Well established APA Div. 12
Klerman, G. L., Weissman, M. M., Rounsaville, B. J., & Chevron, E. S. (1999). *Interpersonal psychotherapy of depression: A brief, focused, specific strategy.* Northvale, NJ: Aronson.	
Beach, S., Sandeen, E., & O'Leary, K. D. (1990). *Depression in marriage: A model for etiology and treatment.* New York: Guilford Press.	
Mann, J. (1973). *Time-limited psychotherapy.* Cambridge MA: Harvard University Press. (Indicated if marital distress is present)	Probably efficacious APA Div. 12
Treatment of Anxiety	
Barlow, D. H., & Cerny, J. A. (1988). *Psychological treatment of panic.* New York: Guilford Press.	Well established APA Div. 12
Brown, T., O'Leary, T., & Barlow, D. H. (2001). Generalized anxiety disorder. In D. H. Barlow (Ed.), *Clinical handbook of psychological disorders* (3rd ed.). New York: Guilford Press.	
Steketee, G. (1993). *Treatment of obsessive-compulsive disorder.* New York: Guilford Press.	
Steketee, G. (1999). *A behavioral and cognitive protocol for the treatment of OCD.* Oakland CA: New Harbinger.	
Shapiro, F. (2001). *Eye movement desensitization and reprocessing: Basic principles, protocols and procedures* (2nd ed.). New York: Guilford Press. (Treatment of PTSD)	Well established Roth & Fonagy (2005)
Treatment of Bulimia	
Fairburn, C. G. (1993). Interpersonal psychotherapy for bulimia nervosa. In G. L. Klerman & M. M. Weissman (Eds.), *New applications of interpersonal therapy.* Washington, DC: American Psychiatric Press.	Probably efficacious APA Div. 12

Table 9.4. (*Continued*)

Manual Citation	Rating
Fairburn, C.G., Marcus, M.D., & Wilson, G.T. (1993). Cognitive-behavioral therapy for binge eating and bulimia nervosa. In C. G. Fairburn & G. T. Wilson (Eds.), *Binge eating: Nature, assessment, and treatment.* New York: Guilford Press.	Well established APA Div. 12
Treatment of Borderline Personality Disorder	
Linehan, M. M. (1993). *Cognitive-behavioral treatment of borderline personality disorder.* New York: Guilford Press.	Well established APA Div. 12
Treatment of Antisocial Behavior in Youth	
Henggeler, S. W., Schoenwald, S., Borduin, C., Rowland, M., & Cunningham, P. (1998). *Multisystemic treatment of antisocial behavior in children and adolescents.* New York: Guilford Press.	Well established Roth & Fonagy (2005)

A unique resource for those working in mental health is Barlow's (2001) *Clinical Handbook of Psychological Disorders* (2001). This book is organized by mental disorder with chapters on the major anxiety and mood disorders, as well as eating disorders, substance abuse disorders, sexual dysfunction, and couple distress. One feature of this book is that each chapter provides a shortened version of the treatment manual for at least one empirically supported treatment. Ideally, clinicians would seek out the original manual for thorough training, but the *Clinical Handbook* provides a starting point.

Once you have found a systematic review relevant to your area of practice, the next step is to look for a citation for the treatment manual in the research studies. Sometimes the systematic review will mention and cite the specific treatment manual. If so, you can get the book through a bookseller. If the systematic review does not list the manual, it will cite the research studies that demonstrate that a treatment works. In that case, get the journal article through your local library or interlibrary loan and look in the methods section to find the citation of the treatment manual used. (Note that this process sounds worse than it is!)

Once you have a treatment manual in hand, then you can proceed to evaluate how it matches your usual way of practicing, the population you serve, and similar issues of goodness of fit. Then you can decide how you want to go about training in the intervention, as described earlier in this chapter. One of the exercises that follows is designed to help you with this challenging task.

As briefly noted earlier, a final resource (see Table 9.4) is a listing of selected treatment manuals and a notation as to which group or authors provided a systematic review of the research evidence for this manual. This list contains all those treatments known to me at the time of press, but it is not systematic or exhaustive. It may, however, save you some time in researching manualized treatments in your area of practice.

SUMMARY

This chapter has taken you through the world of evidence-based practices and treatment manuals and discussed how to proceed with training in one or more treatment protocols. Although evidence is accumulating for the efficacy of a variety of treatments for mental health problems, the application of evidence-based practices in real-life clinical practice continues to be studied. In engaging in the use of evidence-based practices, you are participating in an exciting evolutionary process on the cutting edge of practice. We encourage you to proceed with caution and a critical perspective, engaging in dialogue with your supervisor and other colleagues about how particular evidence-based interventions fit your agency setting and the client populations it serves.

ERNIE—THE YOUNGER YEARS

Catheleen Jordan

Case Description

The client was Ernie Lidquest, a 14-year-old ninth grader. Ernie was brought in for counseling by his mother, Melissa, after marijuana was discovered in Ernie's backpack at school. Ernie told the school counselor that he was "holding the cigarette for a friend" and that it was not his. The police were called, and Ernie was referred for counseling. Ernie's father, Everett, was not present; neither were his older sister and brother (Ann and Todd). Melissa reported that they did not tell Everett about the incident because he would "flip out" and there was "no telling what he would do to both of them." Ann and Todd were twins, age 19. Ann left home the previous year and lived on her own in Las Vegas, while Todd lived at home and was repeating his senior year in high school, hoping to attend the local state university the following year. Melissa said that the best times the family had were eating fried chicken, drinking beer, and arguing about the Dallas Cowboys.

Assessment/Screening and Problem Identification

Ernie and his mother were interviewed separately during the initial visit after it became apparent that Ernie would not talk with his mother in the room. During the assessment interview, Ernie was dressed all in black, and he had a tattoo of a black rose on his shoulder. He said his mother bought the clothes for him but that he had saved his birthday money and allowance for months to afford the tattoo, unbeknownst to his parents, who were unsettled by it. The initial assessment was informed by use of the Integrative Assessment Protocol (Jordan & Franklin, 2003). This instrument provides information on both the intrapersonal and interpersonal issues of clients through client self-reports. The assessment revealed the following:

Ernie did well in school academically; he had an A-average in all his courses and particularly enjoyed story problems in math. He had never been in any trouble at school or with the law before this time. He had many friendships and participated in extracurricular activities, including the science club. He continued to insist that he did not take any drugs but that he knew he made a mistake by putting the friend's marijuana cigarette in his backpack. He said that he had trouble saying "no" to his friends and considered himself to be loyal to a fault. Ernie reported that he was angry with his parents because of his father's bad temper and his mother's unwillingness to stand up to her husband. Ernie said that he was embarassed to bring his friends over to his house because there was "no telling what my dad will say to them." Ernie said that his father had never physically harmed any of the family members but that he said hurtful things to them and got angry "too easily." Ernie felt that he and his mother had been close in the past but that he had lost respect for Melissa over her lack of "backbone." The "backbone of a chocolate éclair," he commented. All the family members were miserable, according to Ernie. His sister, Ann, moved out of the house to get away from the situaton, and his brother, Todd, seemed "depressed."

Melissa verified that Ernie was a good student and had never been in this kind of trouble before. However, his mom was worried that Ernie was in with a "bad group of kids" and could not stand up for himself when they wanted to do something "crazy." Melissa reported similar information about the family dynamics as did Ernie, confirming that her husband was angry and verbally (but not physically) abusive. Melissa was worried about her poor relationship with Ernie. She said that she and Ernie had always been very close but that Ernie wouldn't speak with her anymore, except to yell at her in anger occasionally. Melissa was confused about the reasons for Ernie's anger toward her. Also, Melissa said that she was very dissatisfied about her marriage and had consulted her minister about what to do. The minister advised her that to divorce her husband would be sinful and that she should pray for guidance, including going to more Wednesday prayer meetings.

Intervention Selection

Three problems were identified as the target of intervention and negotiated with Ernie and Melissa. These were:

1. Ernie's lack of skills to resist the peer pressure from his friends. The measurement of this problem consisted of Ernie's keeping a weekly log to document times that he was asked by friends to do something that made him feel unconfortable.
2. Ernie and Melissa's relationship problems. This problem was measured by Hudson's Child's Attitude Toward Mother Scale (Fischer & Corcoran, 2007a).
3. Melissa's marital problems. This problem was measured by the Marital Happiness Scale (Azrin et al., 2006, as reprinted in Fischer & Corcoran, 2007a).

The intervention for the first problem is discussed here. Ernie participated in a social competence training involving three components: cognitive development, problem solving, and social skills training. The intervention selected Social Competence Promotion for Youth, a manualized intervention for treatment for troubled youths discussed by Craig LeCroy (2001). This intervention was selected because of its evidence base, which indicates that it is helpful in treating troubled youths. Following is a description of the social skills training.

Intervention/Treatment

The treatment program includes cognitive development, problem solving, and social skills training. The social skills training component is done in a group setting (LeCroy, 2001). Ernie was one of five boys participating in the social skills group.

After goals are defined and skills selected by youths participating in the training in a group, the following seven steps are used to teach social skills:

1. The social skill to be taught is presented. In Ernie's group, the first skill chosen was resistance to group pressure. The group leader presented the skill and asked whether anyone could give an example. Ernie volunteered his experience with getting in trouble for holding a friend's illegal drugs. The leader then provided a rationale for the skill, gave another example of a situation in which it might be used, and asked the group members for other reasons that or situations in which the skill would be a good one to learn.

2. The social skill of resisting group pressure was discussed. The group leader gave the steps of the social skill: good nonverbal communication (eye contact, saying no, etc.), saying "no" early on, suggesting an alternate to the undesired situation, and leaving.

3. Ernie volunteered to use his problem situation as an example. The group leader modeled how to handle the situation using the skill of resisting group pressure. Other group members volunteered to help role-play the situation. Members then evaluated and critiqued the role play and redid it until they felt comfortable with the new skill.

4. Other members then took turns doing their own role plays while the others observed and gave feedback.

5. During each role play, group members rehearsed the skill and the leader gave feedback. The role play was redone until the actor's behavior was similar to the leader/model's. The goal was overlearning.

6. Group members practiced using their own real-life, complex situations. This important step allowed the members to generate alternate solutions for real-life problems, select solutions, and make implementation plans.

7. Finally, training in generalization and maintenance occured. Overlearning a skill increased the chances of transferring it to real-life situations. The chances for generalization of the skill to real-life situations were increased by the use of varied models, learners, and situations. Homework was assigned; each member made a plan to implement his new skill in his natural environment.

Evaluation

Ernie was involved in evaluating the outcome of his treatment. He kept a log documenting the number of times he felt he was pressured to do something uncomfortable by friends, then logged his responses (both successful and unsuccessful) to the pressure. He brought the log to the treatment session so that each incident could be discussed. Successful attempts were praised and unsuccessful attempts discussed. Unsuccessful attempts became the focus of futher feedback, generation of alternative responses, role playing, and practice.

The intervention resulted in a positive outcome, as indicated by the increased numbers of successful responses to episodes of peer pressure and by self-reports from Ernie. Also, Ernie received no further school reports of violations. The practioner thought Ernie would probably continue cannabis use in the future. Case closed.

Discussion

The group intervention was perfect for Ernie because he was in a group with other boys his own age who also wanted to learn the skill of resisting peer pressure. I believe he made faster progress in the group treatment than he would have made with me alone. Ernie was feeling "let down" by adults in his life (especially his mother) at the point when he entered treatment; however, he had many friends his own age and was comfortable making new friends. Working with others his age was comfortable, as well as motivating, for Ernie.

■ ■ ■

Activities

1. Do you think Ernie was telling the truth about the marijuana? Would you have defined the problem the same way or done something different? If so, what?

2. Are there alternative treatments to increase adolescent resistance to peer pressure that might be equally effective?

3. How would you decide between treatments if more than one evidence-based intervention might be used?

4. Earlier, I discussed the TEST (Coleman 2003, 2004) as a way to facilitate your theory development. It is reprinted here, with the author's permission, and I hope it fulfills its purpose of helping you further develop a

practical theory. Feedback, thoughts, and ideas are welcomed about this training tool.

5. The following form will help you think about each stage of choosing and training in an evidence-based treatment protocol. It is suggested that you work on it, along with your supervisor, probably going back to it several times and revising as you collect new information.

Step 1. *Decide on a client problem area relevant to your internship.* List some possible areas to focus on and ways of conceptualizing the area. Practice may be organized by clients' shared social condition—for example, teen mothers or sexually abused boys. Different researchers may conceptualize the client's focal problem differently. It may help to discuss how to conceptualize the challenges facing your clients with your supervisor, a professor, other colleagues, clients, or community members who share characteristics with your clients.

Step 2. *Get the information you need.* Use the resources listed in this chapter to look for systematic reviews of the area decided on in step 1. For mental health problems, you may find a manual listed in Table 9.4. Consult Chambless and Ollendick (2001), the Cochrane Library (http://www .cochrane.org), the Campbell Collaboration (http://www.campbellcollab oration.org), Nathan and Gorman (2002), or Roth and Fonagy (2004).

If none of these sources have the information you need, go to a literature search using electronic databases such as PsycInfo and Social Work Abstracts.

Make some notes on potential treatments to use, their research support, and the pros and cons for the clients you work with. If possible, discuss the information you are finding with any or all of the people listed at the end of step 1.

Step 3. *Choose a treatment and design a training plan.* Many of you will have identified a treatment manual that will focus your training. Most manuals include a section that describes the training used in the clinical trials of the treatment. In areas in which no clinical trial research has been done or in which research was done but the treatment was not operationalized in a manual, there may be books that describe treatments that have not yet been rigorously tested. Note how you plan to fulfill each of these typical training activities:

- *Content learning*: This will minimally include reading the manual or other materials on the treatment you have chosen and discussing it with your supervisor. Consider also attending workshops or trainings, organizing a training/supervision group to discuss and review the material, or finding and viewing videotapes about the intervention you have chosen.
- *Experiential learning*: This type of learning consists of practicing the techniques and interventions. Supervision and training groups can be an opportunity for role play. Once you have a beginning level of mastery of the approach, supervised cases are essential. Video or audio recording should be considered. Most manuals include measures used to rate taped sessions on how closely the clinician adhered to the treatment described in the manual.

Step 4. *Evaluate.* The use of measures relevant to your client's presenting problem before, during, and after your work together will provide vital feedback on the success of your intervention. Ask for the client's subjective experience of your work together. Throughout the process, discuss in supervision how the work with clients is going, your learning experience, and your evolving understanding and evaluation of the treatment you are focusing on learning.

Theoretical Evaluation Self-Test

CIRCLE the number which best reflects your agreement or disagreement with each item.

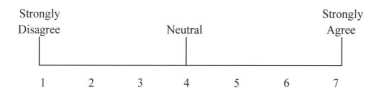

Statement	Rating
1. One central therapeutic factor is the symbolic re-creation of a nurturing caretaker relationship with the therapist.	1　2　3　4　5　6　7
2. The therapist should educate the client about the relationship of patterns of cognition and many mental health problems.	1　2　3　4　5　6　7
3. The therapist's unconditional positive regard for the client is a crucial therapeutic factor.	1　2　3　4　5　6　7
4. It is important for therapists to see clients together with their families.	1　2　3　4　5　6　7
5. The therapeutic alliance is important primarily to provide a foundation for collaborative case management.	1　2　3　4　5　6　7
6. Human behavior is shaped by patterns of reinforcements and punishments in the environment.	1　2　3　4　5　6　7
7. Change occurs in therapy because of the therapist's empathic, non-judgmental, positive attitude towards the client.	1　2　3　4　5　6　7
8. Psychoeducation about the benefits and side effects of medications is an important part of treatment.	1　2　3　4　5　6　7
9. Dreams discussed in therapy can uncover significant unconscious wishes, conflicts and feelings.	1　2　3　4　5　6　7
10. Most psychotherapy theories are distractions from the central task of solving the client's problems.	1　2　3　4　5　6　7
11. Advocacy with other providers on behalf of clients is a central role of the therapist.	1　2　3　4　5　6　7
12. It is important for the therapist to respond to clients with spontaneous, genuine affect.	1　2　3　4　5　6　7

13. Primary emphasis should be placed on the client's interactions with his or her family.	1	2	3	4	5	6	7
14. The role of the therapist is to advise and guide the client.	1	2	3	4	5	6	7
15. Client's problems are often caused by negative patterns of thinking.	1	2	3	4	5	6	7
16. Psychological problems vary with the culture of the client.	1	2	3	4	5	6	7
17. Many mental health problems are effectively treated with medication.	1	2	3	4	5	6	7
18. The therapist should be active, directive and goal-oriented.	1	2	3	4	5	6	7
19. Client's problems are often contributed to by social problems and gaps in the social service system.	1	2	3	4	5	6	7
20. It is important to attend to what the client is projecting onto the therapist.	1	2	3	4	5	6	7
21. The therapist should teach clients techniques to address problem areas.	1	2	3	4	5	6	7
22. When one person in a family is experiencing problems, it is usually the expression of family communication and relationship problems.	1	2	3	4	5	6	7
23. Many clients can benefit from psychiatric medication.	1	2	3	4	5	6	7
24. It is important to assess not only the person seeking services, but his or her environment as well.	1	2	3	4	5	6	7
25. Change occurs in therapy through restoring healthy family structures.	1	2	3	4	5	6	7
26. It is essential for therapists to be aware of the values and worldview of their own culture and how they might affect clients.	1	2	3	4	5	6	7
27. Change occurs in therapy because of the client's insight into characteristic ways of relating with others set in early childhood.	1	2	3	4	5	6	7
28. It is helpful to ask questions to lead the client to realize their mistakes or misperceptions.	1	2	3	4	5	6	7
29. There is evidence that most mental health problems have biological causes.	1	2	3	4	5	6	7
30. Denial, repression, intellectualization and other defense mechanisms are important to understanding psychology.	1	2	3	4	5	6	7

Fold this column, transfer your response, and sum.	COLUMN1	COLUMN2
	To compare scales, Divide each sum by # of items.	Compare your summed scale score to the responses of 130 subjects.
PSYCHO-DYNAMIC		
1_____		
9_____		
20_____		
27_____		Mean (sd)
30_____		
Sum _____	/5 = _____	26.2 (5.2)
BIOLOGICAL		
8_____		
17_____		
23_____		
29_____		
Sum_____	/4 = _____	14.6 (4.0)
FAMILY		
4_____		
13_____		
22_____		
25_____		
Sum _____	/4 = _____	18.2 (4.0)
ECOSYSTEMS		
16_____		
19_____		
24_____		
26_____		
Sum _____	/4 = _____	24.2 (2.6)
COGNITIVE		
2_____		
6_____		
15_____		
21_____		
28_____		
Sum_____	/5 = _____	25 (4.5)
PRAGMATIC		
5_____		
10_____		
11_____		
14_____		
18_____		
Sum_____	/5 = _____	20.1 (5.7)
HUMANISTIC		
3_____		
7_____		
12_____		
Sum_____	/3 = _____	10.4 (2.4)

INTERPRETING YOUR SCORE: The subscales you used to add up your scores (psychodynamic, biological, etc) are derived from a factor analysis of the responses of 130 subjects. See below for sample information (footnote 1).

Column 1 allows you to standardize your subscale scores by dividing the subscale sum by the number of items in that scale. With these 1 item equivalents you can examine which orientations you tend to score more highly on, and which are lower. If you chose to not make the calculation, notice which subscales have 5,4, and 3 items and you can make comparisons within these groups. Some participants have found it helpful to refer back to their responses to individual items to see if there are parts of a theory they tend to agree with more or less.

Column 2 provides the means and standard deviations of the sample of 130 community clinicians. Since these are from one selectively drawn sample, they provide a reference point but are not Anorms@. (These are means of the summed scale scores, not standardized to the 1 item level).

To aid you in interpretation the mean +/- 1 standard deviation would include 68% of the sample, and +/- 2 standard deviations would include 95% of the sample. One caution is that the reliability of the scales is adequate to discriminate group differences, but not individual differences. These scores should be used to stimulate reflection, but not as precise measurements of individual theoretical orientation.

[1] Sample Information: (n=130) Fifty-six (43%) of the subjects were MSW students, and 74 (57%) were practicing clinicians. Ninety-three (72%) were social work associated (students and practitioners) and 37 (28%) were from the other mental health professions. The average age of subjects was 35 (sd=13.7). The average practice experience of practitioners was 13.8 years (sd=11.2).

10 EVIDENCE-BASED PRACTICES FOR AT-RISK VIOLENT AND DELINQUENT YOUTH

JENNIFER ABELOFF

In this chapter you will be introduced to the difference between juve-nile delinquency and conduct disorder in youths. You will learn what the risk factors are for identifying adolescents at risk for delinquency and violence and learn about evidence-based community interven-tions and model programs for at-risk and delinquent adolescents. Finally, this chapter will show you how to develop a learning contract, which will shape your entire internship experience. The chapter ends with activities for learning and a case study.

Many students entering their internships are interested in working on violence prevention with at-risk and delinquent adolescents. This area appears exciting and ripe for us to jump in and make a difference in the lives of adolescents and the greater community. Yet students do not fully comprehend the challenging nature of working with this population. Part of what makes interventions so challenging with this population is the multifaceted nature of their problems. Juvenile de-linquent adolescents possess multiple risk factors, and the complexity of these issues often makes it overwhelming to know where to intervene. Evidence-based community interventions and model programs for at-risk and delinquent adoles-cents are reviewed.

DIFFERENTIAL ASSESSMENT

First, it is important to highlight the distinction between juvenile delinquency and conduct disorder (CD). These youths often share similar challenging and disrup-tive behaviors. Youths with a diagnosis of CD show behaviors such as aggres-siveness toward others, possession of weapons, fire setting, cruelty to animals or persons, vandalism, lying, truancy, running away, and theft (American Psychi-atric Association [APA], 2000). There are two developmental paths for devel-oping CD. CD can begin either early in childhood (early onset), before age 10, or later in adolescence (with no behaviors noted in early years); the latter is called *adolescent-onset CD* (Dishion & Kavanagh, 2003). In contrast, adolescents who are considered "juvenile delinquents" have persistently engaged in a pattern of behavior that violates the rights of others and societal norms over an extended period of at least 6 months. These adolescents may also have diagnoses of CD, but they must have committed at least one delinquent act (Springer, 2004). Therefore, it important that practitioners carefully assess youths in order to make appropriate intervention plans.

RISK AND PROTECTIVE FACTORS

It is important to be familiar with the risk factors for youth violence in order to target interventions. According to Fraser, Kirby, and Smokowski (2004), a risk factor is anything that increases the possibility of a negative outcome. The U.S. Surgeon General specifically defines risk factors in the context of youth violence as "personal characteristics or environmental conditions that *predict* the onset, continuity, or escalation of violence" (U.S. Department of Health and Human Services [DHHS], 2001, chap. 4, para. 7). Although these factors may be correlates of adolescent violence, they are not necessarily the causes.

Protective factors are those factors that mediate or moderate the effect of the risk factors and that result in reducing the risk of the problem occurring. The term *protective factor* is used to describe the personal attributes and environmental conditions that lower the chances of poor developmental outcomes in the presence of risk (Fraser et al., 2004; Thomlison, 2004). The exact nature of the interactional processes among risk and protective factors is unclear. However, it is thought that in the absence of mediating factors, situational circumstances provide the opportunity for problems to emerge. Through a complex and dynamic set of processes, a range of individual, parent, family, and environmental risk and protective factors interact to have an effect on the onset, development, and maintenance of adolescent delinquent problems (DHHS, 2001; Hawkins, Laub, & Lauritsen, 1998).

Risk factors for adolescent violence can be categorized into individual, family, peer, school, neighborhood, and community levels. Individual risk factors include a history of early childhood aggression and disruptive behaviors; antisocial behaviors, distorted attitudes, and irrational beliefs; poor language ability; early juvenile offending and substance use; poor impulse control and low achievement in school; and attention-deficit/hyperactivity disorder (DHHS, 2001; Hawkins, Laub, & Lauritsen, 1998). Parental criminality, violence, and substance abuse; physical abuse and neglect; "poor parenting practices"; family conflict; and low socioeconomic status are familial risk factors for adolescent violence (DHHS, 2001; Hawkins, Herrenkohl, et al., 1998; Moffitt, 1987).

School and peer risk factors include poor achievement and negative attitudes toward school, as well as associations with delinquent peers; lack of popularity and not engaging in appropriate social activities also serve to increase the proba-bility of violence (DHHS, 2001). Being a member of a gang increases the likeli-hood of future violence even more than associating with delinquent peers does (Thornberry, 1998). Living in a neighborhood or community characterized by social disorganization, crime, and the presence of drugs is a community risk fac-tor. In fact, social disorganization may include the youths' exposure to violence in their communities, a risk factor in and of itself for future violence (DHHS, 2001).

The presence of protective factors for adolescent violence can buffer the risk factors. Research identifies five individual protective factors that may interrupt the process. The strongest protective factor in the individual domain may be a youth's disapproval of deviant and violent behavior. Research has cited an above-normal IQ and an orientation toward traditional values and norms as protective factors (DHHS, 2001; Fergusson & Lynskey, 1996; Garmezy, 1985; Rutter, 1985; Werner & Smith, 1982). Whereas some studies have shown that a positive rela-tionship with at least one adult is a protective factor in youth development, other research has not found a connection between such familial factors and adolescent violence (Hawkins, Herrenkohl, et al., 1998; Klein & Forehand, 2000; Rutter, 1979; Werner & Smith, 1992). A youth's commitment to school and involvement in conventional social activities are two other possible protective factors (Jessor, van den Bos, Vanderryn, Costa, & Turbin, 1995; Rae-Grant, Thomas, Offord, & Boyle, 1989). Tables of risk and protective factors can be found at the Internet site for the Office of Juvenile Justice and Delinquency Prevention Model Programs Guide (http://www.dsgonline.com/mpg_non_flash/prevention_risk_factors.htm andhttp://www.dsgonline.com/mpg_non_flash/prevention_protective_factors .htm).

FINDING EVIDENCE-BASED PRACTICES

Before providing specific best practices with this population, you need to review how to access evidence-based interventions in criminal justice in general and, more specifically, within the area of violence and delinquency. First, academic databases that you can access through your university library are a vital resource. Evidence-based resources that are useful in doing these searches include the following databases: Criminal Justice Abstracts, Criminal Justice Periodicals, Social Services Abstracts, and the Social Sciences Citation Index. You can search using keywords such as *evidence based* or *best practices* and *interventions,* along with a keyword that addresses the specific population (e.g., adolescent, youth, delinquent) or service (e.g., prevention, intervention, community based, family) to decide the best course of action. Thus, for example, if you are researching best practices within corrections, you may want to start with the keywords *evidence based, interventions, systematic reviews, meta-analysis, corrections,* and *adolescents.*

The second important resource for information on best practices in criminal justice interventions is reputable Internet sites that provide articles, research, and guidelines to best practices in criminal justice:

- The Campbell Crime and Justice Coordinating Group website. Provides reviews of methods of reducing crime and delinquency (http://www.aic .gov.au/campbell/cj/).
- Center for Evaluation Research and Methodology at Vanderbilt Institute for Public Policy Studies website; Crime, Delinquency, and Antisocial Behavior section. An extensive bibliography of articles that includes many that address the effectiveness of criminal justice interventions (http://www .vanderbilt.edu/cerm/MWL_web_bib.htm).
- National Crime Prevention Council website. Contains a publication section that has research on best practices (http://www.ncpc.org).

A variety of websites, books, and articles contain information on model programs that address violence and delinquency. Although this information is extensive, it is important to remember that all of these classifications are not evidence based, grounded in rigorous evaluations. Some sources that identify model programs include:

- Blueprints for Violence Prevention on the Center for the Study of Prevention of Violence at the University of Colorado's website. Evaluates best practices among youth violence prevention and intervention programs (http:// www.colorado.edu/cspu/blueprints/).
- Roberts, A. R. (2004). Epilogue: National survey of juvenile offender treatment programs that work. In A. R. Roberts (Ed.), *Juvenile justice sourcebook: Past, present, and future.* New York: Oxford University Press. Highlights 10 model programs according to a national survey.
- Strengthening America's Families: Model Programs for Delinquency Prevention website through the Office of Juvenile Justice and Delinquency

Prevention and Substance Abuse Services Administration. Presents evidence-based programs for delinquency and youth violence prevention and intervention (http://www.strengtheningfamilies.org/html/model_programs .html).

- Youth Violence: A Report of the Surgeon General through the Office of the Surgeon General, Department of Health and Human Services. Includes extensive discussion of youth violence as well as an examination of best practices in adolescent violence prevention and intervention programs (http://www.surgeongeneral.gov/library/reports.html).
- Office of Juvenile Justice and Delinquency Prevention Model Programs Guide. Offers a database of evidence-based programs addressing prevention and intervention for at-risk adolescents (http://www.dsgonline.com/mpg_non_flash/mpg_index.htm).
- Bureau of Justice Statistics. *Violence by gang members, 1993-2003* (http://www.ojp.usdoj.gov/bjs/abstract/vgm03.htm).
- Bureau of Justice Statistics. *Family violence statistics: Including statistics on strangers and acquaintances* (http://www.ojp.usdoj.gov/bjs/abstract/fvs.htm).

CHARACTERISTICS OF EVIDENCE-BASED INTERVENTIONS TO REDUCE VIOLENCE

Adolescent violence prevention and intervention programs aim to reduce the risk factors and develop and enhance protective factors at the individual and family levels. Research has identified common characteristics among empirically researched programs (Coyle, 2002). Eight common program elements are necessary for interventions to be effective with at-risk adolescents and to target the risk and protective factors. The eight identified common program elements are as follows:

1. Use problem-solving skills training for anger management.
2. Teach the aggression cycle to gain awareness of the consequences of violence, and use cognitive restructuring to refute beliefs that support violence.
3. Use prosocial skills training and teach how to choose prosocial peer relationships.
4. Focus on effective parenting and bonding for development of positive teen relationships with parents and with nonparental adults.
5. Use parent management training to enhance parental control over adolescents by using structure and limit setting.

6. Focus on strengths and resilience.
7. Provide interventions in multiple domains (e.g., individual, family, peers, community).
8. Use interventions that match the adolescent's individual needs (Coyle, 2002, p. 5–6).

EVIDENCE-BASED CONTENT FOR PRACTICE

Problem-Solving Skills Training

Problem-solving skills training is a cognitively based intervention used to treat antisocial and aggressive youths. Research indicates demonstrated effectiveness of this model with impulsive, aggressive, and conduct-disordered adolescents (Springer, 2004). The strategies focus on the adolescents' thought processes to address deficiencies and distortions in their interpersonal situations. Techniques used include role playing, modeling, feedback, social reinforcement, and therapeutic games (Springer, 2004). Steps in problem-solving skills training are:

1. Defining the problem
2. Identifying the goal
3. Brainstorming
4. Evaluating the alternatives
5. Choosing and implementing an alternative
6. Evaluating the implemented option

Anger Management

Coyle (2002) suggests that effective strategies educate adolescents on the definition of anger and how it is different from aggression, what the possible internal and external cues are that may trigger an angry or aggressive response, how to relax and engage in self-control, and how to accept and appropriately respond to negative feedback, as well as resist taunts.

Refuting Beliefs That Support Violence and Consequences of Violence

Cognitive restructuring is used to teach youths the consequences of violence and to challenge their beliefs about violence. Programs, therefore, should include information on the impact violence has on individuals, families, and communities.

Further, there should be education about violence and self-control, discussion of how cultural issues may influence perceptions of the efficacy of violence, and education in alternatives to violent behavior as a solution to conflict (Coyle, 2002). Adolescents learn to accept responsibility for their actions and change irrational beliefs about violence.

Prosocial Skills Training and Choice of Prosocial Peer Relationships

Social skills training emphasizes choosing positive peer relationships rather than delinquent or deviant ones. Programs address these issues through teaching communication skills, including the ability to give and receive evaluation;, assertiveness and negotiation skills; and conflict resolution techniques. Programs emphasize participation in positive community activities and teach parental monitoring and supervision of adolescents' friends (Coyle, 2002).

Development of Positive Relationships With Parents and Other Adults

Programs focus on adolescent and parent communication skills, listening, and negotiating, as well as increasing the level of emotional support from parents and other adults. One method often used to increase nonparental support is via the utilization of adult mentors (Coyle, 2002).

Structure and Limit Setting

Problem-solving responses and skills in the consistent use of supervision and limit setting are taught to adolescents and parents to establish realistic expectations. As well as the necessity to educate parents, there is a need to educate schools and community settings on the need to set flexible limits and consistent and predictable consequences in order to prevent and reduce youth violence (Coyle, 2002).

Strengths and Resilience

Interventions should be strength-based, identifying and utilizing the talents, skills, and abilities of the individual teens, their families, peers, and communities. Programs treatment plans should set the tone for this approach, focusing on and developing the resilient features and strengths of the adolescent and surrounding supports (Coyle, 2002). Assessments of and interventions with youths and their families need to be individualized, identifying and addressing the specific needs and situations.

Interventions in Multiple Domains

Evidence-based practices focus not only the individual adolescent but also on his or her family, peers, and community and utilize interventions that address these multiple domains (Coyle, 2002).

Parent Management Training

Parent management training is one of the most empirically tested approaches in which parents are trained to use skills for managing their child's behavior, based on social learning principles, and it is highly effective. Used most effectively with parents of younger children, studies suggest that it can also be used with parents of adolescents (Alexander & Parsons, 1973; Dishion & Kavanagh, 2003; Patterson et al., 1975; Pearson, Lipton, Cleland, & Yee, 2002). Parent management training programs teach parents how to discipline more effectively and manage disruptive behaviors and conduct disorders. Parent training consists of four major components: initial assessment of parenting issues, teaching new skills, parents' application (homework, or out-of-session practice) of these new techniques with their adolescent children, and facilitator feedback (Taylor & Biglan, 1998). Core elements of parent training programs include 8–14 weekly sessions of approximately 2 hours each following a treatment or intervention manual for session topics that address information, skills, and strategies for managing child behaviors. Many of the parent training programs evolved from the model developed by Gerald Patterson of the Oregon Social Learning Center (Patterson, 1974).

EVIDENCE-BASED PROGRAMS

Various evidence-based techniques have been associated with effective interventions. Skills training tends to incorporate experiential (e.g., role plays), didactic, and multimedia strategies to provide the content in varied and pragmatic ways. In addition, the cognitive-behavioral approach is used to change not only the behaviors of the adolescents but also their beliefs, attitudes, and thoughts. Additionally, evidence-based programs use a comprehensive model by engaging families and including family therapy (Coyle, 2002).

Effective programs have provided the interventions in a relatively brief time period, in approximately 12 sessions. Programs that target adolescents with more severe risks or histories have found the simultaneous use of multiple interventions in multiple domains to be effective in a time span of 3 to 6 months. As a student you should be aware, however, that there have not been longitudinal studies of these intervention programs. Thus we do not know whether the successes that the youths and families may have gained in the short term were maintained without further support and ongoing services (Coyle, 2002).

The following are three empirically supported violence prevention and intervention programs for at-risk and delinquent adolescents. They are considered among the most effective programs in this area. Although each of these programs has a unique way of approaching adolescent violence, their similarities are most notable in their use of the aforementioned program elements that are essential to successful outcomes.

Multisystemic Therapy

Multisystemic Therapy (MST; Henggeler & Bourdin, 1990; Henggeler, Melton, Brondino, Scherer, & Hanley, 1997; Henggeler, Schoenwald, et al., 1998) is a strength-, family-, and community-based treatment program that targets violent, delinquent, or substance-abusing juvenile offenders between the ages of 12 and 17 who are at risk of being placed out of their own homes. Its multisystemic approach aims to reduce the adolescents' multiple risk factors related to violence and delinquency and to build protective factors within the context of the family, peer, school, and neighborhood (Channing Bete Company, 2004; DHHS, 2001; Henggeler, Mihalic, Rone, Thomas, & Timmons-Mitchell, 1998; Muller & Mihalic, 1999).

Multisystemic therapy is highly individualized and provides its services in the home over a period of approximately 4 months, with multiple weekly contacts between the family and the therapist, approximating a total of 60 hours. Although this is the average service duration, the frequency and duration of the sessions varies according to the needs of the individual adolescents and their families. The treatment is goal-oriented, specifically aiming to improve parental disciplinary practices, enhance family relationships, decrease youths' associations with deviant peers, and increase their interactions with positive peers involved in appropriate activities. Treatment includes support, skill building, cognitive-behavioral therapy, behavioral parent training, structural family therapy, and strategic family therapy. Evaluations of MST have found long-term reductions in adolescent participants' criminal activity, incarcerations, violent offenses, and drug-related arrests (Channing Bete Company, 2004; DHHS, 2001; Henggeler, Mihalic, et al., 1998; Muller & Mihalic, 1999). "To date, MST is the only treatment for serious delinquent behavior that has demonstrated both short and long term treatment effects in randomized, controlled clinical trials with violent and chronic juvenile offenders and their families from various cultural and ethnic backgrounds" (Springer, 2004, p. 267).

For further information on MST, contact:

Marshall Swenson, MSW, MBA
MST Services, Inc.
710 J. Dodds Boulevard
Mount Pleasant, SC 29464
Phone: (843) 856-8226 x 11
Fax: (843) 856-8227
Email: marshall.swenson@mstservices.com
Website: http://www.mstservices.com or http://www.mstinstitute.org

Functional Family Therapy

Functional family therapy (FFT; Alexander, Robbins, & Sexton, 2000; Alexander et al., 1998) is a family-based multistep prevention and intervention program that targets adolescents ages 11 to 18 who are at risk for or are presenting with violent behaviors, delinquency, substance use, disruptive behavior disorder, oppositional defiant disorder, and/or conduct disorder. The interventions are provided in multiple settings, including in the home, clinic, and juvenile court, with the goals of reducing risk factors and enhancing protective factors, as well as engaging and motivating adolescents and their families to change their interactions, communication, and problem-solving methods. The direct services are delivered on average for 8 to 12 hours over the course of 3 months. For more severe cases, no more than 26 hours of direct services are provided (DHHS, 2001; Alexander et al., 1998).

Grounded in learning theory, FFT is a structured, multiphase program consisting of steps that build on one another. The five treatment phases are: engagement, motivation, assessment, behavioral change, and generalization. During the engagement phase, FFT seeks to prevent early program dropout by engaging with the youth and family. The motivation phase consists of increasing the trusting relationship with the therapists in order to enhance motivation. This stage also looks to address and change maladaptive attitudes and beliefs. In the assessment phase, the therapists examine the individual, family, and community relationships, particularly noting the functions of the behavior in these relationships. The behavior change phase, as you can guess, targets altering behaviors through skills training for the adolescents and their parents. It includes basic parenting skills and communication training, as well as contracting techniques.

The final stage, generalization, focuses on providing the families with individualized case management to address the needs of the family as identified in prior phases of work.

Research has provided strong empirical support for FFT. It has been shown to effectively treat adolescents with issues related to violence, including substance abuse, delinquency, conduct disorder, oppositional defiant disorder, and disruptive behavior disorder. FFT has had significant success in preventing reoffending, as well as preventing youths from entering into the adult criminal justice system, and in keeping younger children in the same family unit from entering into the juvenile justice system (Alexander et al., 1998; DHHS, 2001; Muller & Mihalic, 1999).

For further information on FFT, please contact:

Holly deMaranville, Communications Coordinator
Functional Family Therapy, LLC
2538 57th Avenue, SW
Seattle, WA 98116
Phone: (206) 369-5894
Fax: (206) 664-6230
Email: hollyfft@attbi.com
Website: http://www.fftinc.com

CASASTART (Striving Together to Achieve Rewarding Tomorrows)

CASASTART is a school-based, community-centered prevention program that targets at-risk adolescents ages 11 to 13 who live in high-risk neighborhoods. The program aims to prevent or reduce youths' exposure to drugs and criminal activity by addressing the needs and risk factors of the individual adolescents, as well as their families, peers, and communities. Thus, CASASTART strives to reduce risk factors and increase protective factors in order to strengthen families, enhance neighborhood safety, and build resiliency in the youths (Center for the Study and Prevention of Violence [CSPV], 2002–2004; DHHS, 2001; Harrell, Cavanagh, & Sridharan, 1998, 1999; National Center on Addiction and Substance Abuse [CASA], 1996; Substance Abuse and Mental Health Services Administration [SAMHSA], 2006).

In order to meet these goals, CASASTART approaches the prevention of adolescent violence via an intensive, comprehensive community-based model that includes the key members of the community: the schools, law enforcement, health agencies, and social services. Central to CASASTART are the eight core components that address the different risk areas in which the program intervenes (individual, family, peers, neighborhood, and community). The core components are: (1) community-enhanced policing/enhanced enforcement; (2) case management; (3) criminal/juvenile justice intervention; (4) family services; (5) after-school and summer activities; (6) educational services; (7) mentoring; (8) incentives (CSPV, 2002-2004; DHHS, 2001; Harrell et al., 1998, 1999; CASA, 1996; SAMHSA, 2006).

The first component of CASASTART works to increase the police presence in the community, including around schools, and connects the police and neighborhoods to work together on crime prevention and to become more familiar with one another. The second CASASTART core component is intensive case management; each adolescent and his or her family is assigned a case manager to help serve the needs of the family and youth through direct provision of services or linkages to those resources. The case managers have small caseloads of approximately 15 adolescents and families, and they provide an individualized service plan for each. For those youths who are involved or who become involved with the juvenile justice or criminal justice systems, the third core component ensures that the case managers are linked with the courts, increasing the supervision and planning (CSPV, 2002–2004; DHHS, 2001; Harrell et al., 1998, 1999; CASA, 1996; Redd, Cochran, Hair, & Moore, 2002; SAMHSA, 2006).

In order to increase the positive influence of parents and families on youths, the fourth core component, family services, provides counseling services, parent skills trainings, organized activities, and family advocacy on the part of the case managers. In its fifth core component, CASASTART also strives to enhance opportunities for prosocial activities with peers by providing or linking adolescents to recreational, entertainment, and social development activities (e.g., programs on cultural heritage, social problems) in the community. In order to increase the at-risk youths' school performance and commitment, the program also provides educational services as its sixth component; they offer tutoring services and homework assistance, as well as referrals to additional services when necessary. As CASASTART's seventh core component, positive attachments to nonparental adults are fostered via mentoring, in which group or one-to-one relationships with adults are arranged. Finally, in order to promote participation, CASASTART includes the eighth core component, in which monetary and nonmonetary incentives are provided for participation in the activities (CSPV, 2002–2004; DHHS, 2001; Harrell et al., 1998, 1999; CASA, , 1996; Redd et al., 2002; SAMHSA, 2006).

Research supports the effectiveness of CASASTART's eight components, finding that participants demonstrate improved bonds to positive individuals and institutions and decreased attachment to deviant peers and norms, as well as significant decreases in the likelihood that the youths will use gateway drugs or be involved in selling drugs. Moreover, CASASTART adolescents are shown to have lower levels of violent offenses and association with delinquent peers, in addition to experiencing a higher likelihood that they will be promoted to the next grade (SAMHSA, 2006).

For further information on CASASTART, contact:

Lawrence F. Murray, CSW
The National Center on Addiction and Substance Abuse at Columbia University
633 Third Avenue
New York, NY 10017
Phone: (212) 841-5200
Fax: (212) 956-8020
Email: lmurray@casacolumbia.org
Website: http://www.casacolumbia.org

SUMMARY

As you can see, the field of prevention and treatment of adolescent violence is a much more complex and challenging field than many of us first imagine. These teens are faced with layers of risk factors and deficits that we must address in developing prevention and intervention programs. Yet, instead of feeling over-whelmed and frustrated at the complexity of these problems, you can see that turning to empirical research helps us to understand what some effective practices in this field are. Using some of the information that you have gathered from this chapter, therefore, you should have a better sense of what some evidence-based practices are and where to gather further resources on some model programs. With those tools, we hope you are ready to approach this population with realistic expectations and effective approaches.

- For adolescents, cognitive-based interventions are generally most effective when combined with behavioral contingencies in community-based settings (Dishion & Kavanagh, 2003).
- When possible, engage the adolescent's family so that you provide an integrated approach.
- The most extensive interventions researched are parent management training, multisystemic therapy, and problem-solving skills training. Only problem-solving skills training does not place emphasis on the family.

FINDING MITIGATING EVIDENCE

Melissa Kupferberg and José B. Ashford

Case Description

Capital trials consist of two stages. In the first phase of the trial, usually called the *guilt/innocence phase*, the jury is asked to decide whether the defendant is guilty of a capital offense. If the jury returns a guilty verdict for a capital crime, the case immediately proceeds to the *penalty phase* in front of the jury. The same jury that decided the defendant's guilt hears evidence and decides whether to impose the death penalty or a life sentence.

The standard of care in capital cases requires that an in-depth investigation be conducted in the case to develop a reliable biopsychosocial history. This is the crucial first step in determining the range of mitigation evidence that counsel can offer at the penalty phase. The biopsychosocial history also serves the purpose of allowing counsel to rebut, defeat, or mitigate evidence offered by the prosecution as aggravation. Finally, a competent mental health evaluation by psychiatrists, neurologists, psychologists, or social workers requires reliable and independently documented data about the defendant. Only with a properly gathered and documented history can mental health professionals determine the presence, severity, and effect of adverse developmental experiences, mental impairments, community and environmental risk factors, and multigenerational family patterns that affected the defendant's development, behavior, and functioning.

Because attorneys and traditional private investigators do not possess the skills necessary for mitigation investigation, the mitigation specialist is considered the professional on the capital defense team charged with the responsibility of investigating and documenting the defendant's life history. Social workers are often hired as mitigation specialists. The education and training of attorneys and guilt-phase investigators does not include expertise in many substantive areas involving mitigation of punishment, such as trauma, mental health issues, neurological impairment, and the role of culture. Mitigation specialists engage in three essential tasks: collecting and analyzing documentary evidence such as records, locating and interviewing lay witnesses (including the defendant), and advising counsel as to which mitigating information will best support specific legal strategies.

In this case, John Smith was a 47-year-old male facing capital murder charges for the rape and murder of a 21-year-old female. Mr. Smith's background included sexual and physical abuse as a child, perpetrated by his father. In the course of the social history investigation, the mitigation specialist uncovered allegations by several siblings that the defendant was subjected to sexual and physical abuse. In addition, the mitigation specialist learned that the siblings not only observed the abuse but were also victims of abuse by the father.

Assessment/Screening and Problem Identification

Investigation of Mr. Smith's social history requires the mitigation specialist to validate information by collecting verifiable evidence and information to prove or disprove that specific adverse experiences occurred. This legally admissible evidence is collected by interviewing witnesses other than the defendant. As in many cases of trauma, Mr. Smith's family members are reluctant to divulge accurate information about the nature and frequency of the abuse. Interviews about the issues of abuse have disrupted family functioning, and many members of the family have refused to cooperate with members of the defense team. The mitigation specialist must exercise skills aimed at overcoming barriers to disclosure, such as shame, fear, and embarrassment. Multiple and lengthy interviews over time are necessary to create a protective climate that will help reluctant and fearful witnesses provide needed information.

Although the final decision about which evidence to present in the penalty phase is the responsibility of an attorney, the mitigation specialist must help the team identify alternative explanations for the defendant's participation in the crime. This role requires the mitigation specialist to implement hypodeductive procedures in testing the validity of competing theories of why the crime occurred. Returning to the example of Mr. Smith's family, descriptions of child abuse by a few family members would not be sufficient evidence to present. The mitigation specialist must utilize scientific evidence and theory-based propositions in testing the validity of the data gathered in the mitigation assessment process.

The most important contribution of the mitigation specialist to the capital defense team is the utilization of social science knowledge in guiding the investigation of the defendant's life experiences. After a thorough investigation of Mr. Smith's life history in which mitigation themes have emerged, the mitigation specialist also assists the attorney in evaluating which witnesses should testify and how to structure the presentation of witnesses and evidence. This evaluation of potential testifying witnesses includes identifying the need for expert assistance, selecting appropriate experts based on particular areas of scientific expertise, and helping the lawyers prepare those experts to testify.

Intervention Selection

A critical part of the defense presentation of mitigating factors is being able to demonstrate to members of the jury that distal events in Mr. Smith's life have a proximal connection with the crime. There is a substantial body of evidence in scientific literature that shows that child abuse creates devastating, lifelong effects that can, and often do, lead to violent behavior. However, the intervention in this field of practice involves strategizing how to present to the jury this link between Mr. Smith's history of child abuse and the violence involved in his crime.

In addition to the problem of showing a causal link between Mr. Smith's child abuse and violence, the mitigation specialist must be able to assist the defense attorney in anticipating and refuting the prosecution's response to the presented evidence. Prosecutors will likely counter the abuse evidence by suggesting that the abuse is just an excuse for the crime and a way for Mr. Smith to escape personal responsibility for his actions. The prosecutor may also tell the jury that even if Mr. Smith was abused, he still had a choice and that he chose to commit murder. Although the aim of presenting the evidence might be to achieve empathy, this strategy or intervention can easily backfire. The jury needs to evaluate the evidence of abuse, but this information can also be used to help the prosecutor make a case that Mr. Smith poses a continued threat to society as a consequence of his history of abuse. Clearly, child abuse plays a major role in future violent behavior. However, the mitigation specialist must establish the potential effects of the abuse, match those outcomes with the evidence in the social science literature, and relate it to Mr. Smith's negative manner of coping or to the offense for which the death penalty is being sought.

As in all scientific disciplines, mitigation specialists must always look for multiple means to assess information. Melton, Petrila, Poythress, and Slobogin (1997) describe accurate forensic assessment of an individual's development, behavior, and functioning as a comprehensive inquiry utilizing information from a wide variety of sources. This scientific inquiry is divided into collection of third-party information, interviews with the defendant, and other special assessment procedures such as testing (Melton et al., 1997). Therefore, accurate evaluation of the factors interacting in Mr. Smith's life must also follow this course of scientific analysis. Integration of offense-related information with developmental/historical data and prior contacts with relevant helping or enforcement systems must be linked to statistical information contained in the scientific literature. In sum, the presentation of mitigation evidence requires an assessment that includes: corroboration of statements provided by Mr. Smith and his family, combined with the weighing of this personalized data against anecdotal information such as records and lay witness testimony, coupled with

scientific conclusions drawn by appropriate experts identified during the assessment phase of the mitigation process.

Intervention/Treatment

Once the mitigation specialist discovered that Mr. Smith was mistreated as a
child, it was easy to see the devastating impact the abuse had had on his life and
to trace the predictable course of events that culminated in the capital crime.
The United States Supreme Court has made clear that evidence of childhood
abuse is mitigating and must be considered in a death penalty case:

> Evidence about the defendant's background and character is relevant be-
> cause of the belief, long held by this society, that defendants who commit
> criminal acts that are attributable to a disadvantaged background, or to
> emotional and mental problems may be less culpable than defendants who
> have no such excuse. (*Penry v. Lynaugh*, 1989)

Simply presenting Mr. Smith's history of child abuse, no matter how tragic
or compelling, is probably not enough to move a jury to a life verdict. Although
the jury may be swayed by the testimony and moved by the details, the mitigating effect will be lost if they fail to see the causal connection between his
experiences and the capital crime:

> A juror may intuitively understand, based solely on the facts of abuse, that a
> childhood marred by abuse would have been traumatic. That evidence may
> make a juror feel sorry for the defendant, but it is unlikely to cause her to
> vote for a life sentence. The critical part of the defense case for mitigation is
> explaining how and why the defendant's history of abuse caused long-term
> cognitive, behavioral, and volitional impairments that relate to the murder
> he committed. Without testimony establishing this connection, the jurors are
> unlikely to comprehend the significance of the defendant's background in
> their sentencing decision. (pp. 1183–1185; Crocker, 1999)

With regard to Mr. Smith's history of abuse, certain kinds of evidence will
likely be more effective with a jury than others. For instance, if Mr. Smith
denies his history of abuse during his evaluation with the prosecutor's mental
health expert, the evidence has less mitigating potential than if he admits it. It
can be additionally problematic if siblings did not suffer the same frequency or
severity of abuse as Mr. Smith, because it gives the jury the opportunity to
ponder that another family member didn't commit murder and thus that Mr.
Smith's offense behavior must be a result of controllable volition. Finally,
corroborating evidence from a child abuse expert and non-family-member lay

witnesses is likewise important. Mitigation investigation demands a thorough collection of reliable, objective documentation. Independently created records are intrinsically credible and will document events that Mr. Smith and other family members were too young to remember or too ashamed to articulate. This triangulation of life history events is critical in the presentation of mitigating information.

Because other siblings in Mr. Smith's family were abused, the mitigation specialist must identify what made Mr. Smith particularly vulnerable and what made him take a different path in life than his siblings. Mr. Smith's siblings took different turns in their life courses, and that information will be used by the prosecution as evidence that the child abuse was not involved in Mr. Smith's offense behavior. Identifying whether Mr. Smith was singled out for some particular reason, such as preexisting handicaps or behavioral disorders, is also critical in exploring the individual vulnerabilities interacting in Mr. Smith's life. Mr. Smith will likely exhibit psychological disorders that were caused or exacerbated by his abuse. Understanding of the cumulative effect that specific experiences or factors had on Mr. Smith must include a thorough assessment of the literature based on both individual and combined impairments.

Evaluation

Jurors and judges alike will be moved by tragic stories and detailed accounts of biopsychosocial deficits told in the penalty phase of Mr. Smith's trial if they are properly orchestrated and independently documented. Posttrial juror interviews are the best mechanism for assessment of the effectiveness of presented mitigating evidence. The information obtained from interviewing jurors will assist Mr. Smith's future attorneys, in the case of an unsuccessful presentation of information and a subsequent sentence of death. The results can also help attorneys with the appeal process. Juror interviews can also give rise to legal claims of juror misconduct, prejudicial events in the courtroom such as off-the-record comments by the judge, and jury selection issues that may lead to important litigation.

Juror interviews will provide insight into which, if any, presented evidence was persuasive and believable. Presentation of child abuse, in particular, is frequently discounted, as many jurors were abused themselves or have had direct experience with someone who has suffered child abuse. This direct experience often works against the defense's presentation of abuse evidence and underscores the importance of third-party corroboration of abuse and linking of evidence with empirical data and expert testimony.

Discussion

Criminal justice workers and social workers alike who are employed as mitigation specialists are members of a defense team and as such are held to many of the same ethical standards as lawyers. They are protected by attorney-client privilege but often face special ethical challenges because of their own codes of ethics and conduct. The mitigation specialist on the defense team must be aware of the special role he or she is performing in this practice context and how advocacy in the criminal justice system is very different from traditional social service roles and practices.

Despite such differences, the scientific methods do generalize to this practice context. The mitigation specialist is required to keep up with scientific developments and help the defense team members utilize appropriate evidence from the scientific literature in developing relevant mitigation strategies.

■ ■ ■

Activities

1. Assume you are working on the defense team in Mr. Smith's case and that you are performing a collateral interview with a member of his family. This interview is considered very important to the defense strategy for the penalty phase of the case. Let's also assume that this person is Mr. Smith's sister and that while visiting her you observed that the sister's daughter has physically abused her son. When you notice this abuse, you question Mr. Smith's sister about the son's appearance, and she admits that it is abuse but does not want the authorities to know because she fears that the family will lose custody of the boy. Due to the ethical differences in operating as a member of the defense team and an agent of the attorney, the mitigation specialist is unsure how to approach this situation.

   a. What is the mitigation specialist's ethical obligation in this circumstance?

   b. Do her ethical duties differ because she is considered an agent of the lawyer who is responsible for the defendant's case?

     c. If the case is reported, the family can shut down and thus negatively affect the outcome of the defendant's case. Are the standards regarding reporting child abuse different for lawyers than for criminal justice and social workers when it may jeopardize their defendant's defense strategy?

2. To augment information obtained from clinical interview and review of records, the expert hired by the defense team has requested permission to conduct additional psychological testing. Based on the strengths and weaknesses of using these types of tests, what information should the mitigation specialist pass on to the attorney to assist in making the decision of whether to permit such testing?

     a. What are some of the major limitations inherent in the implementation of psychological testing in this practice context because of the different role the mitigation specialist plays on a defense team?

3. How could Mr. Smith's culture affect the expression of certain biopsychosocial factors relevant to mitigation of criminal responsibility? For example, concepts of remorse and shame have great cultural variability. What are some other areas of inquiry that may be obstructed by cross-cultural variables in the mitigation process?

4. Interviewing potential witnesses for Mr. Smith's social history investigation encompasses many kinds of individuals. How does the type of individual being interviewed affect the interviewer's approach? What differences in techniques would the mitigation specialist employ in his or her approach to family member interviews as compared with interviews of neutral, third-party lay witnesses, such as foster care workers or police officers?

5. You are an intern at a high school in a diverse, suburban school district outside a medium-sized city. You have noticed that a large portion of students you are working with have academic learning problems, aggressive behaviors, including conduct disorder, and appear to have attitudes that are conducive to substance use.
   Conduct an Internet search that seeks to answer the following questions:

   a. Is there interplay between learning disabilities in adolescents and violence?

   b. Explain.

   c. What keywords might be the most helpful in researching this question?

6. Conduct an Internet search to answer the following questions.

   a. Brief strategic family therapy is an approach grounded in cultural frame of reference that improves family functioning in families in which parental control and cohesion affect family functioning. Conduct an Internet search on this approach and discuss whether you think it might be considered as a promising intervention to prevent adolescent violence in Hispanic families.

   b. What keywords did you use, and what Internet sites did you access for this information?

The Substance Abuse and Mental Health Services Administration, Center for Substance Abuse Treatment, has issued a 12-session cognitive-behavioral anger management group treatment manual titled *Anger Management: A Cognitive Behavioral Therapy*. You can download the manual at the following website, complete with session content and exercises: http://www.kap.samhsa.gov/products/manuals/pdfs/anger1.pdf

11 IDENTIFYING EVIDENCE-BASED PRACTICE IN CORRECTIONS

DORIS LAYTON MACKENZIE

In this chapter you will learn that relatively few policy decisions regarding corrections use scientific evidence to assist in making informed decisions. This chapter emphasizes the importance of evidence in corrections work if we are to be successful in reducing crime in the community and provides an example of how scientific information can be used to make decisions. An assessment technique designed by University of Maryland researchers is used to assess the effectiveness of correctional strategies, interventions, and programs. Examples in two areas of drug treatment—cognitive skills programs and educational programs—are assessed for scientific rigor to draw conclusions about what works, what doesn't, what is promising, and what we don't know. The assessment technique is described, and summaries of the findings from this assessment are presented. The chapter ends with exercises and a case study.

As prison populations grow nationally and corrections makes up an increasing proportion of state and local budgets, many jurisdictions are seeking to determine whether their funds are being spent effectively. In particular, they ask whether correctional interventions and programs have an impact on later criminal behavior. University of Maryland researchers developed an innovative technique to answer this question in response to a request by the U.S. Congress for a comprehensive evaluation of the effectiveness of more than $3 billion annually in Department of Justice (DOJ) grants to assist state and local criminal justice and community efforts to prevent crime. Congress required the research included in the evaluation to be "independent in nature" and to "employ rigorous and scientifically recognized standards and methodologies." The culmination of this effort was the publication of a more than 600-page report to the U.S. Congress, "Preventing Crime: What Works, What Doesn't, What's Promising" (Sherman, Gottfredson, MacKenzie, Eck, Reuter, & Bushway, 1997). The researchers assessed the quality of the research methods of more than 500 studies of various crime prevention programs. This assessment, along with the direction and significance of the research results, was used to draw conclusions about what works in preventing crime. The Maryland report reviewed the research examining effectiveness in different settings: families, police, community, place, labor markets, and the criminal justice system.

Traditional crime prevention efforts are directed toward those who are not yet involved in crime. In contrast, the University of Maryland researchers used a broader perspective on crime prevention that included any setting that reduces crime in the community. From this perspective, strategies and programs in criminal justice settings (i.e., in the courts and corrections) that focus on reducing the criminal activities of known offenders are included in the definition of crime prevention. That is, because past behavior is the best predictor of future behavior, it is reasonable to attempt to prevent crime by preventing known offenders from continuing their criminal behavior. Because the majority of offenders serve time in the community on probation, parole, or some other type of supervised release and because those who are incarcerated will eventually be released into the community, it makes sense to focus some attention on the possible future criminal activities of these individuals. In one chapter of the report, I focused on crime prevention in the criminal justice system (MacKenzie, 1997).

A later report to the State of Washington Joint Legislative Audit and Review Committee extended these findings by reviewing additional correctional programs (MacKenzie & Hickman, 1998; http://www.evaluatingcorrections.org).

Later, my colleagues extended this work through the use of systematic reviews and meta-analyses (MacKenzie, 2006). This chapter argues for the importance of moving toward evidence-based corrections, reviews the different procedures for assessing what works, and summarizes the work of my colleagues and myself on what works in corrections.

EVIDENCE-BASED CORRECTIONS

Strategies for reducing crime should be based on scientific evidence. With the term *evidence-based corrections,* I am referring to the need to use scientific evidence to make informed decisions about correctional policy (MacKenzie, 2000; MacKenzie, 2001; MacKenzie, 2006). In my review of studies that have examined the effectiveness of correctional programs, interventions, or strategies, I was shocked at how many descriptive studies or poorly done outcome studies are reported in the literature. It is difficult to make decisions about what works if these are the only types of studies available. As I reviewed each topic area (e.g., drug courts, drug treatment, correctional boot camps), I found thousands of published and unpublished studies. However, many of these studies were so poorly designed that it was impossible to rule out alternative explanations for the results. Many others were limited to descriptions of the interventions. Although it is important to have some descriptive studies, it is my belief that they make up too great a percentage of the total and that the literature too heavily leans toward a prevalence of descriptive studies over well-designed outcome studies.

In a recent publication, Sherman (1998) proposed a new paradigm for policing called "evidence-based policing." Correctional decision making based on evidence is equally as important. Such evidence-based corrections would implement guidelines and evaluate the performance of agencies and programs. Evidence-based decision making would use research to guide practice and evaluate programs. It would "use the best evidence to shape the best practice . . . in a systematic effort to parse out and codify un-systematic 'experience' as the basis for decision-making" (Sherman, 1998, p. 4).

The use of evaluation results has been a missing link in correctional decision making. As Sherman (1998) argues, the basic premise of "evidence-based practice is that we are all entitled to our own opinions but not to our own facts" (p. 4). Without help, practitioners do come up with their own "facts" that often turn out to be wrong.

The goal, then, is to use scientific evidence to hold officials accountable for results. Although some would say that correctional administrators currently use evidence to make decisions, there are many obvious examples that this is untrue. A glaring example of how little information is used for decision making became clear to me during a recent study of juvenile correctional facilities. At 47 different facilities, we asked administrators what information they had about what happens to youths who leave their institutions. Did they know if youths were later arrested? Did they know how many returned to their neighborhood schools? Found employment? Attended drug treatment? Administrators in fewer than 10% of the facilities had this type of information available to them. Unquestionably, these individuals viewed their task as one of having an impact on the future behavior of the youths under their care. Yet they had no evidence that anything they did had any effect. There was no way for them to examine whether some new program or procedure had an impact on the youths after they left the facility. Without this feedback about how they were doing, how could they be expected to review and revise their program in order to accomplish their goals?

FOCUS ON RECIDIVISM

In my examination of what works in corrections, I have focused my attention on the impact of the interventions, strategies, or programs on recidivism. Frequently, I am asked why I did not examine other outcomes and whether I believe that other factors are important to consider. I emphatically answer "yes." However, I focus my attention on recidivism for two reasons. First, I believe that the public and many policy makers view recidivism reduction as one, if not the major, goal of corrections. Second, if I attempted to look at all possible outcomes, it would make the results of the impact on recidivism much less clear. Essentially, it would muddy the water. Too often people study intermediate outcomes and assume that these have a certain relationship to recidivism.

Of course, it is important to note that each program or crime prevention strategy has effects other than crime reduction. For example, the analysis of the costs and benefits of a program is critically important in any examination of policy-relevant issues. A high-quality, intensive treatment program for offenders can be relatively costly. The advantages of the program must be weighed against the costs. Such issues, among others, are important in policy decisions. In order to make decisions about whether to continue programs, policy makers must evaluate many factors, including their effectiveness in reducing criminal activity, as well as costs. The problem is that many times other factors confuse the issues, or the crime reduction effect of the program is assumed but not articulated. For these reasons, acknowledging that crime reduction is only one factor among many that are important to consider, I focused my attention on the effectiveness of correctional programs and strategies in reducing criminal activities.

ASSESSING WHAT WORKS IN CORRECTIONS

In my work, I use different approaches to evaluate the research and assess the effectiveness of crime reduction strategies: reviews of the literature, meta-analyses– (a quantitative method used to examine groups of studies), simulation studies, and the scientific methods scoring system that assesses the direction and significance of studies.

Systematic Reviews and Meta-Analysis

Meta-analysis is a method of summarizing, integrating, and interpreting selected sets of scholarly research (i.e., empirical studies that produce quantitative findings; Lipsey & Wilson, 2001). Meta-analysis enables researchers to aggregate the continuously growing body of empirical studies to examine and compare the effects of some intervention. It is a method of encoding and analyzing the statistics that summarize research findings from research reports.

The Campbell Collaboration is an exciting new development in social science research (http://www.campbellcollaboration.org/). The collaboration is designed to facilitate the preparation, maintenance, and accessibility of systematic reviews of research on the effects of social science interventions. One section of the collaboration, the Justice Group, focuses on crime and justice topics.

The Campbell Collaboration follows the precedent of the Cochrane Collaboration in health areas (http://www.Cochrane.org; Petrosino, Boruch, Farrington, Sherman, & Weisburd, 2003). The Cochrane Collaboration was organized to address the concerns of Archie Cochrane, who criticized health care professionals for ignoring scientific evidence. The organization conducts systematic reviews on health care. The reviews are prepared electronically, structured with the same exact detail as earlier reviews, and updated periodically as new evidence becomes available.

The Campbell Collaboration builds on the Cochrane precedent but focuses on what works in social policy. The Justice Group of the collaboration will coordinate the preparation, maintenance, and accessibility of crime- and justice-relevant systematic reviews and meta-analyses.

University of Maryland Scientific Methods Scoring System

The University of Maryland researchers used a two-step procedure for drawing conclusions about what works in crime prevention (Sherman, Farrington, Welsh, & MacKenzie, 2002; Sherman, Gottfredson, MacKenzie, Eck, Reuter, & Bushway, 1997). The first step in this process was to identify a topic area and then to locate and assess each individual study for the quality of the research design and methodology. This assessment indicated the scientific rigor of the study. The second step was to examine each topic area for research quality and the direction and significance of the results. That is, within each topic area, the results of the evaluations were summarized in order to draw conclusions about what works, what doesn't, what is promising, and what we don't know. For instance, all boot camp evaluations were located and each study was assessed for scientific rigor. Following this assessment, the direction and significance of the results were examined.

The review of studies in the criminal justice setting focused on whether the programs reduced criminal activities.

Step 1: Determining Scientific Rigor

The first step in the process of assessing studies for scientific rigor was to locate as many studies as possible within each topic area (e.g., intensive supervised probation, drug treatment, boot camps, etc.). In most cases, we used studies that had been conducted within the past 10 years because older work was less relevant to the present social conditions and correctional programming. Both published and unpublished research reports were included. To be included in the assessment, the study had to include information on criminal activities or recidivism. The scientific rigor of each study was assessed using a form to document research design, selection problems, attrition, statistical analysis, statistical controls, and sample size. The results of the assessment were used to give each study a score for scientific rigor. Scores ranged from 1 to 5, with 5 indicating the most rigor. Studies assigned a particular methods score share the following features:

> *Level 1 Studies.* Some correlation between the program and measure(s) of recidivism. Usually there was no comparison group. Studies in this category were judged to be so low in rigor that they were not used to assess the effectiveness of the correctional programs.
>
> *Level 2 Studies.* These studies indicated some association between the program and recidivism but were severely limited because many alternative explanations could not be ruled out given the research design. Frequently in the correctional evaluations, these studies used dropouts from programs or nonvolunteers as the comparison group, and no variables were included in the statistical analysis to control for initial differences between groups.
>
> *Level 3 Studies.* A comparison between two or more groups, one given the program and one not given the program. The design of the study and the statistical analysis ensured reasonable similarity between the treated group and the comparison(s).
>
> *Level 4 Studies.* Comparison between a program group and one or more control groups, controlling for other factors; or a nonequivalent comparison group that is only slightly different from the program group.
>
> *Level 5 Studies.* The "gold standard," including random assignment and analysis of comparable program and comparison groups, including controls for attrition.

Step 2: Drawing Conclusions About What Works

Clear conclusions about programs that work, don't work, or are promising require a high level of confidence in the research findings. New results continually add new pieces to the puzzle. Old research results must be reconsidered in light of new findings, and these may lead to new conclusions. The best one can claim to "know" about effectiveness is based only on the quality and quantity of the available evidence at one point in time.

Because there are many consequences of claims about "what works," it is important to use a reasonably high threshold for the strength of scientific evidence.

However, the current state of evaluation research creates a dilemma in attempting to draw conclusions. If we use only studies that score at level 5 (i.e., the gold standard) on the scientific merit scale, we would have few evaluations to use in assessing programs. For example, a high threshold in deciding which studies to include in making decisions about what works would require at least two level 5 studies showing that a program is effective (or ineffective), with the preponderance of the evidence in favor of the same conclusions. Employing such a conservative approach to determine what works would leave us with very little research on which to draw conclusions. Obviously, there is a trade-off between the level of certainty in the conclusions that can be drawn and the level of useful information that can be gleaned from the available research. Excluding the findings from studies that score moderately on scientific merit would waste a great deal of useful information. Thus, in order to make use of the available research, the University of Maryland researchers took a middle road between reaching very few conclusions with great certainty and reaching many conclusions with little certainty. This meant that they eliminated studies of very weak methodology.

Studies had to reach the "bar" of scientific rigor with a score of 3 in levels of evidence if they were to be used to draw conclusions about what works. Descriptive or process evaluations and those scoring a 1 on the scale were eliminated from consideration because they could not reasonably be used to determine whether the program was effective in reducing recidivism.

Studies scoring a 2 were very common; however, because many alternative explanations for the results could not be ruled out (i.e., the scientific merit of the studies was so low), we decided to use these only to provide additional information about an area of study (i.e., preponderance of evidence) but not to draw conclusions. Although studies that scored at level 2 lack strong scientific rigor and cannotprovide the sole basis for conclusions about effectiveness, they do provide some worthwhile information. This is particularly true in program areas in which very scant evaluation research exists. These admittedly weak studies may be the only information available. In program areas that are more well researched, level 2 studies become part of the preponderance of evidence, but they do not serve as the primary source of evidence. Here, the findings are given reduced weight relative to those of more scientifically rigorous evaluations.

Studies scoring 3 or higher were used to draw conclusions about the effectiveness of a program in reducing recidivism. We developed decision rules using scientific strength and substantive findings from the available evaluations and classified each program area into one of four categories: what works, what does not work, what is promising, and what is unknown.

What Works: These are programs that we are reasonably certain reduce recidivism in the kinds of contexts (and with the types of participants) in which they have been evaluated and for which the findings should be generalizable to similar settings in other places and times. Programs defined as "working" must have at least two level 3 evaluations, with statistical significance tests showing effectiveness and the preponderance of all available evidence supporting the same conclusion.

What Does Not Work: These are programs that we are reasonably certain fail to reduce recidivism in the kinds of contexts (and with the types of participants) in which they have been evaluated and for which the findings should be generalizable to similar settings in other places and times. Programs classified as "not working" must have at least two level 3 evaluations, with statistical significance tests showing ineffectiveness and the preponderance of all available evidence supporting the same conclusion.

What Is Promising: These are programs for which the level of certainty from available evidence is too low to support generalizable conclusions, but for which there is some evidence predicting that further research could support such conclusions. Programs are defined as "promising" if they have at least one level 3 evaluation, with statistical significance tests showing their effectiveness in reducing recidivism and the preponderance of all available evidence supporting the same conclusion.

What Is Unknown: Any program not included in one of the preceding three categories is defined as having unknown effects. There is simply not enough research, or not enough research employing adequate scientific rigor, from which to draw even tentative conclusions. Program areas with unknown effects should not be interpreted as ineffective. Succinctly put, the jury is still out.

An advantage of this scoring system with clearly specified decision rules about what works, what doesn't, what's promising, and what's unknown is that any other scientists can attempt to replicate our findings. Obviously, the scoring is based more on the internal validity of the research than on the external validity.

ASSESSING EFFECTIVENESS

Based on the literature reviews, systematic reviews, and meta-analyses and on the previously described decision rules, I reviewed correctional interventions, management strategies, and treatment and rehabilitation programs in order to identify which were effective in reducing the recidivism of offenders and delinquents (MacKenzie, 2006). Hereafter in this chapter I refer to all of these as *programs* or *interventions.* I located 284 evaluations of the programs out of thousands of studies examined. In order to be included in this assessment, the study had to be an outcome study of sufficient scientific merit to permit an assessment of effectiveness.

What Works

At this point in time, the research evidence demonstrates that the following programs were effective in reducing recidivism:

- Academic education
- Vocational education
- Cognitive skills programs
  - Moral reconation therapy
  - Reasoning and rehabilitation
  - Cognitive restructuring
- Cognitive-behavioral treatment for sex offenders
- Behavioral treatment for sex offenders
- Hormonal/surgical treatment of sex offenders
- Multisystemic therapy for juveniles
- Drug courts
- Drug treatment in the community
- Incarceration-based drug treatment

One consistent similarity among the effective programs is that they include human service components, with the exception of the hormonal/surgical treatment for sex offenders. The effective programs are not based on a control or deterrent philosophy. Furthermore, the results are consistent with the results of the theoretical meta-analyses. As found in theoretical meta-analyses such as those conducted by Andrews et al. (1990) and Lipsey (1992, 1995), many of the programs target dynamic criminogenic factors. Furthermore, the effective programs are skill-oriented, based on cognitive-behavior/behavior models, and treat deficits simultaneously (i.e., they are multimodal).

What Does Not Work

In my reviews of the following programs and interventions, I concluded that they were not effective in reducing recidivism:

- Life skills education
- Correctional industries
- Multicomponent work programs

- Psychosocial sex offender treatment
- Residential treatment for juveniles
- Community supervision for juveniles
- Domestic violence treatment using a feminist perspective
- Domestic violence programs using cognitive-behavioral treatment
- Domestic violence programs using arrest interventions
- Boot camps for adults and juveniles
- Intensive supervision
- Electronic monitoring
- Scared Straight

No single explanation seems adequate to explain why these programs were not found to be effective in reducing recidivism. Some possible reasons for these findings may be that the programs: (1) have poor or no theoretical bases; (2) are poorly implemented; (3) focus on punishment, deterrence, or control instead of providing human service or rehabilitation; and (4) emphasize the formation of ties or bonds without first changing the individual's thought processes.

The failure of some programs appears to occur because they have little theoretical basis. For example, psychosocial sex offender treatment and community supervision and residential facilities for juveniles appear to fit this description. I hypothesize that this is the reason for their lack of effectiveness. For example, my review of the juvenile programs found little consistent theoretical basis for the programs. The psychosocial sex offender treatment is based on a psychodynamic theoretical perspective, not on the behavioral or cognitive-behavioral models that have been found to be effective in correctional treatment (Andres et al, 1990; Andrews & Bonta, 1998; Lipsey, 1992).

None of the interventions that focused on punishment, deterrence, or control were found to reduce recidivism. These were major goals of corrections during the 1980s and early 1990s. There is now a sufficient body of research from which to conclude that programs such as boot camps, Scared Straight, arrests for domestic violence, intensive supervision, and electronic monitoring are not effective in reducing recidivism. These programs may fulfill other goals of corrections, but there is no evidence that they are effective in reducing recidivism.

Some research suggests that punishment, deterrence, or control-type programs could be effective if they included human service, rehabilitation, or treatment components. As yet, little research has examined such combined programs. Exploratory research by my colleagues and me on boot camps, as well as research on intensive supervision by Petersilia and her colleagues, suggests that adding human service components to such programs may make them effective in reducing recidivism. However, there is not enough research on these combined programs to permit us to draw definitive conclusions.

When I compared the effective programs with the ineffective programs, I noticed an interesting difference. The effective programs focused on individual-level change. In contrast, the ineffective programs frequently focused on developing opportunities. For example, the cognitive skills programs emphasize individual changes in thinking, reasoning, empathy, and problem solving. In comparison, ineffective programs, such as life skills and work programs, focus on giving the offenders opportunities in the community. Based on these observations, I hypothesize that effective programs must transform the individual. This change is required before the person will be able to take advantage of opportunities in the environment.

INDIVIDUAL TRANSFORMATIONS

Most criminologists obtained their training in sociology departments. Not surprisingly, their theories emphasize the importance of the social conditions in determining criminal behavior (Andrews & Bonta, 2003). Recently, criminologists have emphasized the importance of attachment in a variety of social institutions, such as marriage, work, or school. Such ties are expected to reduce the person's criminal activities. For example, in their life-course theory, Sampson and Laub (1995) propose that changes in social bonds explain continuity and change in offending. Individuals form bonds with social institutions, and as bonds strengthen, social capital increases. This capital supplies resources to solve problems. Dependence on capital means that much is jeopardized if it is lost. As bonds form and social capital increases, criminal activity becomes more costly. The establishment of meaningful social bonds during adulthood can function as critical life events or turning points at which offenders begin to conform and to turn away from criminal activity. Ties or bonds to social institutions influence behavior both during long periods of the life course (Sampson & Laub, 1995) and in relatively local life circumstances (Horney, Osgood, & Marshall, 1995; MacKenzie, Browning, Skroban, & Smith, 1999; MacKenzie, Gover, Styve, & Mitchell, 1999). However, little is said in these theories about the mechanisms that lead to the changes in ties or bonds. The question is, what happens within the individual to bring about changes in ties and bonds?

I propose that individual-level change must precede changes in ties or bonds to social institutions. The social environment may be conducive to the formation of ties, but at some individual level the person must change if the bond is to form. In order to get along with family, keep a job, support children, or form strong, positive ties with other institutions, the person much change in cognitive reasoning, attitudes toward drug use, antisocial attitudes, reading level, or vocational skills. This conclusion is supported by the finding that effective programs are those that have a human service component. The programs need to change the individual and not just provide opportunities for the formation of ties or bonds.

Perhaps the best example of the difference is marriage. Marriage is a social institution and, for males, it is associated with a decrease in criminal activity. Using an extreme example, I demonstrate how just changing the social environment does not appear to be a reasonable correctional intervention. From the point of view of bond theorists, a reasonable intervention for corrections might be to have parties to introduce the offenders to women who eligible for marriage. That is, because marriage is associated with a decline in criminal activity, one might want to maximize the chances that these offenders would find someone to wed. The transformation theory would say that the individual must first change so that he or she is ready to marry and move away from criminal activity before marrying. The individual-level change results in both the movement away from crime and the formation of the social ties of marriage.

Incapacitating Offenders Who Continue to Commit Crimes at High Rates

Research on the effects of incapacitation does not lend itself to the scoring and decision rules described earlier because most of the studies use simulation-type models to estimate the crime reduction effect of incapacitating offenders. For this research, I reviewed the literature and from this review concluded that there is evidence that locking up offenders who are not at the end of their criminal careers is effective in reducing crimes in the community. Studies investigating the effectiveness of this strategy show that there are advantages to locking up the high-rate career criminals who commit serious crimes. The difficulties are identifying who these high-rate offenders are and the diminishing return of invested dollars with the increased incarceration rates.

CONCLUSIONS

Policy makers and correctional decision makers have made little use of science to try to inform their decisions. There is an extensive body of research literature that can be used to assess the effectiveness of various correctional programs. One problem with the literature is that the evaluations vary greatly in scientific merit. Some evaluations are descriptive and cannot be used to judge effectiveness; similarly, other evaluations are of such poor scientific quality that they should not be used for decision making. This chapter presents a method for assessing the literature by not only using the direction and size of the effects of a program on recidivism but also weighing the studies by their scientific merit. If we are to advance our knowledge about ways to effectively change delinquents and offenders, it is imperative that we move toward evidence-based corrections. Decisions would be made on the basis of research evidence, both basic and outcome research.

■ ■ ■

Activities

Choose one of the programs from the following list that were identified as effective in reducing recidivism. Bring your responses to the practicum setting or class on a PowerPoint for presentation. This is an opportunity to share program effectiveness information with colleagues and others to learn about best practices. You may also repeat this presentation in the classroom. Review the components that make this program effective:

1. Identify the program—title, name of authors, goal, and objectives.

2. Using the levels of evidence identified in this chapter, at what level of evidence is this program rated?

3. Summarize the research studies that indicate the effectiveness of the program. Be sure to include the authors, study populations, type of research design, sample size, and outcomes.

4. Identify the theoretical perspective or approach in the program.

5. Describe the population at risk that the program is most suited for, including the specific problem or difficulties of those to be served.

6. Describe the setting, structure, and format of the program.

7. Describe the program leader and role.

8. Outline the features of the service, such as duration of program, timing, or when it is to be initiated, staffing and staffing characteristics, and any special training required of staff.

9. How are recipients of the service identified? Include your references and Web resources and links.

Effective Programs

1. Academic education

2. Vocational education

3. Cognitive skills programs

   a. Moral reconation therapy

   b. Reasoning and rehabilitation

   c. Cognitive restructuring

4. Cognitive-behavioral treatment for sex offenders

5. Behavioral treatment for sex offenders

6. Hormonal/surgical treatment of sex offenders

7. Multisystemic therapy for juveniles

8. Drug courts

9. Drug treatment in the community

10. Incarceration-based drug treatment

What Does Not Work

Choose a colleague or partner to work with on this activity. Find out whether your community funds any of the following programs that are not identified as effective. Discuss a plan for how you might help these programs to improve or to transform into a program that works. What are the steps you might propose to reach this goal? Who would you talk to? Choose one program and discuss this with your colleagues, supervisors, or classmates.

1. Life skills education
2. Correctional industries
3. Multicomponent work programs
4. Psychosocial sex offender treatment
5. Residential treatment for juveniles
6. Community supervision for juveniles
7. Domestic violence treatment using a feminist perspective
8. Domestic violence programs using cognitive-behavioral treatment
9. Domestic violence programs using arrest interventions
10. Boot camps for adults and juveniles
11. Intensive supervision
12. Electronic monitoring
13. Scared Straight

A JAIL DIVERSION INTERNSHIP: BRIDGING THE CLASSROOM AND PRACTICE

Marian Dumaine

The Context

Carlos Rodriquez, a first-year social work intern, was given an assignment in his internship seminar class that required him to critically analyze a case situation by responding to the following questions:

1. What does empirical research suggest about your client group: prevalence, profile, psychosocial factors?
2. What challenges is your client likely to encounter?

3. How would you apply theories learned about human behavior to increase your understanding of the case situation?
4. What policies, laws, and ethical issues most directly affect your client?
5. What evidence-based practices are recommended for your client?

Case Description

Carlos, an intern, is placed at HELP NOW, a jail diversion program for clients
charged with misdemeanors and diagnosed with severe mental illness and
substance abuse problems. The agency's mission is to prevent criminalization
of the mentally ill by offering clients linkage to mental health services instead of
serving time in jail. Without the services of HELP NOW, these clients are often
isolated in jail, receive little stimulation, and may require seclusion and restraint.
The end result is often that these clients experience an intensification of symptoms, are not given psychotropic medication, leave the jail without tools needed
to survive in the community, become homeless, and are subsequently rearrested.

Carlos selected the case of Francisco Diaz for his assignment and was given
the psychosocial assessment included at the end of this section. The assessment was developed by Francisco's case manager after consulting records in
the courts and mental health centers and speaking with Francisco's father,
therapist, and boarding home manager.

Intern's Initial Response

After Carlos was given the class assignment and case, he felt overwhelmed, but
he decided to consult both his field instructor, Mr. Henry, and his seminar
instructor, Professor Ospina, to determine what additional information was
needed and what resources were available and to clarify his immediate responsibilities to the client.

He was given several suggestions:

1. Read the case situation and identify questions to review with his field
   instructor.
2. Closely review the grant submitted by HELP NOW for additional information about the intent of the program, the client population, and recommended services.
3. Consult the agency library to assess resources.
4. Develop an action plan to respond to each question of the assignment.
5. Review and use relevant material from his classes on human behavior,
   psychopathology, social policy, criminal justice, and research.

6. Meet with the librarian to improve his skills in conducting literature searches.

Actions Taken

Carlos's seminar instructor, Professor Ospina, told him that the assignment was lengthy, should be completed in stages, and would take several months to complete. She said that the process used to undertake the assignment was important, that he was learning a critical-thinking and case-planning process that he could apply to all cases throughout his professional career. Carlos decided to outline his plan for tackling the assignment and to review his outline with Mr. Henry and Professor Ospina. His outline follows:

I. Preparatory actions
   a. Compile questions about the case situation.
   b. Read grant and highlight relevant areas
   c. Gather pertinent notes and textbooks from classes in human behavior, psychopathology, social policy, criminal justice, and research
   d. Schedule training in library to conduct literature review
   e. Select keywords for literature search
II. Profile of client
   a. Conduct a literature search of peer-reviewed material at the agency and the library
   b. Focus on clients with severe mental illness and substance abuse who have had legal charges
   c. Look for client characteristics and treatment challenges
III. Human behavior
   a. Determine theories applicable to understanding case situation
   b. List relevant questions about the case situation
IV. Social policies
   a. Review social policy class notes for information about policies related to mental health, substance abuse, and criminal justice
   b. Review grant application for information about criminalization of the mentally ill
   c. Describe key policies and their impact on client
V. Evidence-based practices
   a. Conduct a thorough literature search of interventions for clients diagnosed with co-occurring disorders of severe mental illness and substance abuse

b. Assess the relevant effectiveness of each intervention and its applicability to case situation

c. Review results with field instructor and discuss implementation potential with client

Outcomes

Carlos followed his plan, beginning with the preparatory actions indicated in his outline. In addition, he visited community agencies that have provided services to Francisco and met with mental health and substance abuse planning boards. He also attended a project leadership team meeting whose mission is to ensure a comprehensive continuous integrated system of care for individuals with co-occurring disorders.

Carlos then formulated a treatment intervention plan with Francisco and linked him to a crisis center, a day treatment program, and a community mental health center. In addition, he visited him frequently at his boarding home and worked with his case manager to develop and implement plans to try to prevent continued substance use and homelessness, to reinforce the need for medication compliance, and to increase his support system.

Carlos learned that many other individuals had similar problems of severe mental illness and substance abuse. In fact, he read that substance abuse has become so prevalent among the mentally ill that substance use is assumed, that it is considered an expectation rather than an exception (Minkoff, 2001). Many, like Francisco, are homeless, evidence greater potential for violence and self-injury, and find themselves in the criminal justice system. Furthermore, these individuals have an increased risk of HIV infection, medical illness, and early mortality, and they have more problems obtaining meals, managing money, and maintaining stable housing (Dumaine, 2003). These clients present with treatment challenges because interventions have generally not been effective; they are often in crisis, unable to meet their basics needs, and caught in a revolving door from the hospital to the community agency or residence to the street (Drake et al., 2001).

The human-behavior section of Carlos's assignment resulted in his application of the ecological perspective (Corcoran & Casebolt, 2004) to this case situation. First, Carlos expanded his knowledge about the medical model, diagnostic classifications using the DSM, and the role of medication in the treatment of mental illness. He learned about the disease model of alcoholism, as well as the effects of cocaine use. Carlos began to compare the medical model with the ecological perspective and discussed differences with his field instructor. He looked at research about the complex etiology of mental illness and substance abuse and became more informed about empirically supported biopsychosocial causation theories. Carlos was interested in the dynamic vulnerability formulation (Anthony & Liberman, 1986; Zubin & Spring, 1977) because it helped to explain Francisco's symptoms and the importance of improved coping skills and social supports, as well as reduced stressors, in preventing future crisis episodes. Carlos also examined articles about risk assessment and risk and protective factors (Corcoran & Casebolt, 2004).

Many social policies affected his client that were related to deinstitutionalization of the mentally ill and other laws. However, lack of coordination of care between the two service systems with separate funding streams and treatment philosophies seems to present the greatest problem (Drake et al., 2001).

A literature review (Dumaine, 2003; Drake et al., 2001; Minkoff, 2001) of interventions with co-occurring disorders of severe mental illness and substance abuse revealed recurrent themes:

1. Continued assertive outreach is needed to engage these clients in treatment.
2. During the early stages, engagement is the treatment.
3. Expectations for positive treatment outcomes need to be reframed to reflect a long-term perspective, with realistic short- term goals based on client state of readiness, because treatment is difficult, dropout is high, and many clients continue to evidence increased psychiatric crises and impaired functioning levels despite treatment. Expecting total abstinence from substances, particularly during the early stages of treatment, is unrealistic.
4. Leverage is useful in countering the clients' reluctance to become consistently involved in treatment.
5. Linkage, coordination, and integration of treatment services is needed to help these clients locate, access, and use community services.
6. A long-term stage approach to recovery should be adopted.
7. Additional community resources are needed to provide supports.

Evaluation

Carlos met with his field instructor to assess what he had learned from his class assignment. Questions posed and summarized responses follow:

1. What have you learned about yourself as a professional social worker?
   a. I need to take time to prepare my responses to clients, to consult empirical literature and colleagues.
   b. Setting short-term goals helps prevent feeling overwhelmed.

2. What have you learned about the client population?
   a. The clients have complex needs that require a coordinated systems approach.
   b. Daily survival is often a struggle for these clients.
3. How would you assess your effectiveness with your client?
   a. I would examine abstinence, avoidance of crisis episodes, and daily functioning skills.
   b. I need to research feasible outcome measures.
4. How would you apply this learning process with other clients?
   a. I would follow the same steps, consulting materials from my classes, colleagues, and the literature.
   b. I would compose outlines to guide me in the process.
5. How would you maintain proficiency in working with clients?
   a. I would continue to consult the research, listen to clients, and network with other agencies and service providers.
   b. I would attend specialized continuing education programs.

▪ ▪ ▪

Activities

1. Complete the class assignment relating to a client you are working with at your internship.

2. What barriers do you think you might encounter in advocating for the use of evidence-based practices at your agency?

3. What strategies might you use to overcome the agency's reluctance to implement evidence-based practices?

Psychosocial Assessment of Francisco

History of Illness

At age 16, Francisco attempted suicide by overdose. He began using cocaine 2 years later. Hospitalizations began in his early 20s, when he was actively delusional and believed the Lord was influencing him and telling him to take his clothes off in public to be pure. He was admitted nine times to psychiatric hospitals, including ABC Hospital, because of medication noncompliance and inappropriate behaviors (e.g., preaching door to door) prior to admission to State Hospital in 2000 following arrest for exposure of sex organ and disorderly conduct. At that time he stated that the devil was following him, that he needed to offer himself as sacrifice as in Biblical times, and that the police department was against him because he was the son of God. Francisco required several weeks to stabilize once hospitalized. He then went to live at a boarding home but has continued to have periods of decompensation requiring crisis visits and hospitalization. In addition, during the past 3 years he has often denied the need for medication and would stop taking his medications, begin using cocaine and alcohol, and live on the streets. The result was frequent arrests for charges that included disorderly conduct, battery on a police officer, and robbery.

In his late teens, he was shot during a drive-by shooting. His brother died a few years before, also allegedly shot. His parents divorced during the past few years after a tumultuous separation. His father is presently recovering from prostate surgery.

▪ ▪ ▪

Presenting Problems and Significant Events

Francisco continues to hear voices saying that he is a sinner, exhibits delusional thoughts about being Jesus Christ, is hyperverbal with loose associations, and reads the Bible several hours each evening. He has been at Bench County jail the past 2 days, subsequent to a breakup with his girlfriend at the boarding home, medication noncompliance, and cocaine use, all leading to decompensation: threatening others and reporting that the Lord has chosen him to save the world.

Risk Assessment

Suicidality/Self-Injurious Behaviors

He is not presently suicidal but, when psychotic, has threatened to cut his own throat as a sacrifice to the Lord (in 1990, before state hospitalization).

Homicidality/Violence

He has been threatening others who interfere with the Lord's work, and when psychotic in the past, he has been hyperverbal and agitated, often engaging in violent encounters with others.

Victim or Perpetrator of Neglect, Abandonment, or Abuse (Physical, Emotional, Sexual)

His father was allegedly physically abusive with Francisco, beating him with an electrical cord on three occasions after he lied. After the third incident, Francisco went to live with his maternal grandmother, and his parents divorced shortly afterward.

Witness to Domestic Violence

It is not known whether Francisco ever witnessed violent exchanges between his parents or whether he has been violent with his girlfriend.

Trauma

His brother died a few years ago as a result of a gunshot wound. Circumstances are not known. They were very close.

General Strengths/Assets

Francisco presently verbalizes the need for treatment. He has future goals and attends to personal hygiene and grooming independently when stable. He verbalizes his thoughts to others.

Areas for Growth/Development

Francisco needs to increase his understanding of the rationale for medication and continued treatment involvement. He also needs to increase awareness of the consequences of drug use and its effect on his psychiatric stability.

Functional Assessment Rating Scale

1	2	3	4	5	6	7	8	9
No problem		Slight problem		Moderate problem		Severe problem		Extreme Problem

<u>9</u>   1. Emotional/Behavioral/Treatment Compliance/Insight: Francisco has stopped taking his medication repeatedly in the past. Presently appears delusional, hypervigilant, religiously preoccupied, grandiose, hyperverbal, with thought derailment.

<u>4</u>   2. Family Relationships/Support/Stressors: Oldest male of 3 siblings; 1 brother allegedly murdered 3 years ago; parents divorced and his

grandmother died in 2001 (they were close). Father just had prostate surgery. Mother lives in Virginia and has little contact with Francisco.

_6_ 3. Health (Medical and Dental): Francisco takes medications regularly for hypertension. However, he does not eat nutritiously and often fails to follow up with tests for blood sugar levels, which are reportedly high.

_3_ 4. ADL Functioning/Ability to Care for Self: Although Francisco can independently attend to personal hygiene, this area tends to be neglected when psychiatric symptoms worsen.

_7_ 5. Social Network/Interpersonal and Conflict Resolution Skills: Francisco's interactions with peers are often conflictual, as he has anger outbursts, can be verbally abusive, has a low frustration tolerance, and often alienates others.

_5_ 6. Residential/Living Situation/Homeless/Shelter: Francisco lives in a supervised boarding home when not incarcerated. However, he frequently leaves the home and has been found roaming the streets at night and living under bridges. He repeatedly requires prompting to initiate and complete basic living tasks when not taking his medications.

_5_ 7. Vocational Activities/Training/Interests: Francisco has not been employed with the exception of 4 months (part time) at a restaurant wrapping silverware (supported employment). He has never followed through with referrals to vocational rehabilitation.

_4_ 8. Financial Resources/Budgeting: Francisco receives SSI. His father is payee. He has difficulty budgeting his spending money.

_8_ 9. Intellectual Functioning/Educational Level/School Placement and Adjustment: Francisco worked toward his GED in the past but did not complete the educational program. He left school after the 10th grade. There are reports of his having been truant frequently from school and having difficulty concentrating. He has not expressed an interest in returning to school at this time.

_8_ 10. Alcohol/Substance Abuse and Recovery Activities: Francisco has a history of ongoing alcohol and cocaine use. His last known use was 2 days ago. He has been treated at Refuge Residential Program (2001), and Abstinence, Inc. (2002). He reports feeling "strange" in AA meetings.

_4_ 11. Legal: Francisco had a prior arrest for disorderly conduct and exposure of sex organ in 2000 and frequent recent arrests for charges including disorderly conduct, battery on a police officer, and robbery. He is presently incarcerated.

_2_ 12. Recreation: Leisure Interests/Hobbies/Talents: Francisco likes photography and drawing, but he reportedly has not engaged in these activities for 2 years.

<u>6</u>   13. Cultural/Religious Beliefs and Traditions: Francisco has attended Catholic mass on Sundays whenever possible. He states that his higher Power knows all of his deeds, including sinful ones. He prays daily.

<u>6</u>   14. Transportation Means/Mobility: Francisco is fearful of using public transportation on his own.

Summary of Visit in Jail

Francisco was reading the Bible when the worker arrived; he was somewhat guarded and hesitant to open the door. He questioned the worker about becoming his own payee, and during a discussion of the guidelines and procedures involved in changing payee, he accused the worker of being "in cahoots" with his father. It was necessary to terminate the visit prematurely due to Francisco's agitation level.

Justification for Continued Services

Francisco has not been able to maintain himself in the community on medication for longer than 6 months in the past 5 years. Without treatment, supervision, and structure, he has, by history, endangered the safety of himself and others (e.g., threatening others and making statements about offering himself up for sacrifice).

AXIS I:	Schizophrenia, Paranoid Type	295.30
	Polysubstance Abuse	305.90
AXIS II:	None	V71.09
AXIS III:	Noninsulin-dependent diabetes, Hypertension	
AXIS IV:	Severe: breakup with girlfriend, illness of father, incarceration	
AXIS V:	35	

EVIDENCE-BASED PRACTICES FOR RISK ASSESSMENT

JILL S. LEVENSON

This chapter reviews risk assessment factors for criminal offending and actuarial risk assessment tools associated with recidivism in offender populations. Reliability and predictive validity of actuarial instruments for assessing the risk of recidivism for sexual offenders is presented also. This chapter summarizes lessons for practice and includes learning activities and a case for study.

Practitioners are often called on to provide predictions of the future dangerousness of convicted sex predators. To address this objective, considerable effort is being placed on moving from using clinical assessments of sexual offenders, which have proved to be highly inaccurate, to using actuarial tools to improve predictive accuracy (Glancy & Regehr, 2004). As a criminal justice professional, you may be called on to assess the likelihood that someone will commit a future crime or to predict the recurrence of criminal activity in an offender. It is a huge challenge to improve accuracy. The purpose of this chapter is to provide guidelines for valid and reliable tools for assessment of sexual predators that will contribute to improved accuracy of predictions. However, there are several caveats to add at this point. First, only those persons with training and expertise in this area should administer these tools, because the outcomes have implications for individual and community safety. Second, the courts do not uniformly accept these measures as reliable, and therefore it is suggested that these measures be used in conjunction with other clinical assessment tools to provide a complete picture of the potential of the person for recidivism. Third, actuarial tools may not meet the standard for admissibility in the courts (Glancy & Regehr, 2004).

ACTUARIAL RISK ASSESSMENT TOOLS

Actuarial prediction is a scientific method of estimating an individual's risk for something based on *actual* outcomes (hence the term *actuarial*). It has been used in the insurance industry for decades to adjust premium rates based on an individual's risk for making a claim. When you call a car insurance company to get a quote, they ask you some questions, such as "How old are you?" and "How many accidents or speeding tickets have you had?" These questions are designed to determine your "risk factors" for having an accident and costing the insurance company money. By studying past accidents, researchers have asked, who has the most accidents? and have found, for instance, that young males have more accidents than older females. So, if you are a male under the age of 25 years old, you have two "risk factors." If you also have previous speeding tickets or accidents, you are very high risk indeed—and you will pay more money for insurance than an older woman with no tickets! By assessing the risk factors a driver might possess, insurance companies calculate an "actuarial score" to determine an individual's similarity to the "class" of people that have the most accidents. The actuarial method can be used to predict with certainty that any given individual will act in a particular way. It can also estimate the probability that a particular individual will make a future insurance claim.

Medical doctors use actuarial methods. By studying heart disease, for instance, researchers have learned that many people who have heart attacks also have high cholesterol, a family history of heart disease, a history of smoking, and obesity. The more of these risk factors you have, the more likely you are to have a heart attack. Your doctor can even predict how likely you are to have a heart attack by factoring those items into an equation. In fact, you can go on the Internet, plug in your risk factors, and be given a percentage that represents your chance of having a heart attack!

Actuarial methods are increasingly being used in the behavioral professions, such as criminal justice, psychology, and social work, to determine appropriate interventions based on the assessed risk of a particular future behavior. The earliest known empirical study in predicting criminal behavior occurred in 1928. A sociologist named Ernest Burgess developed a scale in which he simply counted the presence or absence of 21 factors that experts considered to be associated with favorable or unfavorable parole outcomes and applied them to parolees (kind of like a checklist—does the parolee have this factor or not?). Clinical judgments (without the checklist) were also made about the parolees by three prison psychiatrists. Burgess then researched the probation success of the offenders under study and determined which of them actually successfully completed their probations without further arrest. The psychiatrists were found to be slightly more accurate in predicting parole success but quite inferior in predicting parole failure. In other words, anyone using the checklist did better at predicting that a parolee would commit a new crime than did psychiatrists with years of experience. Burgess concluded that even this primitive actuarial method was superior to subjective impressions in its predictive accuracy.

Paul Meehl's 1954 book, *Clinical Versus Statistical Prediction,* reviewed 20 such comparative studies and found that, in every case, the actuarial method was equal or superior to informal clinical judgment. Meehl proposed that statistical methods are consistently more accurate than professional judgment, inspiring (not surprisingly) a backlash of resistance from the psychological community and a rash of empirical comparisons. It soon became clear that actuarial methods performed consistently and significantly better than clinical judgment (Grove & Meehl, 1996).

Swets, Dawes, and Monahan (2000) assert that actuarial methods can raise the accuracy of predictions by setting statistical thresholds for decision making and by standardizing factors that professionals readily recognize as key diagnostic features. Grove and Meehl (1996) agree that relying on anecdotal evidence in making decisions is too subjective and may have grave consequences for clients or communities. They further advocate the use of actuarial methods to inform sound policy decisions and say that to use the less scientific of two prediction procedures in the development of social policy and intervention services is not only inefficient but unethical.

Now that you understand the concepts of risk factors and risk assessment, let's turn now to looking at research-based risk factors for certain types of criminal behaviors and tools that are available to help you, the criminal justice professional, to assess risk.

RISK FACTORS FOR GENERAL CRIMINAL BEHAVIOR AND RECIDIVISM

Longitudinal research studies have consistently identified risk factors for criminal offending. Some important historical risk factors for criminal offending include (Farrington, 1999):

- Impulsivity
- Low intelligence or educational attainment
- Having a parent or sibling who has been convicted of a crime
- Poor parental supervision
- Being harshly disciplined as a child
- Parental conflict or divorce
- Low income

- Living in poor or overcrowded housing
- Large family size
- Having delinquent friends
- Living in a high-crime community

These risk factors are well established, but it is unclear which of them are truly causal or how they interact with each other to increase risk. Although many theories exist that hypothesize how personality, family, peer, school, and community factors influence the development of criminal behavior, more research is needed on understanding the specific effects of each risk factor. Although these risk factors are important in understanding the development and prevention of criminal behavior, in your criminal justice career, you will be more likely to be called on to assess the likelihood of recidivism.

Recidivism refers to the recurrence of criminal behavior as measured by a rearrest or a new conviction. In other words, recidivism risk assessment pertains to the question of which criminals, once arrested, will be most likely to go on to commit new crimes. Risk factors for violent recidivism include (Douglas & Webster, 1999):

- Previous violence
- Early onset of violent behavior
- Unstable relationships
- Employment instability
- Substance use
- Major mental illness
- Psychopathy
- Early adjustment problems
- Prior violations of probationary supervision

We now examine three risk factors related to criminal recidivism: psychopathy, mental illness, and substance abuse.

PSYCHOPATHY, ANTISOCIAL PERSONALITY DISORDER, AND RECIDIVISM

Psychopathy is related, but not identical, to antisocial personality disorder as defined by the *Diagnostic and Statistical Manual of Mental Disorders* (*DSM-IV-TR*; American Psychiatric Association, 2000). Antisocial personality disorder is described as a chronic pattern of behavior that includes criminal acts, deceit-fulness, impulsivity, aggressiveness, disregard for safety, irresponsibility, and lack of remorse. Antisocial personality disorder generally has an early onset and begins with conduct problems in childhood and adolescence. Hare, Hart, and Harpur (1991) differentiate psychopathy from antisocial personality disorder, although their research has demonstrated that the behavioral factors of psychopathy, in-cluding an impulsive, irresponsible, criminal, and unstable lifestyle, are positively correlated with a diagnosis of Antisocial personality disorder.

Psychopathy, a syndrome characterized by a combination of interpersonal, affective, and behavioral characteristics, is made up of two stable types of factors:

1. Affective and interpersonal deficits (a lack of emotion and personality traits that interfere with the ability to build healthy relationships)
2. Social deviance (socially unacceptable behavior)

Psychopathic individuals are largely unable to feel empathy, guilt, remorse, or fear of being caught, and thus they are inclined to indulge their desires for im-mediate gratification impulsively, manipulatively, and without inhibition. Psy-chopathic qualities also render a person undeterred by the threat of punishment, less likely to contain aggression, and more likely to obtain gratification oppor-tunistically. These characteristics lead a psychopathic individual to violate the norms and rules of society, as well as the rights of others.

The *DSM-IV-TR* (2000) estimates that 50–80% of criminal offenders and fo-rensic patients are diagnosed with antisocial personality disorder. About 30% of these individuals meet the criteria for psychopathy. However, studies suggest that approximately 90% of all criminals classified as psychopathic also meet the cri-teria for antisocial personality disorder. That is, most individuals with antisocial personality disorder are not psychopaths, but most psychopaths engage in an-tisocial behaviors. Psychopathic individuals are much more likely to commit vi-olent crimes than nonpsychopaths and are estimated to be responsible for more than half of all serious crimes committed. They are also highly likely to recidi-vate. Some recent research studies have indicated that psychological treatment may actually exacerbate their danger: that is, some treated psychopaths reoffend at higher rates than untreated psychopaths.

Psychopaths are not your run-of-the-mill criminals. Hare (1999) describes psychopaths as human predators who coldly, callously, and ruthlessly use charm, deceit, manipulation, threats, intimidation, and violence to dominate and control others and to satisfy their own selfish needs and desires. As a criminal justice professional, it is important that you become familiar with the concept of psychopathy so that you can correctly identify these individuals, for they are likely to be the most difficult clients you encounter. Psychopaths are far more practiced and skillful at lying than you are at detecting lying; the psychopath can fool anyone, even experienced probation officers and clinicians. What is most deceiving about the psychopath is how normal, and sometimes how likable, he or she appears to be. This manipulative charm may convince criminal justice workers, probation officers, clinicians, and lawyers to protect him or her from "malicious others" who are "falsely accusing" him or her of wrongdoing.

Most, though not all, psychopaths will display some criminal history (Hare, 1999). Typically, psychopaths will have excuses for their criminal activities and will blame police, prosecutors, victims, or associates for the criminal charges. Any significant criminal history and any inconsistencies in the offender's story, no matter how minor, should be further explored by a criminal justice worker who suspects that he or she may be dealing with a psychopathic individual. Frequently, only an objective comparison of his or her version of events with those of official records, documents, victims, and collateral contacts will uncover the manipulative, personable psychopath.

The Hare Psychopathy Checklist—Revised (PCL-R)

The Hare Psychopathy Checklist—Revised (PCL-R; Hare, 1991) is a personality and behavioral assessment of psychopathy that is useful for assessing any offender with a significant criminal history. The PCL-R was not designed to be a risk assessment instrument but rather a tool that measures a clinical construct. However, psychopathy scores have proven predictive of future criminal behavior. Use of the PCL-R is limited to those who possess advanced degrees in the social, medical, or behavioral sciences and who have received specialized training in administering the PCL-R. However, criminal justice workers can benefit from becoming familiar with its constructs and understanding its interpretation, in case it should be referred to in an evaluation of an offender.

The PCL-R assessment procedure consists of an interview with the offender, which allows the interviewer to elicit historical information, as well as to observe the individual's interpersonal style. Next, a review of available collateral information is conducted, including criminal records, presentencing reports, institutional progress reports, probation or parole records, interviews with family members, and results of psychological or psychosocial assessment reports, to obtain additional information and to compare the individual's self-report with other versions.

The PCL-R is made up of 20 items in two categories that have been determined by research to be related to psychopathy: interpersonal factors and behavioral factors. Interpersonal factors refer to the individual's personality traits and style of relating to others, including glibness, grandiosity, pathological lying, manipulativeness, lack of remorse, shallow affect, callousness and lack of empathy, and failure to accept responsibility. Behavioral factors include risk taking, parasitic lifestyle, poor behavioral controls, promiscuity, childhood conduct problems, lack of long-term goals, impulsivity, irresponsibility, history of short-term relationships, juvenile delinquency, parole failure, and criminal versatility (Hare, 1991).

The offender's total score is compared with a cutoff score recommended by Hare (1991) as indicating the "prototypical psychopath." Percentile ranks are also given for comparison of the offender's score with those of samples of prison inmates and forensic patients. The PCL-R score can then be incorporated into an overall assessment of risk for future criminal behavior. PCL-R scores have been found to be predictive of future violent and nonviolent crime. Several research studies have found that offenders who score in the top third of the distribution of scores were nearly three times more likely than those in the bottom third to violate the conditions of their release and almost four times more likely to commit a violent crime. Across several studies, the PCL-R has been found to accurately predict recidivism more than 75% of the time (Monahan & Steadman, 1994).

The Psychopathy Checklist: Screening Version (PCL-SV; Hare, Cox, & Hart, 1994) is a shorter measure of psychopathy that can be used by bachelor's-level and nonclinical practitioners who have participated in a minimal training.

MENTAL DISORDERS AND RECIDIVISM

Research indicates that 20–40% of people with severe mental illness are arrested during their adult lives, usually for nonviolent offenses (Swanson et al., 2001). An estimated 16% of persons currently in U.S. jails and prisons are mentally ill, and about half of them were incarcerated for nonviolent offenses (Swanson et al., 2001), such as theft, burglary, larceny, forgery, substance-related offenses, driving while intoxicated, vagrancy, trespassing, disorderly conduct, vandalism, and prostitution. Chronic mental illnesses such as schizophrenic disorders and bipolar mood disorders are likely to interfere with decision making, perception, and judgment. Three factors appear to significantly increase the likelihood of arrest or police contact among the mentally ill:

- Substance abuse
- Medication noncompliance
- Violence

Involuntary outpatient commitment (OPC) is a new legal intervention designed to prevent recidivism in chronically mentally ill individuals who are unwilling or unable to seek and adhere to psychiatric treatment. OPC means that a court orders an offender to obtain outpatient treatment in the community, monitored by a designated agency. In some jurisdictions, special judges preside over "mental health courts" intended to divert mentally ill offenders into community-based, supervised treatment and away from traditional criminal justice systems. Preliminary studies suggest that OPC decreases the risk of arrest by improving compliance with psychotropic medications, improving access to substance abuse treatment, increasing clinical intervention during crises, and intensifying case management services.

SUBSTANCE ABUSE AND RECIDIVISM

Research has found that approximately 53% of criminal offenders use drugs and alcohol. This group of offenders is more likely to be rearrested than offenders without substance abuse problems (Gorski, Kelley, Havens, & Peters, 1995). Substance abuse impairs judgment and lowers inhibitions, making individuals less able to control their behaviors. Alcohol and drug abusers with criminal histories frequently also demonstrate antisocial behaviors and attitudes, further interfering with their ability to regulate their behavior.

Addiction is a complex disease that is influenced by a wide range of biological, social, psychological, and environmental factors. Substance abuse is often triggered by stressors, such as

- Anxiety
- Isolation
- Positive and negative social pressures
- Associating with people who use drugs and alcohol
- Depression

Criminal offenders may be more likely to use substances due to the range of psychosocial stressors that are related to the development of both substance abuse and criminal behavior.

Research studies of relapse (a return to substance use after a period of abstinence) in general substance-using populations suggest that about two-thirds of addicts who receive treatment will relapse several times before obtaining full recovery. Substance-abusing criminals relapse at even higher rates. Factors that contribute to general criminal behavior, as well as to the potential for relapse, include:

- Poor family relationships
- Lack of prosocial support systems
- Educational and vocational deficits
- Employment problems
- Multiple contacts with the criminal justice system
- Inability to handle anger and stress
- Inability to handle high-risk situations that lead to relapse (Gorski et al., 1995).

Substance-using criminals are often arrested for specific crimes, such as drunk driving, public drunkenness, assault, selling drugs, or illegal activities used to support the drug habit. They are also likely to be arrested for offenses related to or resulting from an inability to meet responsibilities due to substance addiction, such as failure to pay child support, contempt of court, and probation violations (Gorski et al., 1995).

MENTAL ILLNESS, SUBSTANCE ABUSE, AND VIOLENT CRIMINAL RECIDIVISM

The relationship between chronic mental illness, substance abuse, and violent recidivism appears to be a strong one, suggesting that groups with dual diagnoses are especially prone to volatile behavior. A *dual diagnosis* is one in which an individual is diagnosed with having both a major mental illness, such as schizophrenia or a mood disorder, and a substance abuse disorder. That the combined effect of mental illness and substance abuse is strong is not surprising given the impairment in judgment, inhibition, perception, and impulse control associated with each of these conditions.

In a series of studies funded by the National Institute of Mental Health, called the Epidemiologic Catchment Area (ECA) project, university-based research teams set out to explore the prevalence of violent behavior among groups of mentally ill persons, substance-abusing persons, and the general population (Silver & Teasdale, 2005). They conducted surveys asking whether or not the respondent had ever used a weapon, been in more than one fight with someone other than a spouse or partner, spanked or hit a child, hit or threw things at a spouse, or gotten into physical fights while drinking. These items were combined in various ways to test different criteria of violence. For instance, by asking about just the first two items, the researchers sought to discriminate general violence from family violence. Adding the second two questions identified family violence, and adding the fifth question was designed to screen for violence related to substance abuse.

Researchers found from asking the first two questions (designed to screen for random violence, which they assumed to be most feared by the public) that 7.3% of violence was perpetrated by individuals with no diagnosis compared with 16% committed by persons with mentally illnesses, 35% by substance abusers, and 44% by individuals with dual diagnoses. Adding the other questions resulted in increased prevalence, with similar linear progression among the groups (Monahan & Steadman, 1994). Among groups with psychiatric diagnoses, the prevalence of violence was less than 2% for those with no diagnosis, less than 4% for those with mental illnesses, 10.5% for substance abusers, and 14% for those with dual diagnoses. However, because the mentally ill account for such a small proportion of individuals, it appears that violence among mentally ill people occurs less frequently than it does in the general population.

In summary, the vast majority of mentally ill people do not commit violent acts. The attributable risk for violence associated with mental illness is between 3 and 5%. Mentally disordered individuals with substance abuse disorders are significantly more likely to be violent than those with mental disorders alone.

VIOLENT CRIMINAL RECIDIVISM RISK ASSESSMENT INSTRUMENTS

The Historical, Clinical, and Risk Management Violence Risk Assessment Scheme (HCR-20)

The HCR-20 (Webster, Douglas, Eaves, & Hart, 1997) is an instrument that measures 20 historical, clinical, and risk management factors that have demonstrated an empirical correlation with violent recidivism. Historical items are static and therefore unchangeable; clinical items are dynamic and refer to current emotional functioning, such as lack of insight, negative attitudes, active symptoms of mental illness, impulsivity, and treatment failure. The risk management scale attempts to predict adjustment to the community by assessing the feasibility of plans, exposure to destabilizers, personal support, compliance with remediation, and stress (Douglas & Webster, 1999).

Although the HCR-20 has not yet undergone enough study to demonstrate consistent predictive validity, it does display robust interrater reliability (.80;

Douglas & Webster, 1999) and moderate correlations with other risk assessment instruments. Some studies show that offenders who score above the median are four to six times more likely to commit subsequent violent crimes than those who score below the median.

The Violence Risk Appraisal Guide (VRAG)

The VRAG is a 12-item actuarial tool for predicting violent criminal recidivism that incorporates the PCL-R into its scoring structure. Total scores are grouped into levels of probability of violent reoffending over a 10-year period. The VRAG has been shown to be reliable and valid with both mentally disordered and non–mentally disordered offenders. The VRAG has been published in the book *Violent Offenders: Appraising and Managing Risk* (Quinsey Lalumiere, Rice, & Harris,1995). Because it requires the administration of the PCL-R, users must have advanced degrees in mental health and special training. However, familiarity with the VRAG can help you, the criminal justice professional, to understand the meaningfulness of the VRAG when you see it included in an assessment.

The Level of Service Inventory—Revised (LSI-R)

The LSI-R (Andrews & Bonta, 1995) is a measure of criminal risk and need for treatment based on assessment of antisocial cognitions, antisocial peers, history of antisocial behavior, and antisocial personality, and it is used to determine supervision requirements. Elevated LSI-R scores have been shown to be indicative of parole violations and recidivism.

RISK FACTORS FOR SEXUAL OFFENSE RECIDIVISM

Risk factors for sexual reoffending have been found to fall into two main categories (Quinsey, Lalumiere, Rice, & Harris, 1995; Hanson & Bussiere, 1998). The first cluster of risk factors relates to sexual deviance—specifically, sexual attraction to children or other nonconsenting partners. The second cluster of risk factors centers around psychopathy, which was covered in a previous section—interpersonal, affective, behavioral, and criminal characteristics related but not identical to those of antisocial personality disorder.

In a recent research study sponsored by the Canadian government, 61 recidivism studies involving almost 29,000 sexual offenders were analyzed using a statistical procedure called meta-analysis. Meta-analysis is a method of combining multiple, independent research studies to create a large sample by which various factors can be analyzed with enough power to produce statistically significant results. In this manner, Hanson and Bussiere (1998) were able to isolate factors that are most strongly related to sex offense recidivism. In other words, the offenders who were rearrested were more likely to possess certain characteristics than those offenders who were not arrested again.

Those factors that were shown to be most predictive of reoffense for identified sex offenders include:

- Sexual deviance as measured by phallometry (a device that measures erectile response)
- Prior sexual crimes
- Prior nonsexual criminal behavior
- Offender being under age 25
- Victims being male
- Victims being outside family, strangers, or acquaintances

The likelihood of future sexual offending has been shown to increase with an increase in the number of risk factors and with the number of prior offenses. Child molesters at highest risk appear to be young; they prefer male victims; they molest children outside of their families; and they have a prior history of sex crime perpetration. Rapists who assault strangers and who have a history of past criminal behavior and/or past sex crimes appear to be at highest risk.

Although use of violence does not, surprisingly, increase the risk of future sex crimes, rapists do tend to use more aggression than child molesters do. Child molesters use a process called "grooming," by which they befriend potential child victims and their families, gain their trust, and use nonsexual behaviors such as bathing, swimming, or wrestling to desensitize children to touch. The Internet has become, in the past few years, an increasingly popular manner by which sex offenders prey on children, primarily through chat rooms and by viewing child pornography.

Dynamic (changeable) factors that increase the likelihood of sexual reoffense include treatment failure, ongoing substance abuse, continuing antisocial behavior, attitudes tolerant of sexual assault, and access to children (Hanson & Harris, 1998). Dynamic risk factors appear to be most useful for identifying the imminence of reoffense. Identifying dynamic factors is also essential in determining appropriate areas for treatment intervention and supervision, as an offender can modify such factors and thus decrease his risk of offending in the future.

Researchers point out that estimates of risk to reoffend must always be considered underestimates of the actual likelihood of sexual reoffending. Recidivism has historically been defined as rearrests or reconvictions rather than as simply engaging in subsequent acts of sexual assault. It is well known that many sex offenses are never reported and that, among those that are, many are not adjudicated for a variety of reasons and some are downgraded to other, nonsexual crimes. In fact, recidivism rates always underestimate any type of criminal reoffending because they cannot account for those offenders who commit crimes but are not caught.

RISK ASSESSMENT INSTRUMENTS

By combining risk factors into scales, then weighting and testing the scales for predictive accuracy, several researchers have developed actuarial risk prediction instruments for sexual reoffense. Scoring a convicted sex offender on these instruments allows his risk for sexual recidivism to be estimated by referring to the recidivism rate of other convicted sex offenders with similar characteristics or risk factors.

Rapid Risk Assessment for Sex Offense Recidivism (RRASOR)

From a selected subset of factors identified in Hanson and Bussiere's (1998) meta-analysis, Hanson (1997) developed an actuarial risk assessment instrument called the Rapid Risk Assessment for Sex Offender Recidivism (RRASOR). The RRASOR weighs four factors known to correlate significantly with recidivism: prior charges, age under 25, male victims, and extrafamilial victims. The combined factors are scored on a scale of 0–6, with 0 representing low risk and 6 indicating the highest risk. Each factor is worth 1 point, except for prior charges, which can have value of up to 3 points, depending on the number of prior arrests. (It is important to note that all officially documented prior charges are counted, even when the offender denies committing the offense.) Hanson (1997) reported that "each increase in value of the risk scale was associated with an orderly increase in the sexual offense recidivism rate" (p. 18). The rates were less than 7% for those individuals with no known risk factors, and they increased to over 70% among offenders scoring 5 points or more. The instrument appears to be more predictive for child molesters than for rapists (Hanson, 1997).

Other Actuarial Assessment Instruments for Sex Offenders

The STATIC-99 (Hanson & Thornton, 2000) measures the same factors as the RRASOR but includes additional factors related to general criminality, noncontact offenses, and lack of adult relationships. The STATIC-99 is now the most universally accepted instrument in sexual predator evaluations in North America. Researchers at the Minnesota Department of Corrections (Epperson, Kaul, & Hesselton, 1998) have combined indicators of sexual deviance, indicators of antisocial behavior, and factors pertaining to response to treatment to create a risk assessment instrument called the Minnesota Sex Offender Screening Tool—Revised (MnSOST-R). The MnSOST-R scores offenders on 16 static and dynamic factors found to have maximal predictive power. The MnSOST-R cannot be used with incestuous child molesters, because the sample on which it was developed included only extrafamilial molesters.

These actuarial instruments have the benefit of being relatively easy to use with minimal training; they are designed to be interdisciplinary and do not necessarily require an advanced degree or a mental health license. The RRASOR and the STATIC-99, along with scoring instructions, can easily be downloaded from the website of the Solicitor General's Office of Canada (http://ww2.psepc-sppcc .gc.ca/publications/corrections/199902_e.pdf).

RISK FACTORS FOR DOMESTIC VIOLENCE RECIDIVISM

Criminal justice professionals may find themselves working with domestic abusers. It is important to understand that domestic violence is not about marital troubles but about a serious impulse control problem on the part of the abuser. Domestic violence represents a repetitive pattern of behavior that escalates over time, the purpose of which is to allow the abuser to obtain complete power and control over the victim through intimidation, degradation, economic control, and physical violence. Domestic abuse occurs not only in marriages but also in dating relationships, gay and lesbian relationships, and adolescent relationships. Although women sometimes abuse men, the vast majority of domestic abusers are male, and women are seven times more likely than men to be killed or severely injured in a domestic violence incident. One in three female murder victims is murdered by her intimate partner (Bureau of Justice Statistics, 2000).

Some people wonder why battered women don't just leave their batterers. This question is complex and is influenced by many emotional, psychological, social, familial, and financial factors. However, many women don't leave because they are afraid to; they believe that the abuser will come after them and hurt them or kill them. In fact, research suggests that women are more likely to be killed after or while in the process of leaving a violent relationship. When the woman leaves, the batterer loses control. So he does what he usually does to maintain control—he increases his violent behavior.

Children in homes in which domestic violence occurs are also at risk. Criminal justice professionals who suspect that a child is being abused or is at risk due to domestic violence in the home should contact their local child protection agency. You, as a criminal justice professional, are, by law in all 50 states, a mandated reporter of child abuse and neglect. Check your state statutes and reporting procedures to more fully understand your responsibilities.

Risk factors for recidivistic domestic abuse have been found to fall into four main categories (Kropp, Hart, Webster, & Eaves, 1999):

- Criminal history
- Psychosocial adjustment
- Spousal assault history
- Factors related to the most recent alleged offense

These factors are discussed in more detail subsequently. They help to predict which domestic batterers are most likely to continue and escalate their violent behavior. Becoming familiar with these factors may help you to detect a high-risk domestic violence situation before tragedy strikes. Domestic batterers with a prior criminal history are at increased risk for future domestic assault. Repeat batterers are more likely to have assaulted family members, strangers, or acquaintances in the past and are also more likely to have previously violated their probations. These men are poor compliers with conditions of court orders, bail, and probationary supervision, suggesting that they tend to disregard rules and consequences.

Psychosocial factors are also related to battering. Repeat offenders are likely to have had chronic relationship and employment problems. One of the most predictive factors for repeat intimate offenders is that they often witnessed violence in their homes growing up or were abused as children. Research has also shown that substance abuse, recent suicidal or homicidal intent, history of psychotic or manic symptoms, and impulsivity or behavioral instability are all associated with domestic violence.

A history of past domestic assault is a powerful predictor of future domestic assault. Risk factors include past perpetration of physical assault, sexual assault, sexual jealousy, and violations of "no contact" orders or restraining orders. Any past use of weapons or credible threats of death, in addition to recent escalations in the frequency or severity of violence, indicate a high likelihood of future domestic violence. Men who minimize or deny their domestic violence histories, blame the victims, or demonstrate attitudes that condone intimate violence are at high risk.

Assessing the most recent offense or allegation is crucial. If the most recent incident included severe physical or sexual abuse, injury requiring medical attention, use of weapons, threats of death, or violation of protection orders, risk is greatly increased. Other considerations, such as a history of stalking, sadistic tendencies, presence of weapons in the home, or a history of torturing or disfiguring a partner, should also be carefully explored.

The Spousal Assault Risk Assessment (SARA)

The Spousal Assault Risk Assessment (SARA; Kropp et al., 1999) is an instrument that assesses the risk of future domestic violence. It is a checklist made up of 20 items that have been shown through research to be empirically related to future domestic assault crimes. It is completed by conducting structured interviews with both the batterer and the victim, as well as consulting official records. Any conflicting information should be resolved by attempting to confirm facts with various sources. The score is totaled, and guidelines are given for placing the total score in a high-, moderate-, or low-risk category. Kropp et al. (1999) found that 60% of recidivists scored in the high-risk range, 33% fell into the moderate-risk range, and only 7% scored in low-risk range. The SARA has also been found to be positively correlated with the PCL-R and the VRAG.

The SARA is not restricted in its use to any particular professional group. It is recommended, however, that users have training or work-related experience in the social sciences or corrections, as well as formal training and experience in the area of domestic violence.

PRACTICE LESSONS

Risk factors are characteristics that increase the probability of an outcome occurring. Static factors are demographic (such as age or gender) or historical (such as prior history of criminal arrest) factors that remain constant and that are, by definition, unchangeable. Dynamic factors can be changed as a result of some intervention. When unchanged, they increase the risk for a particular behavior.

Risk assessment is the process of determining and predicting risk for some particular outcome based on factors that are known to be related to the outcome. There are three approaches to conducting risk assessments: research-guided clinical judgment, actuarial assessment based on statistical outcomes, and adjusted actuarial assessment.

The most important risk factors for criminal offending include impulsivity, low intelligence or educational attainment, having a parent or sibling who has been convicted of a crime, poor parental supervision, harsh discipline, parental conflict or divorce, low income, poor housing, large family size, delinquent friends, and living in a high-crime community. Risk factors for violent reoffending include past violence, early violence onset, relationship and employment instability, substance use, mental illness, psychopathy, and prior parole failure.

1. Recidivism refers to the recurrence of criminal behavior as measured by a rearrest or new conviction. The HCR-20, the VRAG, and the LSI-R are tools used to predict future violent criminal behavior.

   Psychopathy is a syndrome characterized by a combination of interpersonal, affective, and behavioral characteristics and made up of two stable types of factors: affective deficits (lack of emotion) and social deviance (socially unacceptable behavior). The Hare Psychopathy Checklist—Revised (PCL-R) is an assessment of psychopathy and is predictive of future criminal behavior. The PCL-SV (Screening Version) is a shorter tool for assessing psychopathy and can be used by a wide range of professionals with minimal training.

2. Three factors appear to significantly increase the likelihood of arrest or police contact among the mentally ill: substance abuse, medication noncompliance, and violence.

3. Substance-using criminals are often arrested for specific crimes, such as drunk driving, public drunkenness, assault, selling drugs, or illegal activities used to support the drug habit. They are also likely to be arrested for offenses related to or resulting from substance addiction, such as failure to pay child support, contempt of court, and probation violations.

4. Offenders with dual diagnoses are especially prone to volatile behavior. A dual diagnosis is one in which an individual is diagnosed with having both a major mental illness, such as schizophrenia or a mood disorder, and a substance addiction.

5. Static factors that were shown to be most predictive of reoffense for identified sex offenders include sexual deviance, prior sexual crimes, prior nonsexual criminal behavior, offender being under 25, victimizing males,

and victimizing extrafamilial individuals, strangers, or acquaintances. Dynamic factors include treatment failure, ongoing substance abuse, continuing antisocial behavior, attitudes tolerant of sexual assault, and access to children. Three actuarial risk assessment instruments can be easily used by criminal justice workers to assess risk for sexual offense recidivism: the RRASOR, the STATIC-99, and the MnSOST-R.

6. Risk factors for recidivistic domestic abuse have been found to fall into four main categories: criminal history, psychosocial adjustment, spousal assault history, and factors related to the most recent alleged offense. The Spousal Assault Risk Assessment (SARA) is an instrument that assesses the risk of future domestic violence.

THE ASSAULT

Mandy Davis

Case Description

Kathy was a 22-year-old female university student who was seen at the emergency room after she reported being raped. At the hospital a sexual-assault nurse-examiner, police officer, and volunteer victim's advocate saw her. Kathy requested that someone contact her the following day, and the volunteer referred the case to Alison, who was completing her internship as a victims' advocate for a local nonprofit family service agency.

Assessment/Screening and Problem Identification

Alison contacted Kathy and offered to meet with her to provide information about her rights and available services. Kathy agreed to meet if her roommate could also attend. In preparation for the meeting, Alison reviewed the volunteer's report and learned that Kathy had reported being sexually assaulted at a college party. After the assault, she confided in her friend, who recommended they go to the hospital. At the hospital, Kathy received a sexual assault forensic exam and spoke to the police. The report recommended that Kathy receive follow-up medical care and counseling.

Kathy requested that her friend stay with her during her meeting with Alison. Kathy apologized for her appearance and stated she had not been sleeping or eating. Kathy said that she had given the police information about the suspect and was now terrified about what would happen. She was questioning whether she had made the right choice, saying, "I should have just kept my mouth shut, no one's going to believe me, I feel like I am going crazy." Kathy further reported that the detective had called her twice but that she could not handle the stress of talking to her and was not sure she should have pressed charges. Kathy had not been to class in 2 days and was concerned she would fail her classes.

Intervention/Treatment

Several issues surfaced during the first meeting with Kathy, including her safety, her physical and mental health, her decision about pressing charges, and her course work. Alison's first concern was Kathy's safety, and with the client's permission, she contacted the police to find out the status of the case. The officer reported that the suspect had been identified but that they needed to interview Kathy before approaching the suspect and that she had not returned any of their calls. Alison explained that Kathy was staying with a friend and was fearful of pressing charges. The officer sympathized but encouraged Alison to "convince her" to press charges because they could do nothing unless this happened.

Alison was experiencing a typical challenge when responding to rape: balancing the needs and rights of the victim with the desire to hold offenders accountable. Alison was aware that she was feeling angry about what had happened to Kathy and would like to see the offender held accountable, but she also respected the fear and terror that deterred Kathy from pressing charges. In reviewing the literature, Alison knew that the decision to report and participate in the criminal justice system was dependent on several variables, including the characteristics of the rape, demographics of the victim, psychological factors, social support networks, beliefs about the court process, fear, and self-blame (Cluss, Boughton, Frank, Stewart, & West, 1983; Steketee & Austin, 1989). She also discovered that a primary complaint from victims was that they were not kept informed of the process or decisions made about their case (Frazier & Haney, 1996).

Understanding her role as an advocate, Alison focused on promoting Kathy's safety and providing her with the information necessary to make an informed decision about continuing with the criminal investigation. During this initial meeting, Alison informed Kathy of her rights and told her about the judicial process and about victim's compensation. Alison also provided her with information about typical reactions to rape and developed a self-care plan for the next few days that addressed where Kathy would stay and problems with eating and sleeping and provided Kathy with a 24-hour crisis line number she could call. Kathy agreed to Alison's checking in by phone the following day and to meeting in person again in a few days.

Alison met with Kathy a second time to check on how she was doing and to review the information about the criminal justice process. Kathy reported that she was able to eat a bit more and was still having difficulty sleeping but felt safer at her friend's home. Kathy and Alison discussed the pros and cons regarding moving forward with the criminal investigation. Kathy said that she wanted the offender to be punished but was afraid that she would not be believed because she had been drinking that night and that she was fearful of retaliation. Kathy decided that she wanted to meet with the police, but only if Alison and Kathy's friend could be there. During this meeting, Alison also provided referral information for medical follow-up and completed the application for victim's compensation.

Alison was concerned that she was not adequately addressing Kathy's psychological needs because of the time needed to coordinate services and monitor the case process. She discussed this with Kathy, and they decided that Kathy would attend the rape survivors' support group and continue to meet with Alison. They would reassess the situation in a few weeks to see whether a referral for individual counseling services was needed.

Findings

The suspect was eventually apprehended, and because he was already on probation for an unrelated offense, he was held in custody until the trail. Kathy continued to attend the rape survivors' group and reported that this was helpful. Alison and Kathy maintained contact regarding the case. Kathy had been provided with a phone number that she could call anytime to find out whether the suspect was still in custody, and Alison received regular updates from the court advocate regarding the suspect's location. Kathy's symptoms steadily improved, but they began to worsen as the trial approached.

▪ ▪ ▪

Activities

1. How might have this case have turned out differently if Alison had not been involved?

2. Alison was faced with several responsibilities in her role as a victim advocate. What were these responsibilities? How would you prioritize services and why?

3. Within the multiple disciplines that respond to sexual assault, there are two desired outcomes: victims' well-being and offenders' accountability. Discuss instances in which these two desired outcomes may complement each other and in which they may conflict.

4. When can a victim of crime make an informed decision, and what is necessary for her or him to do so?

5. How can Alison monitor Kathy's symptoms to determine whether further counseling would be helpful?

6. In her role of a victim advocate, how might Alison's intervention change if Kathy decided not to press charges?

7. What might have changed if the suspect had not been in custody or had never been identified?

Reflection activity

Why do you think it is important for a criminal justice professional to use risk assessment strategies that are guided by research?

Experiential activities

1. Read the following case scenario and use the RRASOR (Hanson, 1997), given in Table 12.1, to calculate the offender's score and estimate his risk for reoffense. (Note: Remember that scores are derived from official documents, *not* offender self-reports. Also, *prior* offenses

refer only to charges or convictions that *came before* the most recent arrest).

You are a probation officer and have been assigned a new offender on your caseload. He is a 45-year-old white male who was just released from prison following a conviction for molesting his 6-year-old daughter. On reviewing his records, you see that, while he was in prison, a 10-year-old boy from the neighborhood alleged that the offender had sexually abused him. Although your client admits to abusing his daughter, he denies abusing the other child, even though he pleaded guilty to the charge "to avoid the trauma of another trial."

Table 12.1. RRASOR

Risk Factor	Instructions	Score
Age < 25	0 = no 1 = yes	
# of prior arrests for sex crimes	0 = none 1 = 1 conviction or 1 – 2 charges 2 = 2–3 convictions or 3 – 5 charges 3 => 3 convictions or >5 charges	
Male victims	0 = no 1 = yes	
Extrafamilial victims	0 = no 1 = yes	
Total Score		

Score	5-year Recidivism Rate	10-year Recidivism Rate
0	4.4	6.5
1	7.6	11.2
2	14.2	21.1
3	24.8	36.9
4	32.7	48.6
5	49.8	73.1

2. You are a worker in an involuntary outpatient commitment (OPC) program in which you provide case management for mentally ill clients who are being diverted from the criminal justice system. Your new client is diagnosed with bipolar disorder and is prescribed lithium. The client complains that he does not like taking the medication because it makes him gain weight. When you visit his home, you detect an odor of alcohol and see beer cans in the garbage bin. What is the most appropriate risk assessment strategy, and why?

   a. Research-guided clinical judgment

   b. Actuarial assessment

   c. Adjusted actuarial approach

3. List and explain the risk factors that exist in the preceding case.

Self-Assessment

List and describe the ways in which your own personal values and experiences could potentially interfere with risk assessment. Give an example.

Part III   Using Evidence in Practice

13 GATHERING YOUR OWN EVIDENCE

KEVIN CORCORAN *and* BARBARA THOMLISON

This chapter discusses ways to determine whether your clients are changing or have changed. This determination requires that you have evidence of decreases or increases in a client's problems and behaviors and evidence that a goal has been attained.

OUTCOMES OF ALL SORTS

By now you have come to realize that your field experience consists of real-life interventions that affect people's daily living and quality of life. We trust you have seen how important and powerful social work and criminal justice interventions are to society, to your own community, and—most important—to your clients. The two primary and summary lessons to be gleaned from your practice so far are: (1) there are outcomes that are expected, delineated, and enumerated with the client that are based on a thorough assessment and accurate diagnosis; (2) your interventions are targeted with structured protocols tailor-made to reach the outcomes. That is, regardless of whether you are placed in a criminal justice or social work setting, your assessment of the client and his or her social environment will lead to, if not dictate, your intervention and treatment protocol, which is designed for the purpose of reaching observable goals or outcomes.

The focus of this chapter is how to monitor the client's progress in order to discern whether change has resulted from your efforts and from the intervention. The most likely change you will want to observe is change in the problem and the attainment of your client's goal or goals. Inevitably, monitoring a client's progress and goal attainment will provide evidence of the results of your application of that intervention. Your own evaluation of your client's progress is in itself valuable evidence of an intervention's effectiveness. You may even be able to develop 1 of the 10 single-case studies needed to support the evidence-based-practice claim, as we discussed earlier. In all cases, you will have a goal to attain, and it is useful to monitor the extent to which your client's problems decrease in response to the intervention designed to attain that goal and the final outcome of actually reaching the goal. Assessing the progress and attainment of these outcomes is also a useful way to be accountable as a practitioner (Bloom, Fischer, & Orme, 2006).

Although it is undoubtedly an oversimplification, there is an interaction between your client's problems and reaching the goal of an intervention. That is, as the frequency, intensity or duration of the problems decrease, attainment of the goal concomitantly becomes closer. Therefore, we examine how to observe client problems and how to measure goal attainment separately, but please bear in mind that the two occur in tandem.

There are probably as many outcomes of a social work or criminal justice intervention as there are people who receive the services. This is an overstatement, but because every client is unique, you must approach every outcome of an intervention as a new and unique experience. You know it will be one for most of your clients. The desired outcomes may include fewer family fights, more cooperation and courtesy between youths in a group home, clean urine samples for an adult on probation or parole, or just about any mental health and health condition imaginable. The first step in gathering your own evidence is to define the problem and goals in observable terms. In part, this will help you monitor your client's progress, which itself helps facilitate the effectiveness of an intervention. It is easier to see change in a concrete and observable goal (e.g., increased self-efficacy in a particular circumstance) than in nebulous goals (e.g., improved self-esteem) or even ephemeral ones (e.g., enhanced sense of self). The outcomes should clearly delineate how the client will be *different* in an affect he or she experiences, an action he or she takes, or cognitions he or she has. The desired behavior, whether it involves affects, actions, or cognitions, should be defined in quantitative terms. These terms specify the frequency, intensity or magnitude, or duration of the affect, action, or cognition to be changed.

At this point it is important to remember that measurement of a problem or treatment goal is simply a system for observing a client's feelings, thinking, and actions. Moreover, these behaviors, which pretty much encompass all of human behavior, are observable only in terms of how often they occur (i.e., frequency), at what degree (i.e., magnitude or intensity), and for how long (i.e., duration).

The frequency, intensity, or duration of a cognition, affect, or action must be quantified in order to monitor the possible change. The quantified behaviors can then be monitored by noting increases or decreases in frequency, intensity, or duration of affect, action, or cognition. The quantification of the behavior may be done with a variety of assessment instruments, and we recommend short instruments and individualized measures.

One of the more commonly used types of instruments is the Rapid Assessment Instrument (RAI), which tends to be a single-focus measurement of a particular client's conditions. There are a variety of sources for RAI, as illustrated in Table 13.1. Some are narrowly tailored to a particular client condition, such as anxiety, aggression, or depression. Others include a wider scope of conditions for couples, families, and children and conditions of adulthood.

Table 13.1 Selected Volumes Since 1970 on Measurement Devices

Volumes reprinting measures

Cautela (1977, 1981)
Cone (2001)
Feindler & Rathus (2003)
Grisso, Vincent, & Seagrove (2005)
Hudson (1982)
Lopez & Snyder (2000)
McCubbin & Thompson (1991)
McCubbin et al. (1996)
McDowell & Newell (1996)
Moos (1974, 1975, 1979)
Rathus & Feindler (2004)
Robinson & Shaver (1973)
Sajatovic & Ramirez (2001)
Schutte & Malouff (1995)
Turk & Melzack (2001)
Wilson & Keane (2004)

Volumes describing and referencing measures

Anastasi (1988)
Andrulis (1977)
Beere (1979)
Bellack & Hersen (1988)
Briere (2004)
Brodsky & Smitherman (1983)
Chun, Cobb, & French (1975)
Chun, Organista, & Marin (2003)
Ciarlo et al. (1986)
Comrey, Barkey, & Galser (1975)
Conoley & Kramer (1989, 1995)
Dana (1993)
Donovan & Marlott (2005)
Fredman & Sherman (1987)
Goldman & Busch (1978, 1982)
Goldman & Sanders (1974)
Goldston (2003)
Grotevant & Carlson (1989)
Hammill et al. (1989)
Hersen & Bellack (1988)
Holman (1983)
Johnson (1976)
Johnson & Bommarito (1971)
Kamphaus (1996)
Kestenbaum & Williams (1988)
Lake, Miles, & Earle (1973)
McDowell & Newell (1987, 1996)
McReynolds (1981)
Miller (1977)

Mitchell (1985)
Olin & Keatinge (1998)
Reynolds & Kamphaus (2003)
Sawin & Harrigan (1994)
Scholl & Schnur (1976)
Southworth, Burr, & Cox (1981)
Sweetland & Keyser (1991)
Thompson (1989)
Touliatos, Permutter, & Strauss (1990)
van Riezen & Segal (1988)
Wetzler (1989)

Other volumes discussing measurement methods

Ackerman (2006)
Antony & Barlow (2004)
Beutler & Groth-Marnat (2003)
Ciminero, Calhoun, & Adams (1977)
Cone & Hawkins (1977)
Goldman, Stein, & Guerry (1983)
Goldstein & Hersen (1990)
Groth-Marnat (2003)
Gumbiner (2003)
Haynes (1978)
Haynes, Heiby, & Hersen (2003)
Haynes & Wilson (1979)
Hersen (2004)
Hersen & Bellack (1988)
Hilsenroth, Segal, & Herson (2004)
Jacob & Tennenbaum (1988)
Lambert, Christensen, & DeJulio (1983)
Lauffer (1982)
Lidz (2002)
Mash & Terdal (1988)
Merluzzi, Glass, & Genest (1981)
Ogles, Lambert, & Fields (2002)
Ogles & Masters (1996)
Ollendick & Hersen (1992)
Pecora et al. (1995)
Ramsay, Reynolds & Kamphaus (200X)?
Reynolds & Kamphaus (1990)
Reynolds & Kamphaus (2002)
Rutter, Tuma, & Lann (1988)
Sederer & Dickey (1996)
Suzuki, Meller, & Ponterotto (1996)
Urbina (2004)
Vance & Pumarieqa (2001)
Waskow & Parloff (1975)
Woody (1980)

RAIs have several advantages when used in your internship. First of all, they take up very little time and provide valuable quantified reference points about your client's condition or the goal of the intervention. You can instruct your client on how to use an RAI, score the instrument, and have an index of the client for use over the course of treatment in less than 5 minutes. Additionally, RAIs provide enormous benefit in monitoring the impact of the intervention, providing feedback on your client's progress, and evidencing accountability. Like many others (e.g., Bloom et al., 2006), we also recommend RAIs over other measurement tools because they have the advantage of being an efficient way of assessing your client without expensive training or elusive interpretations of costly instruments.

Furthermore, RAIs provide unique accessibility to conditions that are difficult, if not impossible, to observe. These may include the juvenile justice client's efforts at impulse control or a mental health client's feelings of depression. You may be able to observe a couple quarreling, but you simply cannot see how intensely they feel angry, threatened, or hurt; nor can you see what each is thinking about the other, the circumstances, or his or her own behavior during and after the quarrel. In fact, with the exception of overt behaviors, much of the cognition and affect that are the focus of criminal justice and social work are observable only to the client. RAIs allow you access to these experiences by allowing clients to report the magnitude, frequency, or duration of what they did (i.e., actions), how they felt (i.e., affects), or what was going through their minds (i.e., cognitions).

You will find that RAIs allow access to sensitive information that your client may be reticent to mention—especially early in the professional relationship when trust is still being established. RAIs help overcome some of this initial barrier to disclosure. For example, a teen is more likely to indicate severity of alcohol drinking on an RAI than to acknowledge a drinking problem to you. This is also the case with many other sensitive matters, such as sex, emotions, interpersonal relationships, fantasies, failures, and just about any other matter for which one sees a professional helper. Often your client will downplay the significance of his or her presenting problem, but he or she might disclose more on a standardized questionnaire.

An additional advantage of RAIs is comparability over time. Using the same instrument each time to assess the client's condition or goal allows for scores to be compared over the course of the intervention. This is accomplished by simply plotting the scores on a graph, with the horizontal axis representing the course of treatment and the vertical axis, scores on the RAIs. This procedure is illustrated in figure 7.2, which monitored the progress of Ernie Lidquest after he finally sought treatment for his cannabis abuse. We discuss this further later in this chapter in terms of how to interpret scores.

We do not want to oversell RAIs. They are not without limitations. One primary limitation is that RAIs were developed with a group of clients who are fairly homogenous; that is, your client will never be quite like the research participants from whom the reliability and validity estimates of the instrument are derived. The samples used to develop an instrument may be too uniform and may be distinguishable from and to dissimilar to the condition of your client. The research may suggest that an instrument is accurate (estimated via validity procedures) and consistent (estimated with reliability procedures), but it may be based, for example, on a sample of veterans of the armed services, or on younger or older people, or on males instead of females, or on European Americans rather than persons of color or different nationalities. There are all sorts of other dimensions that make you wonder whether the instrument is appropriate for your client's problem or treatment goal. These differences will likely mean that the RAI is not quite as good when used with your client as it is when used with the research sample. This problem is easily addressed by judicious interpretation of the scores. The scores are simply supplements to your professional judgment and should not be a substitute for it.

Another disadvantage of RAIs is that some clients simply are unable to consistently or accurately complete the instrument. This includes very young children, some persons with traumatic brain injuries or severe mental health conditions (such as a psychotic state with acute exacerbation or major depression), some persons with learning disabilities or cognitive impairments (such as dementia or drug-induced psychosis) and hostile and distrustful youths. At other times and in some settings the RAI is useless, as it might not reveal accurate information. For instance, it is quite imaginable that the test would not elicit any meaningful information from an alcoholic in denial, from an inmate preparing for parole who wants to fake a positive condition, or from persons who fake negative in order to be referred for services. Many other examples can be imagined, and this is simply another reason we stress that any measurement tool is only an aid to your professional judgment.

A final disadvantage of RAIs is their availability. By this we mean not having access to too few instruments but to too many. The number of RAIs available for social work and criminal justice has increased dramatically. There are literally thousands of RAIs, and for just about every conceivable mental health condition and presenting problem one can find a number of good instruments that have at least some support for their validity and reliability. The advantage is knowing that a useful tool is available, but the drawback is the number to choose from. It is much easier to select one instrument if only a few are available, such as in the case of suicidality, than to choose from hundreds, as in the cases of anxiety, depression, and assertiveness. To make matters worse, most of the RAIs are scattered throughout the literature and on the World Wide Web.

With so many RAIs available, it is hard to find the best one for your and your client's purpose. We suggest you begin with a good compendium of measures for a variety of client conditions or problems. If you are working with particular types of clients, such as victims and perpetrators of intimate partner abuse or people with anxiety disorder or depression, then we suggest you get a copy of a compendium that focuses more exclusively on domestic violence, anxiety, or depression. Table 13.1 provides a list of recently published volumes, including some that cover a wide range of human conditions and some that are focused on particular conditions. Only a few of these actually provide the instruments for you to examine. Thus, regardless of whether you need to examine a wide range of human conditions or to focus on a narrow condition, we suggest you obtain a compendium that actually reprints the instruments.

INDIVIDUALIZED MEASURES

In addition, you can ascertain a measurement of your client and his or her condition with instruments that are particular to the individual. We show you how to develop two different types of individualized measures both for client problems and for the outcomes or goals of the interventions. The two procedures we demonstrate are direct observations instruments (DOIs) and what are typically called self-anchored rating scales (SARSs). Either can be used to ascertain quantitative reference points for comparing change in a client problem or attainment of a goal.

A DOI simply describes the client's problem or treatment goal in a clear, objective, and complete manner (Corcoran, Gingerich, & Briggs, 2001). All three of these criteria are necessary for a useful description that allows you to directly observe the cognition, overt action, or affect. By *clear* we mean that the description of the problem or goal is cogent enough so that others who might see it would agree that it is an accurate description. For example, a description of the goal of improving self-esteem is not clear, as the definitions are diverse and mean something quite different to different people. In contrast, to describe the goal as competent behavior and emotional comfort in specific social settings might be clearer once the definitions of *competent* and *comfort* are described and the social settings delineated. For example, for an at-risk young woman in a Police Athletic League, defining *competent behavior* as *assertiveness* may make the goal clearer.

The description of competence might involve initiating a game with other youths and the youth's feeling of calmness and lack of anxiety while asserting herself. One could easily agree that for the particular youth who is shy and socially withdrawn, initiating a basketball game with others illustrates a degree of social competence. Similarly, others might very well agree that the youth's self-observation of feeling calm in contrast to a rapid heart beat, sweaty palms, and shortness of breath shows signs of progress.

In addition to being clear, the description must be objective. By *objective* we mean that the behavior being described is in fact directly observable by either your client or a relevant other, such as you, a parent, a teacher or coach, or others in the client's social environment. For example, a couple, Bill and Betty Bickermore, who have the goal of improving communication, would not have an objective description that is observable if the goal were defined as Bill' "trying" to "listen more." An objective description would be one in which both Bill and Betty agree on the desired duration of time that they actually sit down facing each other, using good communication skills such as eye contract, active listening, and self-disclosure. Either would be able to measure the time of the conversation and the use of the appropriate communication skills.

Or consider the youth who does not comply with parental instruction regarding homework, a frequent source of family conflict. A description that simply says "study more" is not objective. The youth may simply say "I am studying" as he or she stares at the textbook, daydreaming about a date on Friday night or about a fashionable outfit to wear to school the next day. In contrast, an objective definition of "studying more" would involve a particular period of time during which a predetermined number of pages would be read, followed by a 3-minute summary of the content by the youth to one of his or her parents.

Finally, in addition to clear objectives, the description must be complete. By this we mean that it should be a thorough or exhaustive definition of the affect, overt action, or cognition. A complete definition is one that includes all the ranges of overt action, attributes, or elements of the behavior. For example, the definition of "studying more" would not necessarily be complete if it included only the number of pages readwithout detailing the different classes for which he or she is to study more. How many math problems are to be completed? How many new words are to be used in a conversation for a vocabulary or literature class? Or how many times does the youth turn in the homework for all of his or her classes? Similarly, if Bill reads the newspaper while Betty talks, then says, "I am listening," he is not listening effectively nor disclosing his own thoughts and feelings. The definition of listening should be completed by including such elements as that Bill will discuss his thoughts and feelings with Betty.

The development of a clear, objective, and complete description of a behavior should be done in cooperation with your client and possibly some relevant others, and copies of the completed description should be made. As an example of an observation, an adjudicated youth who is in a group home may make direct observation of the intensity of his or her feelings and thoughts about being given the "lights out" command. The youth might observe the intensity of angry feelings about being told what to do or may observe the frequency of his or her resentment over interpreting the rules and regulations as infantilizing. In contrast, the intern in this setting may observe the duration of time it takes for the youth to actually go to bed, teeth brushed and actually in bed without distractions such as televisions, stereos or iPods. Either the youth or the intern could observe the problem, such as the oppositional behavior, or the goal, such as getting the youth to comply with rules in a nonoppositional manner. Only the youth can observe whether he or she has less anger and fewer resentful thoughts.

With a clear, objective, and complete description of the problem or goal, either the client or a relevant other can readily count the number of times the behavior occurs, the intensity of that behavior, and the duration of time of the behavior lasts. Consider the example of a toddler who has temper tantrums. A parent or child care worker could count the number of tantrums a day, the loudness of the child's screams, and the duration of time before the child stops.

A variation on DOIs is the well-established and researched goal attainment scaling (GAS; Kiresuk, Smith & Cardillo, 1994). A GAS differs from the direct observation approach in that it includes five descriptions of the goal in observable terms in which the different descriptions reflect different frequency, magnitude, or duration of a goal. Additionally, you will find that by developing a GAS it is easier for you and your client to establish the goal of the intervention and that you are much more concrete about your expectations of the outcomes of the intervention. Thus, the GAS is a clinical tool, as well as an assessment tool.

As was the case with DOIs, the descriptions of the goal must be clear, objective, and complete. The descriptions should delineate the particularities of the outcomes with five descriptions that reflect variance in the outcome. The typical GAS defines levels of outcome as (1) least favorable, (2) less than expected, (3) expected, (4) more than expected, and (5) most favorable. The levels of outcome are scored from 1 to 5, although some authors suggest a $-2, -1, 0, +1$ and $+2$ scoring system. This suggested scoring system has the advantage of reflecting less-than-expected and more-than-expected outcomes in negative and positive numbers, although the system is limited in that successful attainment of a goal is scored as zero.It does not matter what numbering system you use, but we suggest you and your client derive one that is meaningful to your client.

In many cases the client's goal is attainable only after he or she has mastered intermediate goals, such as the case of Bill and Betty Bickermore, who want to improve communication. In this case the clients must first learn the rudimentary skills of communication, such as active listening and other communication skills that were covered in chapter 10. In these cases (and we think it is more common than not to have an intermediate goal), you will need to develop a GAS for the intermediate goal, along with one for the ultimate or outcome goal of the intervention.

Once developed, it will be necessary for the client or a relevant other to observe and rate the change or progress. This might be done once a day, once a week, once a month, or whenever it is meaningful within the context of the goal. At a minimum, we think you should monitor the attainment of the goal at least in the middle, near the end, and at the end of the intervention, with a follow-up assessment after the program of change has terminated.

With each assessment, the information should be used in a discussion with your client about his or her progress and any impediments to the goal. This is valuable information that facilitates the intervention and the professional relationship. This is especially so for the end and follow-up assessments, when the decision to terminate is made chiefly on the amount of change that has occurred. The GAS helps you overview and review the client's progress.

Another individualized rating scale is the self-anchored rating scale (SARS). A SARS is typically a single-item index on which the client or relevant other (e.g., a spouse or family member your field supervisor, who may rate your performance in the internship) assesses the client's performance on a continuum. The continuum of ratings is anchored with descriptions that describe differences in the problem behavior or intervention goal. The descriptions of different attributes on the continuum must be written in concise language that is, once again, clear, objective, and complete.

Because the scale is a single item, it takes but seconds for the client to observe his or her affect, behavior, or cognition. As such, SARS are particularly valuable when observing a behavior that occurs often and that need to measure several times during a day. Generalized anxiety, obsessive-compulsive rumination, and swearing would be examples of events that might warrant observing several times a day. Since SARSs can be completed in a matter of a second or two, time certainly is not an impediment to completing the measurement instrument.

SARS are also narrowly tailored to fit the specific nuances of the presenting problem or treatment goal. A SARS allows you to observe, measure if you will, a variety of particular client problems, such as the ability to abstain from drinking alcohol or calling one's sponsor before drinking. SARS may also be developed for more general conditions, such as the quality of life for an immigrant family or a general sense of satisfaction with the social services. SARS are especially helpful for behaviors that are covert and only observable to the clients, such as feelings of depression or self-defeating cognition or criminal thinking. Clearly, there is considerable utility in SARS, such that it is referred to as an all-purpose measurement tool.

Like all measures of human behavior, SARS will quantify some affect, action, or cognition. Each of these dimensions of human behavior will be observed in terms of its frequency, intensity, or duration. With the alcoholic in recovery, the behavior to be observed may be how frequently the client thinks of drinking throughout the day. Alternatively, if this were your client, you might wish to measure the intensity of the desire to drink alcohol. Finally, you might want to ascertain how long the thoughts about drinking last, that is, duration.

The SARS is easy for you and your client to develop. The exercise at the end of this chapter is designed facilitate the development of SARS. In general, the first thing you and your client must do is have a clear, objective, and complete description of what is to be rated. Next, it is necessary to decide what range of scores to use to reflect the variance in the problem or goal. For example, with very young children, a scale from 1 to 3 may be sufficient, as distinctions from 1 to 5 or more may be beyond their cognitive ability to discriminate. For adults, some recommend scores that range from 1 to 9 or 1 to 10 (Bloom et al., 2006). In our opinion, there is no set range of scales or levels of description. The variability should be determined by your client's ability to distinguish the levels of his or her affect, overt action, or cognitions.

Once the description is clear, objective, and complete and you have selected a range of the variable to be observed, it is necessary to anchor the endpoints with appropriate descriptions. We suggest that you also anchor the middle point with a description, which greatly enhances the consistency and accuracy of the SARS. The SARS is now ready for your client to use in observing him- or herself in order to collect observations for evaluating the outcomes of any intervention, program, or social service.

CASE EVALUATION TECHNIQUES IN THE PRACTICUM

So far we have covered how to observe clients' problems and goals with measurement tools. But the question has to be, what do we do with those observations or scores from the instruments? First of all, they must be organized in a manner that reflects the course of time in exposure to an intervention or program. The various organizational structures are single-subject research designs. Single-subject designs are simply the procedures by which you decide to organize the intervention and make the observations. If you observed your client only during the course of the intervention or program, it is called an "intervention-only" design, or a B design, with B standing for the intervention phase. If you were able to have your client complete an assessment tool while he or she was on a waiting list, you would have a no-intervention baseline, and this is called an AB design. If, after a while, your intervention changed and a new one was started, it would be an ABC design, with C standing for the second intervention. There are, of course, many different single-subject designs, as thoroughly covered in Bloom et al. (2006). We suggest, however, that your purpose is not to necessarily have the best design but to use the one that truly reflects the course of the intervention or program. In other words, let your actual work with the client dictate what design you are to use.

The evidence from the routine monitoring, with scores on an RAI, DOI, GAS, or SARS, constitutes some of the information you will use to determine whether your client changed and reached his or her goals. The data and your evaluation of them should be reviewed frequently with your field instructor. This will not only help master the interventions but also allow both of you to see strengths to be developed and weaknesses to be addressed.

INTERPRETING THE EVIDENCE

As you may imagine, we think it is best to systematically observe your client over the course of the intervention or program: at intake, before intervention, during the intervention period, and after intervention as a follow-up. We say at intake *and* before intervention because a couple of ways exist to estimate the magnitude, frequency, or duration of your client's problems before seeking criminal justice or social work services.

The task at hand is taking the numerous observations and interpreting what they mean. This task is greatly aided by simply plotting the observations or scores from the measurement tool on a graph or chart. On the bottom line of the chart, the X axis, you delineate time, such as weeks of treatment or months of incarceration. On the left vertical, or Y, axis, you demarcate the range of scores on the assessment instrument. (Most of the examples in this chapter have been scored on scales from 1 to 5, 1 to 7, or 1 to 10.) When you have two measures with different score ranges, such as a 1–5 GAS and a 0–10 RAI, you can use the left axis for one of the ranges of scores and the right axis for the other scale's score range. This allows you to plot observations from two instruments with distinct score ranges on a single graph. This is illustrated in figure 7.2, which monitored Ernie Lidquest's treatment for cannabis dependency. The left axis quantifies the amount of marijuana smoked, and the right axis quantifies the number of days of abstinence. Scores for each are still plotted left to right on the X axis, which is organized over time.

In and of itself, the score on any measurement tool means nothing. The quantitative score from any assessment tool is simply a number. A score is a reference point or indicator of something pursuant to the change process. It is not the actual problem or condition; just a marker of the intensity, frequency, or duration of the affect, action, or cognition.

A number, then, is actually quite meaningless. A score becomes meaningful only in comparison with some other number. To say that Davis has a depression score of 13 means nothing. It is meaningful relative to the scores of 20 and 30. There are two ways to make this comparison: by comparing the scores with the scores from a population and by comparing the client's scores with other scores collected on the instrument.

You may want to compare your client's scores with those of a research sample in order to see whether he or she is similar to a clinical sample or distinguishable from a sample of the general population. This type of comparison is called a "norm-referenced comparison." Because individualized rating scales are designed for the particular client, there are no norms, so norm-referenced comparisons are impossible.

Norm-referenced comparisons are possible with most RAIs. This use of an RAI, for example, might be necessary in order to compare a risk assessment of a youth in custody with those of others released from detention or in order to determine whether the youth should be released. Norm-referenced comparisons also help facilitate a diagnosis by determining whether your client's scores are similar to those of others with the same or similar condition. Another clever use of norm-referenced comparisons is to illustrate the necessity of services by showing a managed care organization that the client's condition is sufficiently different from the general population or sufficiently similar to a clinical sample. It would be hard for a gatekeeper in managed care not to authorize services if you illustrate that your client's scores are severe compared with scores of those without the condition (i.e., a general population sample) and quite similar to scores of those already receiving treatment (i.e., a clinical sample; Corcoran & Vandiver, 1996).

The more typical use of RAIs and individualized measures is to compare your client's scores with his or her own scores over the course of the intervention and afterward. This process is called "self-referenced comparison." Self-referenced comparisons are possible with individual rating scales and RAIs. This use of individualized rating scales or RAIs allows you to monitor the client's progress from before the intervention begins to the period of its application and afterward to see whether the change has had any lasting effect. The scores, data or evidence if you will, should provide valuable information to discuss openly with your client as indicators of change. This process should occur throughout your work with the client.

In essence, self-referenced comparisons allow you to determine how much different your client is relative to him- or herself. A norm-referenced comparison, in contrast, allows you to say how similar or different the client is compared with a clinical sample or the general population.

The primary benefit of comparing scores over the course of treatment or exposure to a social service or program is that you will have a more objective validation of how the client has changed, if at all.

Although these data can be statistically analyzed in a variety of ways, simply visually interpreting the change over the course of the intervention will illustrate whether meaningful change is occurring. In essence, it is far easier to obtain a statistically significant change than a clinically significant change, and visual analysis helps determine whether change was meaningful. The reason is that the test of clinical significance is not one of probability, as it is with statistical analyses, but what we like to call the "inner-ocular posttraumatic significance test." That is to say, clinical significance should be so obvious that it hits you right between the eyes.

SUMMARY OF PRACTICE EVALUATION

The most rudimentary questions that should be addressed by the plotted observations are: (1) Did scores on the problems that should decrease over the course of the intervention go down? (2) Did scores that should increase, such as the attainment of a goal, go up? (3) Were these patterns significant enough to be meaningful? In other words, are the outcomes clinically significant? This is a question best answered not by mere numbers or scores on a scale but by your professional judgment and your client's personal opinions.

All of the preceding may be summarized into what we playfully call the DOG model. It includes just three elements: a design (i.e., "D") for collecting observations, an observation system (i.e., "O") for measuring the client problem or goals, and a mechanism for interpreting the scores, which we believe is simplest if charted on a graph (i.e., "G"). Frankly, all of the preceding, and the essence of all single-subject evaluation in the human services, is some variation of the designs, observations, and interpretation of the observations.

CLIENT/CONSUMER: _____

PROBLEMS: 1. _____ 2. _____ 3. _____

GOALS: 1. _____ 2. _____ 3. _____

TX 1. _____ 2. _____ 3. _____

PLANNED NO.
OF SESSIONS: 1. _____ 2. _____ 3. _____

DATE | NOTES:

S
C
O
R
E
S

S
C
O
R
E
S

1 2 3 4 5 6 7 8 9 10 11 12 13 14 15 16 17 18 19 20 21

Figure 13.1 Case Summary Form

Figure 13.1 is the Case Summary Form, which is intended for your use. It has an area for charting the observations and spaces for a summary of the observations and interpretation. We suggest that you use it as a summary form in your case records. We hope you use it regularly with your clients and that it helps manage what might have seemed a daunting challenge in learning to be an effective and accountable professional in social work or criminal justice. We encourage you not to be overwhelmed by all of this discussion but to realize it is simply a DOG: a Design, a systematic way of Observing the problem or the goal, and interpreting the observations by charting the scores on a Graph. In summary, there are all sorts of outcomes for all sorts of clients in social services, whether in the justice system or in social work. We think you will find it valuable to routinely monitor your client with at least one or two RAIs that ascertain the client's condition. The results of this monitoring provide the evidence that will allow you to determine whether you were successful in implementing the intervention. The results will help tell you whether your client has changed or not.

IT'S MY PLEASURE

Bruce A. Thyer and M. Elizabeth Vonk

Case Description

One of us (MEV) was a social worker employed at a university student counseling center, where I undertook the treatment of Beth, a 25-year-old graduate student who referred herself to the center because of her long-term fear of vaginal penetration, a fear of such severity that it precluded her having penile intercourse with a man and kept her from obtaining routine gynecological care. In seeking a resolution of this problem, Beth had had three prior episodes of psychodynamically oriented psychotherapy at ages 17, 20, and 21, all of which failed to provide relief. She initially traced the onset of her fears to around age 15, when she began her menstrual cycle and became very frightened on trying to insert a tampon for the first time. She was unsuccessful at this attempt and subsequently used menstrual pads. At age 17 she needed a pelvic examination and became very frightened in the physician's office, refusing a vaginal examination. Her medical doctor then referred her for her first episode of psychotherapy, which lasted for about 3 months of weekly sessions. Treatment focused on possible relationship issues with her stepfather. She ended therapy to begin college.

At ages 20 and 21, she again sought help via psychodynamic psychotherapy, prompted by her involvement with men with whom she desired a sexual relationship; she remained too fearful to consummate a relationship. Neither course of treatment produced the desired result.

At age 22, her vaginal penetration fears were exacerbated when she sought treatment for a vaginal yeast infection. Despite her professed severe anxiety, the physician insisted on inserting a speculum into Beth's vagina. Beth was unable to tolerate this and terminated the examination. The physician was unsympathetic and told her that she would never have "normal relations" with a man. Beth described this experience as terrifying. At age 23 she was able to tolerate the use of tampons, and through the help of a sympathetic relative and a supportive medical doctor, Beth underwent a pelvic examination to completion. She sought treatment now at age 25 because she remained a virgin with an intact hymen, but she was in a committed, intimate heterosexual relationship and wished to overcome her fears of vaginal penetration so that she could undertake conventional sexual intercourse with her boyfriend.

Assessment/Screening and Problem Identification

Initial assessments were undertaken during two sessions and solely involved a clinical interview, with no use of any formal diagnostic tests or rapid assessment instruments. Beth's reported severe fear of vaginal penetration extended to penises, fingers, and vaginal specula. She was able to use tampons at the time she sought help but had only been able to do so since age 23, having been afraid prior to that time. She did experience sexual arousal during sexual activities that did not involve vaginal penetration, and she was orgasmic; these factors tended to exclude the *DSM* diagnoses of female sexual arousal disorder, or female orgasmic disorder (American Psychiatric Association, 2000). Dyspareunia (genital pain associated with sexual intercourse) and vaginismus (recurrent or persistent involuntary contraction of the perineal muscles surrounding the outer third of the vagina when vaginal penetration with penis, finger, tampon, or speculum is attempted) were also explored and ruled out. There was no history of panic-like symptoms, apart from the excessive fears when vaginal penetration was attempted, so panic disorder was also excluded. The client did meet the criteria for specific phobia, so the principle of etiological parsimony (Epstein, 1984) suggested that this be our initial presumptive diagnosis.

Arriving at a formal provisional diagnosis, of course, does not necessarily imply any correct etiological understanding, but further clinical interviews with Beth disclosed some possible leads. When she was queried about her initial sexual experiences, she spontaneously related that her mother had told her of an episode that occurred when Beth was 4 years old. Beth had been climbing on some playground equipment and fell, tearing the wall of her vagina. This injury had been repaired through surgery, but Beth denied any memory of the episode, claiming only being able to recall lying on an examination table with intense pain in her genital area. It is well established that traumatic childhood events can lead to the development of severe fears experienced by adults (Davey, 1992; Ollendick, King, & Murius, 2002), so once again the principle of parsimony suggests that the phobia she experienced as an adult related to vaginal penetration was etiologically linked to this childhood traumatic injury.

Intervention Selection

When Beth sought help, we were unable to locate any published reports involving the treatment of persons with similar problems (fears specific to vaginal penetration). Given our hypothesis that Beth's difficulties met the *DSM* criteria for a specific phobia, we turned to the available evidence-based clinical research literature regarding the treatment of these types of disorders. At that time, the American Psychological Association's Task Force on Promotion and Dissemination of Psychological Procedures found that the technique of graduated real-life exposure therapy conducted in natural environments was a "well-established treatment" (Task Force, 1995, p. 23) and was indeed the best supported intervention in terms of evidence-based practice. This conclusion has not changed over the past 10 years:

> A consensus has developed that the treatment of choice for specific phobias is exposure-based procedures, particularly in vivo exposure. Exposure has been shown to be effective for a wide spectrum of specific phobias . . . in vivo exposure is generally accepted as the most powerful treatment for specific phobias. (Barlow, Raffa, & Cohen, 2002, p. 315)

Fortunately, an extensive literature describes the rationale and conduct of real-life exposure therapy (e.g., Thyer, 1987), and we drew on this to design the course of treatment suggested to Beth.

Intervention/Treatment

The social worker explained her tentative case formulation, etiological hypothesis, and proposed course of treatment (graduated real-life exposure therapy), emphasizing that this approach was the one apparently best supported by contemporary empirical research into the causes and treatment of phobias. Beth agreed to the following plan. She was asked to undertake some real-life homework exercises, initially alone, and then later involving her boyfriend. She was to practice inserting just the tip of her finger into her vagina, to leave it there for 10 minutes if possible, and to rate her maximum experienced anxiety on a 10-point scale (described later). The first week she did this three times; the second and third weeks, twice and once, respectively. Her maximum reported anxiety declined from 8 during the first session of the first week to 1 during her single session in the third week. Homework sessions 3 and 4 involved her inserting her finger more fully into her vagina and beginning some in-and-out motions. This she was able to do without any setbacks, and she noted that the experience was pleasurable. Session 6 involved recruiting her boyfriend to insert his finger, under her careful instruction, and to move it in and out as she had herself. The first time this was accomplished, her anxiety peaked at 4, but it declined to 0 by the third session with the boyfriend. During her seventh and eighth office visits, she did not engage in any homework (her boyfriend was out of town), but during her ninth office visit, she reported that she and her boyfriend had gotten "carried away" and actually had intercourse twice. The first time induced a maximum anxiety score of 1 and the second time a simple 0. During her tenth and eleventh office visits, she reported enjoying anxiety-free intercourse with her boyfriend, and this was also true during the twelfth visit, which took place 2 months after her first experience with intercourse involving a penis. At this point she claimed that "It's just not a problem any more!" She subsequently broke up with her initial boyfriend and enjoyed anxiety-free penetrative sexual intercourse with a new boyfriend, suggesting that treatment gains both were maintained and also generalized to other partners. She had been carefully counseled by the social worker regarding safe sex practices in the early stages of treatment and reported consistently using condoms.

Evaluation

A relatively simple B single-subject evaluation design was undertaken to assess the apparent effectiveness of treatment. In a B design, systematic measurement of a given variable is undertaken at the same time that treatment is initiated. Such repeated measures, graphed over time and visually evaluated, can indicate whether the problem is improving, deteriorating, or not appreciably changing (see Thyer, 2001). Given the private nature of Beth's presenting problem, assessment of her overt behavior via direct observation was not possible, nor was a direct measure of her primary complaint, subjectively experienced anxiety, available. Thus we relied on the client's self-reports, provided during weekly counseling sessions, and also systematized by her use of a 0- to 10-point scale, with 0 indicating the absence of any anxiety and 10 meaning panic-stricken, to assess her subjective state while undertaking her homework assignments. These self-reported ratings have been shown to correlate reasonably well with physiological measures of anxiety (see Thyer, Papsdorf, Davis, & Vallecorsa, 1984). The data were displayed on a graph in our original report of this case (Vonk & Thyer, 1995) and presented a clear picture of declining anxiety scores.

Discussion

Since this client was originally treated and reported on in the literature, we have been able to locate a narratively reported case history published earlier (Frutiger, 1981) involving a woman with a similar problem treated in a similar manner. Evidence-based practice (EBP) does not assert that all treatments provided to clients must be those proven to be useful through well-crafted randomized controlled clinical trials. Rather, EBP indicates that treatments should be based on the best available evidence, and we believe that this was the case in the care and evaluation of Beth. Given the absence of a substantial body of research involving the treatment of vaginal penetration phobias, we replied on the most closely related body of clinical research evidence, that involving specific phobias in general. Evaluating the outcomes of one's own clinical work is another feature of EBP, and we tried to fulfill this suggestion through our use of a systematic measure of anxiety, its repeated use for measurement, graphic display, and, ultimately, publication in a peer-reviewed professional journal.

▪ ▪ ▪

Activities

1. Here is a study question that is also useful as a group discussion question. What options do you have if a careful review of the evidence-based literature fails to uncover any positive outcome studies directly related to your client's issue?

2. Review the websites for the Cochrane and Campbell Collaborations (http://www.cochrane.org; http://www.campbell.org). Are there any existing

systematic reviews that deal with a clinical issue you are interested in? Print out the synopses of those that are of interest. You have just begun to collect some evidence-based interventions. We suggest that you start a filing system as you gather more and more.

3. Consider the case presented in this chapter.

    a. Define the outcomes or goals other than those covered.

    b. Is the target that is to be changed going to increase or decrease in frequency, intensity, or duration?

    c. Use the information from the last question to quantify the behavior that is to be increased or decreased in its frequency, intensity, or duration.

    d. Use the completed form for a group discussion or for supervision in your field setting.

4. The following two protocols are designed to help you develop SARS and GAS.

Assume that your field placement assigns a junior high school student who is doing poorly in school (seventh grade), has few friends, and generally stays by himself during free periods, such as lunch and study hall. He is generally very shy. You have established the goal of increasing his assertive behavior and peer interaction while maintaining his feelings of comfort and calm. Some of the structured activities are designed to enhance his school performance, such as interaction with lab partners in science or with study groups in social science and classroom participation in a variety of courses.

Question 1. In this school-based internship, what is the best design for gathering evidence and evaluating the effectiveness of your intervention?

Question 2. Develop and record here two self-anchored rating scales, one for the client's primary problem and another for the treatment goal.

- Develop a goal attainment scale for the problem.
  Assume that you are seeing this youth twice a week for 45 minutes during the fall term. Both of you have the holidays off, and you return to continue the work after the 4-week December holidays. During the recess you have the youngster continue to monitor his shyness, anxiety, and

assertiveness. Of course, the monitoring continues once the holiday recess is over and the intervention continues.

- How can you take these circumstances and create an ABAB design?

- Draw a chart of this ABAB design, paying particular attention to the time on the X axis.

- On the chart or graph, identify the "zone of success," and discuss in the classroom or with your field instructor why this is truly a "clinically significant" outcome. What do you think about this frequency, intensity, or duration of the problem or goal?

Consider the case of Ernie. Was there a decrease in his problem? Was there an increase in the goal? Were these trends meaningful?

Direct Observations

In order to develop direct observation systems, you must work closely with your client and his or her significant others in the social environment. We have delineated this process into steps, with space for you and your client to actually develop a direct observation system that is clear, objective, and complete.

Step 1. The first step is to have your client or relevant other write a 25-word description of the problem behavior or intervention goal. The instructions to the client and others who are delineating the problem or goal should be: "In the following space, write a description of the problem you wish to change or the primary goal you intend to reach in the course of our professional relationship."

Step 2. Now have your client discuss with you all the elements or attributes of the problem or goal of treatment. You should actively participate in this discussion, treating it as a brainstorming session, in order to be certain the description is complete. Your description might also include a relevant other, such as a parent, partner, teacher, or, yes, even you, the intern. Record your ideas and the client's ideas in the space provided.

- What are your suggestions or suggestions from relevant others?

- What are your client's suggestions?

- What are those elements or attributes that the client, you, and relevant others all agree about?

Step 3. Based on the preceding description and review of it in step 2, either you or the client should revise the description in the following space:

Step 4. In a discussion with your client, ask and answer the following questions:

   a. Is the description of the problem or goal one that others would agree with? That is, is it clear? __ Yes ___ No

   b. Can someone, such as the client him- or herself or you, the intern, truly observe the description? That is, is it objective? __ Yes __ No

   c. Have you included all aspects, elements, or attributes of the problem or goal? That is, is it complete? __ Yes ___ No

Step 5. Depending on the answers to step 4, revise the direct observation description one more time.

Step 6. Now that you have a workable description of a problem or primary goal, you will need to determine who will make the observations and when the observations will be made. We cannot overstate the importance of specificity with this step. To facilitate this, answer the following particular questions.

   a. Who will use the observation system? In the following space, record the name of each person who will use the description to observe the problem or goal.

   b. When will it be used? On which days of the week will the observations be made?

   Monday   Tuesday   Wednesday   Thursday   Friday   Saturday   Sunday

   Circle all that apply

c. At what time or times of the day will the observations be made?

_____ A.M.

_____ P.M.

Record each specific time of the day separately for observations that are to be made more than once in the morning or afternoon.

Step 7. Now that you have a good description for direct observations of a problem or goal, there is one more step. It is actually the hardest of them all: for your client or relevant other, such as yourself, use the instrument as specified in step 6. In other words, "just do it!"

14 GUIDELINES FOR ASSESSING COMPETENCIES

Preventing Good Placements From Going Bad

BARBARA THOMLISON *and* KEVIN CORCORAN

*All students will be assessed on their performance during the internship
on an established set of criteria for the expected comspetencies. This
is as an integral part of the practicum experience. Assessment and
evaluation is a form of feedback about one's performance and developing
competencies, and it is necessary for practical, professional, and
ethical reasons. However, assessment of learning poses challenges for
supervisors and students due to the inherent problems associated with the
measurement of competencies when a learning plan or learning contract is the basis for measuring outcomes. Guidelines are presented in
this chapter for assessing your accomplishments and determining your
further development as a professional.*

WHAT IS THE PURPOSE OF ASSESSMENT?

Assessment is a complex process that should be about enhancing your learning.
Its purpose includes:

1. Providing a means by which students are graded or evaluated.
2. Providing a means by which students receive feedback on the quality of
   their learning.
3. Enabling supervisors to evaluate the effectiveness of their teaching.
4. Maintaining professional standards (Singh, 2002).

Assessment is a process that should be an ongoing component of practicum
learning. Progress meetings are designed to highlight and review your developing
competencies. As a form of feedback on your progress, assessment starts when
you begin your internship, and it continues throughout, with at least two formal
structured review or assessment meetings during the internship—identified as
the midterm and final evaluation reports.

347

ELEMENTS OF A SATISFACTORY
PROGRESS ASSESSMENT

Good assessments result from the following qualities of the supervisory relationship:

1. Assessment focuses on what has been learned, not what is taught, and has a student-centered approach rather than a supervisor-centered approach.
2. From the beginning, students know specifically what they will be assessed on and how; there shall be no surprises about the process or expected outcomes.
3. Assessment is linked to the learning plan, the objectives, the assignments, and the learning outcomes.
4. Student self-assessment is used, as greater learning occurs when students learn to evaluate their own strengths and deficiencies in a realistic manner.
5. Assessment is bidirectional, not unidirectional from supervisor to student (Singh, 2002).

ELEMENTS OF AN UNSATISFACTORY
PROGRESS ASSESSMENT

Assessments of student performance that do not promote learning are observed to have the following qualities:

1. Not allowing students to make mistakes and to reflect on the mistakes.
2. Assessing the wrong competencies, or assessing the same competency repeatedly so that a realistic view of a range of competencies is not achieved.
3. Placing undue reliance on theory or practice without enabling students to make the link between theory and practice.
4. Limiting and not providing regular feedback.
5. Focusing too heavily on the performance criteria and not the learning (Singh, 2002).

The assessment process comprises three elements: (1) preassessment activities, (2) the assessment report and meeting itself, and (3) postassessment activities. Both you and your supervisor engage in preassessment meeting activities to set the expected outcomes. Remember the learning plan you developed at the beginning of the internship? This document will be used to measure your expected outcomes and your actual achievements. Preparation activities for the assessment and assessment meeting include organizing and reviewing information about your knowledge, practice skills and abilities, and results to date. In the review meeting, both you and your supervisor will assess your progress and reach conclusions about whether you are "putting it all together" as you move toward becoming a professional. Postevaluation activities focus on self-reflection and on organizing yourself for continuing improvement. Your performance in the internship will be evaluated on the expected and relevant criteria set by your program. Program performance criteria will be used to guide assessment of your progress.

PERFORMANCE FEEDBACK

Assessing your learning requires you to pay attention to how well you are able to describe how you have been thinking about what you do, what you know, and the results you have achieved. This is also called *performance feedback*. Feedback is a form of communication to transmit information about the results of actions to the person who performed the actions—in this case, information is communicated to you, the student. Feedback is used to help students make changes or corrections to improve their work. It can be used in the following ways:

- to modify practice skills
- to increase the likelihood of continued learning for improvement
- to help students recognize patterns that need improvement
- to give students positive indicators of areas in which there is evidence of learning and development in their knowledge and in their ability to achieve appropriate practice outcomes.

Learning and making progress are highly individualized processes. Depending on his or her stage of learning, each student is also working at acquiring differentskills or competencies. Learning is an ongoing cyclical process that begins the moment you start your internship. Performance feedback and learning will come from many sources, both yourself and others. It also comes from engaging in the learning activities suggested in this book, from exploring your values and beliefs, and from critically thinking about your assignments, projects, and experiences. The assessment format suggested in this book is to be used as a guide or trigger in preparing for your evaluation meeting. Each educational program will have a specific evaluation form, but the core elements of practice will be consistent: (1) acquiring knowledge, (2) acquiring and applying skills, (3) personal development, and (4) professional development. Use the evaluation form that is specific to your internship to prepare for the performance assessment of your competencies. Remember, the assessment of competencies will focus on what you know, what you have been doing, and what the resulting outcomes are. Criminal justice programs will emphasize difference competencies than social work programs.

Assessing progress can have a significant impact on you. Therefore, it is important how performance assessment is given and received if you are to benefit from assessment feedback. Guidelines for giving and receiving feedback follow:

- *Clarity and specificity*. Be clear and specific about the accomplishments and outcomes. What was done correctly, adequately, and accurately? Identify how you did it so you will be able to keep on doing it. Understand the steps or thinking that went into attaining the competency. If a learning objective was not demonstrated, then clearly specify the area that needs improvement. For example, what specific task or behavior needs to be demonstrated to raise your performance to a satisfactory or acceptable level of performance?
- *Individualization*. Identify your unique strengths and abilities, including the knowledge mastered, and the areas of responsibility you accepted for your learning.
- *Honesty and constructiveness*. It is important to receive authentic and genuine feedback so that you have an accurate picture of your strengths and areas that require improvement. When a supervisor provides information about your performance that may seem unclear to you, ask for examples both of strengths and areas requiring attention. In the same way, if there is an identified problem area, you will need to ask for ideas or suggestions for how to improve or correct that area.
- *Positivity*. Always end on a positive note, identifying your intentions for ongoing learning and development.

HANDLING FEEDBACK CONSTRUCTIVELY

Start thinking about the review of your competencies early in the practicum; in fact, if you are keeping the narrative accounts of your practice as suggested in this book, your task is easier. When the midterm assessment arrives, there should be essentially no surprises about your progress. It is common for students to feel somewhat anxious about receiving an evaluation. Typically, this situation elicits a range of feelings, emotions, and even value conflicts for students. To manage these thoughts and feelings, consider the type of constructive feedback you would give yourself about your development. This exercise is helpful in anticipating the feedback your supervisor will give you during the assessment meeting. Having a clear and balanced view of your abilities allows you to proactively participate in the assessment and evaluation meeting as a well-prepared professional. Constructive feedback will take the form of noting specific positive aspects of your performance and specific suggestions for improvement. Students often interpret the suggestions for change and improvement as criticism. Critical comments should be avoided and balanced with suggestions and examples for improvement.

Reflect on your preferred learning approach and the qualities associated with these styles, as discussed in chapter 4. Some students' learning styles focus on only grades and criticism. Such students cannot see the big picture regarding their progress. Decide ahead of time how you handle constructive feedback. Do you focus on concerns? Is it hard to keep your feelings under control? Personalize or take responsibility for your feelings and reactions. Assess your style and determine what you need to do in advance to handle this communication. Some students like to ask for more details or examples or to ask what solutions are needed to solve a problem. You can keep a cool head by planning. Ask questions about any observations that are unclear to you. Request clarification and ask for suggestions; it is proper to do so. Do not be argumentative, and *compromise when appropriate* if you and your supervisor see your performance differently. If you can spot your setbacks and concerns in advance and propose suggestions for improvement, then you are well on your way to handling feedback constructively.

ASSESSING COMPETENCIES

What have you learned? You know a great deal, and since day 1 of the practicum, you have been thinking critically about your competencies, and you have been documenting your progress for a record of accomplishments over the course of the internship. Critically reflect on your successes and setbacks. How might you have done something differently? Learning comes also from acting and responding to feedback about mistakes and successes and from what you understand about these events. Discovering *all* of your strengths and concerns is not necessary and is usually impossible. Remember, your supervisor will offer observations and feedback about your progress using the criteria developed by the program. Together, you will identify critical incidents that were turning points in your learning.

Reviewing the Learning Plan

When evaluating your knowledge and skills, start with the learning plan and goals you set for yourself. What did you do during the internship to meet your learning needs? Be honest about your learning and progress as you review the information sources: your journal, your cases and notes, and your logs, records, and practice portfolio. What did you actually do? What did you hope to do? What explains any discrepancies? What did you do that was not planned? Were interventions based on client circumstances, evidence-based practice, and safety? Did your practice meet professional standards of care? Were you professional while providing the practice? Did you respond to diverse client needs by developing culturally competent or culturally sensitive responses? Cultural competence includes the knowledge, skills, and attitudes or beliefs designed specifically for the client.

Reviewing the Evidence

What are the results of your individual and collective practice assignments? The best way to review your results will be to organize your successes, accomplishments, and setbacks under each performance criteria on your evaluation form. The task is to pull out from these various documented sources some critical incidents that illustrate progress, change, and results. Construct information to create an integrated view of your performance. Identify repeated patterns and use of skills across assignments. This indicates strong and consistent use of professional knowledge and skills. Review these incidents and markers of learning with a comparative analysis of your written learning plan. What do you think about the results? Are you pleased? Are you concerned about some aspects of your development? If so, what areas raise questions for your ongoing development? Reflect on your learning goals, and then identify opportunities from your assignments that demonstrate the repetition or maintenance of skills and knowledge. Did you demonstrate the application of these skills to new situations? In other words, were you able to generalize your achievements or change across time and across assignments and tasks? Are positive patterns and competent skills repeated? Incorporating new learning *repeatedly* into practice demonstrates integration of learning and promotes improved performance. If you needed to unlearn certain patterns and skills, did this also occur? Questions to ask yourself as you reflect on what you know, what you did, and your achievements or results include:

1. What have I learned?
2. What are my successes?

3. What were my setbacks?
4. What kind of a problem is there (if at all)?
5. Where does the problem occur?
6. When does the problem occur?
7. What does it add up to?
8. What do I need to do more of?
9. What do I need to do differently?
10. How will I know when I achieve my goals? (Reimer et al., 1999, p. 167).

In general, the written assessment report will include comments on your performance as a member of the internship setting, your performance on assigned tasks or projects, and your ethical and professional behavior, motivation, attitude, and ability to get along with clients, staff, and others, as well as your potential for ongoing work in the field (Gordon, McBride, & Hage, 2001).

THE ASSESSMENT MEETING AND EVALUATION

Usually students have two formal assessment or evaluation meetings, as required by their educational program. The midterm assessment meeting occurs about midway through the practicum. The final assessment of learning occurs at the end of the internship. Some programs may require additional assessment times, and some students may need additional assessment meetings. Common processes in evaluation meetings include bringing all of the information concerning student accomplishments together to review. In some situations, the evaluation interview will include you and your supervisor and a faculty member from your university or college.

The Assessment Meeting

Arrive at the meeting with your written performance assessment, notes, and other material you wish to discuss as part of the evaluation. Your supervisor will come to the meeting prepared with the same evidence of your practice. Both you and your supervisor will discuss the findings. Positive comments will be balanced with concerns about improvement. Request clarification and information where appropriate, and balance talking and listening in a way that increases the likelihood of obtaining an informed perspective about your performance. A written evaluation is the result. You may receive a grade, a credit, or some other designation such as pass/fail, satisfactory/unsatisfactory, or need for improvement.

Valued information about outcomes and learning for improvement will be given in the evaluation interview. At this point, you have information about your practice knowledge, skills, and competencies.

Postassessment Reflection

Now that you have a clear picture of your developing professional competencies, you should sit quietly to reflect on the content. This is a good time to record your reactions to the assessment and evaluation in your journal. It is also a good time to reread the written report. Dialogue with yourself and listen to the response. Observe your emerging strengths and speak to the positives. For areas of practice that require improvement, what are your options? The evaluation will guide your next steps in learning. Given your achievements, what do you need to do to move forward? This, of course, will depend on whether you received a satisfactory or an unsatisfactory assessment. A good strategy for assessing the outcomes of the evaluation meeting and report includes the following steps:

1. Summarize. Briefly list the conclusions and milestones achieved.
2. Be realistic. Do not overgeneralize or overstate concerns or strengths.
3. Make a conceptual map. Draw a map depicting the steps needed to reach your goals; include a timeline.
4. Reflect. Review your learning objectives and recalibrate your course if needed.

THE EVALUATION REPORT: PERFORMANCE CRITERIA ACHIEVED

The majority of interns receive positive assessments of their overall performance expectations and requirements, indicating that their actual performance goals on relevant and established program requirements were achieved. Based on the assessment meeting and the written assessment report, you may have agreed in total or in part with the evaluation. If this report is the midterm assessment, then you still have time to improve your competencies. If this report is the final assessment, the area of concern may not be so problematic as to impede your progress. Feedback serves as a reminder of specific areas you need to pay attention to. If you are at the midpoint, you may revise any parts of your learning plan in order to continue to make progress toward fully achieving the performance objectives. Common areas in which interns may receive suggestions about performance improvement include: (1) increasing specific knowledge; (2) practicing specific skill sets, such as assessment, written reports, or cultural and diversity competency; (3) reflecting on practice judgments or decision-making processes, such as course of treatment or technical competencies; and (4) interpersonal skills, such as attitudes and inappropriate emotional reactions; concerns about ethical or professional behavior. There may be tasks to learn or unlearn, and receiving a positive assessment does not mean that you can now sit back and relax for the next half of the term. It is a time for achieving excellence and pursuing professional behaviors at the highest levels. Achieving change and maintaining the desired behaviors, skills, and attitudes is just as important for the next phase of the internship.

THE EVALUATION REPORT: PERFORMANCE CRITERIA NOT ACHIEVED

In cases in which a student receives a progress report at the evaluation interview that is unfavorable, the supervisor has usually provided earlier feedback that problematic behavior or performance was present in the course of the internship. This is not easy to hear. Annually, approximately 3–5% of students receive reports indicating that they have not met the performance criteria for varying reasons (Falender & Shafranske, 2004). If this is a midterm report, feedback is given to help students make the necessary changes prior to the final report. Remediation steps are usually suggested, but an internship site has no obligation to do so unless the student shows that he or she will be able to perform the essential functions with reasonable accommodation or within the designated time frame. If you have received information about your lack of progress and don't know what necessary steps to take to improve, talk it over with your supervisor or the faculty instructor assigned to the internship site. It may be possible to work out a plan for the specific learning in question. If you are not sure whether the feedback in your report constitutes a warning of lack of progress, that too requires that you clarify the feedback with your supervisor and faculty instructor. *Do so immediately.* On the other hand, some students worry needlessly because they have interpreted any constructive feedback as negative. In either situation, you must seek clarification.

If you are a student who received an unsatisfactory progress report, it is, of course, very disappointing and stressful. But the issue is the persistence of problematic behaviors, ethical issues, or incompetent behavior that may need attention. After all, client safety or harm must be considered above all. A student's *attitude* toward learning can often warrant an unsatisfactory progress warning, particularly if responses to suggestions for change are always met with contradiction or anger. If you received such feedback, then your supervisor experiences you as difficult to teach, someone who may be reluctant to listen or to complete tasks, and this lack of progress toward learning goals and objectives places you at risk of not completing the internship and perhaps even at risk for failing the internship.

What does "performance criteria not achieved" really mean? The following list of options is possible:

1. It may be a warning, suggesting that unless major changes in behavior and attitude are forthcoming, a failing grade for the internship course will be assigned.
2. It may mean that you cannot proceed further at this point, especially if safety is a major concern.
3. It may indicate you have failed to meet the performance standards in significant areas that require you to withdraw from the internship. The program may or may not allow for an appeal of the failing grade. Some programs may allow you the opportunity to repeat part or all of the internship.
4. It may indicate that you cannot proceed and may even have to withdraw from the program. It may also mean that you are not suitable to the profession, and if this is the case, it can indeed be a very distressing time for you.

Some common student difficulties that may result in an unfavorable assessment report include:

1. Case decision errors, lack of timely attention to a case, failure to perform appropriate checks or follow-up on cases, or unsafe conduct
2. Unprofessional or unethical behavior or both
3. Insufficient knowledge base, resulting in serious problems in decision making
4. Inability to recognize difficulties and make changes, which consistently negatively affects the quality of services delivered
5. Interpersonal difficulties that interfere with practice decision making.
6. Failure to ask for assistance as needed
7. Unsuitability to the profession (Lamb, Cochran, & Jackson, 1991; Reimer et al., 1999, p. 171).

WHEN GOOD PLACEMENTS GO BAD

There are several reasons that good placements do not work out.

Mismatch

The internship site, the supervisor, or both may have been a mismatch. If this describes the situation you experienced, then immediately discuss the matter with the faculty supervisor assigned to your internship to decide whether the site can be salvaged and your placement restructured in order to meet your amended learning plan. If this is not possible, then determine whether there is an appeal process to advocate for a new internship site or for withdrawal of the grade or to deal with other issues that are relevant to consider about your progress, remediation, or both in the program. Check the student academic handbook or internship handbook to see whether there is a deadline for initiating a formal appeal process regarding the internship course. Before rushing to initiate this option, it is advisable to review the assessment report again and reflect on the expressed concerns cited by your supervisor. Scrutinize the quality of the supporting evidence for the concerns. Are the concerns valid? This review may support your decision to engage in an appeal, or it may lead to a decision to take the course again. It is understandable to feel upset and even a bit defensive. Be honest with yourself. Repeating the course (the internship), if that is the option chosen, may be beneficial in the long run. Realizing that you need to make some changes in your behavior is a wake-up call and is distressing, but it is not a catastrophe or the worst that can happen.

Suitability

Is this career for you? Perhaps not. You and your supervisor may have concluded from your assessment that you are not suited to the professional program. The reasons may not be at all clear to you, or you may have discovered that the personal and academic characteristics needed for this discipline are not a good fit for you. Contact the faculty advisor for academic advising and discuss the possibility of transferring your credits to another program. If this is the case, you have learned a great deal.

Readiness

Are you ready for professional practice? Evidence suggests that helping professionals who are experiencing personal stress are less psychologically available to assist other people (Lamb et al., 1991). This may place others at risk of harm and affect your motivation to learn. If you are preoccupied with your personal stresses, then consider the need for time out from the educational program. If this describes you, then inquire as to whether you can take a leave of absence for a term, and consider this a positive action for both yourself and those you are working with.

There are many reasons that a student may not be suitable for a program, and it is helpful if you can determine this with your faculty instructor, internship coordinator, or other educational or career advisor. This can be an opportunity for further learning and development. As discussed in other parts of this book, from failures and setbacks, some of the most meaningful learning emerges. This may not be evident to you now, but this critical learning event may redirect your pathway to a place where you are more suited and successful.

SUMMARY

Guidelines for assessing your competencies are based on a communication and feedback cycle for continuous learning. Preparing for assessment of your progress involves careful preparation and attention to your documented work assignments and engaging in critical analysis of your practice.

1. Review what you know.
2. Review what you did.
3. Decide where you need to go in developing competencies.

Critical appraisal promotes self-improvement, and the following guidelines are suggested toward this end:

- Change your focus from *what* you are thinking to *how* you are thinking.
- Critical thinking improves assessment, planning, and intervention for practice.
- Feedback in the form of evaluation is the planned opportunity to enhance your knowledge acquisition, performance assessment, and personal and professional growth.

THE REHABILITATIVE IDEAL AND THE
DISSIMILARITIES IN CRIMINAL JUSTICE
AND SOCIAL WORK PRACTICE

Barbara Thomas

Case Description

The client was a 47-year-old Caucasian male expecting to be released from a state prison. This client had been incarcerated since 1992 for a murder. The client was released in 1998 and rearrested for parole violation, which resulted in a conviction for corruption of a minor. During his initial and second incarcerations, there were no medical records identifying his health status as HIV-positive. The client sought medical testing specifically for HIV/AIDS as a result of spending a part of his sentence time in a prison in which 85% of the inmates were HIV-positive. The state mandated HIV testing on admission into the assigned correctional facility, along with other criteria that were to be completed before the inmate could be integrated with the general population. It was apparent that the client, who was diagnosed with HIV-positive infectious disease status, had engaged in unprotected sex after being integrated into the general population. The client did not have an external support system, and over the previous 30 years he had lost both parents to death.

Since his incarceration, he had lost contact with community friends. He did not have any religious affiliation and stated that he did not know what the inside of a church looked like, that his parents had forbidden his attendance at religious practices and activities.

This case illustrates linkage coordination (LC) with this client. The intervention had many false starts, with three postponed release dates. The linkage coordinator attempted to relink community services in 2004, and the client's release date was postponed again. In 2005, the coordinator received a projected release date in March of 2005. The medical infectious disease nurse received a projected released date of May 5, 2005, and the client and assigned parole officer received a projected release date of May 25, 2005.

The LC intervention is a three-step process. The first step is client orientation and enrollment. The second step involves exchanging information, including community appointment dates, times, and locations and answering additional questions the client may have. It is important to note that linkage coordinators schedule community appointments with both physicians and specialized social workers based on release date and community location immediately after release. Therefore, it is critical to have an accurate release date, in addition to release location. The release date and community location facilitate the linkage process for optimum use of community resources. The LC was done by a student intern in a master of social work program. She had participated in several other interviews and had shadowed the complete process a number of times. Her assignments included the LC intervention.

The client visits are all conducted within the prison. The interview is facilitated within the medical section of the institution. The environment is conducive to confidential interviews. A room with a door is provided, with a security guard located outside of the interview room for the safety of both the coordinator and the inmate. Only the medical staff within the prison and the LC staff have knowledge of the inmate's medical status, promoting client confidentiality. Clients who accept LC services are required to complete a release of information form. This signed document facilitates the services provided by the linkage coordinator. The services include providing copies of the inmate's medical records for the physician and social worker, scheduling community appointments, and speaking with the parole board and parole officers as needed.

Assessment/Screening and Problem Identification

The psychosocial assessment form was completed to assist the social worker when addressing mental health needs and in developing a case plan for appropriate services.

Intervention/Treatment

The first step is a 1.5-hour face-to-face interview between the community linkage coordinator and the inmate.

1. CL staff provides an overview of the program—the history of program, the capacity of services with benefits, the locations of programs, and how to access information for services.
2. The inmate has the choice to accept or reject the program services. If services are rejected, the inmate is provided with program pamphlets and brochures for future orientation after release. If services are accepted, the inmate completes a program intake packet to complete the enrollment process and orientation.
3. CL staff obtains copies of the prison medical file and forwards copies to a community social worker and appropriate health care providers.
4. CL staff assess the inmate for additional social services needed, such as medical treatment, housing, nutrition, transportation, and all areas that

could affect HIV/AIDS treatment and the continuum of care. This information is subsequently provided to the community social worker to initiate linking with additional community services.

The second step is a 1-hour interview in which (1) CL staff provides the client with appointment dates, times, locations, contact numbers, and the name of the HIV/AIDS social worker in the community; (2) CL staff provides the same information about the HIV/AIDS physician and related medical providers; (3) CL staff reminds the client that support calls will be made by the program after the inmate is released; this is part of the CL intervention compliance program.

The third step is a series of three telephone contacts: (1) the first call is made within 24–48 hours of release to remind the client of appointments and answer any questions; (2) the second call is made within 24–48 hours of appointment to answer questions and remind the client of the appointment and the follow-up appointment phone call; (3) the third call is made within 7 days to follow up on the appointment and provide the client with appointment dates, times, and locations of community-based services. These calls allow the linkage coordinator to facilitate the continuum of care that was initiated and implemented by the prison. The phone calls are placed after the inmate's release date in order to assist the client in establishing a sense of investment and maintaining a stable health status. The support phone calls can span more than 30 days after release, depending on the scheduled appointment dates. If the client's phone number is not working, the office assistant sends a general letter requesting that the client contact the linkage coordinator. The mailing also confirms the client's address. Assuming that the phone number is a working number, a second phone call is placed 2 days before each appointment to answer questions and to remind the client of the appointment.

The coordinator places a final call after both appointments have been attended, as a follow-up. The final call includes gathering information from the client to complete a telephone survey. According to CL program intervention, the client is considered to be linked to community services.

Evaluation

The final LC call determines whether the goal of providing community linkage was reached. The client is asked to answer questions about the results of the intervention and whether the client was satisfied with the results. The expected results of the intervention are that the client was linked to community-based services, including medical and social services, and that copies of the prison's medical care records were forwarded to the social worker and the physician to facilitate the continuum of care. In response to LC services, the client was asked to state that he agreed to and accepted the scheduled community-based services and that he had completed the AIDS Drug Assistance Program (ADAP) application for financial assistance for HIV/AIDS-related prescribed medications and was asked to give written permission, by signing a release of information form, to access additional services to facilitate the HIV/AIDS-related continuum of care. It would appear that the client generally endorsed the linkage and acceptance of services.

▪ ▪ ▪

Activities

The following are discussion issues for use in peer supervision or classroom discussion. Space is provided for notes.

1. Discuss the options the LC student intern could explore to assist with establishing an external support system.

2. Discuss the possible implications that could result from the LC student intern's not having a correct release date and what preventive steps the student could take to obtain the correct information. Discuss the possible obstacles that could occur in securing additional community services for the client.

3. Develop a comprehensive case plan that includes medical, housing, external support system, and employment. Prioritize tasks from the case plan and utilize a behavioral theory that supports your rationale for doing so.

Inventory of What You Know and What You Can Do

Prepare for your assessment of competencies by considering the following items.

1. Identify practice skills and examples of them that you do well.

2. Identify practice skills that you could have done differently or skills in which you need to improve your performance. Provide an example for each one.

3. Consider developing a scale to measure your level of performance for the preceding skill situations. You could scale yourself from 1 to 5 and describe what your performance at a certain level looks like. It is best to anchor your scale by defining what performing at levels 1 and 5 on your scale would look like. For example: "The internship has helped me to gain new insights into the court settings," with a score of 1 designated as "not at all" and 5 as "very much." You may set a 3 rating as about halfway between your defined levels 1 and 5.

4. What techniques have you developed to reframe criticism that help you to deal with the situation of concern and learn from it? How would this be helpful for your assessment meeting at midterm? At the final assessment meeting?

5. Keep a cool head; stop, calm down, and think! What strategies could you use to remember this?

6. Finally, do more of the same if it is working well, and try another way if it is not!

Evidence From Practice

Guidelines for thinking critically about the explanations of your strengths and areas of concern may be clustered into at least three categories: changes in attitude and beliefs; changes in skills; and changes in behavior. Three types of evidence can be used to assess changes in each of these areas.

1. *Narrative sources* of evidence can be identified from your journal, in which you identify themes and patterns repeated in practice and your reflections on these entries.

2. *Objective sources* of evidence might be ratings from assessments completed on clients or assignments or other projects undertaken at the internship and graded by those who viewed your work. A taped recording may also be evidence of performance skill changes.

3. *Pragmatic evidence* can be identified as the increased ease with which you are able to perform practice or performance skills due to changes in your skill and confidence levels.

Under each of the following categories, list at least one expected attitude, skill, or behavior, the type of evidence (pragmatic, etc.), a brief description of the evidence or counterevidence, and the conclusions you might draw from the evidence (i.e., your strengths or areas of concern).

Changes in Attitude or Beliefs

1. *Attitude or belief* (e.g., increased self-awareness, self-confidence, help seeking)

2. *Evidence type* (narrative, objective, and pragmatic or combinations)

3. *Counterevidence*: (e.g., feedback from supervisor after being observed with a client)

4. *Conclusions*: Describe your strengths and or concerns regarding how you have changed in this attitude.

Changes in Skills

1. *Skill* (e.g., increased skills, communication skills).

2. *Evidence type* (narrative, objective, and pragmatic or combinations)

3. *Counterevidence*: (e.g., feedback from supervisor)

4. *Conclusions:* Describe your strengths and concerns regarding how you have changed in this skill.

Changes in Behavior or Performance

1. *Behavior or performance* (e.g., increased knowledge and critical thinking skills, a sense of humor)

2. *Evidence type* (narrative, objective, and pragmatic or combinations)

3. *Counterevidence*: (e.g., feedback from supervisor)

4. *Conclusions:* Describe your strengths and concerns regarding how you have changed in this behavior.

5. How do you think the reliance on types of evidence is related to your preferred learning style?

Reviewing Your Evidence

The first set of questions will help you to collect and review journal writings as part of the preassessment process. The second set of questions addresses journal entries at postassessment.

Preassessment Review

1. What have I learned?

2. What are my successes?

3. What were my setbacks?

4. Where and when do the problem(s) occur? Is there a pattern?

5. What does it add up to?

6. What do I need to do more of?

7. What do I need to do differently?

8. How will I know when I achieve my goals?

Postassessment Review

1. Compare your assessment of your strengths and your concerns to the strengths and concerns raised by your supervisor. How are they similar and dissimilar?

2. Did you over- or underestimate your knowledge, abilities, or performance in an area? Describe the situation.

3. Is this assessment similar to other assessments you have received?

15 FROM INTERNSHIP TO EMPLOYMENT

Preparing Your Practice Portfolio

BARBARA THOMLISON *and* KEVIN CORCORAN

In this chapter we examine the ending your internship and—ideally—your procuring satisfactory, professional employment. We consider some of the best practices for transitions and endings in the professional relationship, including guidelines for terminating with clients, with supervisors, and with the staff and field site. We provide guidelines for reviewing your accomplishments in the internship and how to develop a professional portfolio that will greatly help you as you seek employment.

The goal of this book has been to guide you through the internship and to develop proficiency in applying an evidence-based focus to practice. Learning about evidence-based practice resources prepares you for a smooth transition from the internship to employment, equipped with real skills for real work settings. Evidence-based practice skills substantiate the competencies you acquired during the internship. These competencies include not only the knowledge and skills of a practitioner in social work or criminal justice but also personal and interpersonal qualities that will prepare you to practice in various settings. The internship has been supplying you with a conceptual framework for practice, with a research-based approach to finding the most effective interventions for client problems and challenges, and with a scholarly approach to professional behavior, values, and ethics. Conceptual and assessment tools have been provided to motivate you to continue applying this approach as you end the internship and transition to employment. You are now prepared to commit to becoming a competent professional, armed with the necessary tools.

Opportunities and challenges were no doubt present, and we hope that, based on your discoveries from these experiences, you are more encouraged to seek consultation and supervision and to engage in evidence-based practice as a normative part of professional practice. Students always report the internship as one of their most critical learning experiences, likely never to be forgotten, unlike other courses. The internship experiences are given a special place in students' memories. We trust that your experiences have been special, too.

The purpose of this chapter is to highlight and review the key issues learned from your internship and to consider how you may best present yourself for a professional career and employment. It is now time to consider what is necessary to make the transition to your next challenge: ending the internship and seeking employment. Before you leave your internship, some matters require attention.

BEST PRACTICES IN TRANSITIONS AND ENDINGS

The transition from intern to professional is marked by the termination of the internship and the acceptance of the responsibilities associated with a professional career. Nevertheless, in moving from intern to professional, students are still expected to finish their assignments, complete daily log sheets, terminate appropriately with clients and colleagues, and prepare to "unhook" from your main lifeline: your supervisor. In addition to focusing on these tasks, you also need to consider your personal goals and achievements. Preparing to leave your clients, instructors, and internship typically elicits a range of emotions and even conflicts for students. You can prepare for termination. Your focus will shift to making transitions to new experiences and support systems.

A search for evidence-based termination practices has highlighted gaps in research that identifies effective interventions. Therefore, the information provided here relevant to termination is based on the best available evidence and expert consensus guidelines.

Guidelines for Terminating With Clients

As a student, you begin terminating with clients the moment you start the internship. The internship is a brief, time-limited experience, with known start and completion dates. Goal setting and planning for termination are normally part of the steps taken with each client contact. Progress on cases is, of course, not always a straightforward matter; changes may not occur as planned, and cases may need to be transferred to other practitioners or referred to other agencies for ongoing service. In essence, the actual practices of criminal justice and social work are never as easy as they seem in textbooks and classroom discussions.

For clients, each contact or task you engage in with them has a beginning and an ending—in a sense, a termination. When clinical goals have been reached, you end your contact with the client. Skills for ending with clients include reviewing the process, analyzing and evaluating changes and accomplishments, and summarizing and evaluating (Cournoyer, 2000, pp. 371–392). The possible options for clients are (1) referral to another service, (2) transfer to another practitioner, (3) closing of the case, or (4) discontinuation by the client, perhaps without notice, as often happens.

In order to thwart discontinuation, it is helpful to review what has been accomplished and, if necessary, how the client is going to continue to receive help. It may include introducing the client to a new practitioner or linking the client to another setting. It is helpful to remind clients several weeks prior to your leaving that this will happen. You and your clients prepare for ending, and in many cases this can be quite emotional for both of you. Clients share many personal and intimate concerns, and they come to view you as a caring, helpful, and trustworthy person who listened to them. Therefore, transitions may be difficult and can represent a host of feelings, thoughts, and experiences to you and the client. To increase the likelihood of engagement with the new person, try to introduce the client firsthand to the practitioner who will be assuming your responsibilities. Personal introductions smooth the transition for clients and are more likely to ensure continuity. Successful transitions require well-developed ending skills, which often are taken for granted but are seldom taught explicitly. Transitions are a process, not an event; a transition cannot be handled in one meeting because it typically affects many areas of the client's life simultaneously.

Not everyone handles a transition in the same manner, and different individuals will experience transitions in very different ways. There is no one way that is best for all clients, as the context will be different for each and require different transition skills (Hiebert & Thomlison, 1996).

Guidelines for Terminating With Your Supervisor

The process of ending contact with your supervisor will be parallel to the way you end with your clients. Similarly, you need to review your learning goals, placement contract, and progress, to analyze and evaluate your accomplishments, and to summarize practice goals for ongoing personal and professional development (Cournoyer, 2000, pp. 371–392). Learning and development do not end when you leave the internship, and reviewing where you are prepares you to continue long after leaving the internship.

Students always receive final evaluation reports from their supervisors, as required by their academic programs. The final evaluation report signals the formal termination of the internship. No matter what your relationship with and feelings toward your supervisor were, a review is completed. You may want to use the following questions to focus the review:

1. What was helpful, great, or wonderful?
2. What skills and knowledge were used effectively?
3. What skills and knowledge development still need to be refined?
4. What else could have been done to extend your learning?
5. What the lessons were learned from the internship learning assignments?

If possible, it also is helpful to provide summative feedback to your supervisor about the internship site, the assignments, and the learning activities. This is a form of constructive closure to the working relationship that you had with your supervisor. Supervisors also want to review the experience and understand how they helped and what else may have increased your learning. If any unfinished matters or issues were never discussed, try to talk about them now and resolve them. The purpose is not necessarily to change opinions or positions. It may simply be a matter of agreeing to disagree and leaving some issues at that, as a form of resolution. If you have constructive comments to offer about the internship site, *give recommendations* for or examples of how the situation might be changed or improved. Balance concerns with positive exemplars. It is important to leave the internship site and supervisor in a positive light. A supervisor may be called on to write you a potential recommendation. In any case, she or he is a "colleague" in the same profession, and you never know when your paths may ntertwine in the future. The unwritten protocol is to provide *appreciation* to your supervisor as part of the ritual associated with leaving. This expression can take the form of a card, personal comments, lunch, or other symbol of thanks.

Guidelines for Terminating With the Internship Staff and Site

In addition to reviewing your learning process, you need to show gratitude to staff members and other professionals in the internship setting who have provided help and support in your learning. Expressing appreciation for the time and opportunities provided by these colleagues is necessary. You may find yourself working with these professionals on committees or in a collaborative situation, or you may work with their clients in some context in the future. In fact, you probably will discover this to be the case. These contacts form the basis of future community-based networks and support systems for you. Reviewing your reactions and feelings about the setting is an important activity in your deliberations about future opportunities for work and learning. Students often express thanks to others in the setting through a small token of appreciation—a cake, card, book, or chocolate.

TRANSITION AND CONTINUITY

As you begin the transition to leaving the internship, it is necessary to also review what you know and consider as your accomplishments. The internship has set the stage for you to continue your professional development, experience new supervisors, and even find intentional mentors for ongoing learning and challenges. The lesson to learn here is that you are always leaving situations and beginning new ones. You are readjusting both to the situation you are leaving and to the situation you are about to start. Skills learned in the internship are transferable to other settings. Linking skills and processes from past learning to new learning is a way of investing in and building on your knowledge structure. This includes using the evidence-based resources discussed in this book. These resources can be applied to your new employment setting.

Lessons Learned and Lessons Applied

What is a lesson learned? A lesson learned is knowledge or understanding gained from the internship experience. It may be positive, negative, or both, but it must be significant, valid, and applicable to other situations and experiences. Lessons learned from the internship need to be turned into lessons applied to other situations and settings if they are to be helpful. The purpose of reviewing your accomplishments for lessons learned is to promote the recurrence of successful outcomes and preclude the recurrence of unsuccessful outcomes. Review your journal, case notes, logs, contracts, and midterm and final evaluations and determine the lessons you learned from your experiences. Some guidelines to developing your list of lessons learned follow:

1. What were the discoveries and joys of learning in practicum? (e.g., it's okay to be unsure of yourself, just don't let your anxiety control you.)
2. What were your fears and dreams? (Actions create reality, so test out your ideas.)
3. Who listened to you? (Sometimes you need to talk things out, sometimes you need to think, but above all it is important to listen first.)
4. What actions did you take? (It takes actions to make things change.)
5. What did you learn that you love to do? (Through the various cases and assignments, through the opportunities and challenges, the cases won or lost, you remain confident that you love to do this work.)
6. Practice makes perfect. (Persistence wins out, so when cases are difficult, don't give up.)

7. Take a lesson from Charlie Brown: "Dance with your dog. Smile . . . it makes people wonder what you're up to." (Allen, 2001)

Learning is never finished, so resist the temptation to feel as if you must tie up all the loose ends. Instead, create an inventory for future work. Make a note in your journal of skills and behaviors you still need to work on and experiences that need repeating for consolidation. Acknowledging your strengths and evolving concerns is more helpful. It is not unusual to feel as if you are not ready to move on. Students often feel that they need more time in an internship. In fact, your supervisor will likely think you could benefit from more time in the internship. This is normal, and it is not to take away from what you know. Practice does make you more nearly perfect, but there will be plenty of time for that in the next phase of your learning.

The most important discovery you have learned may be that you can be both a vulnerable learner and a competent student at the same time. You have learned about practice, evidence-based resources, your own learning and teaching styles those of your supervisor, and the context of learning. These skills will prove influential in endless ways as you handle the many transitions and challenges ahead.

ENCORE! GUIDELINES FOR MAINTAINING YOUR ACCOMPLISHMENTS

1. *Maintaining skills.* When you first learn a skill, it is not part of everyday usage or part of your practice repertoire of competencies until it is repeated. Skills need to be practiced and generalized to many other contexts. Therefore, review your inventory of skills from your practice assignments and your journal and make an inventory of these to put in the portfolio discussed later. You can build on these for your next practicum or place of work. The more you practice your competencies and skills, the more you will stand out among your peers, and the more competent you will become.

2. *State of mind.* Stress is a normal part of everyday life, but in the helping professions, practitioners are exposed to stress in many different and continuous ways. Chronic exposure to stress can cause burnout, and it can affect your state of mind. It can change you from a caring individual to an apathetic person if it is not addressed. Regardless of whether the stressors come from your personal or professional life, excessive stress or ongoing

stress is the result of ineffective coping strategies. Learning to reduce stress is the key to preventing burnout. Self-care is probably the single most important strategy you can focus on to prevent burnout. Your sense of well-being starts with finding time for yourself, getting a good night's sleep, and finding ways to relax. "Running on empty" is a sure sign of a life on the verge of a meltdown. Read your body's signals and look for the hassles that contribute to the stress and ineffective coping. Self-care means finding a balance, or feeling centered spiritually. Be clear about your values. Rest, proper nutrition, exercise, and a little fun are in order. Assess what you do for fun or "down time." If you find that you can't make changes, talk to your supervisor, locate other sources of support, or even seek professional guidance.

3. *Smart practice.* You may feel that you did not receive all of the experiences you hoped for, or you may have had to undergo experiences that you had no choice but to face. All of your experiences contribute to learning, even when they have not been ideal. Although you really wanted to spend extra time working in the courts, for instance, the homeland security experience turned out great and provided valuable learning in the area of prevention services.

4. *Critical reflection.* Reviewing your accomplishments is a form of critical reflection and decision making. It is a continuous assessment of your actions and decisions and leads to self-understanding.

THE PRACTICE PORTFOLIO: EVIDENCE-BASED PRACTICE ACCOMPLISHMENTS

Portfolios are used to illustrate achievements, learning, competence, talent, and potential (Cournoyer, 2000). A portfolio is a structured collection of labeled evidence and critical reflection on that evidence. It comprises numerous items rather than a single piece of work. It is produced and presented to show evidence of specific learning or to demonstrate that learning outcomes have been achieved. For your purpose, the portfolio will cover practice skills and emphasize your abilities as a professional social worker or criminal justice student. Portfolios contain a collection of exemplars of your work, your self-assessment and orientation to practice, evaluations, and letters of commendation. Essentially it is a "life book" of your professional learning history that specifies your record of accomplishment.

Portfolio use is relatively recent in social work and criminal justice, having been more commonly used by designers, artists, actors, and others to display their successes. Increasingly, employers want to see what applicants can do, as well as what they know, and to this end the portfolio can support and demonstrate a wide range of personal, professional, and academic capabilities. It can evidence work accomplished and learning achieved (Cournoyer & Stanley, 2002). However, some still question the validity and reliability of portfolios as a method of judging achievement of learning goals (Learning and Teaching Support Network [LTSN], 2001).

Documenting your practice in the form of a practice portfolio has extensive benefits. All students and professionals need to have a record of learning and practice accomplishments. Portfolios require gathering and presenting both evidence and elements of critical reflection or commentary. Examples of your work may be integrated into the portfolio or presented as a separate element in its own right. Students must gather the evidence together into a coherent story of learning, of testing new ideas and discarding others. Portfolios are compatible with Kolb's learning inventory that suggests that learning takes place only when learners reflect on the experience.

Structuring an Evidence-Based Practice Portfolio

Evidence-based practice portfolios can be structured in many ways: according to learning outcomes, knowledge outcomes, professional practice, service accomplishments, or other features such as professional experiences. Evidence usually combines all or several of these elements, depending on your program. Regardless, the structure should be clear and explicit; the overall aim is to create a readable and accessible portfolio. In addition, the evidence should be labeled and put into sections in the portfolio. Label the items, and create a table of contents. Items should be labeled with dates, name of the person who produced the work, title, and identification of the work's form (e.g., paper, essay, assessment of client, segment of a log recording, etc.). If the work is collaborative, all authors are listed. Websites, CD-ROMs, and other identified pieces of work are labeled. Critical reflection notes should accompany the pieces of evidence. Your portfolio will be unique. You can set up this record in many ways. The record of practice profile should, at the very least, include the following:

1. Title page with name and date
2. Table of contents identifying documents included
3. Your resume

4. Letter of submission, if applicable
5. Statement of introduction and presentation of yourself; a personal statement
6. Learning products, with each section starting with a self-reflective review
   a. Case exemplars
   b. Self-assessment
   c. Checklist of evidence-based skills
   d. Special knowledge acquired
   e. Sample assignments completed that illustrate best practices
   f. Review of your journal, log sheets, or other entries that show how you constructed knowledge among cases or across clients
   g. Review of your course outlines for knowledge acquisition
   h. Other illustrations (teaching, coaching, cooperative learning, mastery of procedures, etc.)
   i. Evaluations or assessments of learning
   j. Course syllabus if necessary to illustrate learning outcomes
   k. Course papers, assessments, or other critical reflections
   l. Career directions

The record of your practice is a summative evaluation of your learning and can be used from year to year during your employment. It should, therefore, be maintained well into your career. Keeping an updated portfolio is important, and therefore you will want to update this regularly. You can add other items to personalize your portfolio and make it unique while emphasizing your competencies.

SUMMARY

In order to transition from internship to employment, make note of the following key points:

- Recognize the limits of your ability.
- Use setbacks as opportunities for learning.
- Recognize that supervision is a necessity.
- Prevent job stress.
- Enhance and maintain the values, knowledge, and skills of a professional.
- Remember that the quality of *becoming* rather than *being* captures the meaning of *professional* or *expert*.
- Develop a culture of thoughtfulness in your practice behaviors.

Learning as a journey is a process of change. Helen Harris Perlman (1989) a well-known social work educator, eloquently speaks of our journey:

> If looking back represents a reluctance to leave the known for the unknown, if it expresses a fear of present prospects, if it is a temptation to escape the here-and-now reality and thus becomes a deterrent to looking ahead with courage, it is to be deplored. If, however, it is a way of gaining perspective, a means by which we may recognize and thus avoid earlier errors of judgment and action, or if, in reverse, it is a means by which to identify and preserve what is still to be developed further, if, in short, we look to the past as a way of seeing more clearly and penetratingly its meanings, and uses for our immediate present and near future, then it may serve us well. So my malaise is temporarily put to rest, and I look back in order to see ahead. (Perlman, 1989, pp.1–2)

MULTISYSTEMIC THERAPY IN ACTION

Jennifer Powers

Case Description

Justice Time, a probation officer, referred 16-year-old Scott to Cathy Whinebach for services. Mr. Time explained that Scott had faced numerous charges since the age of 14 that ranged from trespassing to a more recent charge of grand larceny. In addition to these charges, Scott's mother, Lila Goynes, and stepfather, Alex Goynes, reported that Scott did not follow his curfew, did not respect their authority, and was generally defiant. To further complicate matters, during a visit with his probation officer Scott admitted to using marijuana.

Scott resided with his mother, stepfather, and younger brother in Charleston, South Carolina. His mother remarried 5 years previously, following a contentious divorce from Scott's father. Prior to the divorce, Scott witnessed his father sexually and physically abusing his mother for 10 years. His father now lives in Indiana with his new family and has infrequent visits with his son. Given the severity of Scott's charges, his illegal drug use, and his family history, he was ordered to participate in the juvenile drug court program and to receive treatment for his drug use and delinquent behaviors. The initial assessment diagnostic criteria qualified Scott and his family for multisystemic therapy (MST).

The intervention chosen for Scott and his family follows the nine principles of MST, a well-specified and research-focused approach to treating families and youths with severe emotional and behavioral problems. Treatment is intensive and requires on-call coverage 24 hours a day, 7 days a week, by a master's-level therapist. An MST therapist strives to assess systems—caregiver, school, family, peer—factors and determine a *fit*, or ways in which these systems contribute to the problem.

Assessment/Screening and Problem Identification

Cathy began her assessment by gathering information from key informants, such as schoolteachers, family members, and Mr. Time. After the necessary releases were signed by Scott's mother, informants were asked a series of open-ended questions that were helpful in determining the fit for Scott's delinquent behaviors.

Through more formalized instruments, Scott and his caretakers provided detailed information about the extent and history of Scott's drug use and any family history of psychiatric/health problems. A genogram was also completed that detailed significant persons and events in Scott's life. The strengths and needs of the systems that affected Scott's behavior were also assessed in reference to family dynamics, school involvement, neighborhood resources, and mental and emotional status of the individual and the family. With a caseload of only five families, Cathy was able to dedicate the time needed to complete a detailed assessment that spanned a 3-day period and would continue as needed.

A written assessment of the problem behaviors, treatment expectations, and MST goals was submitted for review to the drug court coordinator. Using her clinical judgment, along with information gathered during the assessment, Cathy determined that the proximal fit factors for Scott's delinquent behaviors were negative peer involvement, ineffective parenting, and lack of involvement in extracurricular activities.

Intervention Selection

Using an ecological model, the therapist applied multisystemic therapy (MST). MST draws from a number of evidence-based approaches. In Scott's case, those interventions targeted each specific system that was contributing to his behaviors. After prioritizing the drivers for Scott's delinquent behaviors, Cathy decided to target the family system, as well as using individual interventions for Scott's drug use.

By following the MST model of applying evidence-based strategies, Cathy sought interventions that were problem focused and change oriented. To achieve this, she found it necessary to use a combination of structural family therapy, solution-focused problem solving, and communication training. Interventions within those frameworks complemented the nine principles of MST (see Table 15.1).

Table 15.1. MST Treatment Principles

Principle 1: The primary purpose of assessment is to understand the fit between the identified problems and their broader systemic context.

Principle 2: Therapeutic contacts emphasize the positive and use systemic strengths as levers for change.

Principle 3: Interventions are designed to promote responsible behavior and to decrease irresponsible behavior among family members.

Principle 4: Interventions are present focused and action oriented, targeting specific and well-defined problems.

Principle 5: Interventions target sequences of behavior within and between multiple systems that maintain the identified problems.

Principle 6: Interventions are developmentally appropriate and fit the developmental needs of the youth.

Principle 7: Interventions are designed to require daily or weekly effort by family members.

Principle 8: Intervention effectiveness is evaluated continuously from multiple perspectives with providers assuming accountability for overcoming barriers to successful outcomes.

Principle 9: Interventions are designed to promote treatment generalization and long-term maintenance of therapeutic change by empowering caregivers to address family members' needs across multiple systemic contexts.

Source: Henggeler & Borduin (1990); Henggeler, Mihalic, Rone, Thomas, & Timmons-Mitchell (1998).

Intervention/Treatment

The first system that Cathy targeted was the family. As noted in the assessment, Ms. Goynes was unable to establish and enforce rules for her son. After gathering input from Scott and his caretakers, they developed a behavioral plan linking immediate consequences and rewards to behaviors. During the process, Scott's input was encouraged and praised by the MST therapist. In a second and third visit that week, Cathy applied communication training by role-playing with Scott's mother effective ways of enforcing the plan. The role-playing continued until Cathy was confident that Scott's mother and stepfather followed through with the contract.

Cathy's ongoing assessment of the family suggested that Ms. Goynes' cognitive distortions about Scott's behavior posed a significant barrier to improving parenting. To successfully engage Ms. Goynes in improving her parenting skills, Cathy used cognitive-behavioral therapy (CBT). Ms. Goynes had said, "Scott is old enough to know how to do right. He's just trying to get me upset."

By using CBT, Cathy's goal was to help Ms. Goynes develop a more realistic view of her son's motivations and circumstances.

After consultation with her supervisor and a review of the literature, Cathy knew that Scott's negative peer group had to be addressed. In addition to disallowing contact with negative peers on the behavioral contract, Cathy and Scott's mom set out to locate activities for Scott in which he would be able to interact with a prosocial peer group. After 2 weeks of searching, Scott chose to join a martial arts club, where he would spend 2 to 3 days after school each week. The rest of his days were filled with homework, household chores, and time with his grandmother.

Concomitant with the MST interventions, the therapist relied on empirically supported interventions provided by the Charleston Juvenile Drug Court. This program furthered the efforts of the MST team by using court-supported graduated sanctions and rewards. For example, as Scott's family progressed through the drug court program, his curfew was extended, and he received gift certificates as rewards. If any of the rules were not followed (positive drug screen, failure to abide by curfew, inability to follow house rules), the drug court judges could order him to community service or to the Charleston County Juvenile Detention Center for a specified amount of time.

As part of the home-based services, the therapist targeted Scott's drug use, using individually oriented strategies. As part of an NIDA-funded research grant, Cathy's agency integrated current empirically supported approaches with behavioral interventions called the community reinforcement approach (CRA). This approach included weekly random drug screens, vouchers for drug refusal, weekly homework assignments geared toward identifying triggers for using, and a self-management plan.

Evaluation

The MST/CRA approach to treatment targeted key outcomes. The specific measurements tracked the reduction of substance abuse, of criminal activity, of mental health symptoms, and of juvenile justice placements. Tools used to gather data included a self-report substance abuse measure; biological assays (urine analysis); a self-report delinquency scale used to tract antisocial activities; charges, arrests, adjudication, and placement records; and a child behavior checklist consisting of caregiver ratings of child behavior functioning (Achenbach, 1991).

Three months after the family successfully graduated from the drug court program, Ms. Goynes reported that Scott continued to meet his goals and found a job working with children at the martial arts school. He is also considering applying for a scholarship for college. From Scott's perspective, the key to his success was finding something that made him feel good about himself. In the spring, he plans to compete with other martial arts teams across the country.

Discussion

At first glance, this case may appear simplistic. It is important to note, however, that the intervention with Scott's family is extremely intensive and requires a team effort. A typical week spent with Scott and his family included meetings at drug court, frequent home visits lasting anywhere from 1 to 3 hours at a time, several phone calls, regular supervision, and court staffings. The average time spent on the Goynes family totaled 10 hours per week.

In supervision, Cathy said that she had learned that a major key to success is flexibility and creativity. Initially, Scott's mom showed reluctance to cooperate with the stated goals, and Scott's behavior remained unchanged. As this became more apparent to Cathy, she knew she had to switch gears and focus on engagement factors. This was accomplished by demonstrating to Ms. Goynes that Cathy was sincere in her efforts by structuring her schedule to accommodate Ms. Goynes's, by continuously praising Ms. Goynes for her efforts, and by helping her with transportation as needed. Cathy also realized that as her confidence improved, so did the family's engagement and that the more engaged Scott's parents were, the more likely they were to enforce rules for their son.

▪ ▪ ▪

Activities

1. Should the therapist have contacted Scott's father and included him (via telephone) in the treatment process?

2. Why did Cathy decide not to focus on past events?

3. What may be some reasons that Ms. Goynes was reluctant to engage in the treatment plan?

4. Why did the therapist choose to include Scott's input in the behavioral plan?

5. Now that Scott has graduated from the drug court program and the intense MST intervention is completed, are there services that Scott and his family may still need? What services are needed and why?

6. This exercise will give you the opportunity to create a practice portfolio that incorporates an inventory of skills, accomplishments, and exemplars from your internship experience. Use the portfolio to track your career accomplishments and to illustrate products developed. The portfolio can be used to illustrate your work and evaluations, and you can include self-assessments that represent your perspective. This information could be kept in your practice portfolio for future reference and updating.

   Put the materials in a three-ring binder with a table of contents and place materials under relevant sections (e.g., case exemplars, service commitments, papers written, evaluations from clients and supervisors, a personal statement or philosophy about approaching work, evidence-based skills, etc.).

   Three areas should be covered: practice, service, and professional experiences. You can also add your own unique sections. Follow the preceding guidelines, but at the very least use the following headings:

   • Title page with name and dates

   • Table of contents identifying documents included

   • Your resume

   • Letter of submission, if applicable

   • Statement of introduction and presentation of yourself; a personal statement

   • Learning products, with each section starting with a self-reflective review

     a. Case exemplars

     b. Self-assessment

    c. Checklist of evidence-based skills

    d. Special knowledge acquired

    e. Sample assignments completed that illustrate best practices

    f. Review of your journal, log sheets, or other entries that show how you constructed knowledge among cases or across clients

    g. Review of your course outlines for knowledge acquisition

    h. Other illustrations (teaching, coaching, cooperative learning, mastery of procedures, etc.)

    i. Evaluations or assessments of learning.

    j. Course syllabus, if necessary, to illustrate learning outcomes.

    k. Course papers, assessments, or other critical reflections.

    l. Career directions.

• Practice and skills

    a. Describe your preference for working with a particular client or population based on significant past or present experience.

    b. Describe the experiences that have informed your preferences.

    c. What theoretical orientation or intervention approach is most interesting to you?

    d. Describe a situation in which you demonstrated the level of proficiency that could be labeled "expert." You can limit the skill or skills, that you needed to draw on, depending on your practice experience. Describe the criteria you used to assess your level of competence as expert.

• Service involvement

    a. Volunteer and board experiences

• Professional experience

    a. Previous professional experiences or volunteer experiences you have had

    b. Course work and workshop training

    c. Educational programs and special classes taken, as certain courses may be specifically relevant to future positions

• Career plans

    a. What future directions do you aspire to?

    b. What level of involvement and responsibility would you prefer in employment?

16 RESOURCES FOR APPLYING BEST PROFESSIONAL PRACTICES

CATHERINE N. DULMUS *and* KAREN M. SOWERS

By the time you read this portion of the book, you are likely getting ready to end your internship. We hope you learned a lot, acquired skills for competent professional practice, and found your decision to enter the human services rewarding. Specifically, we hope you learned the importance of selecting and implementing evidence-based interventions that best answer the practice questions at hand. Above all, it was our goal to demonstrate that practice settings require adherence to evidence-based protocols with a dose of flexibility to adapt these practices to rapidly changing service environments while improving the quality of service to clients. We also hope this book has helped make your internship successful.

In all likelihood, the primary reason that your successful learning experience in the field will be successful is your direct contact with clients and your supervisor and reflecting on what you did to bring about change for the client system. Your case assignments probably stood out as key to your learning, and similarly the cases in this book illustrate the challenges of consolidating knowledge, practice, and working in complex environments and settings. For this reason we end with a summary of evidence-based resources and with a case by Franklin and Linseisen. The selected evidence-based resources provide the foundation and stimulation for analyzing the case that follows or cases that you are currently concerned about. This case is a little longer than the others, but it reflects the many aspects of what we have tried to accomplish in book. We think you will find Cynthia Franklin and Tammy Linseisen's case a good illustration of issues of ethics, supervision, using effective interventions, and seeing a client through the intervention process. In other words, this case represents all the issues associated with evidence-based practices.

RESOURCES FOR BEST PRACTICES WITH INDIVIDUALS

Web Sites

- Campaign for Mental Health Reform. (1999). *Evidence-based services and emerging best practice for treating mental disorders in adults and children.* Retrieved March 13, 2005, from http://www.mhreform.org/policy/ebs.htm.
- Information for Practice: http://www.nyu.edu/socialwork/ip
- American Medical Association: http://www.ama-assn.org/
- National Criminal Justice Reference Service http://www.ncjrs.org/ or http://www.ojjdp.ncjrs.org/
- Child Welfare League of America: http://www.cwla.org
- American Society on Aging: http://www.asaging.org/
- National Institute on Drug Abuse: http://www.nida.nih.gov/PODAT/PODAT10.html#Relapse
- National Institute of Mental Health: http://www.nimh.nih.gov

Books

Bloomquist, M. L., & Schnell, S. V. (2002). *Helping children with aggression and conduct problems: Best practices for intervention.* New York: Guilford Press.

Drake, R. E., Merrens, M. R., & Lynde, D. W. (Eds.). (2005). *Evidence-based mental health practice: A textbook.* New York: W.W. Norton & Company.

Gambrill, E. (2006). *Social work practice: A critical thinker's guide* (2nd ed.). New York, NY: Oxford University Press.

Gibbs, L. E., (2003). *Evidence-based practice for the helping professions: A practical guide with integrated multimedia.* Pacific Grove, CA: Brooks/Cole-Thomson Learning.

Kazdin, J. R., & Weisz, J. R. (Eds.). (2003). *Evidence-based psychotherapies for children and adolescents.* New York: Guilford Press.

Klosko, J. S., & Sanderson, W. C. (1999). *Cognitive-behavioral treatment of depression.* Northvale, NJ: Aronson.

McGinn, L. K., & Sanderson, W. C. (1999). *Treatment of obsessive-compulsive disorder.* Northvale, NJ: Aronson.

MacKenzie, D. L. (2006). *What works in corrections: Reducing recidivism* Cambridge University Press.

Roberts, A.R., & Greene, G. (Eds.). (2002). *Social workers' desk reference.* New York: Oxford University Press.

Roberts, A.R., & Yeager, K.R. (Eds.). (2004). *Evidence-based practice manual: Research and outcome measures in health and human services.* New York: Oxford University Press.

Roberts, A.R., & Yeager, K.R. (Eds.). (2006). *Foundations of evidence-based social work practice.* New York: Oxford University Press.

Rowland, N., & Goss, S. (Eds.). (2000). *Evidence-based counseling and psychological therapies: Research and applications.* Philadelphia: Routledge.

Rygh, J. L., & Sanderson, W. C. (2004). *Treating generalized anxiety disorder: Evidence-based strategies, tools, and techniques.* New York: Guilford Press.

Journal Articles

Beyer, M. (2003). *Best practices in juvenile accountability: An overview.* Washington, DC: U.S. Department of Justice, Office of Justice Programs, Office of Juvenile Justice and Delinquency Prevention.

Dulmus, C. N., & Smyth, N. (2000). Early-onset schizophrenia: A literature review of empirically based interventions. *Child and Adolescent Social Work Journal, 17* (1), 67–92.

Dulmus, C. N., & Wodarski, J.S. (2002). Six critical questions for brief therapeutic interventions. *Brief Treatment and Crisis Intervention, 2* (4), 279–286.

Hoagwood, K., Burns, B., & Kiser, L. (2001). Evidence-based practice in child and adolescent mental health services. *Psychiatric Services, 52*(9), 1179–1189.

Lynam, D. R., Milich, R., Zimmerman, R., Novak, S. P., Logan, T. K., Martin, C., Leukefeld, C. & Clayton, R. (1999). Project DARE: No effects at 10-year follow-up. *Journal of Consulting and Clinical Psychology, 67,* 590–593.

Petrosino, A., Turpin-Petrosino, B., Buehler, J. (2003). "Scare Straight" and other juvenile awareness programs for preventing juvenile delinquency. Campbell Collaboration Review. The Campbell Library. http://www.campbellcollaboration .org/doc-pdf/ssrupdt.pdf

Wilson, S. J., Lipsey, M. W., & Soydan, H. (2003). Are mainstream programs for juvenile delinquency less effective with minority youth than majority youth? A meta-analysis or outcomes research. *Research on Social Work Practice, 13*(1), 3–26.

RESOURCES FOR BEST PRACTICES WITH FAMILIES

Web Sites

- Thornton, T. N., Craft, C. A., Dahlberg, L. L., Lynch, B. S., & Baer, K. (2000). *Best practices of youth violence prevention: A sourcebook for community action.* Atlanta, GA: Centers for Disease Control and Prevention, National Center for Injury Prevention and Control. Retrieved December 6, 2006, from http:// www.cdc.gov/search.do?action=search&queryText=best+practices&x= 10&y=8

With the homicide rate for youth under the age of 19 averaging nine deaths a day over the last decade, the CDC's Injury Center announces the release of the 216-page publication, entitled *Best Practices of Youth Violence Prevention: A Sourcebook for Community Action (Best Practices). Best Practices* is the first of its kind to look at the effectiveness of specific violence prevention practices in four key areas: parents and families; home visiting; social and conflict resolution skills; and mentoring. These programs are drawn from real-world experiences of professionals and advocates who have successfully worked to prevent violence among children and adolescents. As a CDC publication, the sourcebook also documents the science behind each best practice and offers a comprehensive directory of resources for more information about programs that have used these practices (Thornton et al., 2000).

Books

Corcoran, J. (2000). *Evidence-based social work practice with families: A lifespan approach.* New York: Springer.

Corcoran, J. (2003). *Clinical applications of evidence-based family interventions.* New York: Oxford University Press.

Dulmus, C. N., & Rapp-Paglicci, L. A. (Eds.). (2005). *Handbook of preventive interventions for adults.* New York: Wiley.

Fergusson, D. M., & Mullen, P. E. (1999). *Childhood sexual abuse: An evidence based perspective.* Thousand Oaks, CA: Sage.

Kendall-Tackett, K. A. (Ed.). (2004). *Health consequences of abuse in the family: A clinical guide for evidence-based practice.* Washington, DC: American Psychological Association.

Rapp-Paglicci, L. A., Dulmus, C. N., & Wodarski, J. S. (Eds.). (2004). *Handbook of preventive interventions for children and adolescents.* New York: Wiley.

Thomlison, B. (2007). *Family assessment handbook: An introductory guide to family assessment and intervention.* 2nd edition. Belmont, CA: Brooks-Cole.

Wodarski, J. S., Wodarski, L. A., & Dulmus, C. N. (2003). *Adolescent depression and suicide: A comprehensive empirical intervention for prevention and treatment.* Springfield, IL: Thomas.

Journal Articles

Groza, V., Maschmeier, C., Jamison, C., & Piccola, T. (2003). Siblings and out-of-home placement: Best practices. *Families in Society, 84* (4), 480–491.

McKay, M., & Bannon, W. (2004). Engaging families in child mental health services. *Child and Adolescent Psychiatric Clinics of North America, 13*(4), 905–921.

RESOURCES FOR BEST PRACTICES WITH GROUPS

Web sites:

Promising Practices Network:
http://www.promisingpractices.net/

The Promising Practices Network (PPN) website highlights programs and practices that credible research indicates are effective in improving outcomes for

children, youth, and families. The information pertains to children from the pre-
natal period to age 18, as well as the families and communities in which they live.

National Institute of Mental Health (NIMH):
http://www.nimh.nih.gov/

Search site by keywords "evidence based" or "best practices." The National Institute of Mental Health (NIMH) is one of 27 components of the National Institutes
of Health (NIH), the federal government's principal biomedical and behavioral
research agency.

Books

Child Welfare League of America. (2004). *Best practices in behavior support and intervention assessment*. Washington, DC: Author.

Lyman, L., & Villani, C. (2004). *Best leadership practices for high-poverty schools*. Lanham,
MD: Scarecrow Education.

Macgowan, M. J. (in press). *A guide to evidence-based group work*. New York: Oxford
University Press.

McLean, P. D., & Woody, S. R. (2001). *Evidence-based principles for substance abuse
prevention*. New York: Oxford University Press.

Potocky-Tripodi, M. (2002). *Best practices for social work with refugees and immigrants*.
New York Columbia University Press.

Vance, H. B. (Ed.). (1998). *Psychological assessment of children: Best practices for school
and clinical settings*. New York: Wiley.

Journal Articles

Molina, I., Bowie, S.L., Dulmus, C.N., & Sowers, K.M. (2004). School-based violence
prevention programs: A review of selected programs with empirical evidence. *Journal of Evidence-Based Social Work: Advances in Practice, Programming, Research, and
Policy, 1* (2/3), 175–190.

Molina, I. A., Dulmus, C. N., & Sowers, K. M. (2005). Secondary prevention for
youth violence: A review of selected school-based programs. *Brief Treatment and
Crisis Intervention, 5*(1), 95–127.

Pollio, D. E. (2002). The evidence-based group worker. *Social Work With Groups,
25*(2), 57–70.

Other

Coalition for Evidence-Based Policy. (2003). *Identifying and implementing educational
practices supported by rigorous evidence: A user-friendly guide*. Retrieved March 18,
2006 from: http://www.ed.gov/rschstat/research/pubs/rigorousevid/rigorousevid
.pdf

Contents include:

I. The randomized controlled trial: What it is, and why it is a critical factor in establishing "strong" evidence of an intervention's effectiveness.

II. How to evaluate whether an intervention is backed by "strong" evidence of effectiveness.

III. How to evaluate whether an intervention is backed by "possible" evidence of effectiveness.

IV. Important factors to consider when implementing an evidence-based intervention in your schools or classrooms.

Appendix A: Where to find evidence-based interventions

Appendix B: Checklist to use in evaluating whether an intervention is backed by rigorous evidence

RESOURCES FOR BEST PRACTICES WITH COMMUNITIES

Web Sites

Thornton, T. N., Craft, C. A., Dahlberg, L. L., Lynch, B. S., & Baer, K. (2000). *Best practices of youth violence prevention: A sourcebook for community action.* Atlanta, GA: Centers for Disease Control and Prevention, National Center for Injury Prevention and Control. Retrieved March 13, 2005, from National Center for Injury Prevention and Control Web site: http://www.cdc.gov/ncipc/dvp/bestpractices.htm.

Books

Burns, B. J., & Hoagwood, K. (2002). *Community treatment for youth: Evidence-based interventions for severe emotional and behavioral disorders.* New York: Oxford University Press.

Journal Articles

Bond, G. R., Rollins, A. L., Rapp, C. A., & Zipple, A. M. (2004). How evidence-based practices contribute to community integration. *Community Mental Health Journal, 40*(6), 569–589.

Embry, D.D. (2004). Community-based prevention using simple, low-cost, evidence-based kernels and behavior vaccines. *Journal of Community Psychology, 32*(5), 575–591.

Other

Education Review Group. (2004). *The effects of school-based social information processing interventions on aggressive behavior.* Retrieved March 12, 2005, from http://www.campbellcollaboration.org/doc-pdf/agbhprt.pdf.

Extremely violent events in schools in recent years have drawn popular attention to issues of school safety. Sensationalized reports of extreme violence sometimes create the impression that violence is pervasive in schools and instill fear in the minds of parents, students, and teachers. While this fear is understandable, the instances of violence that fuel this fear are few and far between and not typical of school misbehavior; for example, less than one percent of the children who are murdered annually are murdered while at school (DeVoe, et al., 2003; Education Review Group, 2004).

RESOURCES FOR PROFESSIONAL ORGANIZATIONS

Web Sites

Blueprints for Violence Prevention. (2006). OJJDP identification of research-based effective programs. Retrieved December 06, 2006 from http://www.colorado.edu/cspv/blueprints/index.html

CDC Community Guides. (2006). Guide to Community Preventive Services at the U.S. Centers for Disease Control and Prevention conducts systematic reviews of available scientific literature to determine what this evidence shows about the effectiveness of public health interventions in preventing violence, primarily violence by and against juveniles. Retrieved December 06, 2006 from http://www.thecommunityguide.org

What Works Clearinghouse. (2006). A central, independent and trusted source of scientific evidence of what works in education. Retrieved December 6, 2006 from http://www.w-wc.org/

Books

Guimon, J. (2004). *Relational mental health: Beyond evidence-based interventions.* New York: Kluwer Academic.

Journal Articles

Barkham, M., & Mellor-Clark, J. (2003). Bridging evidence-based practice and practice-based evidence: Developing a rigorous and relevant knowledge for the psychological therapies. *Clinical Psychology and Psychotherapy, 10*(6), 319–327.

Manela, R. W., & Moxley, D. P. (2002). Best practices as agency-based knowledge in social welfare. *Administration in Social Work, 26*(4), 1–24.

THE MULTIDIMENSIONAL CLIENT AND FAMILY

Cynthia G. S. Franklin and Tammy Linseisen

Case Description

Jeremy Gonzalez was a 15-year-old Latino male who was currently living with his maternal grandmother Edna Santos, his stepgrandfather Juan Santos, his 22-year-old maternal uncle Pito, and his 7-year-old female cousin Lili. Jeremy has an open case with Children's Protective Services (CPS) because his mother could no longer control his behaviors in her home. Jeremy has a history of becoming violent with his mother, and he has been arrested three times over the past 3 months by juvenile authorities in his hometown for possession of marijuana, breaking and entering into a neighbor's home, and domestic battery against his mother and sister in the home. The juvenile court judge ordered that CPS become involved in the case, asking CPS to secure alternative placement for Jeremy, because the court determined that Jeremy's mother was not able to control his behavior in her home.

Jeremy was placed in a local therapeutic foster home with foster parents who were specially trained to manage youths with behavioral and emotional difficulties. He ran away after living there only 2 days and was found by police 3 days later, more than 100 miles from his hometown, and under the influence of both drugs and alcohol. Jeremy was then placed in a locked treatment facility more than 150 miles away from his home. He remained in this facility for approximately 1 month before finding a way to escape his locked environment and run away from this facility, as well. Jeremy returned to his mother's home by hitchhiking and walking, and she notified the police after he arrived. The police arrested him and locked him into a juvenile detention center until he could be seen again by his presiding judge.

According to case records, Mrs. Santos, Jeremy's grandmother, attended the juvenile detention hearing, even though the hearing occurred more than 4 hours from her home and she was able to attend with only one day's notice. She pleaded with the court to allow her grandson to live with her, indicating that she would be able to manage him without problems due to the closeness of their relationship. Mrs. Santos stated that she had been involved in the raising of her grandson from the time he was very young and that he had been successful living with her in the past. Jeremy agreed that he would be willing to live by his grandmother's rules, go to school, attend outpatient drug treatment, take any prescribed medications, and involve himself in therapy. Mrs. Santos tearfully explained to the court that she was afraid for Jeremy's life if he lived anywhere except with her. The judge surprisingly ordered that Jeremy should leave the custody of the detention center and live with his maternal grandmother pending an approved home study by the local CPS office in her hometown. A home study is an assessment of the home environment and family system in which a child is being placed to live. The study determines that the home is an appropriate placement for a child and that the family will be able to meet the child's needs sufficiently. The assessment also determines that there is a goodness of fit between the child and the caregivers. The judge allowed Jeremy to move into his grandmother's home immediately, though, prior to the home study being completed.

Assessment and Problem Identification

Twenty-three-year-old Valeria Gonzales, a Latina graduate social work intern at the local CPS office, was assigned the home study for this family as her first case in the internship. Jeremy had been living in his grandmother's home for approximately 3 months when the home study was assigned. On receiving the case assignment, Valeria read the case file and was struck by the grandmother's obvious care and concern for her grandson. She also noted that it seemed that Jeremy would have to live in a juvenile detention facility until he was 18 if his grandmother did not "step up" to take care of him. Valeria contacted Mrs. Santos, introduced herself, and spoke of the home study procedure. She obtained a mailing address for Mrs. Santos and indicated that she would be sending a number of social history forms for her to complete. Valeria then set the first meeting for 1 week from that day and obtained directions to Mrs. Santos's home, which was located about 20 miles from the CPS office.

Valeria brought the case to her individual supervision meeting and discussed her plan for the first interviews of the home study process. Valeria's field instructor asked Valeria to contact members of Jeremy's treatment team, such as his juvenile probation officer, his case worker from his hometown, and his current school counselor in order to obtain more information about the family's involvement with their agencies and about Jeremy's current level of functioning in his placement with his grandmother.

Intervention Selection

Valeria traveled to Mrs. Santos's home to complete the first interview, but on arriving at the home, she learned that Mrs. Santos was not there. Her adult son, who lives in the home, informed Valeria that a case worker working with the family from the community had called to reschedule the appointment, but Valeria had never received any such message. She returned to the agency and determined that her voice mail was not functioning.

Intervention/Treatment

Feeling guilty, Valeria called Mrs. Santos again, apologized profusely for the voice mail problems that prevented Mrs. Santos from reaching her, and rescheduled the appointment for 2 days later. When Valeria arrived at Mrs. Santos's home for this appointment, the community-based case worker, Norma, was present, along with the family, for the interview. Valeria did not know what to do, and because she already felt bad about her voice mail problems, she did not want to ask the case worker to leave. After all, it appeared the family wanted the case worker to be with them.

Valeria asked to interview Mr. and Mrs. Santos first, and once they were alone (with the community-based case worker), she asked Mrs. Santos for the forms that were supposed to have been completed before the meeting. Mrs. Santos indicated that she had not known that the forms were supposed to be finished for the meeting and that she did not have them completed. Valeria began to wonder whether she had not told the family that the forms were to be ready at the time of the first interview, questioning her own memory and effectiveness at this point. Mrs. Santos apologized profusely for not having the forms ready, and she touched Valeria on the knee and said, "Oh, *muchachita*, you know how we Latinas are—we are always late!" Valeria felt closer to Mrs. Santos at this point, and she was pleased that Mrs. Santos was not angry with her for making so many mistakes.

As she began her interview, Valeria realized that the television was on in the room and that the family occasionally laughed at the program showing. Again, though, she was not sure whether this was acceptable or not. She assumed that this meant the family felt comfortable with her there and took it as a good sign. Valeria conducted the home study interview with the couple and then with Mr. and Mrs. Santos individually. Mrs. Santos answered each question with vivid examples of her own history and family stories to illustrate each of her points. She often went on tangents, and Valeria struggled to redirect her or keep her on topic. Valeria thought it was very important to build rapport, and she felt disrespectful if she interrupted. Besides, she wanted the family to like her. The interviews continued for more than 4 hours, and finally, Valeria, feeling terrible, told the family that she had to go. She reported to the family that she would have to return for another interview with the adult son, the granddaughter, and Jeremy, as well. Valeria left the home in the dark and was late to a personal appointment because her meeting with this family had not ended at the scheduled time. She found herself feeling frustrated and irritable, but she decided that the reason was her time management problems.

Valeria was exhausted after this long interview, but she explained to her field instructor later that Mrs. Santos seemed "really nice" and that she could tell that they "connected" during the home study. Her supervisor asked her to think about this further and to stay aware of her feelings. She shared all of the positive events of the interview process with her field instructor. Valeria wondered if it had been appropriate to discuss vintage clothing as a common interest with Mrs. Santos, but she decided it was not a necessary topic for supervision. Valeria assumed that she was using self-disclosure to build rapport. She mentioned to her peers how much she liked her first client and stated that Mrs. Santos is "kind of like a grandmother figure to me."

The Santos family cancelled the next two appointments with Valeria. One appointment was cancelled 2 days in advance and the other at the time she arrived at the home. Valeria met with Jeremy at school, and he stated that he was having no problems living with his grandmother. He also told Valeria how much he loved his grandmother. Jeremy's counselor was not available to discuss Jeremy's school progress, but the community-based counselor, Norma (who had attended the family's home study interview), was housed at the school and saw Valeria in the attendance office. Norma approached Valeria and reported openly in the office area that Jeremy was functioning "so well" in his grandmother's home. She stated that even though he had been arrested the previous Friday for truancy and public intoxication, that had been his only problem in more than a month. Valeria felt shocked by this new information and did not know what to say. She thanked Norma for the information and hurriedly left the school.

Valeria contacted Mrs. Santos and asked her about Jeremy's recent arrest. Mrs. Santos immediately dismissed the arrest, minimizing Jeremy's responsibility and blaming Jeremy's doctor for going on vacation without calling in refills for Jeremy's medication first. Mrs. Santos told Valeria that it was all a mistake and that if Jeremy had been on his medication, no problems would have occurred. Valeria felt relieved.

Evaluation

Valeria went into her field instructor's office for their regularly scheduled supervision hour. Her field instructor asked for an update on the Santos home study, indicating that the study was due in only 3 days. Valeria told her supervisor that she had not even completed her interviews at this point because the family had had conflicts with the previous two appointments that had been set and that she did not have the information forms yet, either. The supervisor asked what Valeria had learned from her contacts with the people who were involved collaterally with Jeremy's case, and Valeria admitted that she had not contacted them. When asked, Valeria explained that she had become so overwhelmed by the need to accomplish her interviews with the family members that she had forgotten to contact others. She also admitted that everything had seemed to be going so well that she had not been sure whether collateral contacts were necessary. The supervisor then informed her that the juvenile probation officer had called and said that Jeremy has been arrested four times in the previous 3 months while living with the Santos family, including one time for stealing and selling Mrs. Santos's pain medication. The probation officer also said that Mrs. Santos seemed to be protecting Jeremy from the authorities, keeping him from accepting responsibility for his difficulties. According to the probation officer, she rescued Jeremy and explained away his deeds as if they were "just a misunderstanding."

The field instructor asked Valeria to reflect on the information she had just heard and how it fit with the information she had obtained so far from the family. Valeria told her supervisor that she was very worried that Jeremy would have no place to go but jail if Mrs. Santos could not raise him, and she also expressed concerns for Mrs. Santos's feelings. As Valeria and her supervisor sat together in silence, Valeria felt shocked and embarrassed because she suddenly realized that she had not been objective when working with Mrs. Santos and had allowed her own feelings about this family and Jeremy's case to interfere with her professional skills and responsibilities.

Discussion

A review of current literature offers considerable information on the interpersonal skills needed to be effective in interviewing and family practice (Jantzen, Harris, Jordan, & Franklin, 2006; Drisko, 2004). More than 50 years of clinical, process-outcome research have pointed to the importance of the helping relationship and have defined the characteristics of relationships that are needed to be effective with clients (Assay & Lambert, 2000; Drisko, 2004;

Luborsky, McLellan, Diguer, Woody, & Seligman, 1997; Orlinsky, Ronnestad, & Willutzki, 2001). As Wampold (2001) points out that, the essence of effective intervention is embodied in the clinician. Research suggests that accurate empathy, positive regard, warmth, and congruence are the importance characteristics of interpersonal relationships with clients (Assay & Lambert, 2000). Beginning social workers some times mistake rapport building and the desire for clients to like them for these characteristics. Nothing could be further from the truth, however. Instead, appropriate empathy, positive regard, and congruence require boundaries, setting limits, and providing structure for client contacts. Structure is as essential to building effective relationships with families as being a warm and caring person. Evidence-based models within family intervention have demonstrated the need for the social worker to take leadership and provide structure during family interviews (Alexander & Sexton, 2002; Sexton & Alexander, 2002). Family practitioners who use structured skills, along with showing appropriate empathy, are found to be much more effective with families than those who only show compassion and are likable, for example. The social work student in the previous case study did not set the appropriate boundaries or structure for her roles and intervention. Let's look at some interpersonal and clinical interviewing skills that might have helped her be more effective in her job.

In the helping professions, it is widely understood and accepted as best practice that the use of professional boundaries is critical when working with clients. Peterson (1992) explains that "boundaries are the limits that allow for a safe connection based on the client's needs" (p. 74). Strom-Gottfried (1999) discusses these boundaries that separate the client and the social worker: "not in a cold or hierarchical fashion, but rather, with the intent of preserving and promoting the helping relationship" (p. 439). A number of Valeria's actions might have been considered violations of boundaries in the worker-client relationship. Strom-Gottfried (1999) indicates that violations "fall generally along a continuum from rather benign mistakes such as personal revelations by the worker or the failure to set appropriate limits, to clearly exploitive acts such as engaging clients in business deals or pursuing sexual relationships" (p. 439). Valeria's inability to hold the family to their scheduled appointments and paperwork deadlines provided the family with little structure within which to work. The Santos family pushed the boundaries in many areas, and Valeria did not set necessary limits, decreasing the family's confidence in her power and authority and reinforcing Valeria's role as a "grandchild," rather than as professional helper. This also affected Valeria's own view of herself as a professional, diminishing her professional objectivity and interfering with her ability to critically assess the Santos home as an appropriate placement for Jeremy.

Professional boundaries and interpersonal skills issues coalesce with relationship issues in the family that the social worker interviewed. In order to be an effective helper, social workers must anticipate what interpersonal issues that they may encounter in a particular family. They must manage those issues using their own interpersonal skills. One way of learning how to be interpersonally effective is to draw on existing empirical knowledge of family interventions. For example, the social worker in the case study was entering a Hispanic family system in which there was an adolescent with drug abuse problems. Evidence-based approaches for engaging and interviewing this type of family have been developed (Szapocznik & Williams, 2000). If the social worker had applied this evidence-based knowledge, she could have been better prepared to manage the interpersonal issues in this type of family interview. For example, in families in which there is adolescent substance abuse, it is not unusual to encounter protective mechanisms and violations of hierarchy (authority structure) and inappropriate boundary functioning. The social worker might have used this information to realize that the grandmother might be inappropriately involved with her grandson, protecting her grandson, even minimizing his problems by making excuses for his behavior. The social worker might have also been aware that grandmother was likely a very caring and powerful figure in the family but might be involved in a rescuing triangle (a three-person system meant to manage conflict or stress) between her daughter and grandson. The triangle represents a violation in boundaries and authority roles within that family. The boundary and authority problems are exemplified by the grandmother's assuming an inappropriate and ineffective parental role while at the same time the mother also assumes an ineffective and incompetent parenting role toward her son. Research indicates that this type of family system often does not provide enough parental control over children. It leaves the teenager in charge and may foster out-of-control behavior, for example (Sells, 2001).

The Center for Family Studies' research (2001) on Hispanic families with adolescents who abuse substances suggests that in order to effectively engage these families in intervention, hierarchical functioning issues, including protective functions and boundary issues, must be addressed from the beginning contact. In this case, for example, the grandmother appeared to be acting to protect the teenager, and the mother had relinquished an effective and competent parenting role. These family issues would suggest that it might be important for the social worker to align herself with the grandmother, because the grandmother was the one with the power in the family; but at the same time the social worker must thoroughly assess the functions of the grandmother's protective role and how that this role might affect her caretaking effectiveness with her grandson. Effective parenting for teenagers, for example, not only requires nurturance but also clear expectations, consistent consequences, and parental control. Another way of saying this is that too much caring is not very caring. The social worker would want to assess these parenting skills to determine the appropriateness of the placement. It might also be important to invite the youth's mother to the interview so that the social worker could assess the relations between the grandmother and her daughter and determine what might be involved in engaging the mother in a more active and competent parental role with her son.

Jeremy's problems and family issues would suggest that the social worker might also expect such a family not to have clear boundaries and that these boundary issues might press on the social worker, trying to draw her into boundary violations such as caring too much and not providing enough authority and structure to the interview. As was noted earlier, it appeared that Valeria allowed herself to be drawn into an inappropriate relationship with the grandmother. Valeria also felt incompetent to accomplish her goals and functions with the family. It is interesting to note that the daughter also felt incompetent to accomplish her parental functions with the grandson. One might hypothesize that this relationship between Valeria and the grandmother might also mirror the relationship between the grandmother and her daughter.

Maintaining goal directness is an important way to become more interpersonally effective with clients, and this issue is important to the case being discussed. Donahey and Miller (2000) propose that client goals should be the focus of any kind of intervention and that this applies regardless of theoretical orientation. For a social worker to be interpersonally effective, he or she must conduct an interview with a purpose in mind and structure the interview in such a way that he or she can achieve that purpose. Social workers must not allow the family system or the situation at hand (e.g., child at risk of going to jail, miscommunication, other social workers) to keep them from accomplishing the purposes of their family contact. In the case of the CPS client, it is important for the social worker to balance the goals of the client with the goals of the agency. In this case scenario, the goal of the client was to get custody of her grandchild, Jeremy. But the goal of the agency was to determine whether that was the best decision for the adolescent. When working with clients, social workers can identify goals with such questions as "How did you hope that I might be of help? What is your goal for my visit? What did you hope/wish/

think would be different as a result of my coming here today? How will you know when this visit is worth your time?" Although it is essential for social workers to understand and honor the goals of clients, it also important for the social worker to track his or her own goals and purposes. The social worker may ask these types of questions to stay on track toward the agency goals and in their roles. What is the purpose of my contact with this family? What has to happen today for me to help this family? What do I need to come out of this interview with to do my job well? What tasks are at hand? What is the best way for me to accomplish today's tasks?

In the previous case study, Valeria, the social work student, might have been more interpersonally effective if she had focused on the goals at hand, thus setting an appropriate professional boundary by sticking to the agenda and staying on track in the interview. She might have confronted the grand-mother about the cancelled appointments by telling her that if she did not finish her family study, it could not be determined whether Jeremy could live with the grandmother or not. She might say that it was her understanding that that was what the grandmother wanted. To set another appropriate boundary and to keep the interview on track, Valeria might have asked the grandmother to turn off the television during the interview or to move the interview to another room so that they could focus on the important information. Valeria might have also set boundaries for the information given, saying, for example, that she enjoyed getting to know the family but that it was important to finish the information she needed for her assessment. She might have reinforced this approach by telling the client how much time they had for the interview and sticking to that time schedule. To increase her interpersonal effectiveness, it was essential for Valeria to take charge of the interview and to proceed to ask the questions and get the information she needed in a timely fashion. It was necessary for Valeria to quickly stop Mrs. Santos from running on with her stories and to swiftly remind her, when necessary, that she had to stick to the agenda of asking the questions and getting the information.

Conclusion

Assessment of worker vulnerability allows constructive critique and future prevention of similar errors by this student. Several factors increased Valeria's vulnerability for boundary violations. First, she was just beginning as a student intern in her first graduate field placement. She may not have yet had the opportunities to learn all the evidence-based family interviewing skills that she needed to work with this type of challenging family. Her lack of knowledge and experience put her at an disadvantage. Because Valeria was a novice, she might have needed to check in with her supervisor more frequently. She likely wanted to do a good job, however, and this may be why she did not ask for more help. Performance anxiety, form being new as well as from wanting to excel, sets students up to make mistakes. It is not uncommon for a new or seasoned practitioner to contend with feelings of wanting to be liked by his or her clients. Workers generally come into this line of work to help, and if a practitioner is at odds with his or her client, it seems less beneficial to everyone involved. Next, Valeria is Latina, and her first case at the agency involved a family of the same ethnicity, a minority that has endured much social injustice and that has struggled significantly within the dominant culture's institutions of power. Valeria might have overidentified with the client and her struggles, influencing Valeria to bend the rules and provide opportunities for the client that she might not have had otherwise. Finally, Valeria's personal feelings about Jeremy going to jail decreased her objectivity and made her vulnerable to manipulation and opinion, rather than practicing fact finding and critical assessment of Jeremy's needs and whether they could be met in this environment. Her personal worries about this being the "client's last chance for a home" influenced her decision making in a way that, ultimately, was not in his best interest but that made her feel better about the decision being made. There is no magic solution for improving the types of learning and interpersonal effectiveness issues that have been illustrated in this case example. They are normal issues that often emerge in learning how to be an effective social worker. Self-exploration and critique, coupled with ongoing case consultation and close supervision, are the best way to monitor and improve the effectiveness of one's interpersonal skills in interviewing.

■ ■ ■

Activities

1. Assume that you are the worker on this case. You have traveled to the family's home to conduct your first interview. The family has invited a community case worker to sit in on the interview and has left the television on loud. You are aware that these are boundary violations. How do you handle these with the family in a way that does not damage rapport?

2. You remain the worker on this case. You are interviewing Mrs. Santos, and she rambles from topic to topic while trying to answer specific interview questions. Role-play how you might assist her to minimize her tangents and stay focused on the questions you are asking. Again, keep in mind your wish to establish and maintain rapport with this client.

3. As the worker, you have completed your assessment of Jeremy's placement in this home, and you have determined that the family is not able to meet his needs effectively in the placement. The family calls you and asks you what your recommendation in court will be. How do you address this question? What do you say?

REFERENCES

Achenbach, T. M. (1997). *Manual for the young adult self-report and young adult behavior checklist.* Burlington, VT: University of Vermont, Department of Psychology.

Achenbach, T. M. (1991). *Manual for the youth self-report and 1991 profile.* Burlington: University of Vermont, Department of Psychiatry.

Alexander, J., Barton, C., Gordon, D., Grotpeter, J., Hansson, K., Harrison, R., et al. (1998). *Blueprints for violence prevention: Book 3. Functional family therapy.* Boulder, CO: Center for Study and Prevention of Violence.

Alexander, J., Robbins, M., & Sexton, T. (2000). Family-based interventions with older, at-risk youth: From promise to proof to practice. *Journal of Primary Prevention, 21*(2), 185–205.

Alexander, J. F., & Parsons, B. V. (1973). Short-term behavioral intervention with delinquents: Impact on family process and recidivism. *Journal of Abnormal Psychology, 81,* 219–225.

Alexander, J. F., & Parsons, B. V. (1982). *Functional family therapy.* Monterey, CA: Brooks/Cole.

Alexander, J. F., & Sexton, T. L. (2002). Functional family therapy: A model for treating high risk, acting out youth. In F. W. Kaslow & J. L. Lebow (Eds.), *Comprehensive handbook of psychotherapy: Vol. 4. Integrative/eclectic* (pp. 111–161). New York: Wiley.

Allen, J. M. (2001). *Good Grief, You Taught Me a Lot, Charlie Brown!* Retrieved December 6, 2006, from http://www.coachjim.com/articles/charliebrown.html

American Psychiatric Association. (1987). *Guidelines on confidentiality.* Washington, DC: Author.

American Psychiatric Association. (2000). *Diagnostic and statistical manual of mental disorders* (4th ed., text rev.). Washington, DC: Author.

American Psychological Association Task Force on Promotion and Dissemination of Psychological Procedures. (1995). Training and dissemination of empirically-validated psychological treatments: Report and recommendations. *Clinical Psychologist, 48,* 3–23.

Andrews, D. A., & Bonta, J. L. (1995). *The Level of Service Inventory—Revised.* Toronto, Ontario, Canada: Multi-Health Systems.

Andrews, D. A., & Bonta, J. L. (1998). *The psychology of criminal conduct* (2nd ed.). Cincinnati, OH: Anderson.

Andrews, D. A., & Bonta, J. L. (2003). *The psychology of criminal conduct* (3rd ed.). Cincinnati, OH.: Anderson.

403

Andrews, D. A., Bonta, J. L., & Hoge, R. D. (1990). Classification for effective rehabilitation: Rediscovering psychology. *Criminal Justice and Behavior, 17,* 19–52.

Andrews, D. A., Zinger, I., Hoge, R. D., Bonta, J., Gendreau, P., & Cullen, F. T. (1990). Does correctional treatment work? A clinically relevant and psychologically informed meta-analysis. *Criminology, 28,* 369–404.

Anthony, W. A., & Liberman, R. P. (1986). Practice of psychiatric rehabilitation: Historical, conceptual, and research. *Schizophrenia Bulletin, 12,* 542–559.

Appleby, L., Dyson, V., Altman, E., & Luchins, D. J. (1997). Assessing substance use in multiproblem patients: Reliability and validity of the Addiction Severity Index in a mental hospital population. *Journal of Nervous and Mental Disease, 185,* 159–165.

Assay, T. P., & Lambert, M. J. (1999). The empirical case for the common factors in therapy: Quantitative findings. In M. A. Hubble, B. L. Duncan, & S. D. Miller (Eds.), *The heart and soul of change: What works in therapy* (pp. 23–55). Washington, DC: American Psychological Association.

Association for Counselor Education and Supervision. (1995). Ethical guidelines for counseling superviors. *Counseling Eucation and Supervision, 34,* 270–276.

Association of State and Provincial Psychology Boards Task Force on Supervision Guidelines. (2003). *Report of the ASPPB Task Force on Supervision Guidelines.* Montgomery, AL: Author.

Austrian, S. G. (2002). Guidelines for conducting a biopsychosocial assessment. In A. R. Roberts & G. J. Greene (Eds.), *Social workers' desk reference* (pp. 205–208). New York: Oxford University Press.

Baer, R. A., & Nietzel, M. T. (1991). Cognitive and behavioral treatment of impulsivity in children: A meta-analytic review of the outcome literature. *Journal of Clinical Child Psychology, 20,* 400–412.

Baird, B. (2004). *The internship, practicum, and field placement handbook: A guide for the helping professions* (4th ed.). Upper Saddle River, NJ: Prentice Hall.

Barkham, M., & Mellor-Clark, J. (2003). Bridging evidence-based practice and practice-based evidence: Developing a rigorous and relevant knowledge for the psychological therapies. *Clinical Psychology and Psychotherapy, 10*(6), 319–327.

Barkley, R. A. (1987). *Defiant children: A clinician's manual for parent training.* New York: Guilford Press.

Barlow, D. H. (Ed.). (2001). *Clinical handbook of psychological disorders* (3rd ed.). New York: Guilford Press.

Barlow, D. H., Raffa, S. D., & Cohen, E. M. (2002). Psychosocial treatments for panic disorders, phobias, and generalized anxiety disorder. In P. E. Nathan & J. M. Gorman (Eds.), *A guide to treatments that work* (2nd ed., pp. 301–335). New York: Oxford University Press.

Barry, J. M. (2004). *The great influenza: The epic story of the deadliest plague in history.* New York: Viking.

Beck, A. T., Ward, C. H., Mendelson, M., Mack, J., & Erbaugh, J. (1961). An inventory for measuring depression. *Archives of General Psychiatry, 4,* 561–571.

Beck, J. (1995). *Cognitive therapy: Basics and beyond.* New York: Guilford Press.

Beyer, M. (2003). *Best practices in juvenile accountability: An overview.* Washington, DC: U.S. Department of Justice, Office of Justice Programs, Office of Juvenile Justice and Delinquency Prevention.

Bien, E., Anderson, T., Strupp, H. H., Henry, W. P., Schacht, T. E., Binder, J. L., et al. (2000). The effects of training in time-limited dynamic psychotherapy: Changes in therapeutic outcome. *Psychotherapy Research, 10*(2), 119–132.

Bien, T. H., Miller, W. R., & Tonigan, J. S. (1993). Brief interventions for alcohol problems: A review. *Addiction, 88,* 315–335.

Binder, J. (1993). Is it time to improve psychotherapy training? *Clinical Psychology Review, 13,* 301–318.

Black's Law Dictionary (5th ed.). (1979). St. Paul, MN: West.

Bloom, M., Fischer, J., & Orme, J. G. (2006). *Evaluating practice: Guidelines for the accountable professional* (5th ed). New York: Allyn & Bacon.

Bloomquist, M.L., & Schnell, S.V. (2002). *Helping children with aggression and conduct problems: Best practices for intervention.* New York: Guilford Press.

Bond, G. R., Drake, R. E., Mueser, K. T., & Latimer, E. (2001). Assertive community treatment for people with severe mental illness. *Disease Management and Health Outcomes, 9,* 141–159.

Bond, G. R., Rollins, A. L., Rapp, C. A., & Zipple, A. M. (2004). How evidence-based practices contribute to community integration. *Community Mental Health Journal, 40*(6), 569–589.

Brestan, E. V., & Eyberg, S. (1998). Effective psychosocial treatments of conduct-disordered children and adolescents: 29 years, 82 studies, and 5,272 kids. *Journal of Clinical Child Psychology, 27,* 180–189.

Burke, B. L., Arkowitz, H., & Dunn, C. (2002). The efficacy of motivational interviewing. In W. R. Miller & S. Rollnick, *Motivational interviewing: Preparing people for change* (2nd ed. pp. 217–250). New York: Guilford Press.

Burke, B. L., Dunn, C. W., Atkins, D. C., & Phelps, J. S. (2004). The emerging evidence base for motivational interviewing: An analytic and qualitative inquiry. *Journal of Cognitive Psychotherapy, 18*(4), 309–322.

Burns, B. J., & Hoagwood, K. (2002). *Community treatment for youth: Evidence-based interventions for severe emotional and behavioral disorders.* New York: Oxford University Press.

Calhoun, K. S., Moras, K., Pilkonis, P. A., & Rehm, L. P. (1998). Empirically supported treatments: Implications for training. *Journal of Consulting and Clinical Psychology, 66*(1), 151–162.

Canadian Association of Social Workers. (1996). *Code of ethics.* Ottawa, Ontario: Author.

Cavell, T. A. (2000). *Working with parents of aggressive children: A practitioner's guide.* Washington, DC: American Psychological Association.

Center for Family Studies. (2001). *Brief strategic family therapy.* Retrieved October 14, 2004, from http//:www.cfs.med.miami.edu/Docs/Clinical Approach.html.

Center for the Study and Prevention of Violence. (2002–2004). *Blueprints for violence prevention: CASASTART.* Retrieved January 6, 2005, from http://www.colorado.edu/cspv/blueprints/promising/programs/BPP04.html

Center on Alcoholism, Substance Abuse, and Addictions. (2006). Motivational Interviewing. Retrieved December 13, 2006, from http://casaa.unm.edu/info/mi _files/frame.htm

Chambless, D. L., Baker, M. J., Baucom, D. H., Beutler, L. E., Calhoun, K. S., Crits-Christoph, P., et al. (1998). Update on empirically validated therapies: II. *Clinical Psychologist, 51*(1), 3–16.

Chambless, D. L., & Ollendick, T. H. (2001). Empirically supported psychological interventions: Controversies and evidence. *Annual Review of Psychology, 52,* 685–716.

Channing Bete Company. (2004). *Communities that care prevention strategies guide.* Retrieved January 6, 2005, from http://www.channing-bete.com/positiveyouth/ pages/CTC/prevention_strategies.html

Child Welfare League of America. (2004). *Best practices in behavior support and intervention assessment.* Washington, DC: Author.

Cluss, P. A., Boughton, J., Frank, E., Stewart, B. D., & West, D. (1983). The rape victim: Psychological correlates of participation on the legal process. *Criminal Justice and Behavior, 10,* 342–357.

Coleman, D. (2003). Learning about therapy theories: An empirical test of an experiential technique. *Journal of Teaching in Social Work, 23*(3/4), 73–89.

Coleman, D. (2004). The Theoretical Evaluation Self-Test (TEST): A preliminary validation study. *Social Work Research, 28*(2), 117–128.

Conners, C. K. (1997). *Conners' rating scales—revised: Technical manual.* North Tonawanda, NY: Multi-Health Systems.

Corcoran, J. (2000). *Evidence-based social work practice with families: A lifespan approach.* New York: Springer.

Corcoran, J. (2003). *Clinical applications of evidence-based family interventions.* New York: Oxford University Press.

Corcoran, J., & Casebolt, A. (2004). Risk and resilience ecological framework for assessment and goal formulation. *Child and Adolescent Social Work Journal, 21*(3), 211–235.

Corcoran, J., & Springer, D. W. (2005). Treatment of adolescents with disruptive behavior disorders. In J. Corcoran, *Strengths and skills building: A collaborative approach to working with clients* (pp. 131–162). New York: Oxford University Press.

Corcoran, K. (1998). Clients without a cause: Is there a legal right to effective treatment? *Research on Social Work Practice, 8,* 589–596.

Corcoran, K. (2005). The Oregon Mental Health Referral Checklists: Concept mapping the mental health needs of youth in the juvenile justice system. *Brief Treatment and Crisis Intervention, 5,* 9–18.

Corcoran, K., Gingerich, W., & Briggs, H. (2001). Practice evaluation: Setting goals and monitoring change. In H. Briggs & K. Corcoran (Eds.), *Social work practice: Treating common client problems* (pp. 66–84). Chicago, IL: Lyceum Press.

Corcoran, K., Gorin, S., & Moniz, C. (2005). Managed care and mental health. In K. A. Kirk (Ed.), *Mental disorders in the social environment* (pp. 430–442). New York: Columbia University Press.

Corcoran, K., & Vandiver, V. L. (1996). *Maneuvering the maze of managed care: Skills for mental health practitioners.* New York: Free Press.

Corcoran, K., & Vandiver, V. L. (2004). Implementing best practice and expert consensus procedures. In A. R. Robert & K. R. Yeager (Eds.), *Evidence-based practice manual: Research and outcome measures in health and human services* (pp. 15–19). New York: Oxford University Press.

Corcoran, K., & Winslade, W. J. (1994). Eavesdropping on the 50-minute hour: Confidentiality and managed mental health care. *Behavioral Sciences and the Law, 12,* 351–365.

Cournoyer, B. (2000). *The social work skills workbook* (3rd ed.). Belmont, CA: Wadsworth.

Cournoyer, B., & Stanley, M. (2002). *The social work portfolio: Planning, assessing, and documenting lifelong learning in a dynamic profession.* Pacific Grove, CA: Brooks/Cole.

Covington D. L., Justason, B. J., & Wright, L. N. (2001). Severity, manifestations, and consequences of violence among pregnant adolescents. *Journal of Adolescent Health, 28*(1), 55–61.

Coyle, J. P. (2002). *Methods for preventing and reducing violence by at-risk adolescents: Common elements of empirically researched programs.* Buffalo: State University of New York School of Social Work. Retrieved January 6, 2005, from http://www.socialwork.buffalo.edu/fas/smyth/Personal_Web/Projects/Coyle-Preventing%20 and%20reducing%20adolescent%20violence.pdf

Crits-Christoph, P., Siqueland, L., Chittams, J., Barber, J. P., Beck, A. T., Frank, A., et al. (1998). Training in cognitive, supportive-expressive, and drug counseling therapies for cocaine dependence. *Journal of Consulting and Clinical Psychology, 66,* 484–492.

Crocker, P. L. (1999). Childhood abuse and adult murder: Implications for the death penalty. *North Carolina Law Review, 77,* 1143–1222.

Davey, G. C. (1992). Classical conditioning and the acquisition of human fears and phobias: A review and synthesis of the literature. *Advances in Behavior Research and Therapy, 14,* 715–734.

Dear, P. (2001). *Revolutionizing the sciences: European knowledge and its ambitions, 1500–1700.* Princeton, NJ: Princeton University Press.

Derogatis, L. R. (1975). *The SCL-90-R.* Baltimore: Clinical Psychometrics Research.

Derogatis, L. R., Lipman, R. S., & Covi, L. (1973). The SCL-90: An outpatient psychiatric rating scale. *Psychopharmacology Bulletin, 9,* 13–28.

DeVoe, J. F., Peter, K., Kaufman, P., Ruddy, S. A., Miller, A. K., Planty, M., et al. (2003). Indications of school crime and safety. *Education Statistics Quarterly, 5*(4). Retrieved March 6, 2006, from http://nces.ed.gov/programs/quarterly/vol_5/5_4/3_6.asp

Diamond, R. J. (1996). Coercion and tenacious treatment in the community: Applications to the real world. In D. Dennis & J. Monahan (Eds.), *Coercion and aggressive community treatment: A new frontier in mental health law* (pp. 53–73). New York: Plenum.

Dishion, T. J., & Kavanagh, K. (2003). *Intervening in adolescent problem behavior: A family-centered approach.* New York: Guilford Press.

Dixon, L. B., Krauss, N., & Lehman, A. F. (1994). Consumers as service providers: The promise and challenge. *Community Mental Health Journal, 30,* 615–625.

Donahey, K. M., & Miller, S. D. (2000). Applying a common factors perspective to sex therapy. *Journal of Sex Education and Therapy, 25,* 221–230.

Douglas, K. S., & Webster, C. D. (1999). The HCR-20 violence risk assessment scheme: Concurrent validity in a sample of incarcerated offenders. *Criminal Justice and Behavior, 26*(1), 3–19.

Doverspite, W. F. (1990). Multiaxial Diagnostic Inventory: Adult clinical scales and personality scales. *Innovations in Clinical Practice, 9,* 241–263.

Drake, R. E., Essock, S. M., Shaner, A., Carey, K. B., Minkoff, K., Kola, L., et al. (2001). Implementing dual diagnosis services for clients with severe mental illness. *Psychiatric Services, 52,* 469–476.

Drake, R. E., Goldman, H. H., Leff, H. S., Lehman, A. F., Dixon, L., Mueser, K. T., et al. (2003). Implementing evidence-based practices in routine mental health service settings. In R. E. Drake & H. H. Goldman (Eds.), *Evidence-based practices in mental health care* (pp. 1–4). Washington, DC: American Psychiatric Association.

Drake, R. E., Merrens, M. R., & Lynde, D. W. (Eds.). (2005). *Evidence-based mental health practice: A textbook.* New York: W.W. Norton & Company.

Drisko, J. W. (2004). Common factors in psychotherapy outcome: Meta-analytic findings and their implications for practice and research. *Families in Society: The Journal of Contemporary Social Services, 85,* 81–90.

Dukes, R. L., Stein, J. A., & Ullman, J. G. (1997). Long-term impact of drug abuse resistance education, (DARE): Results of a 6-year follow-up. *Evaluation Review, 21*(4), 483–500.

Dulmus, C. N., & Rapp-Paglicci, L. A. (Eds.). (2005). *Handbook of preventive interventions for adults.* New York: Wiley.

Dulmus, C. N., & Smyth, N. (2000). Early-onset schizophrenia: A literature review of empirically based interventions. *Child and Adolescent Social Work Journal, 17*(1), 67–92.

Dulmus, C. N., & Wodarski, J. S. (2002). Six critical questions for brief therapeutic interventions. *Brief Treatment and Crisis Intervention, 2*(4), 279–286.

Dumaine, M. L. (2003). Meta-analysis of interventions with co-occurring disorders of severe mental illness and substance abuse: Implications for social work practice. *Research on Social Work Practice, 13*(2), 142–165.

Dunn, C., DeRoo, L., & Rivara, F. P. (2001). The use of brief interventions adapted from motivational interviewing across behavioral domains: A systematic review. *Addiction, 96*(12), 1725–1742.

Durlak, J., Fuhrman, T., & Lampman, C. (1991). Effectiveness of cognitive-behavior therapy for maladapting children: A meta-analysis. *Psychological Bulletin, 110,* 204–214.

Education Review Group. (2004). *The effects of school-based social information processing interventions on aggressive behavior.* Retrieved March 12, 2005, from http://www.campbellcollaboration.org/doc-pdf/agbhprt.pdf

Elkin, I., Parloff, M. B., Hadley, S. W., & Autry, J. H. (1985). NIMH Treatment of Depression Collaborative Research Program. *Archives of General Psychiatry, 42,* 305–316.

Embry, D. D. (2004). Community-based prevention using simple, low-cost, evidence-based kernels and behavior vaccines. *Journal of Community Psychology, 32*(5), 575–591.

Epperson, D. L., Kaul, J. D., & Hesselton, D. (1998). *Minnesota Sex Offender Screening Tool—Revised (MnSOST-R): Development, performance, and recommended risk level cut scores.* Unpublished manuscript.

Epstein, R. (1984). The principle of parsimony and some applications in psychology. *Journal of Mind and Behavior, 5,* 119–130.

Epstein, R. M., & Hundert, E. M. (2002). Defining and assessing professional competence. *Journal of the American Medical Association, 287,* 226–235.

Eyberg, S. (1988). Parent-child interaction therapy: Integration of traditional and behavioral concerns. *Child and Family Behavior Therapy, 10,* 33–45.

Falender, C. A., & Shafranske, E. P. (2004). *Clinical supervision: A competency-based approach.* Washington, DC: American Psychological Association.

Falvey, J. E. (2002). *Managing clinical supervisor: Ethical practice and legal risk management.* Pacific Grove, CA: Brooks/Cole.

Farrington, D. P. (1999). A criminological research agenda for the next millennium. *International Journal of Offender Therapy and Comparative Criminology, 43*(2), 154–167.

Fenley, M. A., Gaiter, J. L., Hummett, M., Liburd, L. C., Mercy, J. A., O'Carroll, P. W., et al. (1993). *The prevention of youth violence: A framework for community action.* Atlanta, GA: Centers for Disease Control and Prevention.

Fergusson, D. M., & Lynskey, M. T. (1996). Adolescent resiliency to family adversity. *Journal of Child Psychology and Child Psychiatry, 37,* 281–292.

Fergusson, D. M., & Mullen, P. E. (1999). *Childhood sexual abuse: An evidence based perspective.* Thousand Oaks, CA: Sage.

Fischer, J. (1990). Problems and issues in meta-analysis. In L. Videka-Sherman & W. J. Reid (Eds.), *Advances in clinical social work research* (pp. 297–325). Washington, DC: NASW Press.

Fischer, J., & Corcoran, K. (2007a). *Measures for clinical practice and research: Vol. 1. Couples, families, and children.* New York: Oxford University Press.

Fischer, J., & Corcoran, K. (2007b). *Measures for clinical practice and research: Vol. 2. Adults.* NewYork: Oxford University Press.

Fleischman, M. J., Horne, A. M., & Arthur, J. L. (1983). *Troubled families: A treatment program.* Champaign, IL: Research Press.

Fonagy, P., & Kurtz, A. (2002). Disturbance of conduct. In P. Fonagy, M. Target, D. Cottrell, J. Phillips, & Z. Kurtz (Eds.), *What works for whom? A critical review of treatments for children and adolescents* (pp. 106–192). New York: Guilford Press.

Fonagy, P., Target, M., Cottrell, D., Phillips, J., & Kurtz, Z. (2002). *What works for whom? A critical review of treatments for children and adolescents.* New York: Guilford Press.

Forehand, R. L., & McMahon, R. J. (1981). *Helping the noncompliant child: A clinician's guide to present training.* New York: Guilford Press.

Fortune, A. E., & Abramson, J. S. (1993). Predictors of satisfaction with field practicum among social work students. *Clinical Supervisor, 11*(1), 95–110.

Franklin, C., Harris, M., & Allen-Meares, P. (Eds.). (2006). *School social work and mental health workers training and resource manual.* New York: Oxford University Press.

Fraser, M. W., Kirby, L., & Smokowski, P. R. (2004). Risk and resilience in childhood. In M. W. Fraser (Ed.), *Risk and resilience in childhood: An ecological perspective* (2nd ed., pp. 13–67). Washington, DC: NASW Press.

Frazier, P. A., & Haney, B. (1996). Sexual assault cases in the legal system: Police, prosecutor and victim perspectives. *Law and Human Behavior, 20*(6), 607–628.

Frutiger, A. D. (1981). Treatment of penetration phobia through the combined use of systematic desensitization and hypnosis: A case study. *American Journal of Clinical Hypnosis, 23*(4), 269–273.

Furrow, B. R., Greaney, T. L., Johnson, S. H., Jost, T. S., & Schwartz, R. L. (2004). *Health law: Cases, materials and problems* (5th ed.). St. Paul, MN: West.

Gallagher-Thompson, D., & Steffen, A. M. (1994). Comparative effects of cognitive-behavioral and brief dynamic therapy for depressed family caregivers. *Journal of Consulting and Clinical Psychology, 62,* 543–549.

Gambrill, E. (1999). Evidence-based practice: An alternative to authority-based practice. *Families in Society, 80,* 341–350.

Gambrill, E. (2006). *Social work practice: A critical thinker's guide* (2nd ed.). New York: Oxford University Press.

Garmezy, N. (1985). Stress-resistant children: The search for protective factors. In J. E. Stevenson (Ed.), *Recent research in developmental psychopathology* (pp. 213–233). New York: Elsevier Science.

Gibbs, L. (2003). *Evidence based practice for the helping professions: A practical guide with integrated multimedia.* Pacific Grove, CA: Brooks/Cole–Thompson Learning.

Gibbs, L., & Gambrill, E. (2002). Evidence-based practice: Counterarguments to objections. *Research on Social Work Practice, 12,* 452–476.

Glancy, G., & Regehr, C. (2004). Assessment measures for sexual predators. Step-by-step guidelines. In A. R. Roberts & K. R. Yeager (Eds.), *Evidence-based practice manual: Research and outcome measures in health and human services* (pp. 531–539). New York: Oxford University Press.

Goodyear, R. K., & Bernard, J. M. (1998). Clinical supervision: Lessons from the literature. *Counselor Education and Supervision, 38,* 6–22.

Goodyear, R. K., & Nelson, M. L. (1997). The major formats of psychotherapy supervision. In C. E. Watkins, Jr. (Ed.), *Handbook of psychotherapy supervision* (pp. 328–344). New York: Wiley.

Gordon, G. R., McBride, R. B., & Hage, H. H. (2001). *Criminal justice internships: Theory into practice.* (4th ed.). Cincinnati, OH: Anderson.

Gorski, T. T., Kelley, J. M., Havens, L., & Peters, R. H. (1995). *Relapse prevention and the substance abusing criminal offender.* Washington, DC: U.S. Department of Health and Human Services.

Gribbin, J. (2002). *The scientists: A history of science told through the lives of its greatest inventors.* New York: Random House.

Griswold v. Connecticut, 381 U.S. 479 (1965).

Grove, M. G., & Meehl, P. E. (1996). Comparative efficiency of informal and formal prediction procedures: The clinical-statistical controversy. *Psychology, Public Policy, and Law, 2*(2), 293–323.

Groza, V., Maschmeier, C., Jamison, C., & Piccola, T. (2003). Siblings and out-of-home placement: Best practices. *Families in Society, 84*(4), 480–491.

Guimon, J. (2004). *Relational mental health: Beyond evidence-based interventions.* New York: Kluwer Academic.

Hanish, L. D., Tolan, P. H., & Guerra, N. G. (1996). Treatment of oppositional defiant disorder. In M. A. Reinecke, F. M. Dattilio, & A. Freeman (Eds.), *Cognitive therapy with children and adolescents* (pp. 62–78). New York: Guilford Press.

Hanson, R. K. (1997). *The development of a brief actuarial risk scale for sexual offense recidivism* (User Report No. 1997–04). Ottawa, Ontario: Department of the Solicitor General of Canada.

Hanson, R. K., & Bussiere, M. T. (1998). Predicting relapse: A meta-analysis of sexual offender recidivism studies. *Journal of Consulting and Clinical Psychology, 66,* 348–362.

Hanson, R. K., & Harris, A. (1998). *Dynamic predictors of sexual recidivism.* Ottawa, Ontario: Department of the Solicitor General of Canada.

Hanson, R. K., & Thornton, D. (2000). Improving risk assessments for sex offenders: A comparison of three actuarial scales. *Law and Human Behavior, 24*(1), 119–136.

Hare, R. D. (1991). *The Hare Psychopathy Checklist—Revised.* Toronto, Ontario, Canada: Multi-Health Systems.

Hare, R. D. (1999). *Without conscience: The disturbing world of the psychopaths among us.* New York: Simon & Shuster.

Hare, R. D., Cox, D. N., & Hart, S. D. (1994). *Manual for the screening version of the Hare Psychopathy Checklist—Revised (PCL-SV).* Toronto, Ontario, Canada: Multi-Health Systems.

Hare, R. D., Hart, S. D., & Harpur, T. J. (1991). Psychopathy and the *DSM-IV* criteria for antisocial personality disorder. *Journal of Abnormal Psychology, 100*(3), 391–398.

Harrell, A. V., Cavanagh, S., & Sridharan, S. (1998). *Impact of the Children at Risk program: Comprehensive final report: III.* Washington, DC: Urban Institute.

Harrell, A. V., Cavanagh, S., & Sridharan, S. (1999). *Evaluation of the Children at Risk Program: Results 1 year after the end of the program.* Retrieved January 6, 2005, from http://www.ncjrs.gov/txtfiles1/nij/178914.txt

Havinghurst, C. C. (1991). Practice guidelines as legal standards governing physician liability. *Law and Contemporary Problems, 54,* 87–117.

Hawkins, J. D., Herrenkohl, T. L., Farrington, D. P., Brewer, D., Catalano, R. F., & Harachi, T. W. (1998). A review of predictors of youth violence. In R. Loeber & D. P. Farrington (Eds.), *Serious and violent juvenile offenders: Risk factors and successful interventions* (pp. 106–146). Thousand Oaks, CA: Sage.

Hawkins, J. D., Laub, J. H., & Lauritsen, J. L. (1998). Race, ethnicity, and serious juvenile offending. In R. Loeber & D. P. Farrington (Eds.), *Serious and violent juvenile offenders: Risk factors and successful interventions* (pp. 30–46). Thousand Oaks, CA: Sage.

Haynes, B., Devereaux, P., & Guyatt, G. (2002). Clinical expertise in the era of evidence based medicine and patient choice. *APC Journal Club, 136,* A11–A14.

Hellman, S., & Hellman, D. (1991). Of mice but not men: Problems of the randomized clinical trial. *New England Journal of Medicine, 324,* 1585–1589.

Henderson, C. E., Cawyer, C. S., & Watkins, C. E., Jr. (1999). A comparison of student and supervisor perceptions of effective practicum supervision. *Clinical Supervisor, 18,* 47–74.

Henggeler, S. W., & Borduin, C. M. (1990). *Family therapy and beyond: A multisystemic approach to treating the behavior problems of children and adolescents.* Pacific Grove, CA: Brooks/Cole.

Henggeler, S. W., Melton, G., Brondino, M., Scherer, D., & Hanley, J. (1997). Multisystemic therapy with violent and chronic juvenile offenders and their families: The role of treatment fidelity in successful dissemination. *Journal of Consulting and Clinical Psychology, 65,* 821–833.

Henggeler, S. W., Mihalic, S. F., Rone, L., Thomas, C., & Timmons-Mitchell, J. (1998). *Blueprints for violence prevention: Book six. Multisystemic therapy.* Boulder, CO: Center for Study and Prevention of Violence.

Henggeler, S. W., Schoenwald, S. K., Borduin, C. M., Rowland, M. D., & Cunningham, P. B. (1998). *Multisystemic treatment of antisocial behavior in children and adolescents.* New York: Guilford Press.

Henggeler, S. W., Schoenwald, S. K., Liao, J. G., Letourneau, E. J., & Edwards, D. L. (2002). Transporting efficacious treatments to field settings: The link between supervisory practices and therapist fidelity in MST programs. *Journal of Clinical Child Psychology, 31*(2), 155–167.

Hester, R. D. (2003). Physician medical records and the Health Insurance Portability and Accountability Act. *Journal of Health and Social Policy, 18,* 1–14.

Hickman, L. J., Jaycox, L. H., & Aronoff, J. (2004). Dating violence among adolescents: Prevalence, gender distribution, and prevention program effectiveness, *Trauma, Violence, and Abuse, 5*(2), 123–142.

Hiebert, B., & Thomlison, B. (1996). Facilitating transitions to adulthood: Research and policy implications. In B. Galaway & J. Hudson (Eds.), *Youth in transition: Perspectives on research and policy* (pp.54–60) Toronto, Ontario, Canada: Thompson Educational.

Hill, C. E., & Knox, S. (2001). Self-disclosure. *Psychotherapy, 38,* 413–417.

Hill, C. E., Mahalik, J. R., & Thompson, B. J. (1989). Therapist self-disclosure. *Psychotherapy, 26,* 290–295.

Hoagwood, K., Burns, B., & Kiser, L. (2001). Evidence-based practice in child and adolescent mental health services. *Psychiatric Services, 52*(9), 1179–1189.

Hodges, K. (2000). *The Child and Adolescent Functional Assessment Scale self-training manual.* Ypsilanti, MI: Eastern Michigan University, Department of Psychology.

Horak v. Biris, 474 N.E. 2d 13,130 Ill. App. 3d 140 (1985).

Horne v. Patton, 291 Ala. 701, 287 So. 2d 824 (1973).

Horney, J. Osgood, W. D., & Marshall, I. H. (1995). Criminal careers in the short-term: Intra-individual variability in crime and its relation to local life circumstances. *American Sociological Review, 60,* 655–673.

Howard, M. O., & Jenson, J. M. (1999). Clinical practice guidelines: Should social work develop them? *Research on Social Work Practice, 9*(3), 283–301.

Howard, M. O., McMillen, C. J., & Pollio, D. E. (2003). Teaching evidence-based practice: Toward a new paradigm for social work education. *Research on Social Work Practice, 13*(2), 234–259.

Humphers v. First Interstate Bank of Oregon, 696 P2nd, 527 (1985).

Jaffee v. Redmond, 518 U.S. 1 (1996).

Jantzen, C., Harris, O., Jordan, C., & Franklin, C. (2006). *Family treatment: Evidenced-based practice with populations at risk.* Pacific Grove, CA: Brooks/Cole.

Jensen, J. P., Bergin, A. E., & Greaves, D. W. (1990). The meaning of eclecticism: New survey and analysis of components. *Professional Psychology: Research and Practice, 21*(2), 124–130.

Jessor, R. J., van den Bos, J., Vanderryn, J., Costa, F. M., & Turbin, M. S. (1995). Protective factors in adolescent problem behavior: Moderator effects and developmental change. *Developmental Psychology, 31,* 923–933.

Johnson, W. B. (2002). The intentional mentor: Strategies and guidelines for the practice of mentoring. *Professional Psychology: Research and Practice, 33,* 88–96.

Johnson, W. B., & Nelson, N. (1999). Mentor-protégé relationships in graduate training: Some ethical concerns. *Ethics and Behavior, 9,* 189–210.

Jones, S. H., Thornicroft, G., Coffey, M., & Dunn, G. (1995). A brief mental health outcome scale: Reliability and validity of the Global Assessment of Functioning (GAF). *The British Journal of Psychiatry, 166,* 654–659.

Jordan, C., & Franklin, C. (2003). *Clinical assessment for social workers: Quantitative and qualitative methods.* Chicago: Lyceum.

Kadushin, A. (1992). *Supervision in social work* (3rd ed.). New York: Columbia University Press.

Kaiser, T. L. (1997). *Supervisory relationships: Exploring the human element.* Pacific Grove, CA: Brooks/Cole.

Kanfer, F. H. (1970). Self monitoring: Methodological limitations and clinical applications. *Journal of Consulting and Clinical Psychology, 35*(2), 148–158.

Kanfer, F. H. (1979). Self-monitoring: Methodological limitations and clinical applications. *Journal of Consulting and Clinical Psychology, 35,* 148–152.

Kanfer, F. H. (1986). Implications of a self-regulation model of therapy for treatment of addictive behaviors. In W. R. Miller & N. Heather (Eds.), *Treating addictive behaviors: Processes of change* (pp. 29–50). New York: Plenum Press.

Kazdin, A. E. (1994). Psychotherapy for children and adolescents. In A. E. Bergin & S. L. Garfield (Eds.), *Handbook of psychotherapy and behavior change* (4th ed., pp. 543–594). New York: Wiley.

Kazdin, A. E. (1997). Parent management training: Evidence, outcomes, and issues. *Journal of the American Academy of Child and Adolescent Psychiatry, 36,* 1349–1356.

Kazdin, A. E. (2002). Psychosocial treatments for conduct disorder in children and adolescents. In P. E. Nathan & J. M. Gorman (Eds.), *A guide to treatments that work* (2nd ed., pp. 57–85). New York: Oxford University Press.

Kazdin, A. E. (2003). Problem-solving skills training and parent management training for conduct disorder. In A. E. Kazdin & J. R. Weisz (Eds.), *Evidence-based psychotherapies for children and adolescents* (pp. 241–262). New York: Guilford Press.

Kazdin, A. E., & Weisz, J. R. (Eds.). (2003). *Evidence-based psychotherapies for children and adolescents.* New York: Guilford Press.

Kendall-Tackett, K. A. (Ed.). (2004). *Health consequences of abuse in the family: A clinical guide for evidence-based practice.* Washington, DC: American Psychological Association.

Kiresuk, T. S., Smith, A., & Cardillo, J. E. (Eds.). (1994). *Goal attainment scaling: Application, theory and measurement.* Hillsdale, NJ: Erlbaum.

Klein, K., & Forehand, R. (2000). Family processes as resources for African-American children exposed to a constellation of sociodemographic risk factors. *Journal of Clinical Psychology, 29,* 53–65.

Klerman, G. L., Weissman, M. M., Rounsaville, B. J., & Chevron, E. S. (1999). *Interpersonal psychotherapy of depression: A brief, focused, specific strategy.* Northvale, NJ: Aronson.

Klosko, J. S., & Sanderson, W. C. (1999). *Cognitive-behavioral treatment of depression.* Northvale, NJ: Aronson.

Kniskern, D., & Gurman, A. (1979). Research on training in marriage and family therapy: Status, issues and directions. *Journal of Marital and Family Therapy, 5,* 93–94.

Kolb, A. Y., & Kolb, D. A. (2005). *Bibliography of research on experiential learning theory and the Learning Style Inventory.* Cleveland, OH: Case Western Reserve University, Department of Organizational Behavior.

Kronenberger, W. S., & Meyer, R. G. (2001). *The child clinician's handbook* (2nd ed.). Needham Heights, MA: Allyn & Bacon.

Kropp, P. R., Hart, S. D., Webster, C. D., & Eaves, D. (1999). *Spousal assault risk assessment guide.* New York: Multi-Health Systems.

Kutchins, H., & Kirk, S. A. (1997). *Making us crazy: The psychiatric bible and the creation of mental disorders.* New York: Free Press.

L'Abate, L. (2004). *A guide to self-help workbooks for mental health clinicians and researchers.* Binghamton, NY: Haworth.

Lamb, D. H., Cochran, D. J., & Jackson, V. R. (1991). Training and organizational issues associated with identifying and responding to intern impairment: Professional impairment during the internship: Identification, due process, and remediation. *Professional Psychology: Research and Practice, 18,* 597–603.

Larson, D. (1980). Therapeutic schools, styles and schoolism: A national survey. *Journal of Humanistic Psychology, 20*(3), 3–21.

Leccese, M., & Waldron, H. B. (1994). Assessing adolescent substance abuse: A critique of current measurement instruments. *Journal of Substance Abuse Treatment, 11,* 553–563.

LeCroy, C. W. (1994). *Handbook of child and adolescent treatment manuals*. New York: Lexington.

LeCroy, C. W. (2001). Social competence promotion for troubled youth. In K. Corcoran & H. Briggs (Eds). *Social work practice: Treating common client problems* (pp. 199–212). Chicago: Lyceum Books.

LeCroy, C. W. (2007). *Handbook of child and adolescent treatment manuals*. New York: Oxford University Press.

LeCroy, C. W., & Daley, J. (Eds.). (2005). *Case studies in child, adolescent, and family treatment*. Belmont, CA: Brooks/Cole.

LeCroy, C. W., & Mann, J. E. (Eds.). (2007). *Handbook of prevention and intervention programs for adolescent girls*. New York: Wiley.

LeCroy, C. W., & Okamoto, S. (2006). Evidence-based practice and manualized treatment with children. In A. R. Roberts & K. R. Yeager (Eds.). *Foundations of evidence-based social work practice* (pp. 204–213). New York: Oxford University Press.

Leong, G. B., Spencer, E., & Silva, J. A. (1992). The psychotherapist as witness for the prosecution: The criminalization of Tarasoff. *American Journal of Psychiatry, 149*, 1011–1015.

Lewis, P. S., Goodman, S. H., & Fandt, P. M. (2004). *Management: Challenges in the 21st century*. Cincinnati, OH: South-Western College/Thomson.

Linehan, M. (1993). *Cognitive-behavioral treatment of borderline personality disorder*. New York: Guilford Press.

Lipsey, M. W. (1995). What do we learn from 400 research studies on the effectiveness of treatment with juvenile delinquents? In J. McGuire (Ed.), *What works? Reducing offending* (pp. 63–78). New York: Wiley.

Lipsey, M. W. (2002). Juvenile delinquency treatment: A meta-analytic inquiry into the variability effects. In T. D. Cook, H. Cooper, D. S. Cordray, H. Hartmann, L. V. Hedges, R. J. Light, et al. (Eds.), *Meta-analysis for explanation: A casebook* (pp. 83–127). New York: Russell Sage Foundation.

Lipsey, M. W., & Wilson, D. B. (1998). Effective intervention for serious juvenile offenders: A synthesis of research. In R. Loever & D. Farrington (Eds.), *Serious and violent juvenile offenders: Risk factors and successful interventions* (pp. 313–344). London: Sage.

Lipsey, M. W., & Wilson, D. B. (2001). *Practical meta-analysis*. Thousand Oaks, CA: Sage.

Lochner, B. T., & Melchert, T. P. (1997). Relationship of cognitive style and theoretical orientation to psychology interns' preferences for supervision. *Journal of Counseling Psychology, 44*, 256–260.

Loeber, R., Farrington, D. P., & Waschbusch, D. A. (1998). Serious and violent juvenile offenders. In R. Loeber & D. P. Farrington (Eds.), *Serious and violent juvenile offenders: Risk factors and successful interventions* (pp. 13–29). London: Sage.

Luborsky, L. (1993). Recommendations for training therapists based on manuals for psychotherapy reserach. *Psychotherapy, 30*(4), 578–580.

Luborsky, L., McLellan, A. T., Diguer, L., Woody, G., & Seligman, D. A. (1997). The psychotherapist matters: Comparison of outcomes across twenty-two therapists and seven patient samples. *Clinical Psychology: Science and Practice, 4,* 53–65.

Lyman, L., & Villani, C. (2004). *Best leadership practices for high-poverty schools.* Lanham, MD: Scarecrow Education.

Lynam, D. R., Milich, R., Zimmerman, R., Novak, S. P., Logan, T. K., Martin, C., et al. (1999). Project DARE: No effects at 10-year follow-up. *Journal of Consulting and Clinical Psychology, 67,* 590–593.

Manela, R. W., & Moxley, D. P. (2002). Best practices as agency-based knowledge in social welfare. *Administration in Social Work, 26*(4), 1–24.

Mann, J. (1973). *Time-limited psychotherapy.* Cambridge, MA: Harvard University Press.

Marshall, M., & Lockwood, A. (1998). *Assertive community treatment for people with severe mental illness.* London: The Cochrane Library.

Martin, S., Clark, K., Lynch, S., Kupper, L., & Cilenti, D. (1999). Violence in the lives of pregnant teenage women: Associations with multiple substance use. *American Journal of Drug and Alcohol Abuse, 25,* 425–440.

Maxmen, J. S., & Ward, N. G. (1995). *Essential psychopathology and its treatment* (2nd ed.). New York: Norton.

MacDonald v. Clinger, 446 NYS.2d 801 (1982).

Macgowan, M. J. (in press). *A guide to evidence-based group work.* New York: Oxford University Press.

MacKenzie, D. L. (1997). Criminal justice and crime prevention. In Sherman, L. W., Gottfredson, D., MacKenzie, D. L., Eck, J., Reuter, P., & Bushway, S. (Eds.), *Preventing crime: What works, what doesn't, what's promising.* A Report to the U.S. Congress. Washington, DC: National Institute of Justice.

MacKenzie, D. L. (2001). Corrections and sentencing in the 21st century: evidence-based corrections and sentencing. *The Prison Journal, 81,* 299–312.

MacKenzie, D. L. (2006). *What works in corrections: Reducing the criminal activities of offenders and delinquents.* New York: Cambridge University Press.

MacKenzie, D. L., Browning, K., Skroban, S., & Smith, D. (1999). The impact of probation on the criminal activities of offenders. *Journal of Research in Crime and Delinquency, 36,* 423–453.

MacKenzie, D. L., Gover, A. R., Styve, G. J., & Mitchell, O. (1999). A national study comparing the environments of boot camps to traditional facilities for juvenile offenders. Final Report to the National Institute of Justice. College Park, MD: University of Maryland, Department of Criminology and Criminal Justice.

MacKenzie, D. L., & Hickman, L. (1998). What works in corrections? Report to the State of Washington Joint Audit Review Committee. Retrieved February 7, 2007, from http://wwwevaluatingcorrections.org

McCrady, B. S. (2000). Alcohol use disorders and the Division 12 Task Force of the American Psychological Association. *Psychology of Addictive Behaviors, 14*(3), 267–276.

McGinn, L. K., & Sanderson, W. C. (1999). *Treatment of obsessive-compulsive disorder.* Northvale, NJ: Aronson.

McKay, M., & Bannon, W. (2004). Engaging families in child mental health services. *Child and Adolescent Psychiatric Clinics of North America, 13*(4), 905–921.

McLean, P. D., & Woody, S. R. (2001). *Evidence-based principles for substance abuse prevention*. New York: Oxford University Press.

McLellan, T., & Dembo, R. (1993). Screening and assessment of alcohol- and other drug-abusing adolescents: Treatment improvement protocol (TIP) series. DHHS Publication SMA 94–2009. Rockville, MD: U.S. Department of Health and Human Services.

McLellan, A. T., Kushner, H., Metzger, D., Peters, R., Smith, I., Grissom, G., et al. (1992). The fifth edition of the Addiction Severity Index. *Journal of Substance Abuse Treatment, 9*, 199–213.

McLellan, A. T., Luborsky, L., Woody, G. E., & O'Brien, C. P. (1983). Predicting response to alcohol and drug abuse treatment: The role of psychiatric severity. *Archives of General Psychiatry, 40*, 620–625.

McNeece, C. A., Bullington, B., Arnold, E. M., & Springer, D. W. (2002). The war on drugs: Treatment, research, and substance abuse intervention in the twenty-first century. In R. Muraskin & A. R. Roberts (Eds.), *Visions for change: Crime and justice in the twenty-first century* (3rd ed.; pp. 11–36). Upper Saddle River, NJ: Prentice Hall.

McNeece, C. A., & Thyer, B. A. (2004). Evidence-based practice and social work. *Journal of Evidence-Based Social Work, 1*, 7–25.

Meehl, P. E. (1996). *Clinical versus statistical prediction: A theoretical analysis and a review of the evidence*. Northvale, NJ: Aronson. (Original work published 1954)

Melton, G. B., Petrila, J., Poythress, N. G., & Slobogin, C. (1997). *Psychological evaluations for the courts: A handbook for mental health professionals and lawyers* (2nd ed.), New York: Guilford Press.

Meyers, C. & Jones, T. B. (1993). *Promoting active learning: Strategies for the college classroom*. San Francisco: Jossey-Bass.

Miller, W. R. (1999). Enhancing motivation for change in substance abuse treatment. Treatment Improvement Protocol (TIP) Series No. 35. DHHS Publication No. SMA 99–3354. Rockville, MD: U. S. Department of Health and Human Services.

Miller, W. R., & Brown, J. M. (1991). Self regulation as a conceptual basis for the prevention and treatment of addictive behaviors. In N. Heather, W. R. Miller, & J. Greenley (Eds.), *Self control and the addictive behaviors* (pp. 3–79). Sydney: Pergamon.

Miller, W. R., & Rollnick, S. (2002). *Motivational interviewing: Preparing people to change addictive behavior* (2nd ed.). New York: Guilford Press.

Miller, W. R., Toscova, R. T., Miller, J. H., & Sanchez, V. (2000). A theory-based motivational approach for reducing alcohol/drug problems in college. *Health Education & Behavior, 27*, 744–759.

Miller, W. R., Zweben, A., DiClemente, C. C., & Rychtarik, R. G. (1992). *Motivational Enhancement Therapy manual: A clinical research guide for therapists treating individuals with alcohol abuse and dependence*. Rockville, MD: National Institute on Alcohol Abuse and Alcoholism.

Minkoff, K. (2001). Best practices: Developing standards of care for individuals with co-occurring psychiatric and substance use disorders. *Psychiatric Services, 52*, 597–599.

Mithaug, D. E. (1993). *Self-regulation theory: How optimal adjustment optimizes gain.* Westport, CT: Praeger.

Moffitt, T. E. (1987). Parental mental disorder and offspring criminal behavior: An adoption study. *Psychiatry, 50,* 346–360.

Molina, I., Bowie, S. L., Dulmus, C. N., & Sowers, K. M. (2004). School-based violence prevention programs: A review of selected programs with empirical evidence. *Journal of Evidence-Based Social Work: Advances in Practice, Programming, Research, and Policy, 1*(2/3), 175–190.

Molina, I. A., Dulmus, C. N., & Sowers, K. M. (2005). Secondary prevention for youth violence: A review of selected school-based programs. *Brief Treatment and Crisis Intervention, 5*(1), 95–127.

Monahan, J., & Steadman, H. J. (1994). *Violence and mental disorder.* Chicago: University of Chicago Press.

Moras, K. (1993). The use of treatment manuals to train psychotherapists: Observations and recommendations. *Psychotherapy, 30*(4), 581–586.

Mufson, L., Dorta, K. P., Moreau, D., & Weissman, M. M. (2004). *Interpersonal psychotherapy for depressed adolescents.* New York: Guilford Press.

Mullen, E. J., Shlonsky, A., Bledsoe, S. E., & Bellamy, J. L. (2005). From concept to implementation: Challenges facing evidence-based social work. *Evidence and Policy, 1*(1), 61–84.

Muller, J., & Mihalic, S. (1999). *Blueprints: A violence prevention initiative* (OJJDP Fact Sheet #110). Retrieved January 7, 2005, from http://www.ncjrs.org/txtfiles1/fs99110.txt

Munson, C. (1989). Editorial. *Clinical Supervisor, 7*(1), 1–4.

Munson, C. (1993). *Clinical social work supervision* (2nd ed.). New York: Haworth Press.

Munson, C. (2000). Supervision standards of practice. In P. Allen-Meares & C. Garvin (Eds.), *Handbook of social work practice* (pp. 611–632). Thousand Oaks, CA: Sage.

Nathan, P. E., & Gorman, J. M. (Eds.). (2002). *A guide to treatments that work* (2nd ed.). New York: Oxford University Press.

National Association of Social Workers. (1999). *Code of ethics* (Rev. ed.). Silver Spring, MD: Author.

National Center on Addiction and Substance Abuse. (1996). *Comprehensive service delivery program for children at risk.* New York: Columbia University.

Nelson, G. L., (1978). Psychotherapy supervision from the trainee's point of view. A survey of preferences. *Professional Psychology, 9,* 539–550.

Noonan, W. C., & Moyers, T. B. (1997). Motivational interviewing: A review. *Journal of Substance Misuse, 2,* 8–16.

Norcross, J. (1985). In defense of theoretical orientations for clinicians. *Clinical Psychologist, 38,* 13–17.

Norcross, J. C., Santrock, J., Campbell, L. F., Smith, T., Sommer, R., & Zuckerman, E., (2003). *The authoritative guide to self help resources in mental health* (2nd ed.). New York: Guilford Press.

O'Connor, B. P. (2000). Reasons for less than ideal psychotherapy supervision. *Clinical Supervisor, 19*(2), 173–183.

O'Hare, T. (2005). *Evidence-based practices for social workers: An interdisciplinary approach.* Chicago: Lyceum Books.

Ollendick, T. H., King, N. J., & Murius, P. (2002). Fears and phobias in children: Phenomenology, epidemiology, and etiology. *Child and Adolescent Mental Health, 7*(3), 98–106.

Orlinsky, D. E., Ronnestad, M. H., & Willutzki, U. (2001). Fifty years of psychotherapy process-outcome research: Continuity and change. In J. J. Lambert (Ed.), *Bergin and Garfield's handbook of psychotherapy and behavior change* (pp. 307–389). New York: Wiley.

Patterson, G. (1974). Interventions for boys with conduct problems: Multiple settings, treatments, and criteria. *Journal of Consulting and Clinical Psychology, 42,* 471–481.

Patterson, G. R., Reid, J. B., Jones, R. R., & Conger, R. E. (1975). *A social learning approach to family intervention: Vol. 1. Families with aggressive children.* Eugene, OR: Castalia.

Pearson, F. S., Lipton, D. S., Cleland, C. M., & Yee, D. S. (2002). The effects of behavioral/cognitive-behavioral programs on recidivism. *Crime and Delinquency, 48*(3), 476–496.

Penry v. Lynaugh, 109 S.Ct. 2934, 2947 (1989).

Perlman, H. (1989). *Looking back to see ahead.* Chicago: University of Chicago Press.

Peterson, M. (1992). *At personal risk: Boundary violations in professional-client relationships.* New York: Norton.

Petrosino, A. J., Boruch, R. F., Farrington, D. P., Sherman, L. W., & Weisburd, D. (2003). Toward evidence-based criminology and criminal justice: Systematic reviews, the Campbell Collaboration and the Crime and Justice Group. *International Journal of Comparative Criminology, 3,* 42–61.

Petrosino, A. J., Turpin-Petrosino, C., & Buehler, J. (2002). "Scared Straight" and other juvenile awareness programs for preventing juvenile delinquency. *The Cochrane Database of Systematic Reviews* 2002, Issue 2, Art. No.: CD002796.

Platt, S. (1992). *The process of learning in clinical social work students.* Unpublished doctoral dissertation, Smith College School of Social Work, Northampton, MA.

Pollio, D. E. (2002). The evidence-based group worker. *Social Work With Groups, 25*(2), 57–70.

Potocky-Tripodi, M. (2002). *Best practices for social work with refugees and immigrants.* New York: Columbia University Press.

Poznanski, J. J., & McLennan, J. (1995). Conceptualizing and measuring counselors' theoretical orientation. *Journal of Counseling Psychology, 42*(4), 411–422.

Prochaska, J. O., & DiClemente, C. (1986). Toward a comprehensive model of change. In W. R. Miller & N. Heather (Eds.), *Treating addictive behaviors: Processes of change* (pp. 3–27). New York: Plenum Press.

Prochaska, J. O., DiClemente, C. C., & Norcross, J. C. (1992). In search of how people change: Applications to addictive behaviors. *American Psychologist, 47,* 1102–1114.

Prochaska, J. O. Velicier, W. F., Rossi, J. S. & Goldstein, M. G. (1994). Stages of change and decisional balance for 12 problem behaviors. *Health Psychology, 13,* 39–46.

Project MATCH Research Group. (1997). Matching alcoholism treatment to patient heterogeneity: Project MATCH posttreatment drinking outcomes. *Journal of Studies on Alcohol, 58,* 7–29.

Project MATCH Research Group. (1998). Matching alcoholism treatments to patient heterogeneity: Project MATCH three-year drinking outcomes. *Alcoholism: Clinical and Experimental Research, 22,* 1300–1311.

Quinsey, V. L., Lalumiere, M. L., Rice, M. E., & Harris, G. T. (1995). Predicting sexual offenses. In J. C. Campbell (Ed.), *Assessing dangerousness: Violence by sexual offenders, batterers, and child abusers* (pp. 114–137). Thousand Oaks, CA: Sage.

Rae-Grant, N., Thomas, B. H., Offord, D. R., & Boyle, M. H. (1989). Risk, protective factors, and the prevalence of behavioral and emotional disorders in children and adolescents. *Journal of the American Academy of Child and Adolescent Psychiatry, 28,* 262–268.

Rapp-Paglicci, L. A., Dulmus, C. N., & Wodarski, J. S. (Eds.). (2004). *Handbook of preventive interventions for children and adolescents.* New York: Wiley.

Reamer, F. G. (2006). *Social work values and ethics* (3rd ed.). New York: Columbia University Press.

Redd, Z., Cochran, S., Hair, E., & Moore, K. (2002). *Academic achievement programs and youth development: A synthesis.* Retrieved January 6, 2005, from http://www .childtrends.org/what_works/clarkwww/acadach/CAR.pdf

Redondo, S., Sanchez-Meca, J., & Garrido, V. (1999). The influence of treatment programs on the recidivism of juvenile and adult defenders: A European meta-analytic review. *Psychology, Crime, and Law, 5,* 251–278.

Reid, W. J., & Colvin, J. (2005). Evidence-based practice: Breakthrough or buzzword? In S. A. Kirk (Ed.), *Mental disorders in the social environment: Critical perspectives* (pp. 231–247). New York: Columbia University Press.

Reimer, M., Thomlison, B., & Bradshaw, C. (1999). *The clinical rotation handbook.* Albany, NY: Delmar.

Ribisl, K. M., Walton, M. A., Mowbray, C. T., Luke, D. A., Davidson, W. S., Jr., & Bootsmiller, B. J. (1996). Minimizing participant attrition in panel studies through the use of effective retention and tracking strategies: Review and recommendations. *Evaluation and Program Planning, 19,* 1–25.

Ries, R. (1994). *Assessment and treatment of patients with coexisting mental illness and alcohol and other drug abuse.* Treatment Improvement Protocol (TIP) Series 9. DHHS Publication SMA 95–3061. Rockville, MD: U.S. Department of Health and Human Services.

Roberts, A. R., & Greene, G. J. (Eds.). (2002). *Social workers' desk reference.* New York: Oxford University Press.

Roberts, A. R., & Springer, D. W. (Eds.). (2007). *Social work in juvenile and criminal justice settings.* Springfield, IL: Charles C Thomas.

Roberts, A. R., & Yeager, K. R. (Eds.). (2004). *Evidence-based practice manual: Research and outcome measures in health and human services.* New York: Oxford University Press.

Roberts, A. R., & Yeager, K. R. (Eds.). (2006). *Foundations of evidence-based social work practice.* New York: Oxford University Press.

Robinson v. Jacksonville Shipyards, Inc., 760 F. Supp. 1486 (1991).

Roe v. Doe, 400 N.Y.S. 2d. 668 (1977).

Roe v. Wade, 410 U.S. 113 (1973).

Rogers, G., & Thomlison, B. (2000). The write stuff: Documenting learning in the practicum. In R. Power & G. Kenyon (Eds.), *No magic: Readings in social work education* (pp.53–73). Toronto, Ontario: Canadian Scholars Press.

Rollnick, S., & Miller, W. R. (1995). What is motivational interviewing? *Behavioural and Cognitive Psychotherapy, 23,* 325–334.

Rosenberg, W., & Donald, A. (1995). Evidence based medicine: An approach to clinical problem solving. *British Medical Journal, 310,* 1122–1126.

Rosenthal, R. N. (2004). Overview of evidence-based practice. In A. R. Robert & K. R. Yeager (Eds.), *Evidence-based practice manual: Research and outcome measures in health and human services* (pp. 20–29). New York: Oxford University Press.

Roth, A., & Fonagy, P. (1996). *What works for whom? A critical review of psychotherapy research.* New York: Guilford Press.

Roth, A., & Fonagy, P. (2005). *What works for whom?* (2nd ed.). New York: Guilford Press.

Rounsaville, B. J., Chevron, E. S., Weissman, M. M., Prusoff, B. A., & Frank, E. (1986). Training therapists to perform interpersonal psychotherapy in clinical trials. *Comprehensive Psychiatry, 27*(4), 364–371.

Rowe v. Bennett, 514 A2d. 802 (1986).

Rowland, N., & Goss, S. (Eds.). (2000). *Evidence-based counseling and psychological therapies: Research and applications.* Philadelphia: Routledge.

Rutter, M. (1979). Protective factors in children's responses to stress and disadvantage. In M. W. Kent & J. E. Rolf (Eds.), *Primary prevention of psychopathology: Social competence in children* (Vol. 3, pp. 49–74). Hanover, NH: University Press of New England.

Rutter, M. (1985). Resilience in the face of adversity: Protective factors and resistance to psychiatric disorder. *British Journal of Psychiatry, 147,* 598–611.

Rygh, J. L., & Sanderson, W. C. (2004). *Treating generalized anxiety disorder: Evidence-based strategies, tools, and techniques.* New York: Guilford Press.

Sackett, D. L., Rosenberg, W. M. C., Gray, J. A. M., Haynes, R. B., & Richardson, W. S. (1996). Evidence-based medicine: What it is and what it isn't. *British Medical Journal, 312,* 71–72.

Sackett, D. L., Strauss, S. E., Richardson, W. S., Rosenberg, W., & Haynes, R. B. (2000). *Evidence-based medicine: How to practice and teach EBM.* New York: Churchill-Livingstone.

Salyers, M., Bosworth, H. B., Swanson, J., Lamb-Pagone, J., & Osher, F. (2000). Reliability and validity of the SF-12 Health Survey among people with severe mental illness. *Medical Care, 38,* 1141–1150.

Sampson, R. J., & Laub, J. H. (1995). *Crime in the making: Pathways and turning points through life.* Cambridge, MA: Harvard University Press.

Saunders, B., Wilkinson, C., & Phillips, M. (1995). The impact of a brief motivational intervention with opiate users attending a methadone programme. *Addiction, 90,* 415–424.

Seifert, P. (2003). What is HIPAA? *PSR Connections 2,* 3.

Sells, S. P. (2001). *Parenting the out of control teenager.* New York: St. Martin's Press.

Sexton, T. L., & Alexander, J. F. (2002). Family-based empirically supported interventions. *Counseling Psychologist, 30*(2), 238–261.

Shaw, B. F., Elkin, I., Yamaguchi, J., Olmsted, M., Vallis, T. M., Dobson, K. S., et al. (1999). Therapist competence ratings in relation to clinical outcome in cognitive therapy of depression. *Journal of Consulting and Clinical Psychology, 67*(6), 837–846.

Sheidow, A. J., & Henggeler, S. W. (2005). Community-based treatments. In K. Heilbrun, N. E. Sevin Goldstein, & R. E. Redding (Eds.), *Juvenile delinquency: Prevention, assessment, and intervention* (pp. 257–281). New York: Oxford University Press.

Sherman, L. W. (1999). Evidence-based policing. *Ideas in American policing.* Washington, D.C.: Police Foundation. Available at http://www.policefoundation.org/pdf/ Sherman.pdf

Sherman, L. W., Farrington, D. P., Welsh, B. C., & MacKenzie, D. L. (Eds.). (2002). *Evidence-based crime prevention.* New York: Routledge.

Sherman, L. W., Gottfredson, D., MacKenzie, D., Eck, J., Reuter, P., & Bushway, S. (1997) *Preventing crime: What works, what doesn't, what's promising. A report to the United States Congress.* College Park, MD: University of Maryland, Department of Criminology and Criminal Justice.

Shulman, L. (1982). *Skills of supervision and staff management.* Itasca, IL: Peacock.

Shulman, L. (1993). *Interactional supervision.* Washington, DC: NASW Press.

Silver, E., & Teasdale, B. (2005). Mental disorder and violence: An examination of stressful life events and impaired social support. *Social Problems 52*(1), 62–78.

Simmons v. United States of America, 805 F.2d. 1363 (1986).

Singh, G. (2002). Assessment in social work. Retrieved June 5, 2005, from http:// www.swap.ac.uk/Learning/AssessSW2.asp?version=printversion

Slobogin, C., Reisner, R., & Arti, R. (2003). *Law and the mental health system: Civil and criminal aspects* (4th ed). St. Paul, MN: West.

Smith, M. L., Glass, G. V., & Miller, T. I. (1980). *The benefits of psychotherapy.* Baltimore, MD: Johns Hopkins University Press.

Smith, S. R., & Meyer, R. G. (1987). *Law, behavior, and mental health.* New York: New York University Press.

Sobell, L. C., & Sobell, M. B. (1992). Timeline follow-back: A technique for assessing self-reported alcohol consumption. In R. Z. Litten & J. P. Allen (Eds.), *Measuring alcohol consumption: Psychosocial and biochemical methods* (pp. 41–72.). Totowa, NJ: Humana Press.

Social Policy and Social Work. (2001). Social policy and social work subject centre of the Higher Education Academy. Retrieved December 13, 2006, from http://www .swap.ac.uk

Sowers-Hoag, K., & Thyer, B. (1995). Teaching social work practice: A review and analysis of empirical research. *Journal of Social Work Education, 21*(3), 5–15.

Spitzer, R. L., Kroenke, K., & Williams, J. B. (1999). Validation and utility of a self-report version of PRIME-MD: The PHQ primary care study. Primary Care Evaluation of Mental Disorders. Patient Health Questionnaire. *Journal of the American Medical Association, 282,* 1737–1744.

Spivak, G., & Shure, M. B. (1974). *Social adjustment of young children.* San Francisco, CA: Jossey-Bass.

Springer, D. W. (2002). Assessment protocols and rapid assessment instruments with troubled adolescents. In A. R. Roberts & G. J. Greene (Eds.), *Social work desk reference* (pp. 217–221). New York: Oxford University Press.

Springer, D. W. (2004). Treating juvenile delinquents with conduct disorder, attention-deficit/hyperactivity disorder, and oppositional defiant disorder. In A. R. Roberts & K. R. Yeager (Eds.), *Evidence-based social work primer: Outcome measures in health and human services* (pp. 263–274). New York: Oxford University Press.

Springer, D. W. (2005). Treating substance-abusing youth. In C. A. McNeece & D. M. DiNitto (Eds.), *Chemical dependency: A systems approach* (3rd ed., pp. 269–292). Needham Heights, MA: Allyn & Bacon.

Springer, D. W., McNeece, C. A., & Arnold, E. M. (2003). *Substance abuse treatment for criminal offenders: An evidence-based guide for practitioners.* Washington, DC: American Psychological Association.

Stein, D. M., & Lambert, M. J. (1995). Graduate training in psychotherapy: Are therapy outcomes enhanced? *Journal of Counseling and Clinical Psychology, 63,* 182–196.

Steketee, G., & Frost, R. O. (2007). *Compulsive hoarding and acquiring, therapist guide.* New York: Oxford University Press.

Steketee, G. (1999). *Overcoming obsessive-compulsive disorder: A behavioral and cognitive protocol for the treatment of OCD.* Oakland, CA: New Harbinger.

Steketee, G., & Austin, A. H. (1989). Rape victims and the justice system: Utilization and impact. *Social Service Review, 63*(2), 285–303.

Stephens, R. S., Roffman, R. A., & Curtin, L. (2000). Comparison of extended versus brief treatments for marijuana use. *Journal of Consulting and Clinical Psychology, 68,* 898–908.

Strom-Gottfried, K. (1999). Professional boundaries: An analysis of violations by social workers. *Families in Society, 80*(5), 439–449.

Substance Abuse and Mental Health Services Administration. *SAMHSA's* National Registry of Evidence-Based Programs and Practices. Retrieved December 13, 2006, from http://captus.samhsa.gov/national/resources/evidence_based.cfm

Sussex, B., & Corcoran, K. (2005).The impact of domestic violence on depression in teen mothers: Is the fear or threat of violence sufficient? *Brief Treatment and Crisis Intervention, 5*(1), 109–120.

Swanson, J. W., Borum, R., Swartz, M. S., Hiday, V. A., Wagner, H. R., & Burns, B. J. (2001). Can involuntary outpatient commitment reduce arrests among persons with severe mental illness? *Criminal Justice and Behavior, 28*(2), 156–189.

Swets, J. A., Dawes, R. M., & Monahan, J. (2000, October). Better decisions through science. *Scientific American,* 82–87.

Szapocznik, J., & Williams, R. A. (2000). Brief strategic family therapy: Twenty-five years of interplay among theory, research and practice in adolescent behavior problems and drug abuse. *Clinical Child and Family Psychology Review, 3*(2), 117–134.

Szasz, T. S. (1974). *The myth of mental illness: Foundations of a theory of personal conduct* (2nd ed.). New York: Harper & Row.

Szuchman, L., & Thomlison, B. (2007). *Writing with style: APA style for social work.* (3rd edition) Pacific Grove, CA: Brooks/Cole Wadsworth.

Tarasoff v. the Board of Regents of the University of California, 551 P. 2d 334 (1976).

Tate, D. C., & Redding, R. E. (2005). Mental health and rehabilitative services in juvenile justice: System reforms and innovative approaches. In K. Heilbrun, N. E. Sevin Goldstein, & R. E. Redding (Eds.), *Juvenile delinquency: Prevention, assessment, and intervention* (pp. 134–160). New York: Oxford University Press.

Taylor, T., & Biglan, A. (1998). Behavioral family interventions for improving child-rearing: A review of the literature for clinicians and policy makers. *Clinical Child and Family Psychology Review, 1*(1), 41–60.

Teplin, L. A., Abram, K. M., McClelland, G. M., Dulcan, M. K., & Mericle, A. A. (2002). Psychiatric disorders in youth in juvenile detention. *Archives of General Psychiatry, 59,* 1133–1143.

Thomlison, B. (1995). Student perceptions of reflective team supervision. In G. Rogers (Ed.), *Social work field education: Views and visions* (pp. 234–244). Dubuque, IA: Kendall Hunt.

Thomlison, B. (1999). Supervision and consultation. In F. J. Turner (Ed.), *Social work practice: A Canadian perspective* (pp. 505–517). Scarborough, Ontario, Canada: Prentice Hall–Allyn & Bacon.

Thomlison, B. (2000). Descriptive studies. In B. A. Thyer (Ed.), *Handbook of social work research methods* (pp. 131–141) Thousand Oaks, CA: Sage.

Thomlison, B. (2002). Enhancing practice knowledge through supervision and consultation. In F. J. Turner (Ed.), *Social work practice: A Canadian perspective* (2nd ed., pp. 553–564). Scarborough, Ontario, Canada: Prentice Hall–Allyn & Bacon.

Thomlison, B. (2004). Child maltreatment: A risk and protective factor perspective. In M. W. Fraser (Ed.), *Risk and resilience in childhood: An ecological perspective* (2nd ed., pp.89–133). Washington, DC: NASW Press.

Thomlison, B., & Jacobs, R. J. (2006). Developing a systematic evidence-based search plan for a client with co-occurring conditions. In A. R. Roberts & K. R. Yeager (Eds.), *Evidence-based social work primer* (pp.163–181). New York: Oxford University Press.

Thomlison, B., Rogers, G., Collins, D., & Grinnell, R., Jr. (1996). *The social work practicum: An access guide for students* (2nd ed.). Itasca, IL: F. E. Peacock.

Thomlison, B., & Rogers, G. (1995, March). Guidelines for developing cultural competence in field education. Paper presented at the annual program meeting of the Council on Social Work Education, San Diego, CA.

Thornberry, T. P. (1998). Membership in youth gangs and involvement in serious, violent offending. In R. Loeber & D. P. Farrington (Eds.), *Serious and violent juvenile offenders: Risk factors and successful interventions* (pp. 147–166). Thousand Oaks, CA: Sage.

Thornton, T. N., Craft, C. A., Dahlberg, L. L., Lynch, B. S., & Baer, K. (2000). *Best practices of youth violence prevention: A sourcebook for community action.* Atlanta, GA: Centers for Disease Control and Prevention, National Center for Injury Prevention and Control.

Thyer, B. A. (1987). *Treating anxiety disorders.* Thousand Oaks, CA: Sage.

Thyer, B. A. (2001). Single-system designs. In B. A. Thyer (Ed.), *Handbook of social work research methods* (pp. 239–262). Thousand Oaks, CA: Sage.

Thyer, B. A. (2002). Principles of evidence-based practice and treatment development. In A. R. Roberts & G. J. Greene (Eds.), *Social work desk reference* (pp. 739–742). New York: Oxford University Press.

Thyer, B. A., Papsdorf, J. D., Davis, R., & Vallecorsa, S. (1984). Autonomic correlates of the Subjective Anxiety Scale. *Journal of Behavior Therapy and Experimental Psychiatry, 26,* 93–98.

Tompkins, M. A. (2004). *Using homework in psychotherapy.* New York: Guilford Press.

Tourse, R. W., McInnis-Dittrich, K., & Platt, S. (1999). The road to autonomous practice: A practice competency teaching approach for supervision. *Journal of Teaching in Social Work, 19*(1/2), 3–19.

Tripodi, S. J., Kim, J. S., & DiNitto, D. M. (2006). Effective strategies for working with students who have co-occurring disorders. In C. Franklin, M. B. Harris, & P. Allen-Meares (Eds.), *School social work and mental health workers training and resource manual.* New York: Oxford University Press.

Trochim, W. (1989). An introduction to concept mapping for planning and evaluation. *Evaluation and Program Planning, 12,* 1–16.

U.S. Department of Health and Human Services. (2001). *Youth violence: A report of the Surgeon General.* Retrieved January 10, 2005, from http://www.surgeongeneral.gov/library/youthviolence.

U.S. Department of Health and Human Services. (2003). *New Freedom Commission on Mental Health: Achieving the promise: Transforming mental health care in America.* (DHHS Publication No. SMA-03–3832). Rockville, MD: Author.

Van Bilsen, H. P. J. G., & van Emst, A. J. (1986). Heroin addiction and motivational milieu therapy. *International Journal of the Addictions, 21,* 707–713.

Van Bilsen, H. P. J. G., & Whitehead, M. L. (1994). Learning controlled drugs use: A case study. *Behavioral and Cognitive Psychotherapy, 22,* 87–95.

Vance, H. B. (Ed.). (1998). *Psychological assessment of children: Best practices for school and clinical settings.* New York: Wiley.

Vandiver, V. L. (2002). Step-by-step practice guidelines for using evidence-based practice and expert consensus in mental health settings. In A. R. Roberts & G. J. Greene (Eds.), *Social work desk reference.* (pp 731–739). New York: Oxford University Press.

Vonk, M. E., & Thyer, B. A. (1995). Exposure therapy in the treatment of vaginal penetration phobia: A single-case evaluation. *Journal of Behavior Therapy and Experimental Psychiatry, 26*(4), 359–363.

Walk, A. I., Jensen, N. M., & Havighurst, T. C. (1997). Meta-analysis of randomized control trials addressing brief interventions in heavy alcohol drinkers. *Journal of General Internal Medicine, 12,* 274–283.

Wampold, B. E. (2001). *The great psychotherapy debate: Models, methods, and findings.* Mahwah, NJ: Lawrence Erlbaum.

Webster, C. D., Douglas, K. S., Eaves, D., & Hart, S. D. (1997). *HCR-20: Assessing risk for violence* (version 2). Vancouver, British Columbia, Canada: Simon Fraser University.

Webster-Stratton, C., & Reid, M. J. (2003). The incredible years parents, teachers, and children training series: A multifaceted treatment approach for young children with conduct problems. In A. E. Kazdin & J. R. Weisz (Eds.), *Evidence-based psychotherapies for children and adolescents* (pp. 224–240). New York: Guilford Press.

Weiner, B. A., & Wettstein, R. M. (1993). *Legal issues in mental health care.* New York: Plenum Press.

Werner, E. E., & Smith, R. S. (1982). *Vulnerable but invincible: A longitudinal study of resilient children and youth.* New York: McGraw-Hill.

Werner, E. E., & Smith, R. S. (1992). *Overcoming the odds: High risk children from birth to adulthood.* Ithaca, NY: Cornell University Press.

Whalen v. Roe, 410 U.S. 113 (1977).

Wilk, A. I., Jensen, N. M., & Havighurst, T. C. (1997). Meta-analysis of randomized control trials addressing brief interventions in heavy alcohol drinkers. *Journal of General Internal Medicine, 12,* 274–283.

Wilson, S. J., Lipsey, M. W., & Soydan, H. (2003). Are mainstream programs for juvenile delinquency less effective with minority youth than majority youth? A meta-analysis of outcomes research. *Research on Social Work Practice, 13,* 3–26.

Winslade, W. J., & Ross, J. W. (1985). Privacy, confidentiality, and autonomy in psychotherapy. *Nebraska Law Review, 64,* 578–636.

Winters, K. C. (1999). Screening and assessing adolescents for substance use disorders: Treatment improvement protocol (TIP) series 31. DHHS Publication No. SMA 99–3282. Rockville, MD: U. S. Department of Health and Human Services.

Wolpe, J. (1969). *The practice of behavior therapy.* Elmsford, NY: Pergamon Press.

Wodarski, J. S., Wodarski, L. A., & Dulmus, C. N. (2003). *Adolescent depression and suicide: A comprehensive empirical intervention for prevention and treatment.* Springfield, IL: Thomas.

Zubin, J., & Spring, B. (1977). Vulnerability: New view of schizophrenia. *Journal of Abnormal Psychology, 86*(2), 103–126.

INDEX